THE SELF-MADE MAP

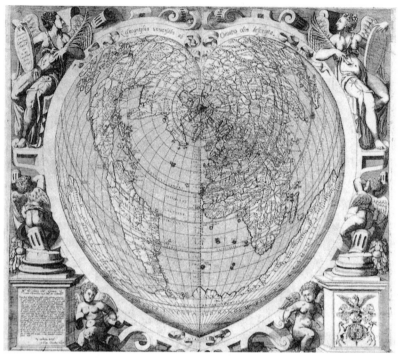

Giovanni Cimerlino's 1566 copperplate reproduction of Oronce Finé's single cordiform map of 1534

THE
Self-Made
MAP

Cartographic Writing
in Early Modern France

Tom Conley

University of Minnesota Press
Minneapolis
London

Grateful acknowledgment is made for the assistance of the following in providing illustrations reproduced herein: the Newberry Library (Figures 1.1–1.6, 3.1–3.5, 3.17–3.18, 3.20, 3.24–3.25, 4.2–4.4, 5.3, 5.9–5.11, 6.15–6.16, 8.1, 9.1, 9.3); the Novacco Map Collection, Newberry Library (frontispiece, Figures 3.19, N.2); the Edward E. Ayer Collection, Newberry Library (Figures 4.1, 5.5–5.7, 6.1–6.14, 6.17–6.20, 6.22, 7.1, 9.2); the Case Collection, Newberry Library (Figures 6.21, 8.3); the Wing Collection, Newberry Library (Figure 8.2); and the James Ford Bell Library, University of Minnesota (Figures 2.1–2.12, 3.6–3.16, 3.21–3.23, 5.1–5.2, 5.4, 5.8, 7.1–7.3).

Every effort was made to obtain permission to reproduce the illustrations in this book. If any proper acknowledgment has not been made, we encourage owners or copyright holders to notify the publisher.

Published by the University of Minnesota Press
111 Third Avenue South, Suite 290
Minneapolis, MN 55401-2520
http://www.upress.umn.edu

Library of Congress Cataloging-in-Publication Data

Conley, Tom.
    The self-made map : cartographic writing in early modern France /
Tom Conley.
        p.   cm.
    Includes bibliographical references and index.
    ISBN 978-0-8166-2700-4 (hc: alk paper)
    ISBN 978-0-8166-7448-0 (pb: alk paper)
    1. Cartography—France—History—16th century.   2. Maps in literature.
I. Title.
GA863.5.A1C66   1997
840.9′003—dc20   96-20302

17 16 15 14 13 12 11 10   10 9 8 7 6 5 4 3 2 1

Contents

Illustrations

Preface and Acknowledgments

The pages that follow grow out of research in early modern French literature, the history of cartography, and readings in psychoanalysis. I always have felt that the seductive appeal and unsettling expression of the arts of the Renaissance are due to various and always mobile articulations of space. In that age, as it seems in no other, writings are *spatially* conceived and materially determined; they explore surfaces and volumes in ways that were perhaps unknown prior to the development of print culture and the discovery of the New World. To see whether and how cartography is a virtual or even a real component of the literary imagination of the early modern age, I have started from the position that textual creations are coordinated as might be both maps and works of art. The question I have asked throughout the study is whether their words and figures are measured, "compassed," or gridded according to procedures that develop on cartographers' tables or in engravers' workshops. And if so, we can be led to wonder what the consequences may be in the more delicate areas of ideology or politics, or even in our drive to exhume the creations of sixteenth-century France.

To approach these questions I have chosen to study a number of works that bear strong affinities with the construction of space in disciplines that pertain to geometry. All of them seem to treat writing—whether words, letters, or inscription itself—as a function of extension. Writing holds, penetrates, delineates, and explores space; it maps itself in relation to an autonomous signature—that of the author, artist, cartographer, or editor—born of the congress of space and discourse. The early modern period witnessed the growth of a composite writing that moves between diagrammatical and discursive inspiration. This writing is decisive for the creation of the self, and it owes much to a new genre that might, for lack of an official term, be called "cartographic literature."

One of the aims of the study is not quite to reconstitute or revive a "geographic literature" of the kind studied so admirably by Père François de Dainville and, more recently and no less compellingly, by Frank Lestringant and Christian Jacob. Following the lead of an intuitive mode of inquiry that reaches back to traditions of new criticism, I have tried to engage cartographical writing *in medias res*, as a close but generally uninformed reader. It seems that much of the pleasure these works afford is due to the ways that they allow us to invent imaginary realms of space through our illusion of having "firsthand" contact with them. For that reason I have chosen to study accessible materials, available wherever possible in inexpensive editions or facsimile copies. Original materials have been transcribed and are followed by my own translations.

This project was begun in the midst of a fellowship offered by the Institute for Research in the Humanities at the University of Wisconsin. The bulk of the research was continued under the auspices of a grant generously offered by the Hermon Dunlap Smith Center for the History of Cartography at the Newberry Library in the spring of 1992. I am deeply indebted to David Lindberg and to David Woodward, at the University of Wisconsin, for the time and interest they took in the project in its early stages.

The triumvirate of James Akerman, David Buisseret, and Robert Karrow has provided untold inspiration and continued guidance. Their generosity, knowledge, and inspiration have been unequaled at all stages of the research and writing.

The Newberry Library fostered much of the research. Instrumental in their help were Arthur Holzheimer, Paul Gehl, Paul Saenger, and the staff commanding the special collections. In Paris, Frank Lestringant and Gisèle Mathieu-Castellani have provided much help in discussions about sixteenth-century writing. I would also like to thank Carol Urness of the James Ford Bell Library for her selfless encouragement and suggestions.

Colleagues in early modern studies who have read and sustained the project include Stephen Bann, Norman Bryson, Marie-Hélène Huet, John Lyons, and Timothy Murray. Without their counsel, the project could not have been completed. I owe much, too, to François Cornilliat, Floyd Gray, Ullrich Lauger, Kathleen McKenna, Andrew J. McKenna, Philip Lewis, Mary McKinley, Réda Bensmaïa, Alice Jardine, and colleagues and students in the Department of

Romance Languages at Harvard University. Biodun Iginla, Lisa Freeman, and the Committee on the University of Minnesota Press have offered generous assistance and encouragement. I am indebted to Kathy Delfosse for her painstaking work of copyediting. Michelle Quade helped finish the photographic work, and Linda Redmund provided a source of electricity when I was editing the manuscript in the Superior National Forest. Above all, Verena Conley sacrificed undue time and energy to see the work through to completion. To her this book is dedicated.

Introduction

Not long ago, David Buisseret posed a fundamental question for historians of early modern cartography: With the exception of Mediterranean navigators' portolano charts or "harbor-finding charts" (Brown 1977: 113), used on sailing vessels, at the beginning of the fifteenth century maps were practically nonexistent, whereas only two centuries later they were the bedrock of most professions and disciplines. Why the sudden birth and growth of mapping? He responded by noting that new worldviews were born for at least five reasons: First, in its admiration for antiquity, the newly intellectual Renaissance esteemed Ptolemy as the world's founding geographer. Up to 1550, the authority of his *Geographia* is evidenced by a fervent production of manuscripts, incunabular editions, and sumptuously printed folios. The rediscovery of Ptolemy triggered innovation in woodcutting, copper engraving, and movable type. Second, with the increasing stress placed on quantification and measurement during the growth of the scientific revolution, the human body and the geographic landscape of the natural world became topics of interest. Third, this was accompanied by refinements in the visual arts. In northern Europe, a "saturated" realism began to animate painted representations of rural and urban life. At the same time, in the south, the invention of artificial perspective led artists to discover ways of gridding and plotting the world before the naked eye. Plotting and perspective owe much, fourth, to the development of estate planning and the definition of private property: Landowners commissioned surveyors to chart their personal holdings and to identify arable tracts of land.

1

And fifth, political unification, or nation building, led administrators and statesmen to use maps to define national boundaries and to construct systems of defense (Buisseret 1992a: 1–2).

A sixth cause might be located in the new importance afforded to the emerging *self* and to the self's relation to the idea of national space. In this domain, which appears to be situated between raw perception and the creative imagination, there seems to be a correlation between mapping and the growth of a new medium—literature—in early modern print culture. New modes of surveying and plotting the world influence representations of the private and public domains of the individual writer. What Erich Auerbach once called the "drama" of European literature (1984) may indeed have been, in the changes between the fifteenth and seventeenth centuries, an unforeseen theatricalization of the self, which acquired a consciousness of its autonomy through modes of positioning that are developed into both textual and gridded representations of reality.

As historians, we are impelled to ask whether certain literary or creative works that sum up the status of knowledge of their times—the "comic epic" of Rabelais, the unreliable *Cosmographie universelle* and the book of "singularities" of the years 1540–1580, the personal essay (whose invention is associated with Montaigne), and even Cervantes's tales of a knight errant's misinformed adventures—are also born of a new cartographic impulse. Can their fortunes be related to changing conditions of information and its dissemination, to new taxonomies, to new relations that individuals hold with space and to an emerging sense of national identity?

The chapters that follow will respond in the affirmative by arguing that cartographic reasoning inspires both the graphic and the imaginary forms of literature. Since literature was a broadly and even ill-defined field in the sixteenth century, it behooves us to ask whether it appealed to mapping to create new forms that account for the new entity, the "self" and the "subject." Like the plotted tract of land, the topographical view, or even the coextensive design of lettering and of image in a woodcut or a copperplate engraving, the self would acquire its identity through the creation of a space that bears the presence or the reminder of the mapping of its signature. The self ascribes to its being the illusion of autonomy and of self-possession when it can be configured as a textual diagram. The "foundational fantasy" that the self endlessly reproduces, to use Teresa Brennan's words (1993: 12), depends on an alliance with a strongly marked geographic consciousness. Specifically, with reference to the literary world of the French Renaissance that will be the area studied in the nine chapters that follow, we can wonder if Rabelais's universe of the 1530s is not only a chorography of Chinon and its environs in the Touraine but also a totality that mimes the construction of a world map that valorizes the author in view of the contemporary politics of statecraft. In a no less ideological way, does Maurice Scève's *Délie* (1544), in effect a geometer's poem, deploy numbers, images, and emblems to locate a mobile site of anguish to project the portrait—of epic and lyrical scope—of a national subject? Are André Thevet's accounts of his travels to "Antarctic" France themselves also voyages that cut a path between experience and fantasy for the sake of producing imaginary conquests in the shape of self-aggrandizement? Are Montaigne's *Essais* dialogical ventures of the self into the meditation, civil strife, and contested space of the France of the 1580s? Is Descartes a cartographer who fashions himself as a surveyor, a topographer, in the double guise of an *ingénieur du roi* and an *ingénieur du moi*? Is Cervantes a cartographer both of the postmedieval Mediterranean and of the pastoral novel? All of these questions are based on the spatial, indeed quasi-cartographic traits of the early modern literary and philosophical canon.

To approach these questions from the standpoint of the production of imaginary space, nation, and selfhood, I would like to set what literary historians have established as masterworks of the Renaissance in the context of mapping and some of its tributary issues. Some points of complementarity and contrast will emerge and show that early modern printed writing and cartography share common problems and goals. They work in concert, but they also crystallize some broader issues that engage concurrent dilemmas about the emergent status of literature, cultural identity, nationhood, and the self-possessed individual. However, before these problems can be addressed, we must create a working concept of cartographic literature. Writings can be called "cartographic" insofar as tensions of space and of figuration inhere in fields of printed discourse. Most printed writing that follows the early modern age conveys effects of recorded speech. Printed characters reconstitute the verbal medium of communication; in printed texts, meaning unwinds or unfolds in the duration of reading or in our fantasy that we hear what is being conveyed through the mechanical technology of transcription. Printed discourse reproduces what seem to be "living" moments of a delivery of meaning from one interlocutor to another. As we read their works, the great authors of the early modern age appear to be "speaking" directly to us over a gap of four centuries, across a transparent page of printed characters that serve as a stenographic relay of their ideas: When we find ourselves aroused by what is being "said" to us, we sense that we participate in an animated dialogue with the writer, whom we bring to life by reproducing in our imagination the primary and living conditions of vocal exchange.[1]

We obey the laws set forth by a rhetorical contract, in which the writing winds through its arguments or unveils its world of meaning according to pre-established orders of narration. As we "listen" to the spoken words through the printed page, we nonetheless discover that our response is tentative, imaginary, seeming forever to be light-years from the context in which the writing originated. The discourse mechanically develops a fully constituted world by dint of its accumulation of meaning, its divisions into parts, its tones or rhetorical colors, and the like, so that that world becomes something akin to an organic whole bearing the signature, if not of its author, then at least of a self-proclaimed authority of an epoch that is either behind its mass or that is being constructed as a result of its accumulated effects. But as the living exchange of interlocution is dramatically reduced in the realm of printed writing, in which an indifferent graphic form conveys speech in a world of silence, the force of communication—or enunciation—is drastically weakened.

Cartographic Writing

It is as this living exchange is reduced that we discover how the presence of *space* in language, what I would like to underscore as a first component of cartographic writing, sends meaning adrift. As soon as we realize that the discursive or vocal order of printed literature happens in no small way to be a product of our imagination, or as soon as a mass of the author's "effects"—not necessarily his or her intentions—is located between meaning and its spatial form (such as the distinction between the content of a discourse and its typographic design) it becomes clear that rhetorical orders are not unrelated to diagrammatic processes. Meaning is produced through both printed and diagrammatic means. Speech is relayed, but it is also rendered visible, or it is organized in accord with categories of extension and volume that share intimate analogy not only with the graphic and visual arts but also with projective and expansive designs that tie cartography to expansion and conquest (Harvey 1989; Woodward 1991). In incunabular and sixteenth-century literature, we behold works that betray the touch of the architect, the stage designer, the painter, and, no less, the cartographer. By virtue of spatial modes of composition, the writer tends to "map out" the discourse of the work before our eyes and to invite us to see the self constituting its being in patterns that move into space by means of diagrammatic articulations.

Produced from the tension between discourse and space are works that on the one hand seek to be complete in themselves. These works are worlds that can be explored and that can be plotted, but that are also, at the same time, determined by visible coordinates that enclose, frame, and even quantify the sum of all their parts. On the other hand, these works seem to find their "bearings" at every moment and place of their composition. Even labyrinthine or encyclopedic compilations—the mobile, ever ambiguous world of Rabelais's four books of *Gargantua* and *Pantagruel*, the plenitude of Thevet's and Belleforest's works, with the same title and of the same year, *La cosmographie universelle* (1575), Montaigne's apparently helter-skelter *Essais*, or Cervantes's account of Quixote's wanderings—designate where they are with respect to their geographic and cardinal indications. No wonder, then, that the great adventure and surprise encountered in the rereading of early modern literature comes from our rediscovery of a process of discovery that *maps its movement as it goes.*

Many literary works of the years 1470–1640 appear to be seeking to contain and appropriate the world they are producing in discourse and space through conscious labors of verbal navigation. Writers borrow from a stock of geometric and cartographic commonplaces (as in new editions of the works of Johannes de Sacro Bosco, Pieter Apian, and Ptolemy) to map out creations that are totalities much greater than their authors' own appreciation or conscious knowledge of them. As fictions with mobile and ever expanding possibilities, these worlds are liable to be explored over and again. They admittedly do not fall under the total control of the author or the reader, but they internalize spatial strategies that, we can surmise, run through books of navigation (*routiers*), island atlases (the genre known as *isolario,* or the book describing and illustrating the islands of the world), sheet maps (topographical views executed by an *ingénieur du roi* or a *maréchal de logis*), cosmographies (compendious creations that combine discourse and map), and full-fledged atlases (such as the *Theatrum orbis terrarum* launched by Abraham Ortelius in 1570).

The cartographic writings of the French Renaissance share a common trait that results from the tensions between discourse and spatial plotting. In almost all of these works, there emerges an often confused, paradoxical, but indelible presence of a signatory "self" in the liminal or marginal areas between represented speech and the space on the page. The self seems to be produced in the form of a *subject* that is ruled by laws of classification or by ideology, such that it can be seen not only as an "author," an "authority," an expert cosmographer or topographer, a savant, or a technician, but also as a paradoxical being divided between a representation of the conflictual relations it is producing—including the conditions of patronage and practice in which the works are crafted—and the composite nature of the simultaneously aural and visual medium of print. The cartographic writer, brimming with self-confidence and offering swashbuckling images of himself (like Thevet or Nicolas de Nicolaï), also witnesses his silencing and alteration in the spatial medium of writing. In response to the loss of control that the medium engineers, we see ever more images of self-authorized creators who are identified as increasingly collective and "national" subjects attached to the geographies that they are both mapping and describing.[2] "Selfhood," "self-fashioning," and their consequent impact on the creation of national subjects become especially visible in the evolution of cartographic writing from the years of humanism to the age of Henry IV and the subsequent growth of French cartography (Brown 1977: 241–52; Buisseret 1992a: 113–20; Konvitz 1987: 1–40).

In what pertains here to the graphic construction of the self, I should like to argue that in this composite genre of writing and mapping, there are some viable relations between historical and psychoanalytic methods. I do not use the word "deconstruction" because, in a work that traces some elements of graphic and textual rhetoric of selfhood, the operating principles of what goes by that term are already at work.[3] The cartographic genre displays, in a nutshell, various images of emergent, autonomous subjects—writers and cartographers alike—whose projected being finds a delicately nascent place in tensions of discourse and space. The self is visible only when it achieves the effect of totality, of having engineered a world through its own labors. Yet, at the same time, in order to bear a signature, the self has to appear to be gratuitous, total, or "self-made" in a space that is granted to be its own. The self makes itself or is made to look self-like when it appears to be a simultaneous cause and effect of a creation that is both total and local. The self's emergence is evinced where discourse and geography are coordinated, and the self becomes autonomous only (1) when it is fixed to an illusion of a geographic truth (often of its own making) and (2) when it can be detached from the coordinates that mark its point of view, its history, its formation, and the aesthetics and politics of its signature.

Third, cartographic writing appears to rehearse what much criticism studies in terms of the birth of the subject and of subjectivity in early modern Europe.[4] Its mixed genre, however, affords an almost instantaneous view of its own development of the subject and subjectivity through its affinities with extension, with national boundaries, with vernacular idioms, and with the conflicts of warring states. The resulting link between cartography, logistics, and polemology (the art of dispute) is no less constitutive of the self and subject. That cartographers and practitioners of spatial writing were exercised in military and diplomatic realms comes as little surprise; neither does the growth of cartographic representation from the volumetric, three-dimensional world of the cosmographer into that of two-dimensional representations of localities as serialized, segmented or "segmentable" units of an infinite possibility of scale and focus.[5]

Here, however, intervenes a psychoanalytic dimension of our project. If the "self" constitutes the field of study to which Freud's science is dedicated, it stands to reason that some unnamed motivation inspires our desire to see how and why cartographic literature may be related to the history of the birth of the subject. What is it that fascinates us about the period attesting to the fabulous growth of cartography? Clearly, it is not that cartographic literature or early mapping develop toward transparency or accuracy from confusion and doubt about the size and shape of the world: This hypothesis would merely reiterate the main lines of a history of science that begins with error and leads either to the illusion of a state of rectitude or to making a fetish of progress and accuracy. It may be that our fascination with early modern mapping has to do with the imagination of psychogenesis in our own, more recent history, a history that involves our own struggles to disentangle ourselves from the vital, narcissistic illusion that the world begins with our birth and expands through our perception of it.[6] Thus we may invest—wrongly or rightly, but not without commitment and conviction—what we discover and relish in the inaccuracy of sixteenth-century projections (of both image and text) with a dialogic character that shares much with the movement of drives, forces, and symbolic forms that we imagine to be constitutive of ourselves. Thus our consciousness is a duplication and a reiteration of a partial and universal history of ourselves (and of the degrees of our narcissism) in a world in which we discover our heritage as gratuitous beings. In the labor of consciousness we realize that we are products of individual and collective histories with complexities that are quite beyond our grasp.

The Relation to the Unknown

In order to specify better the liminal territories between the utter gratuitousness of our birth into the world and the spatial histories that precede us, I would like to borrow four concepts from psychoanalytic theory and then graft them onto a notion of "cartographic writing." In both literature and diagrammatic reason, we witness projects that entail a historical and textual relation among maps, writing, and selfhood. First, in what Guy Rosolato calls one of the basic components of the clinical practice of analysis, the *relation to the unknown* shares much with what might have been one of the principal drives inspiring navigation and the discovery of the world. It entails a subject's ever renewed and renewing encounter with the mysteries that foster a desire to seek a sense of identity.[7] Any vital relation to language and space, to life and death, and to both the imagination and the sensation of objective reality of the world (which defies reduction to language and hence is *real*) is spurred by the unknown. Psychoanalysis takes as its goal, then, the mapping of forces that resemble what drove the cartographers and the omniverously curious thinkers of the sixteenth century—all cast, in manuals of literary history, as visionary writers—to engage their labors with the world. The unknown, graphically inscribed as *terrae incognitae* on the western and southern horizons of early maps, was traditionally included as an important element of the maps' overall depictions. It was to be conquered, or at least to become known insofar as the gain of knowledge would assure the discoverer's founding illusion of immortality. Another unknown continent, for example, the "third world," or *troisième monde,* that readers of Antonio Pigafetta's account of Magellan's voyage (readers such as Lancelot du Voisin, whom we will later encounter) "knew" to exist somewhere beyond the Pacific, was as much an admission of an aporia within reason, a deferral of conquest, as it was a reassuring enigma. Because the unknown was located by being *named,* it became a form of a relation rather than an unfathomable menace or delusion. For writers, it comprised what language always aims at naming without ever being quite able to bring under rational control: In mystical terms, the unknown would be the figure of the human navel behind or within a typographic period. The historian of cartography Christian Jacob reiterates Stéphane Mallarmé's remarks (sketched in *Crayonné au théâtre*) about naming and implantation: "Nomination is a mode of symbolic appropriation that furnishes virgin territories with a memory, with a gridding that dispossesses space of its alterity and that makes of it an object of discovery subjected to the constraints of linguistic reference, that intends that at every identifiable site there correspond a name" (1992: 267). It would be lodged in the corporal space of an image of "man," such as the lettered body in Geoffroy Tory's *Champ fleury* (1529a); located among the bizarre islands that dot the itinerary of the Pantagruelists of Rabelais's fourth book (1548 and 1552); seen in the figure in the landscape of the Rhône valley of *Délie,* the object of the poet Maurice Scève's quest; or found adrift in the currents circulating through an archipelago described in a cosmography, such that the words describing the space turn into the waters that isolate it from greater continents of knowledge. Or it might be the confused, screened image that Montaigne projects of contemporary Paris and of classical Rome at the end of the journey of his essay "De la vanité" (1962: 922–80). As we shall discover, it might also be found in the relation that the cartographer Oronce Finé holds to the shape of his own name in his career as mathematician and topographer.

Rosolato remarks that for Freud, the *relation d'inconnu* includes three perspectives that are in fact rarely studied in the "diurnal" discipline of cartography: an obsession with the trauma and mystery of birth, with the spectral presence of death, and finally, with the vital drives of sexuality, which also include madness (a spatial experience) and the brute resistance that the real exerts against language, knowledge, or representation in general. In the first, or psychoanalytic, instance, the *navel* is construed to be a site where the relation of the unknown has its first noticeable, physical trace. It becomes the site of a ruptured attachment to the world, which philosophers (Marsilio Ficino), poets (among others, Antonin Artaud), and psychoanalysts (Freud) have idealized in similar terms. The unknown declares itself to be what escapes recognition. For the growing subject, it assures a place where sexual difference is erased. In a lexicon that evokes the process of centering and of depicting contour and relief in printed maps, the navel, both a valley and an inverted molehill (what geographers call a *taupinière*), seems to allow for the designation of a place where bodily demarcations can be effaced. It could also be a dot marking an agglomeration, a capital city, or a town.[8] What Rosolato calls "umbilication" draws attention to a hollow (or relief), to a centering without any outlet or issue beyond, "to a 'one-eyed hole,' a hole that is not a hole, a caecum, a blind gut that represents a limit, an anti-abyss, an interruption along a path, a passage into the void through a conceptual impasse" (1978: 257). In this sense, the navel is freighted with cartographic and literary meanings. It invokes an origin of visibility in what is unknown (the path as a *voie*, or a road that is broken, such as the intestinal innuendo of the caecum, a "blind alley" or void in the road map of our entrails), but it is also a pertinent sign of geographic difference between the body, other bodies, and the surrounding world that is visibly defined by shifts, erasures, and undulations of its surface.

Second, the navel also becomes a site where subjects define their lives through the fantasy of losing an appendage (Rosolato 1978: 258). It is the point of separation from the mother, Freud's famous mother earth (*Mutter Erde*), but it is speculating about this point of separation that ties the writer or cartographer to the imagination of his or her presence as a godlike form, as a nurturing force. Allegorical propaganda is quick to argue in a good deal of geographic literature of the Renaissance that national space is miraculously unified, at once maternal and of a common vernacular idiom. By contrast, Freud metaphorically likened the moment of loss or rupture to that of the detachment of a mushroom from its mycelium, in other words, to a subject's birth when he or she grows out of and are broken off from the great webbings of adventitious strands of living matter that grid much of the world's surface.[9] The process of detachment that constitutes every subject's psychogenesis inspires a geographic desire to retrace one's tenuous "roots," which are woven through the visible register of language, the audible areas of images, and along the edges of signifying matter in general.[10]

Third, the navel seems to locate a slit or an opening that is absolutely necessary for a subject to gain a sense of time and place, "such that the unknown, the impossible, are indispensable to all organization of meaning," in which the experience of rupture and lack is opened by the umbilical crevasse that "comprises the hollow, the void that prefigures negation itself that will come in the area of language" (Rosolato 1978: 261). Included are fantasies about return to the womb (or the reassuring rectitude of the map, which is both a maternal and paternal image of seemingly timeless symbolic order). But the search for origins that this view of the navel inspires also carries with it a drive for self-totalization, or of idealization and conquest. The subject desires to be at one with himself or herself, with a language that would be adequate to what it describes, and at one with his or her (self-made) "map," which is the world itself, being at one with the local, national, global, and cosmic space in which he or she visualizes an origin associated with a site of birth.

The concept of a slit or gap can also focus the way a subject lives with oppositions that are essential to the tensions of his or her being: "between the inside and outside, between the visible and the invisible, between what is sure and what is uncertain, what is virgin or not (the mother), what is licit and what is forbidden, what is home-like and the uncanny" (Rosolato 1978: 270). It seems to articulate even the principles of *cardinalization* that a subject uses to gauge his or her whereabouts. The originary gap is used as a point that can be surveyed with a compass, an astrolabe, a magnetic needle, or other instruments of navigation. Thus, when Rosolato remarks that the "quest" after the unknown is "conceived as a possibility of quasi-spatial conquest through the extension of the delimited field of the known in the channel of a *polar relation with the unknown,* according to mappings that envisage the progression of a *deferred* knowledge" (1978: 273, emphasis in the original), he appeals to the very idiolect of technologies that construct early modern space.

The revery of totalization brings the cartographic impulse into the drives that produce the subject. Here two ancillary, but no less cartographic, components mark the figure of the navel as an embodiment of the relation to the unknown. The subject desires to give birth to himself or herself without the intermediary of the parent; the subject feels that the beginning of the world is coextensive with his or her birth; thus, the creation of a "universal cosmography" or of a self-contained sum of a "book of essays" would serve as a realization of an artificial self-birthing and self-monumentalization. It would also be akin to Rabelais's creation of a universe of wise, "Pantagruelic" children that is the book *Gargantua,* or to Montaigne's stillborn but immortal progeny, the male child that replaces (or is the bookish homunculus of) the sibling that will perpetuate his name, immortalized in the shape of the published book of *Essais.*[11] Hence one writes or maps out a limited "totality" as if one were reproducing the travail of the mother in a self-contained act of fertilization, pregnancy, labor, and birthing. With the unknown, "everything that is placed under the term of creation evokes the giving of birth" (Rosolato 1978: 264).

Beyond the form of the navel, the relation with the unknown has a less mimetic and more forceful correlative in its association with the unconscious. Although it is safe to say that the unconscious could not have existed in the epistemological frame of the sixteenth century, it nonetheless cannot fail to be associated with whatever defies fixed meaning (what writers attempt to create in ever recurring, mobile, and modular structures that endow themselves with renewed form), with *terrae incognitae* (illustrated with scenes of cannibalism, vivisection, and death), and with the depiction of mental space. This is exactly where Freud schematizes the unconscious as a great circle that encloses within its area a smaller circle that is the conscious. He constructs the unknown in a way not unlike cosmographers' descriptions of the Ptolemaic universe in early modern print culture.[12] At the same time, the unconscious denotes the erasure of demarcation between life and death inasmuch as it draws the horizon of alterity into the register of life. Time and again, narratives of the Renaissance tell of the construction of the subject through a venture—a plotted itinerary—into the realm of death and back again. These individuals "find themselves" when they establish their bearings within infernal or other regions beyond the known. Rabelais's Epistémon, beheaded or weaned (*la coupe testée,* the antistrophe of *la teste coupée,* in Rabelais 1962: 294–302), in sum, tested when reborn—thanks to Panurge's surgical talent of reattaching bodily members lost on the field of battle—tells of his travels into Lucifer's domain. And, in order to produce a great geography of introspection, Montaigne (1962: 350–60) "invents" a story of his brush with death that recalls the moment he was knocked unconscious upon falling from a horse and taken for dead. A function of life and death delineates both cosmic and affective space.

Frequently, the encounter with death is averred to be an erotic or a mystical event. It shares much with the experience of cartographic literature. The novelty of printed world maps that redrew, varied upon, added to, or took leave of Ptolemaic models could not fail to contain vestiges of a mystical relation with languages and images. For the first time, we imagine, viewers of these new, post-Columbian maps were able to see the totality of the world *from without while within* its confines, with effects no less dazzling than those of our first reception of images of the earth taken from the moon in 1968. Spectators could imagine themselves in the midst of a mystical voyage beyond the confines of a well-beaten space by means of newly known areas being projectively distorted onto flat planes that yielded illusions of a universe of infinite curvature. The viewer of these early maps could thus broach the unknown all the while he or she was leading the grounding paradox of the outside-inside into areas that, at least in narrative and literary domains, could probe confusions of sexual identity, of parentage, of authority, and of kinship within the body of the self. Access to a mystical vision, offered by the impossible "point of view" given to the observer of early world maps, was no doubt gained so quickly that it soon became an object to be purveyed. In this light, mystical effects quickly became commodities of mysticism. Nonetheless, writers who seek to gain worlds beyond reason use the surface of maps to effect voyages on paper and in discourse. The common mystical narrative, which tells of a dedifferentiation of the world and the body and of a contact with supernatural beings, depends on an itinerary *through* space and language. It departs into what is reputed to be a void and is verified by some trace—usually a scar—left on the body of the figure narrating the event.[13]

Cartographic literature would tend, therefore, both to foster and to discredit the mystical relation with the unknown. It fosters the relation insofar as the mix of visible and discursive forms situates or leads the journey into an area where the one is dedifferentiated from the other, in order that a language of enigmas—rebuses, ideograms, hieroglyphics—can convey the incommunicability and fascination that the unknown seems to be offering. But it discredits it insofar as the printed and drafted character of the account has been rationalized, proofread, set in letterpress, and distributed for the sake of gain rather than of encountering the unknown. No wonder, then, that the literature that treats of the *relation d'inconnu* seems to hold a rapport with rational thinking that parallels the evolution of the map from a cosmographic to a geographic instrument. It is in the works of the seventeenth century, reports Michel de Certeau, that one first encounters the term "mystic*ism*," meaning that its status as substantive allowed it to be studied scientifically, as an object, whereas in the works of the Renaissance and before, only adjectival forms of the term had occurred, suggesting that the nonsubstantive status of mystical activities made them more *real* than we might believe (de Certeau 1992: 11–25, esp. 15). The development of atlas-structures and of two-dimensional views confirms a rapid attenuation of the mixture of scientific and mystical dimensions in the history of cartographic literature from the age of the incunabulum to the triumph of Cartesian method. It parallels, too, the shift from a half-named sense of the unknown to a clearly articulated *relation* with the unknown.

The Perspectival Object

A second psychoanalytic concept connected to the nexus of the unknown and part of a greater cartographic infrastructure is the *perspectival object* (*objet de perspective*). This concept has to do with the positioning and mapping of the self in and about the world in its ongoing construction of psychogenesis, and it is tied at once to aesthetics, the history of perspective, and clinical practice.[14] Crafted from clinical experience, literary theory, art history, and linguistic principles, it designates a series of junctures between a viewer and what he or she sees, projects, fantasizes, and remembers, but what also always eludes containment. A *prise de conscience* with the real and with the body's location in the world, the perspectival object is bound to the relation with the unknown at the point where what is taken to be evident or "visible" meets what remains invisible or outside of language. Graphically, it might be compared to the areas in early modern maps where the edges of the stereographically assembled letters that spell "*terrae incognitae*" inform the environing space in such a way that the designation marks an intersection between things known—on the printed, gridded, and colored surface—and things yet to be named. Between what is clearly grasped, that is, the sign of an unknown body of land or water, and what is imagined to be its aspect, its flora, its fauna, and its singularities, the perspectival object remains a site where visual signs and conjecture meet and disappear together.

In a psychoanalytic sense, the concept has ramifications in three areas that are crucial for the formation of the subject. First, when an analysand's discourse resists analysis, it is usually because the patient refuses to draw attention to the ways he or she avoids taking stock of habitual activities. The analysand prefers to adhere to pregiven roles in an imagined "theater" of operations.[15] By holding to a neutrality that does not play into the scenarios he or she is asked to enter, the analyst attempts to exert a subtle and persistent influence so that patients will begin to *see* what is happening in the utterances that have not been adequately heard. Where significant sounds, pauses, or verbal articulations—in conjunctions, phatic signs, or other manifestations of speech—are seen, both analyst and patient can note patterns of deviation or of complicated circuitries of relations with the past and present. Once they are grasped, some of these visible shards or fragments of speech allow the labor of analysis to begin.[16]

The analysand, therefore, begins to cope with his or her formation as a subject when the ostensible transparency of the spoken discourse begins to acquire perspectival traits, which are sensed as knots that show something that language cannot utter but that inheres in the shape or the position of these traits with respect to the verbal surrounding. At a vanishing point that is both changing, mobile, and only fleetingly present in the speech, access is gained to areas that the patient had carefully barred.[17] The patient no doubt refuses to account for these points for many reasons, including the fear of violence or the disabling effect that recognition might change his or her way of thinking and doing. In approaching this anarchic state of things, the patient seeks to find an indiscriminate mix of language and image. It is obtained by the cultivation of a *free attention*, or a mode of "scanning" one's discourse in order to approximate a preconscious feel for the touch, color, sight, and sound of language.[18]

We shall see how perspectival objects tend to "grid" the relation of the visible and the invisible in cartography and writing and how a certain mobility of flux and indeterminacy in their operation quickly sets in and becomes—at least in the world of René Descartes—a subliminal practice, that is, one that is seemingly unconscious, elaborated in order, it appears, to inscribe the presence of a pictorial or topographical unconsciousness in the drift of writing. In every event, in the context of literary and mapped creations, the *objet de perspective* serves as a hinge that binds two different orders. It also draws one area of consciousness into and through another. It shows how the artifact is of an ever composite nature in which differences are of its essence and in which its ideological dimensions are crystallized. What the late J. Brian Harley effectively calls the "hidden agenda" of cartographic practices seems to come into view when this concept is used to study works of the past.[19]

The perspectival object has an added advantage as an analytic tool when it is applied to areas other than psychoanalysis. As we have noted, the concept and its process allow the patient—but also the spectator and the reader—to mark an *active* critical relation with the discourse and images set before his or her eyes. Instead of simply detecting what objects are said to mean, the viewer is urged to look at things *transversally*, from a bias other than what is inferred in a contract of decipherment that follows the codes of the discipline in which it is located. In the terms of what follows, the spectator or reader invents the process of subjectivity when analyzing the differential patterns that are working in the cartographic document. He or she lives through the discovery of a mode of control and of division, that is, through whatever agency is used to divide attention in order to establish relations of perplexity, which are basic to the double binds that constitute ideology and subjectivity.

Thus, we can hypothesize that early modern cartographic literature owes much of its power to its discovery that it can produce ideology through its implementation of myriad double binds: of cosmic and local space, of a viewer included and excluded from the discourse, of weakened deixis (or dialogue), of shifts and transformation of text and figure, of different versions of the same space presented differently in the same atlas (which occurs not only in editions of Ptolemy's work but also in the works of Ortelius and his followers). Drawing on Gregory Bateson (1972: 271–78), Rosolato defines the double bind in decidedly optical terms, "as the mental focalization upon an impasse, an undecidable choice such that it invades one's entire psychic life, even to the point of either paralyzing it, or making necessary solutions of rupture obtained through violence, or of getting out of it through recourse to an originary path [*voie*] outside of its system" (1978: 164). The double bind, he adds, is *power itself.* Those who deploy it—which includes writers and cartographers, the avatars of the image makers of our time—present their interlocutors, their listeners, or their general public with choices that cannot be made, thus diminishing their powers of judgment or response. As in the age of Louis XIV, when cartography flourished in France,[20] the producer of double binds in political and aesthetic spheres seems to have an "excess of mastery" and an "absolute quest of power" (1978: 166).

The *objet de perspective* seems to embody the double bind. When observers use the *objet de perspective* instead of or concurrently with the image maker, they are able to find an escape from the double bind. The exit can take the form of dialogue that puts a visible distance between the object producing the bind and one's own sensibility, discerned in a "vital movement and invention in the direction of the other, in the way that art offers a paradigm for the general process" (Rosolato 1978: 176), meaning that what is felt as other is also a relation being established with the unknown.

So far, we have shown that the perspectival object has served to locate and to mirror the construction of double binds that mobilize subjectivity. We have seen that active use of a doubly bound relation to the visible and the invisible grants agency to the reader, spectator, or analysand. It also points to areas where the pictural, diagrammatic, or nonlinguistic areas of writing are tipped into spaces otherwise occupied by language. A nonverbal fragment, a shard of the real, inheres or is encrusted in discourse so as to make meaning enigmatic or indiscernible, especially in the very areas where a clarity of expression seems to reign. Here there also exists a temporal dimension of the concept. On the analytic stage, patients search for impressions of origins in order to reach thresholds from which they can invent the space of their everyday lives. The perspectival object stipples those areas where a projection of the past is focused and is about to insert itself into the present. It is also a transitional object (Winnicott 1971), in that it releases the patient into a field of dialogical or interdiscursive "play" between impressions and memories.

It would not be wrong to speculate that cartographic writing, because it seeks to account for origins, to chart out the past, and to legitimate the present state of things, is also an object *in* a perspective created for consciously designed programs, mapping out the collective past that the official artisans of national glory would like to project (such as the Trojan origins of the French, as recounted by Jean Lemaire and Pierre de Ronsard). It finds ruins, relics, and residue in antiquities that are charted on topographical views (e.g., those of Gabriele Symeone), in itineraria (such as Charles Estienne's *Le guide des chemins*, 1552), and in toponyms (which Maurice Bouguereau delights in glossing on the verso pages of his *Le théâtre françoys,* cribbed from François de Belleforest). The cartographic project invents a relation with the past by coordinating archaeological and geographic information that builds a case for national supremacy or identity. The latter is confined to local areas that manufactured both a regional and national consciousness within the divisions of religious wars that ultimately established a firm spatial coherence. Early cartographic writing produces a *pact,* of which one might have been unaware, and, in doing so, it promotes an unconscious—a relation of difference with the unknown—which acquires a temporal background at the same time that it develops a spatial sense that will quickly rationalize colonial expansion.

The mass of textual material that accompanies single-sheet or atlas maps tends to reveal its ideological perspective in the gaps between a silent, spatial, schematic rendering of an area (in visual form) and a voluble, copious, emphatic, printed discourse that strives to tell of the invisible history that the image cannot put into words. Thus, if maps seek to create double binds by putting subjects into their place and simultaneously freeing them of that place by virtue of the surrounding variety in or of the image, their historiographical operation also frees their readers from the constraints of a limited or mythic sense of time. The spectator who dwells on the toponym of the "birthplace" he or she sees on the map affirms, "I live here, this is where my forebears have lived, this is where I shall die, next to my kin," and so invests the map with the image of a greater extension of time that is yet another illusion.[21] In short, if the perspectival object is understood in a way that is conjoined to the transitional object, then one can discern correlations between the production of ideology of space and of time in the cartographic institutions of the Renaissance.

It appears, too, that in their strongest expression of power, early modern maps and texts tend to impose upon their users a *projective identification* (McDougall 1991a: 173), an illusion that tells who, where, and what these maps are about, and specifies the power that they wish to appropriate in diplomatic and military areas. But when their users respond with interrogation or play, with distraction or a bent for scanning, or with inversions of text and image, the ideal user (perhaps the historian) evades the constraining effects of cartographic strategies. Double binds give way to a creative reworking that may or may not be channeled into the project of self and nation. When one wanders or gets lost in the space of language, new agency is obtained in the discourse of images; it is a mystical but also a highly coded activity.[22] The perspectival object is the concept that shifts the spectator from a passive role to that of an engaged traveler who moves through the time and space of a given body of words, images, and sensation. The concept offers cardinal points, markers, and signposts that grant passage into vital and marginal areas where imagination, fact, history, and the self are combined.

Pictograms

A third, correlative concept that devolves from the relation with the unknown and the perspectival object is that of the *pictogram*. According to Piera Aulagnier (1975: 81–127), the real labor of analysis begins when a subject discerns fragments of visible writing in the field of memory. These are remainders of a preconscious "grammar" that mediates the trauma of detachment necessary for the process of "shattering into" life (Bersani 1990) and for breaking the dyadic relation of illusory plenitude between the self and an origin that is no less necessary to fuel the drive to live. The analysand glimpses these pieces of writing *as if by chance* in order to discern the universality and fortuitousness of his or her psychogenetic history. That history is universal because it is common and basic to life; fortuitous, because all human subjects pass through the same violence of beginnings. With the aid of the pictogram, patients can reconstruct a geography that becomes far more meaningful than would be an unquestioned acceptance of the names of persons and places that are conferred upon them from without. We can imagine the pictogram to be a mix of alphabetical shapes, a bodily form, a memory of a seemingly archaic past of confusion and violence, and, too, a dedifferentiated form with indiscriminately plastic and lexical attributes. Like the iconic and symbolic force of the navel, or the coordinate features of the perspectival object, the pictogram brings together space, language, and tactility. A private, illegible discourse shunts between the trauma of birth and growth and the onslaught of symbolic forms that continually bombard the growing infant.

The concept would appear to be far from cartographic literature. As adepts of astrology, cartographic authors are obsessed with the time, the place, and the surrounding character of the origins and traits of writing that adorn the images they make of themselves in their works. In his writings, Oronce Finé calls attention to his Dauphinois character (*Finé* being *in* Dau*phiné*), since the hills and valleys of the French Alps were reputedly giving its population mathematical and geographic aptitude available nowhere else in France. The umbilicus of his birthplace at Le Champ-Rouët (near Briançon) figures as a vanishing point in at least one of his projections. And the Dauphinois Nicolas de Nicolaï, who held the position entitled *géographe du roy* under Henry II in the 1550s, takes pleasure in recounting how, "like a dolphin," he swam out of the womb of the same countryside before embarking on a career as a geographer and an emissary for the king. Writers draw attention to their "unique" past, which seems to be congealed in the shape of their names and works. More precociously, in 1529 Geoffroy Tory elaborates a great "pictogrammar" of allegorized letters designed to launch a new typographic style that supersedes and also contains in its form the entire history of antiquity. The letters that he designs grid a national, a humanist, and a vernacular space set in front of what he ascertains to be a recently murky, incunabular past that is visualized in the angularities of gothic type (the *lettre de forme* and the *lettre bâtarde*). The pictogram enables the Renaissance subject to produce the illusion of his or her birth into and out of a national arena.

As with the preceding concepts, the pictogram is mobile. It moves between one register of cognition and another. It resembles the rebus and the calligram (Céard and Margolin 1986; Foucault 1973) in that it conflates language and image and is thus liable to move in many unpredictable directions. In the analytic theater, the pictogram mobilizes wit and laughter, caused by a short-circuiting of rational thinking (Bastide 1970), for the constitution of a psychogeography. Clinical literature reports that in full-fledged cures, the analysts and their patients endure together long hours of unproductive discourse. A necessary tedium gives way, on unexpected occasions, to explosive "connections" that collapse images in memory, current impressions, and fragments of remembered writing. These are illuminations, flashes and dazzles of new awareness, that sally forth when diurnal thinking is momentarily suspended, or when the world of art cuts into that of ideology. Sophie de Mijolla-Mellor notes that "the labor of interpretation consists exactly in opening onto surprise, in the sense of the immediate rediscovery of the known . . . when a suspension of attention allows the labor [of analysis] to be accomplished at an infra-conscious level" (1991: 201–2).[23] An *other* grammar within accepted codes of discourse, the pictogram affords a new consciousness and a sense of animation that comes with a subject's feeling of deracination and freedom from confining areas of language. A subjective and universal sense of history and geography takes root in the explosive traits of languages that confuse pictorial and lexical properties.

It should be noted that the wit of the pictogram animates both imaginary and real movement. Michel de Certeau, in a view of thinking that shares much with Tory's vision of the space of writing, has shown that letters, seen as "textual icons" (such as the butterfly-winged figure of an *angel* concretizing the origin of visibility in a pictorial *angle*), can "initiate other encounters and other spaces" in both the mind and the urge that anyone feels when he or she begins to wander.[24] A movement that issues out of (and that also burrows into) the self begins in the very areas where public institutions strive to impose control.

And the historical evolution of the pictogram in cartographic documents attests to the same ambivalence of image, language, and meaning. Sixteenth-century maps can be identified by a tendency to replace *words,* which occupied much of the surface of earlier models, with initials, abbreviations, or *pictograms* to "air out the field of the map, to remove useless commentaries and suppress words where a sign or an adopted type of letter suffices to designate what is given" (Dainville 1964b, cited by Jacob 1992: 313). They are first mimetic figures, such as of buildings or grapes on vines, but they quickly become ideograms that appeal to subjective memory or that convey, in a blitz, various ideas through a sign that confuses language and image, that disrupts and affirms a state of things. The picto–ideogram becomes a stenographic form that telescopes language and extends into space as it signals a point where memory and national identity are being schematized. It remains, however, descriptive by dint of miming the object, not of translating it into an ostensibly neutral code of signs. As in the psychoanalytic frame, the pictogram stands attached to the place that it both represents and remotivates. Jacob notes that "old maps are preoccupied with information at the specific point where it can be written, only at the very site of its pertinence" (1992: 316).

As in the case of the other concepts enumerated above, the pictogram is also a doubly bound concept. It can spell or map out an area of control whenever the unforeseen relations of images and language become predictable or limiting, such as in the effects of jokes that are used to ensure decorum through humor that muffles wit. In these dominant instances, the pictogram serves the purpose of an ideology: Rabelais exploits humor in *Gargantua* to follow a prescribed order that will mask the twisted and distorted views that are otherwise visible in the same material. The creation of a national space by means of "language maps" (Cave 1991) of humor would constitute a limited use of the pictogram. It would be the continuum of speech where "speaking is not seeing" (Blanchot 1969: 34–35) and where reason prevails. However, when historical and psychoanalytic dimensions are shared, the pictogram locates a point where past and present space can be reinvented. As Aulagnier (1975: 127) and Rosolato (1993: 50) underscore in different ways, the pictogram allows the subject to reach back to what they call the rigid structures of originary fantasm, to the unconscious, and to childhood experiences that precede the acquisition of language. The subject uses the illusion of a given spatial and historical order to create an imaginary world of impressions that tie his or her body to a *mobility* of space and place. New connections are made by virtue of the pictogram that moves between inherited orders of geography and a sense of growth *into* a map that is at once recognizable, collective, and personal.

The Signature

A fourth concept, linked to the pictogram, that serves to define cartographic writing is the *signature*. If we take a historical view of what Joyce McDougall calls the "psychogenetic theater," it appears that the early modern individual attempts to overcome the gratuitousness of his or her being-in-the-world not merely by appealing to religion but also by affixing his or her proper name to signs of works, times, and places. "Maistre Geoffroy Tory de Bourges, libraire et autheur"; "Oronce Finé dauphinois"; "François Rabelais, docteur en medecine et calloier des isles hieres"; "André Thevet, angoumois, cosmographe du roy"; "Maurice Bouguereau, imprimeur & libraire demeurant en la rue de la Scellerie, devant la Trinité" (of Tours)—these and other formulas betray a will to be attached to a world, or a work, at the very moment when there reigns a fragile or tenuous motivation between language and its spheres of reference.[25] The signature would be the point where an act of motivation is recalled in particularly spatial and graphic terms. The signature is not located within the grammatical webbing of a text, nor is it really located within the map; rather, it is affixed to the edges or in the spandrels between a map and its borders. This is an intermediate area where the subject is commodified in the mechanical operation of printed writing. Because the signature is both ungrounded and necessary, it is also a focal point or perspectival object; when it is a topic for play and experiment, its components can easily be recombined and recrafted through appeal to pictogrammar.

The signature marks an axis where the known and the unknown or the visible and invisible tend to meet. It can be serious (François Rabelais), artfully scrambled (Alcofribas Nasier, an almost anatomical anagram of the author's name), demonic in its will to move across a text or an image (Montaigne on the hilly landscape of the *Essais*), or it can serve the royal order all the while it is detached from it (*Oronce Finé dauphinois*, embodying but also deploying the totem of the former dauphin, King Francis I). It is freighted by a sense of motion that, over time, folds upon itself to the point of almost total concealment or absence (René Descartes, who allows us to glimpse the *Discours de la méthode* as a creation mapped about the pictogram of his own name). Because the signature focuses the labors of writing, of mapping, and of wit, it becomes a privileged mark of both the spatialization of language and the obsessions that works of the sixteenth century make everywhere manifest in their authors' attempts to immortalize and monumentalize themselves. In cartography, names and their adjacent dates have *authenticating effects* that valorize the execution of and the labor invested in the drawing, printing, and coloring of maps. They are also sites where falsification is often practiced: Names in copperplate are erased, and dates are changed to give the effect of novelty and freshness to projections not deemed worthy enough to be redrawn. Long before copyright law, the signature became a site of contested authority and of counterfeit.

The signature also engages the doubly bound process of *reiteration*. The "event" of the map and its presentation, or of the self becoming and being the subject of its own cartography, takes place when the signature is seen pertaining to its own divided nature. It can be the time and place of its own performance (Derrida 1972b), but also a figure of contestation. The writer or cartographer labors at creating the aura of the language and the lands of his patron, but he also gains currency, ascendency, and even a sense of adequacy through the gesture and reminder of his own presence located in the inscription. Sometimes the map is implicitly drawn around and about the apparent origin of a secret signature. Like the map or the design of contemporary literary works, the signature embodies a quasi-*diagrammatic* property that is derived from its ambivalent condition of being between spatial form and language. It posits a relation of forces that move along the interstices of the known and the unknown and that, when seen over time, determine a history of forces and of subjects.[26]

To sum up: the relation to the unknown, the perspectival object, the pictogram, and the signature offer viable articulations of two different axes that cross early modern writing and cartography. One involves the creation and re-creation of the "subject" in space and history in both graphic and psychogenetic terms. The individual who comes to be named as such can only do so when he or she gains the required illusion of having a real place in the world or, failing that, of experiencing movement in space and language that redeems the labor of living. Through confronting the unknown, an increasing awareness of a perspectival point is gained in biological and historical time. Travel is offered in the commodities of a new literature of images and maps.[27] A sense of self-distance and power are obtained in the enactment of a signature. These are, to be sure, the material components of autobiography, but also of self-mapping.

The other axis involves a history that sees the birth of the subject at a moment that coincides with the extraordinary growth of cartography in print culture.[28] The time (1460–1640) roughly parallels that of the coming of autobiography, thus hinting that mapping is responsible for the consciousness that leads to the production of the fashioned self. The creation of the subject is buttressed by the subject's affiliation with the mapping of the world. Such are the broad theoretical lines that inform the arguments in the chapters that follow.

Approaches

The chapters that follow will navigate between seemingly literary artifacts and cartographic documents. In the mixed and often confused matter of sixteenth-century writing, in which form is at once virtual and material and structure is always mobile, I would like to contend that cartographic writing possesses nascently programmatic—or covertly diagrammatic—configurations. Cartographic writing serves as a guide or compass for verbal plotting, but it also betrays its agendas by turning the reader's gaze toward a productive consideration of its visible form. Inversely, cartographic materials of the period are riddled with the dialogue—and dialogic echoes—of writing that is disruptive in different ways. Where they are endowed with an authority of silence, maps of the period also speak with powerful and mystical voices. They comment on their form; they question the impossible finality of their diagrammatic construction through a third or supplementary voice heard in the language hidden between its printed words and images. Those voices can sometimes be detected with the aid of the concepts adumbrated above, but they are not always a function of them. They display and speak of their own relations with themselves.

The study moves from documents that imply a mapping impulse in language and picture to those that consciously—if furtively—fold that impulse into their design. Earlier works evince a cartographic consciousness and a sense of selfhood in the ways that their discourse is gridded or allegorized through appeal to spatial rhetoric. First, the paintings of Jean Fouquet, the tales of *Les cent nouvelles nouvelles* (1462 and 1486), and the poetry of Jean Molinet (ca. 1475–1485) translate a diagrammatic consciousness in shapes that belong both to manuscript and incunabular cultures. They mark an awareness of travel and of a growing sense of national space that must be circumscribed in the staging of their performance as objects given to be seen but also to be read, both silently and aloud. Second, Geoffroy Tory's project of welding perspective to language announces a quasi-cartographic mode of writing that will dominate most of the sixteenth century. In chapter 3, we shall see how Oronce Finé shares and mobilizes much of Tory's labors in cartography, the woodcut, and the art of the printed book. Rabelais's global vision may find, then, a cartographic parallel in the maps and texts of Oronce Finé.

As we move into the reign of Henry II and Catherine de Medici, we witness a moment of experiment in writing and cartography. It yields cosmographies and the *isolario,* or "island atlas," of cartographic writing that attest to the relation between mapping and early ethnography. It takes the form of compositely drawn travel books, initial signs of a discourse of singularity, that break and combine diagram and writing (André Thevet's *Cosmographie de Levant* of 1554 and *Les singularitez de la France antarctique* of 1557, as well as *Les navigations, peregrinations, et voyages . . .* of Nicolas de Nicolaï, published five years later). We shall see that the years of civil war show how the birth of the self and of an ideology of nation are comparable, and we shall see that the new form of a self-produced "geography" of writing emerges when Montaigne's *Essais* (1580, 1588, and 1592) are set adjacent to the first French text-atlas, Maurice Bouguereau's *Le théâtre françoys* (1594). Finally, after Henry IV's model of statecraft is set in place, when fortification, centralization, and extensive rebuilding of national borders are undertaken, the itinerary of the self becomes complete: In the form of his *Discours de la méthode,* Descartes—his name being the perspectival signature of his existential relation with space—displays to his public the image of an autonomous geography of writing, or a text that tells about how it is to become a self-made map.

I

Franco-Burgundian Backgrounds: Some Figural Relations with Space

Representations of space in late-medieval French painting provide some indication of the development of cartographic writing. We know that the landscapes in the works of the Limbourg brothers and Jean Fouquet are tied to the saturated symbolism of their northern predecessors, the van Eyck brothers and their followers, in whose paintings every visible detail is invested with symbolic meaning. Analogies congealed in the paint and varnish are the physical signs of a language of abstraction within the images before our eyes. Details accumulate, their sum generating comparisons and relations all over the painted surfaces where they are located. The viewer faces the dilemma not only of having to decipher encrypted signs that seem to be held within forms that give depth to the landscape but also of determining how each sign is set in other—no less encrypted—dimensions of spatial relations. The paintings seem to be multilayered "texts" that can be read and seen in various ways at once.

The same paintings, however, yield to perspectival systems that allow the eye to gather in a glance the entirety of both their meanings and their spatial arrangements. The fifteenth-century French masters appear to drain the northern landscape of some of its allegorical density by placing within the Flemish landscape a systematic, quasi-Albertian conception of space that follows the mode of representation that Filippo Brunelleschi had theorized in the 1420s. Coordinate systems tend to grid what comes to the naked eye, or what the eye reaches out to grasp. A French style emerged when the followers of the "International Style" brought together two vastly different ways of representing the world. Erwin Panofsky calls the French role one of *mediatrix et pacis vinculum,* in which the respectively meditative and affective traits of the van Eycks and the Master of Flémalle (Robert Campin) are synthesized (1971: 307), and in which the nation is, so to speak, "infiltrated by shock troops trained in the camps of the Flémalle master and Jan van Eyck, swamped by a massive army of Rogerians [followers of Rogier van der Weyden] and held by a post-Rogerian occupation force" (308). In a word, France not only mediates two strains of representation that come from the Netherlands, but it does so by means of its proximity to Italian styles that protect the nation from aesthetic invasions from the North.

At least two different cultural systems are mixed. On the one hand, we see how French painting seeks new and innovative solutions by combining different styles, and on the other, we witness different types of figuration working through each other. In the evolution of late-medieval French painting, northern and southern modes are synthesized, but so are multifarious relations of space and of textual inscription. Between the one and the other we can perceive the nascent presence of a cartographic space defined by the emergent webbings that are themselves defined by identities and differences of verbal and figural forms. It is also a space in which the coming of the Renaissance is felt when a pictorial order of discourse begins to mark the representation of time. The movement of discrete units of language seems to supplant the abstraction of meditation on meaning. A mapping of space is accomplished when *passage* defines the representation of accumulated details. In the words of Pierre Francastel,

> Here we touch on one of the great distinctions between the figurative system of the quattrocento and the Middle Ages. In Italy, a single way of attaining the projective montage of the elements of the language of painting pertains at once to things spiritual and temporal. In the (the Master of Flémalle's) Mérode altarpiece, the imaginary circuit that we follow in order to take account of the work is marked by the presence of three places, but also of three temporalities—the figurative, the mythic, and the real—and of three projective solutions: the abstract cube, intellectualized space, and space studded with imaginary objects. (1967: 247–48)

All the things that we behold in the field of view of a painting like Campin's *Mérode Altarpiece* are juxtaposed, and what might seem to be an idea of instantaneous, fixing, and unifying vision cannot quite be felt or discerned. A figurative language is held in what is implied to be a highly paratactic articulation of space and symbol. The array of things that we see in the works of the Master of Flémalle, or in the oeuvre of van Eyck "incarnates the spirit of its place; but this place is eradicated, at the same time, in front of the actualization of the invisible" (250) that we behold. What the northern tradition encodes in painting in spiritual terms contrasts with Masaccio's discovery of an area of "the visual and even the tangible" (251). In other words, the field of figuration, the wall, that is for northern art the "site of an exchange of values between the tangible and the spiritual" becomes, in the south, "the field of a visual illusion" (251).

A French Model: Jean Fouquet

Jean Fouquet locates a point where these identities and differences of visual and lexical shapes begin to intersect. With calculated combinations of writing and of painting, as if anticipating a synthesis of landscape painting and cartographic representations of space and place names, Fouquet defines a field of meditation in compositions that draw on the perspectival modes of quattrocento Italian artists and the symbolic realism inherited from the van Eycks and the Master of Flémalle. Fouquet, born in Tours about 1420, lived in Italy (Rome, Florence, and Naples) from 1442 to 1447. He returned to France, went to Paris, and in 1461 he returned to Tours to finish a construction for the entry of Louis XI to the city. From 1470 to 1474 he completed a painting for the new order of the Knights of Saint Michael, a book of hours for Marie de Cleves, another for Philippe de Commynes, and a model for the tomb of Louis XI. In 1475, awarded the title of *peintre du roi*, he was commissioned to decorate a dais celebrating the arrival of the king of Portugal to Tours. He probably died shortly thereafter (Pächt 1940–41; Castelnuevo 1966).

Fouquet's work varies in genre, in style, and in its articulation of the circumstances surrounding its making. The artist executes both miniatures and portraits with the same mastery of detail and polish that had been the trademark of the International Style in France throughout the first half of the century. But Fouquet's training in Italy brought new and timely inspiration that inflects the constructions of space that came to dominate art, poetry, and narrative in the later years of the fifteenth century. In *Livre d'heures d'Etienne Chevalier* (ca. 1450), Fouquet appears to mix realism and heraldry, as had the Boucicaut master and the Limbourgs before him (Panofsky 1971: 60); in the *Heures,* the effect of realism and coded figuration mixes schematic and realistic modes. In the *Nativity of Saint John the Baptist* (Figure 1.1, finished about 1450), the tiled floor serves as a grid and a perspectival device on which are seen the daily chores of preparing water and drying linen in the guise of the symbolic presence of baptism. Two frames, enclosing a heraldic initial and a lamb representing Christ, float, as if in trompe l'oeil, in an intermediate space

Figure 1.1. Detail of *Nativity of Saint John the Baptist* (Jean Fouquet, *Les Heures d'Etienne Chevalier*)

between the scene and the spectator. So also do the wooden panels, crowned with ogee arches, illustrating three moments of the saint's life, held by two angels in the lower area, in an effect of *repoussoir*. The tiled floor on which the angels are kneeling gives way to the space of the realistic depiction above at the same time that it introduces the more abstract, diagrammatic forms that en-code the announcement of "things to come" in the three moments of the saint's life, in the heraldic signs above, and in the letters that appear to be woven into the cloth of the baldachin over the bed attended by ladies in waiting. We behold the scene from the "bird's eye view" that characterizes a carto-graphic tradition; at the same time, the space, imbued with naturalistic detail, serves to bring forth a presence of writing and of mute signs that turn the work into a flat, paginal surface on which are written heraldic forms and place names. The point where spatial illusion and the flat, gridded qualities of the scene seem to meet is at the tip of the chronicler's stylus, which traces a letter on a parchment sheet resting on his crossed legs. Two ways of looking at space are mixed: One, illusionistic, belongs to the tradition of genre painting and of landscape that is not distant from the topographical domain; the other, figural and lexical, requires the viewer to decipher the characters of a language that seems to be encrusted in the image. Although the perspective is only vaguely Italian, the lines of force converge from the corners of the rectangle to the face and halo of the Madonna in the upper center of the depiction.

The illusionistic quality that the nascent vanishing perspective confers upon the both singular and quotidian scene is more directly actualized in the *Annunciation* (Figure 1.2, 16.5 × 12 cm). Here, the Italian system is set in a late-Gothic church seen beneath the heraldic frame of a basket-handle arch. A southern mode that is shaped to the proportions of "man" is applied to the mystical space of a northern interior. The lines in the design of the floor, like those of the window sills at the lower edge of the clerestory, move toward the background, where a sculpted figure, possibly of Moses, stands under a taber-nacle and holds the Holy Tablets. The ridge rib that traverses the four bays of the vaulted ceiling (not visible here) has the same effect (especially when the eye connects the lines of the pendant chandelier to the dais supported by four columns in the space between the altar and the sculpture set against the east wall). All the illusion of a depth and volume infused with mysterious light is countered by the projective signature of the painter, which takes the form of bodies that resemble sculpted forms that we "read" in serial progression from foreground to background.[1] Eight statues (two of which are melded into the wall, ostensibly "fudged," evidence of the painter's indecision about effacing or retaining them in the first bay of the apse) on the north and south walls of the chapel are placed on spiral columns under the shafted mullions that bisect the lancet windows above.

Flattening and scattering the portrayal is the spatial configuration of writ-ing. The words of the annunciation, scripted in gold letters below the picture (and separated by the "diaphragm" of a gold bar over the blue background on which they stand) give way to a closed book at the lower left corner, garnished with green clasps on a red binding, that is placed on a carpet whose rectangu-lar border is written in several alphabets. On the carpet reposes (if we read the

Figure 1.2. Detail of *Annunciation* (Jean Fouquet, *Les Heures d'Etienne Chevalier*)

spatial syntax without regard to the depth of field) an open book, set on the opposite side of the Virgin Mary to mark a passage from a "closed" to an "open" state of being. The miraculous conception is conveyed through the figure of the book, which can be opened and closed without loss or damage.

The sight line established by the corners of the two books and the gutter between the pages of the open volume in the back leads indirectly to the tablets in the background. The angel's index finger, in fact, points not only to the passage of the Holy Spirit through the glass above but also to the writing on the tablets in the background. Since her gesture pertains to a weakened or ambivalent deixis, she points both to the spatial mystery of the church, a "saturation" of meanings that convey Christian teaching, and to the production of figural traits that establish lines of tension on a flat surface. The contrastive effect of centering gained from an Italian perspective in a northern chapel is subtended by the relation of volume and of writing. The picture celebrates the character of writing in space and in sculptural illusion as much as it deals with a sacred narrative.

Fundamental, however, is the inscription of the difference between writing and volume at privileged areas that cue the identity and difference of figural and pictorial surfaces. The process shares much with what will ground the relation between language and space in cartographic writings. In the second annunciation of the collection (Figure 1.3, 16.5 × 12 cm), the same problem is articulated through the contrast of a spherical disposition of the braided rug in opposition to the Italianate marble panels of the wall, which recede obliquely toward a vertical bar of vanishment. The "lenticular" traits of northern painting are felt in the curve of the ground, but they are opposed to the flat quality of the wall, which is divided by pilaster strips. The words of the annunciation, written in the space of the picture, hover over the open book placed between the angel and the Virgin. Its characters are seen obliquely, as a dividing line that "cuts" the space being traced by the gutter of the book that defines the lines of entry into the room. The point where the elements of the picture converge is the book, set in the center in the shape of a lozenge, which emphasizes the overall scenography.

Other illustrations betray the same play between writing and space. In the lozenge-like figure of writing, central to the image of *François de Rochechouart Receiving a Letter,* in the *Grandes Chroniques de France* (Paris: B. nat. Ms. Fr. 6 465, ill. in Fabbri 1966: 5), the placement of the note at the abyssal point in the image, at the meeting of the diagonals drawn between the four corners of the image, gives force to the quadrant of hands that frame the white rhombus at the center. This rhombus contrasts with the stone lozenge above it that figures in the realistic depiction of the refortification of the town's walls, which is no doubt included to contrast the reality of contingent human activity to the heraldic lozenge that is held by two angels in a vignette in the border below. History thus moves from the effect of human action—with the names marked in the blazon of Rochechouart in the border—to the narrative of the depiction and to the collective, national campaign of building walls and ramparts. Language, reality, and action are mapped out as different entities in the historical scene construed to be of a single surface. The art of illumination that Fouquet

Figure 1.3. Detail of second *Annunciation* (Jean Fouquet, *Les heures d'Etienne Chevalier*)

establishes seems to reduce the haptic experience of seeing and reading to a division between language and maps that is coordinated in nascently carto-graphic ways. Otto Pächt (1986: 200–202) has shown that with the advent of Fouquet and the Master of Mary of Burgundy, arrangements of border deco-ration, script, and picture in illuminated manuscripts reveal that "the book housed a picture *as an alien body*" (200). A gap between looking and reading initiated a greater rift by virtue of the division of labor among the illuminator, the scribe, and the decorator. Each held a different relation to the page he or she was crafting. Fouquet deployed the page as "a common denominator in picture, ornament, and script." Most lexical and pictorial values were registered on a single surface that, because of the relation of writing to its placement in the picture, both fostered and occluded illusionism. Space beyond the frame, such as a landscape, was now pulled up to the surface of the page, as if it were the ground for a topographical view. But the script, though strategically placed in the image, remained "marooned like an island in the dividing wall of space" (201). Writing was located both within and outside the image, but it also served to plot and to map out spatial and ideological relations in the visual field.

Wit and Rivalry: The Portrait of Guillaume Juvénal des Oursins

The most salient instance of writing inflecting the construction of space and of history can be found in Fouquet's great portrait of Guillaume Juvénal des Oursins (Figure 1.4, 92 × 74 cm, ca. 1460). Oursins, a descendant of an Italian bourgeois family, was a powerful chancellor of France. Rendered to convey a sense of force and strength, the face is treated in detail that rivals the work of Jan van Eyck and Rogier van der Weyden, its lines and wrinkles brought forward by the implied black frame of the marble cartouche on the wall behind him. Pilasters set between black marble panels on either side display two pairs of bears holding the Oursins' coat of arms and, so it appears, the upper edge of the painting. In the floral pattern of the grotesques, eight other little bears roam, graze, or strut about. These are *oursins*, animalcules that literally convey—or derive from—the family name. But as *les oursins* crawl about the surround of the portrait, their presence also seeps into the cloth and texture of the work. Oursins sports a quasi tonsure that matches the fur collar and cuffs of his ample robe. The fuzzy, almost prickly feel of the fur and hair seems to make Oursins an effect of the name that he bears.

At the juncture of the collar, below the chancellor's ample chin, a cub seems to emerge from the brown mass of lines and colored hatchings (Figure 1.5). At a point comparable to those where writing and letters are set in a perspectival fashion in other works, the name and the figure of *oursins* is both centered on and scattered about the surface. A mystical effect of a saturated allegory, the spiritual presence of the chancellor, pullulates in the flora and fauna, but it is also charted according to a series of quadrilaterals. The portrait is "written" all over with rebuses that define and fragment the pictorial space. The heavy ring that is placed below Oursins's right elbow is reminiscent of the letter O, within whose cavity we perceive an ursine mouth; the great *ourlets,* or hems or

Figure 1.4. Detail of the face in the portrait of Guillaume Juvénal des Oursins (Jean Fouquet)

folds, make the name used to describe the stitching of the fabric identical to the hide of the animal in question. There is so much identity of words and things that, in the wit of the image, Oursins begins to resemble the mammal of his own name.

The play of writing in and about the portrait begins to chart the picture with pertinent linguistic features. They are both coordinated and dispersed in pictograms that circulate in the image, allowing a relation of difference and of analogy to run through the painting. A subtle device that might accompany

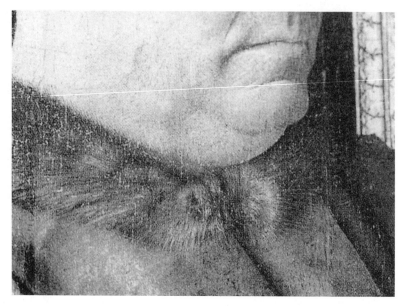

Figure 1.5. Detail of ermine coat in the portrait of Guillaume Juvénal des Oursins (Jean Fouquet)

the portrait—or offset the serious expression on the patron's face—in fact seems to be essential to the construction of a gridding or a mapping of writing in pictorial space. The quasi-heraldic play of the rebus that sanctifies and multiplies the chancellor's attributes also turns him into an ambiguous figure that belongs to a greater "idiolect" of forms that confuses the person and the decor (Figure 1.6): The bear that is both domesticated and savage, which runs through literature from Eustache Deschamps to Charles d'Orléans, inscribes a signature that conflates humanity and bestiality. The portrait seems to establish a relation of ambivalence between a nominal origin and a real effect insofar as Fouquet is pushing further—even collapsing—the distinction that the Limbourg brothers had drawn between the lives of the lower, animal classes of humans and their counterparts of the nobility.[2] Here, Fouquet continues in the line of the International Style, in "an inflationary spiral of overstatement" (Panofsky 1971: 68), but he also initiates a rivalry in which the artist outdoes the sitter's—Oursins's—own desire to be seen through the purchase and execution of the self-portrait. The painter outdoes the patron by mastering an idiom of his own specialty. As we shall see, the same problem will characterize the signature of sixteenth-century cartographers—among them Oronce Finé— who also produce the effect of controlling their media by deploying a wit that

Figure 1.6. Detail of bears on pilaster strip in background of the portrait
of Guillaume Juvénal des Oursins (Jean Fouquet)

exploits figure, rebus, and space both to please their patrons and to underscore
the technology of a representation of which the patron may have little knowledge. In the worlds of both the painter and the cartographer, a technical and
iconographic expertise places the artisans above their patrons, but social orders
dictate that the artisans remain below. The options that remain for expression
include the mapping of other kinds of language—cartographic writing—in
space and picture, or vice versa, and an overproduction of mimicry and simulated forms. Like what we see encrusted in Fouquet's portrait of Chancellor

Oursins, daring torsions define the relation of picture and discourse. Now we can see if, in the media of writing and poetry, at a concurrent moment, identical effects of centering, scatttering, and diagrammatic play are at work.

A Nascent Grid of Narrative

The *nouvelle* of the incunabular era appears to put into a spatial configuration of words some of what Fouquet inherited from the International Style and the conjunction of northern and southern constructions of perspective and landscape. If the advent of monocular perspective was decisive for shifts in style and organization of space in painting and plastic representation in general, its impact must also have been felt in other media and in different areas of early modern culture (Edgerton 1975: 99, 164). We are now poised to ask whether printed discourse also internalizes the dialogue between northern and southern views of form. Paleographers have shown that a common *spatial* consciousness binds the manuscript to the incunabulum (Saenger 1982, 1989). Can we not also hypothesize that some of the effects, on the one hand, of the inventions of Brunelleschi and Leon Battista Alberti in the south and, on the other, of French and Flemish painters in the north mark that spatial consciousness of writing? If so, the coordination of language and space would define an area where cartographic principles are almost unconsciously embedded in written discourse.

Narrative might constitute an area where two or three vastly different systems of articulation work with and against each other, where one mode, be it language or perspective, affects the composition of the other.[3] After his journey to Rome in the years 1445–1448, Fouquet, with the completion of the *Livre d'heures d'Etienne Chevalier*, brought to French soil a fresh acquaintance with artificial perspective. In the new work, Fouquet's illustrations are "seen as coinciding with the surface of a page pierced by pictorial space" (White 1987: 225). At the same moment, pictorial depth and the graphic ground of writing begin to intermingle.

But is textual space, like the space that is accorded to illustration, also "of a pictured world as things seen through a window" (White 1987: 225)?[4] In the inverse of Fouquet's placement of writing at strategic points in his paintings, does language conceive of figural signs, at once lexical and pictorial, that advance or betray spatial and visual problems that will inflect cartographic writing? Does the emergence of perspective work in accord with *brevitas* or a self-contained style of narrative "pictures"? If so, the discourses that define—and are defined by—their borders would be no less inflected by cardinal design.

And, further, the tendency to *grid* pictorial space might extend to the surfaces on which language is inscribed.

At this point, we begin to discern how manuscript or printed discourse might, first, be arranged in accord with a system of receding planes and vanishing points while, second, it depicts a single surface (its imprint on parchment or paper) that extends a flat surface on which all of its signs and marks are of "equipollent" value. A textual configuration can be conceived in terms of visible and invisible "plot points" that become narrative or episodic hinges as its signifiers share an equal charge all about the narrative surface. Stated in cartographic terms, a *nouvelle* can be seen both as a "center-enhancing" and a "route-enhancing" *map* of language while, at the same time, its descriptive means are invested into every available fragment of expression. The resulting equivalence of intensity can also confer upon it a gridded form that distributes values equally over its surface.[5] According to this scheme, no trait or printed character would have greater value than any other; every piece of expression would be liable to receive or convey the same signifying charge as the whole.

Such appears to be the shape of *Les cent nouvelles nouvelles*. Presented to the Burgundian court in 1462, at roughly the same time as the high points in the career of Fouquet, the collection differs vastly from Italian models such as the *Decameron*, which uses an organizing cornice to set forth a finite number of tales (one hundred) in a coherent frame (a pastime among the nobility as they waited for the plague to abate in Florence). Whereas Giovanni Boccaccio's organizing scheme would be comparable to a narrative border that surrounds the ensemble, the same number of tales in the anonymous Burgundian collection, piled together with little rhyme or reason, would approximate the sensation of "empirical" space and time as they were known in northern aesthetics. In this system—if it can be called a system—the narrators are many (thirty-six) and lack any distinguishing characteristics; they share a setting that our romantic reveries inspire us to imagine as a fireside or *veillée*. While they have historical identities, their discourse betrays no variety of styles or signatures. A geography is vaguely intimated by Burgundian and Flemish place-names marked here and there in the incipits, with excursions to France and, infrequently, to countries north, south, and west. The events narrated comprise a fantastic melange of unchecked desire that mixes folklore with shards of historical events. The tales are, in the words of Erich Auerbach, "anything but literary" (1956: 282). Scenarios include tricksters tricked, priests practicing everything but what they preach, husbands cuckolded, women seduced and abused; coprophilia and castration reign supreme, and the tales paint uncommon pictures of excess. The elegant or "intermediate" style of the Italian model in narrative seems light-years away from the design of this rough-hewn collection.

The composition shares an affiliation with the International Style and the works of Fouquet. Drawing on the *fabliau* and *lai* (Dubuis 1973: 302–3, 359) and restricted to a transalpine milieu, the tales seem to defy their Italian counterparts. Because these tales of lust in the lower and middle classes are told and transcribed in the Burgundian court, they belong to the tradition, opened by the Limbourgs, in which the author and audience derive a vicarious pleasure from the representation of a class opposite or other than their own. The fabled lust of the *gente rustique* and of commoners becomes the ground for the delight of courtesans who amuse themselves with a mixture of "half sympathetic and half amused, half supercilious and half nostalgic" interests (Panofsky 1971: 71).

But when seen in the context of the revolutions of gridding, of perspective, and of the mediation of northern and southern modes of spatial representation, the tales appear to mix elements of narrative with elements of the kind of latent mapping that we saw at work in Fouquet's paintings. The history of the collection intimates that the tales were written with a strongly pictorial consciousness. Not only do they "represent" excess against a backdrop of daily life, but they are also written in order, literally, to be pictured. The Glasgow manuscript (1462) is studded with racy illuminations that recall the illustrations accompanying manuscripts of the *Roman de la rose*. The history of the first printed editions of *Les cent nouvelles nouvelles* shows that editors sought to publish a composite of narrative text and woodcut figures. Antoine Vérard's first edition (Paris, 1486) included woodcuts taken from other works (Sansi 1992: 69). He printed another edition soon thereafter, but only at the turn of the century did the work reach a broader public. Illustrations were included in Nicolas Desprez's edition (Paris, 1505), as well as those of Michel Lenoir (Paris, n.d.), Jehan Trepperel (Paris, n.d.), Jehan Petit (printed by Desprez, n.d.), Olivier Arnoullet (Lyon, ca. 1530), and Jacques Aubert (Rouen, ca. 1540) (Jacob 1858: xxiii–xxiv). *Les cent nouvelles nouvelles* must have been attractive for printers wishing to experiment with text and illustration. Comprised of finite units of text with many sites available for illustration, a serial work of this kind would offer compositors and typographers material for extensive experiment with textual and visual relations. In the early editions, the narrative seems to be infused with the nascent or real pictorial matter. Even in modern renditions, a coextension of images and diegetic material is evident.

The setting and diegesis of the fiftieth tale may serve to indicate why:

La L^e Nouvele
par Monseigneur de la Salle, Premier Maistre d'Hostel de Monseigneur Le Duc
Comme jeunes gens se mectent voulentiers à voyagier, et prennent plaisir à veoir et sercher les adventures du monde, il y eut n'a guères au païs de Lannoys le filz d'un laboureur qui fut depuis l'eage de dix ans jusques à l'eage de vingt et six tousjours hors du pays; et puis son partement jusques a son retour, oncques son pere ne sa mere n'en eurent une seule nouvelle: si penserent plusieurs foiz qu'il fust mort. Il revint après toutesfoiz, et Dieu scet la joye qui fust en l'ostel, et comment il fut festoié à son retour du tant pou de biens que Dieu leur avoit donné. Mais qui le vit voluntiers et en fist grand feste, sa grand mere, la mere de son pere, luy faisoit plus grand chere et estoit la plus joyeuse de son retour; elle le baisa plus de cinquante foiz, et ne cessoit de loer Dieu qu'il leur avoit rendu leur beau filz et retourné en si beau point. Apres ceste grande chere, l'heure vint de dormir; mais il n'y avoit à l'ostel que deux lictz: l'un estoit pour le pere et la mere et l'autre pour la grand mere. Si fut ordonné que leur filz coucheroit avecques sa taye, dont elle fut joyeuse; mais il s'en fust bien passé, combien que pour obéir il fut content de prendre la pacience pour ceste nuyt. Comme il estoit couché avec sa taye, ne sçay de quoy il luy sourvint, il monta dessus. "Et que veulz-tu faire? dit-elle. — Ne vous chaille, dit-il, ne dictes mot." Quand elle vit qu'il vouloit besoigner à bon escient, elle commence de crier tant qu'elle peut après son filz, qui dormoit en la chambre au plus près. Elle se leve de son lit et se va plaindre à luy de son filz, en plorant tendrement. Quand l'autre entendit la plainte de sa mere et l'inhumanité de son filz, il se leva sur piez très courroussié et mal meu, et dit qu'il l'occira. Le filz, oye ceste menace, si sault sus, et s'en picque par derrière et se sauve. Son pere le suyt, mais c'est pour neant: il n'estoit pas si radde du pyé comme luy; il vit qu'il perdoit sa peine; si revient à l'ostel et trouva sa mère lamentant à cause de l'offense que son filz avoit faicte. "Ne vous chaille, dit-il, ma mère, je vous en vengeray bien." Ne sçay quants jours après ce pere vint trouver son filz, qui jouoit à la paulme en la ville de Laon; et tantost qu'il le vist, il tire bonne dague et marche vers luy et l'en cuide ferir. Le filz se destourna, et son pere fut tenu. Aucuns qui là estoient sceurent bien que c'estoit le pere et le filz. Si dit l'un au filz: "Et vien ça; qu'as tu meffait à ton pere, qui te veult tuer? — Ma foy, dist-il, rien. Il a le plus grand tort de jamais; il me veult tout le mal du monde pour une pouvre foiz que j'ay voulu ronciner sa mere; il a ronciné la mienne plus de cinq cens foiz, et je n'en parlay oncques ung seul mot." Tous ceux qui oyrent ceste response commencerent a rire de grand cueur et dirent bien qu'il estoit bon homme. Si s'efforcerent a ceste occasion de faire sa paix a son pere, et tant si employerent qu'ils en vindrent au bout, et fut tout pardonné d'un costé et d'aultre.

[The Fiftieth Tale
by Monseigneur de la Sale, first Maître d'Hôtel of Monseigneur the Duke
As the youthful breed eagerly starts to travel and takes pleasure in seeing and seeking the adventures of the world, not long ago there lived in the Laonnois region a plowman's son, who, from the age of ten years up to the age of six and twenty, was always out of the country; and, from his departure until his return, neither his father nor his mother had any inkling of his whereabouts. On several

occasions they even thought he was dead. All the same back he came, and God only knows the joy that reigned in the house, and how he was celebrated upon his return with the gift of as many goods that God had ever bestowed upon them. But the one who saw him most eagerly, and who was overjoyed, was his grandmother, the mother of his father, who feasted the most and who, about his return, was happier than everyone else. She kissed him more than fifty times, and endlessly praised God for bringing back to them their handsome son and returning him in such fine condition. After these great festivities, there came the time to sleep, but in the house only two beds were available: One was for the father and the mother, and the other, for the grandmother. So it was ordered that the said son would go to bed with his grandmother, and that made her joyous; but he would have easily been done with the event, but for the sake of the company he was happy to pass the night in patience. After he had gone to bed with his ancestor, I don't know what came over him. He climbed right on top of her: "Now what are you doing?" she said. "Don't be bothered," he said, "don't utter a word!" When she saw that he really wanted to mount her, she began to cry as loud as she could to her son, who was asleep in the adjacent room. And she got out of her bed and went off, weeping tenderly, to the doorway to complain to her son. When the other heard the mother's sobs, and of his son's inhumanity, he jumped to his feet, angered and ruffled, and said he would kill him. The son heard the threat, jumped up, and went out the back way. His father followed him, but for naught: He wasn't so swift afoot; he saw that he was wasting his time; so he came back home and found his mother in lament because of the offense that his son had made toward her. "Don't be bothered, mother," he said, "I'll avenge you." A few days later, I'm not sure how many, his father happened to find his son, who was playing tennis in Laon; and no sooner did he see him than draw his dagger and march toward him, readying to strike a deadly blow. The son turned around, but his father was held back. Some who were there were sure that it was the father and the son. "Now what the hell," said one of them to the son, what did you do to irk your father so as to make him want to kill you?" "Goddamn it," he said, "nothing. He's way out of line! He wants to heap on me all the evil of the world for one little time that I wanted to ride astride his mother; he rode on mine more than five hundred times, and I didn't have one word to say about it!" Everyone who heard this remark began to laugh with joy. And they used the occasion to bring peace, and the partners were pardoned on one side and the other.][6]

One of the shortest narratives in the collection, the fiftieth tale projects a common joke as a recent *fait divers* occurring in the Soissonnais. Roger Dubuis ranks the tale among what the post-Victorian age would call the most "obscene" of the entire collection. A terse introduction leads directly to the son's bon mot at the conclusion, the "filth" of incest constituting the overall "picture" that the narrative initially stages and then resolves. A ludicrous mise-en-scène betrays a desire to share with the reader a mockery of psychology and, further, to violate its codes. When seen in the context of the "gravity" of the son's transgression of the incest tabu, the greatest of all interdictions, the art of brevity becomes the central concern of the narration (Dubuis 1973: 64, 114, 115).[7] The tale would exemplify the search for a "*pointe*," a bon mot, or a synthesis where narrative and wit are alloyed. The son's parting shot indicates that the diegesis is organized around a fulcrum, or *point de bascule.* Although the turning point of the fiftieth tale falls at the end, in others it is located elsewhere—anywhere—according to the given form of the tales and their staging.

The concept of a narrative fulcrum implies that a relation of mapping and narrative is being staged, a relation in which stories organize their diegetic material according to perspectival loci that constitute keys that at once open and close the overall narrative structure, or else mark the plot points of a subjacent diegetic itinerary. What Dubuis calls the *pointe* or *point de bascule* tells where the discourse in fact *emerges into visibility* and how it is mapped. These loci denote exactly where the abstraction of the mise-en-scène is conveyed and betrayed by graphic modes of organization, and where the latent identification with perspective, dialogic tension, and narrative time is marked.

The tale has a confined, almost quadrilateral aspect that can be scanned in a glance. Its edges are in play with a strange deictic twist at the center of the story. In the very middle, when the story tells of the son nestled in bed with his grandmother, all of a sudden the narrator enters into the picture in order to note that natural laws are thrown topsy-turvy; at the same time, the first-person voice, the cause and imaginary origin of the story, is inscribed where causality is erased: "Comme il estoit couché avec sa taye, *ne sçay de quoy* il luy sourvint, il monta dessus." An enigma is set at the axis in such a way that the entire tale appears to develop from this median point.

But when we note that the deictic shift is plotted at a narrative vanishing point, the same formulation recurs below, following the father's promise to take revenge on the son: "*Ne sçay quants* jours après ce pere vint trouver son filz" seems to confirm the presence of the center by underscoring the formula, "Ne vous chaille," which recurs adjacent to the first-person expression. On the first occasion, the father's son implores the grandmother "don't be bothered" while he climbs on top of the old lady; on the second, the father, the son of the violated grandmother, implores the victim "don't be bothered" about the cause of the son's offense "*à cause de* l'offense que son filz avoit faicte" (emphasis added). The reuse of the same expression indicates that the tale is fabricated through the erasure and reinscription of causality and that the total social fact that the tale is satirizing is treated in a confusion of literal and figurative meanings.

The physical center of the story is taken to be the literal moment of incest, whereas its reinscription marks the oedipal or figurative consequence that will be negotiated in the public confrontation at the tennis arena in Laon. In the minimal expression, however, the narrator's avowal that "I don't know what came over him" underscores a writing of legalistic precision that spatializes familial relations. Within the family romance, we witness the expression of a relation with the unknown. But at the same time, to the contrary, where familiar relations are specified, they are also confused.[8] The deictic marker, Dubuis's *point de bascule,* is now taken in a graphic sense; it is almost a rebus signaling the overlap of the visual and aural traits of discourse. The narrative turns on the apposition *sa grand mere, la mere de son pere* to state that the story deals with the patrilineal or directly oedipal grandmother. Clarification in the enunciation is undone by the confusion of names and familial roles in the serial aspect of the sentence articulated, it appears, to produce a simultaneously visual and oral rhyme:

> sa grand *mere,* la *mere* de son *pere,* luy faisoit plus grand *chere.*

This distinguishes one son from another and a perspective of three generations in the diegesis, only, however, in order to stage confusion elsewhere. When "si fut ordonné que leur filz coucheroit avecques sa taye," for a moment, because of the confusion of antecedents to which "leur" could refer (the father? the son?), the reader cannot tell if the son is a product of the relations of the father and the mother or of the father and the grandmother. A shadow of paternal doubt is cast elsewhere in the narrative when, in contiguous space, the deictic mark, "son filz," refers at once to the father and the son: "Elle commence de crier tant qu'elle peut après son filz. . . . Elle se leve de son lit et se va plaindre à luy de son filz."

The narrative appears to establish a scumble of filial relations through a spatial and serial tactic. Blurring the distinction between father and son also invites the reader to play with spatial and grammatical distinctions that set humanity apart from bestiality. As we have seen, the serial disposition of vocables invites a scansion whereby contiguity entertains a scheme of identity. As soon as the father hears his mother's complaint (literally), the discourse slips into abstraction, implying—but never stating—that he also discerned (figuratively) his son's "inhumanity":

> Quand l'autre entendit la plainte de sa mere et l'inhumanité de son filz, il se leva sur piez très courroussié et mal meu, et dit qu'il l'occira. Le *filz, oye* ceste menace, si sault sus, s'en picque par derrière et se sauve. Son pere le suyt, mais c'est pour neant: il n'estoit pas si radde du pyé que luy; il vit qu'il perd*oit sa peine,* se revient

à l'ostel et trouva sa mère lamentant à cause de l'offense que son *filz* av*oit* faicte.
(Emphasis added)

At first we cannot discern who is "l'autre." Does it refer to the father, to the son, to ourselves, or to a dialogic effect that would make each a function of the other? Only in the movement of the characters does the familial picture fall into place as an effect of the initial and necessary confusion. The following sentence indicates that the father's "son," like the listener or reader of the story, hears the grandmother's complaint without the father seeing him. In this sentence sequence, the father, who is characterized by *voice-off*, is contrasted to the figure of the son, who is, as it were, *image-in*. At this axial moment, the confusions of nomination also project into the verbal register. The son who "hears" the menace is simultaneously likened to a molting goose ("mal meu"), and to a monstrous chimera of human and birdlike aspect, and it is at this moment that, as good readers who cast aside the fantasies that the narrative elicits in us by visual and oral homonyms, we make sense of the causal order by repressing what visible characters led us to imagine. Here the son-goose figure is cast aside, like the confusion of father-and-son in "l'autre." But the beast reappears in the image of the antagonist enacting on his own body what he had done with his grandmother ("si sault sus"), sticking himself from behind ("s'en picque par derrière") and darting—or quickly waddling—away. In the graphic matter, the father resembles this monster since he did not have muscles erect enough ("n'est*oit* pas si radde") to follow and because he lost both pain and feathers.[9] The father seems to "owe" his condition to his gooselike form, such that "il per[pere]doit[oye] sa peine" can be inferred in the area scanned in silence between graphics and the vocables.

The narrative keeps an exact tally of its quanta of energy and their transfer from one site to another. The relation of the narrative to an "account" (by which the *nouvelle*, or *conte*, is likened to a *compte*, or inventory, of transgression) is sought in the flickers of interior duplication that reflect the tale's own form. If a poetics of *Les cent nouvelles nouvelles* can be sought in the praxis of its narration, its method is concretized in the rapport of diegesis, spatial placement, and numbers and in its play on calculation. The combinations foster growth, with addition and multiplication being valorized over subtraction or division.[10] Because of its setting in the middle of the entire volume, the tale draws what might be an originary meridian on which is placed a vanishing point.

The serial disposition of the characters of the story implies that distinctions between human and beast, like those among the three generations of the plowman's family, are both held and collapsed into an indiscriminate form of writing. A scenario of the object relations in a family romance is visibly played out in the graphic register. It may also be that the obvious technique of perspectival centering, which brings the narrator into view—as we have observed in Fouquet's portrait of the "bestial" character of Juvénal des Oursins—invites the eye to move about peripherally and to confuse the relational (or familial) registers of illusion that are being staged. Shards of words elicit connections among different areas of the text in ways that might be likened to a transgression or violation of the laws of grammar. Hearing his mother's account of the act of incest, the enraged father "se leva sur piez tres-*cour*ROUSSIÉ et mal meu" (literally, "co-horsed and coerced"), but he is corrected, and the son turns his anger into an economy of frigging: "Il me veult tout le mal du monde pour une pouvre foiz que j'ay voulu *ronciner* sa mere; il a *ronciné* la mienne plus de cinq cens foiz."

Words beget one another in ways that cannot be ordered unilaterally; *courroussié* signals *ronciner*; the blow that the father wants to strike (*ferir*) upon his son precipitates laughter (*fait rire*). Or, if bestiality is suggested by the confusion of the son and a bird (*le filz, oye*), then *oye* can be seen rippling through the story by analogy, suggesting that what we hear (*ouïr*) happens to be what our mind's eye sees as a mix of human and bird. Visual reminders occur everywhere in the tale, right from the incipit, which defines the relation of seeing and hearing:

> Comme jeunes gens se mectent voulentiers à v*oy*agier et prennent plaisir à v*eoi*r et sercher les adventures du monde, il y eut n'a guères au païs de Lann*oys* le filz d'un laboureur . . . si pensèrent plusieurs f*oiz* qu'il fust mort. Il revint après toutesf*oiz,* et Dieu scet la j*oye* qui fust en l'ostel, et comment il fut fest*oié* à son retour.

Echoes and redundancies of forms within and across words break the links we tend to establish when we associate causality with narrative development. If the graphemes *oie, oiz,* and *oye* are traced through the text, a loosely "gridded" appearance of the writing results from the implicit lines that tie them together, making the discourse emerge into visibility. When the protocartographic character of the writing is brought forward, at least three other features further complicate the tale.

One, which results from the blurring of human and beast, involves both a conflation and a separation of figures and ground of writing. An overall effect of lust prevails. Force burgeons everywhere—in the narrative, personages, deixis, words, letters, and even punctuation marks. The father's *pyé* can be seen simultaneously as a foot, a teat, an erogenous tip, or apical meristem. It shifts between the subsumed figure of a pen inseminating a page with ink, the *laboureur's* plow, and the dagger that the father will brandish before his son. The surrounding erotic ambience inspires the reader to visualize all the masculine and feminine shapes that are both in and represented by the discourse as part of an indiscriminately generative form. We gaze upon the central axis marked by the narrator—*ne sçay de quoy*—while we also discern a presence of force multiplying its effects *all over* the narrative surface. In the statement of the grounding enigma are embedded its umbilical form (which gives life to the tale), a pictogram that associates the production of the tale's telling and hearing, its animality (*quOY*), and the spatial signature that assures its iterability. The axial enigma opens the tale onto its willful confusion of visual and oral "tracks" for the purpose of moving us toward a threshold beyond which we behold a language of unbridled nature.

Second, if the story can be seen "gridding" images of boundless erotic force, it displays an art of generation or multiplication that proceeds from the differences it inscribes in its form. We discern these areas wherever the story eagerly confuses words, letters, and ciphers. What distinguishes a "natural" from a "technical" discourse in our world seems, in the Franco-Burgundian context of the fifteenth century or in French incunabular culture, so mixed that an infinity of possible shapes can be generated from the given elements of the narrative.

And third, in the fiftieth tale, discourse is riddled with numbers. Akin to nongrammatical signs, numerical shapes are pictograms embedded in the writing. They imply that the story tells of the production of excess and of the ways that balance can be equitably restored. Here one—but only one—son spends his adolescence (sixteen years) "hors du pays." He never gives his parents even one account of his fortunes. Within the discourse, meticulous attention is paid to the relation between an event and a dispensation of energy. Numbers translate the problem into intermediate signs. The tale tells of something that takes place "une foiz," but until it reaches its denouement, the son's parents "pensèrent plusieurs foiz qu'il fust mort"; however, he returns "après toutesfoiz" ("later all the same" but also "after each and every time") before the grandmother welcomes the prodigal child's return by kissing him "plus de cinquante foiz," a point marked near the center of the narrative. At the conclusion, the son's quid pro quo equates the "one little time" ("une pouvre foiz" a dilative and erotic moment, if the rhetoric of orthography invites us to see *ouvre* in *pouvre*) he spent with the father's mother to the "more than five hundred times" that the father mounted the son's mother without the son's uttering "one word." The wit of the joke brings the world back to order. But whereas his speech is expressed in the silence of writing, the play of figure and discourse allays the difference between the verbal performance and its printed condition. A debt of five hundred to one is erased in the explosion of *graphic* wit that brings the world back to order.

If the collection can be imagined as being bisected by this story, the fiftieth tale is likely to serve as a *mise en abîme,* also a perspectival object, that organizes the infinite scatter of events and places on either side. The grandmother's fifty kisses cannot fail to recall the number—fifty—of the tale. And the recurrence of *nouvelle,* which pertains to the title of the collection, within the story reflects the whole on the surface of one of its smallest parts: The son's father and mother had not even "une seule nouvelle" of his travels all the while the narration takes place under the sign of "La Lᵉ nouvele." That the son was happy to spend the night with the old lady ("fut *content* de prendre la pacience") is also reflective of the story *telling* of initial violence and the conquest of peace. Numbers and digital forms make up an ensemble of loose connections and recurring forms that imply a gridding of traits that are charged at once with lexical and numerical value.[11] The choice of the ultimate act of transgression, which happens to be the relation with the unknown or the umbilicus of the tale; violation of the law of incest; narrative and satire of the oedipal paradigm; confusion of humanity and bestiality—all indicate that the thematic material is also placed at a center from which all other tales appear to radiate. Site and treatment suggest that this tale is a model or a creative paradigm at the center of the collection.

The variety of human experience that the sum of the stories displays is loosely gridded by a latent perspectival and cartographic scheme. We tend to get our bearings through the serial form and the extensive play of language, picture, and figure. The most graphic illustration of the relation of navigation and narrative movement may reside in the opening sentence, which now merits yet another reading. In the mix of forms before our eyes, the initial formula, "Comme jeunes gens se mectent à voyager et prennent plaisir à veoir et sercher les adventures du monde," is set in motion with the inscription of the first letter, a "historiated" or pictogrammatic sign that both launches and summarizes—or resumes, as might the incipit of a *rondeau*—the form of the entire collection. At the same time, "Comme jeunes gens" indicates that an extended comparison will equivocate on the process of metaphor by implied allusion to the biblical tale of the prodigal son. A new, mercantile inflection of adventure is also implied. Former travels of knights errant are now oriented, the context tells us, toward the commercial world. The highly material ambience allows the sum of the stories to be reflected in an initial. The Roman numeral C can be detached from *Comme* as a cardinal sign of the sum of the collection, while at the same time it figures as a letter in the lexical order.

Hence, the economy of the tale's geography: The plateau of the Soissonnais on which perches the city of Laon becomes the point of eminence or the vanishing point at the center, L, around which, like an annulated form, the collection turns. *Lannoys* marks the space and time both of this tale and the sum by inscribing a halfway point in the itinerary (fifty, or L) and extends the figure of the whole as a yearly cycle or ring (*année, annel, annoys*) conventionally associated with the figure of one hundred. The son travels everywhere and nowhere within the confines of a prearranged cartography visible less to him than to the reader who follows his movement, which leads from the world in general, *le monde,* to the Lannoys. A pictorial landscape is implied, in which the reader or viewer gains an unforeseen visual mobility.[12]

Such play of letter, number, and toponymy also configures the greater economy of the tale's wit. Narrative demands that a dilemma, the presence of the unknown, or an imbalance be shown in exposition in medias res or through descriptive elaboration. The same rule holds for the first sentence of this tale, except that the conflict is denoted less in content than in its *form* of enunciation. Something goes awry in the comparison: The initial part of the simile that thematizes youth and worldly adventure is not quite complemented by a predicate that follows or is adjacent to the subject. "Not long ago, . . . in the Laonnois region," a statement that ostensibly locates the narrative site, floats ambiguously in respect to the "adventures of the world" just mentioned. Logically, the scope of travel about the world at large cannot be contained in the Lannoys, especially if this young man's adventure lasts sixteen years and occurs "tousjours hors du pays." A paradox is marked in that what took place in the Lannoys, which probably refers to battles on the borders of France and Burgundy, also took place outside of the Lannoys.

The statement can be interpreted in two ways. First, it may be that the boundary that we find separating a part from a whole or a topographical view from a cosmographic perspective constitutes a misreading. Second, in accord with the graphics of the tale, the skewed geography begs the reader to find the dilemma of the tale in the visual register, in areas within and between the written shapes that convey the exposition. If, historically, adventure had connoted the enterprise of battle (Nerlich 1988), then the conflict that is being posited might also include war in both local and broader senses: "Il y eut n'a *guères* au païs de *Lannoys*. . . ." Since the spacing of letters and words promotes ambivalence, the statement implies that lately there was "war" in the Lannoys region in the 1450s, and that possibly (the cipher L both belonging to and liable to be

detached from its substantive) *noise* (L*annoys*) or conflict of seasons or generations reflects universal turmoil.[13] For that reason, it follows that the son was
always *hors du pays*, in battle with the French in defense of the Burgundian
kingdom. The expression plays on geographic displacement and the wild, im-
balanced character of the medieval designation of adolescence that now veers
toward history.

Literally horny, "hors de lui-même," the son brims with erotic energy. His
condition also describes the imbalance of nature that seems to be both cause
and effect of the crippled logic of the initial simile. A picture of force is described *en sourdine*, as it were, in order to be potentiated in the narrative and
then consumed in the wit of the final quid pro quo. The explosion literally
brings the reader back to the place whence the tale departed, except that the
telling has resolved the cosmic imbalance inscribed at the beginning. The wit
indicates, finally, that two modes of creation confirm the dialogic pattern of
the tale. The text impels the reader, first, to behold written or printed language
that maps its totalities everywhere in and through its tiniest shards and fragments, and second, to note that the interstices between oral report and visible
form are the beginning of a narrative map at once local, historical, and universal. Third, the fiftieth tale displays such an economy of narration that it seems
to be the original *meridian* of the collection, the initial and dividing line that
draws both within and beside itself the laws of construction inspiring the
scheme. A point of origin to which all other tales respond, like a vertical axis
of the kind of topographical map that Pieter Apian, Oronce Finé, and other
cartographers would soon theorize in the 1520s and 1530s, the tale grids its
discourse and sum of stories as an infixed totality of events that recount
and renew the world. A cosmography of language and events, *Les cent nouvelles nouvelles* offers countless pictures of worlds within its modular, variable,
and reproducible form.

A Poetic Map: Jean Molinet

Les cent nouvelles nouvelles configures an infinitely possible "pixellated" space—
that is, composed of many pixel images—of human action in a loosely equipollent composition. Its lines of construction can be seen from afar, in the
shape of the whole and, at the same time, within the frame of single tale units
and even graphic shards. There results a variety of picture and a topography
that blends mapping, language, and landscape. In order to see if Franco-
Burgundian writing displays a nascently cartographic style in other areas, we
can turn to the lyrical creations of Jean Molinet, the most commanding poet

and chronicler of the Burgundian court in the last quarter of the fifteenth century. Born in the Boulonnais region of northwestern France, Molinet became a canon in the college church of Valenciennes before replacing Georges Chastellain as historiographer and poet at Dijon during the reign of Charles the Bold. Founding a first generation of "Grands Rhétoriqueurs," a group of poets who would soon inspire Jean Lemaire, Jean and Clément Marot, and Rabelais, Molinet's work became a poetic standard against which contemporary verse was measured. His style was followed and adapted well into the sixteenth century.

Molinet infuses discourse with pictorial and graphic values. And, like future cartographers, Molinet figures among the poets who relate the act of writing to an invention of space that is defined by alterity. "Narrowly constrained by the cultural milieu in which they belong," the Grands Rhétoriqueurs "never fail to seek occasions to find a place to camp, in clandestine fashion, *outside of it*: [They are] rooted in a stable and ponderous tradition, but in obstinate revolt against it" (Zumthor 1978: 278, emphasis added). The poetry allows Molinet and his fellow travelers a means of escaping from their milieu, while at the same time it allows them to be imprisoned in that "other world," the text itself, which their writing produces (279). Each poem becomes a map, an island, or an isolated space in which a circuit or path is traced through a body of language. Like that of *Les cent nouvelles nouvelles*, the language reflects both the infinite expanse and the limits that the acts of reading and writing are charting. A sense of compression is gained where verbal graticules, cross-hatched tracings, numbers, lines of vanishment, perspectival objects, pictograms, and enigmatic centers abound.

One of Jean Molinet's most circumstantial poems is, in fact, a grid. A piece of ciphered verse, it begins to make sense only when the reader imagines the composition as the product of at least two superimposed checkerboards. One, of lexical order, comprises the narrative that leads the reader from the incipit to the final word, *advint*, which falls at the end of the fourteenth line:

> Un Dictier Joyeux
> Un homme est pendu au gibet,
> Me dict ung tres ort quodlibet.
> Qu'as tu ores, quoquin, quetis,
> Qui les brayes secs n'as toudis,
> Car foire au cul as en septembre,
> Octobre, novembre, decembre.
> On se doit monstrer doux et gent
> Tres amiable a toute gent;
> En purgatore seront mis

Quoquins et qui hait ses amis;
Toudis scet Dieu que jadis wit
De sens fut Adam et seduict
D'Eve en paradis neuf, ou vint
Sathan, par qui ce mal advint.

[A man who hangs at the gallows
Tells me the dirty ditty that follows.
What's wrong? What's your gripe?
You, with pants that smell quite ripe,
Your breeches are messy in September,
October, November, and even December.
You should be seen sweet, even comely,
Affable to everyone for, namely
Purgatory will be the end
For whoever hates a friend.
God only knows what a jerk
Was Adam when he went berserk
By Eve in Paradise, where Satan went,
And so then did he evil invent.][14]

The poem works simultaneously on two registers. The one, which rehearses a sermon telling of the Fall of Man, admonishes an interlocutor (implicitly, we the readers) for failing to obey codes of propriety. On display is a fairly topical dialogue that moves across the barrier between life and death. A man hanged, privy to the workings of the afterlife, asks the reader (because the deictic positions marked in the first two lines are ambivalent, "Me," line 2, could refer to Molinet, a scribe, or even to us) a playful riddle ("quodlibet") that is crafted to strike fear into our souls. The lesson that the question preaches superimposes three unrelated truisms: (1) The fool who soils his breeches from the time of harvest to Christmas is told to look alert, clean, and affable; (2) whoever hates his or her friends will find a station in Purgatory; and (3) everybody knows how Eve's seduction spelled trouble in Paradise. No logical connection links any of the three statements; each remains a textual layer of couplets piled below a debate between a dead criminal and a poor soul who does not know how to regulate his bodily functions: The butt of the farce is told that, by setting aside the fruits of harvest for consumption during the thin months of winter, he will be incontinent in the fall and dead in the spring. A lesson about potentiation, a half-baked joke, and a song of the morality of seasons, the poem treats of an economy of bodily and social orders.

The paratactic effect of disjoined statements that follow upon one another, like one textual surface glued over the other, betrays the ciphered design that appeals to the visual frame of the verse, its latent gridding, and its confusion of symbolic and numerical signs. The poem inscribes a function of counting from one to twenty:

> *Un* [1] homme est pen*du* [2] au gibet,
> Me dict ung *tres* [3] ort quodlibet.
> *Qu'as tu ores* [4], quo*quin* [5], quetis,
> Qui les brayes *secs* [6] n'as toudis,
> Car foire au cul as en *septem*bre [7],
> *Octo*bre [8], *novem*bre [9], *decem*bre [10].
> *On se* [11] doit monstrer *doux e*[12]t gent
> *Tres* [13] amiable a toute gent;
> En pur*gatore se*[14]ront mis
> Quo*quins e*[15]t qui hait *ses* [16] amis;
> Tou*dis scet* [17] Dieu que ja*dis wit* [18]
> De sens fut Adam et seduict
> D'Eve en para*dis neuf* [19], ou vint
> Sathan, par qui ce mal ad*vint* [20].

The poem underscores its diagrammatic condition when it is seen as a function of enumeration. The narrative of admonishment, which leads to visions of guilt and the underworld, finds itself countered by a simple numerical progression that is additive—or generative—in the very places where the sermonic tones would be subtractive or negative. The poem is literally coordinated by the isomorphic traits of number and letter that celebrate the paginal surface of the poem to the detriment of the imaginary volume of the Christian cosmos.

The ludic character of the poem, however, suggests that the mechanism that is set in place exceeds the order that it follows. In the Christian scheme of the cosmos, the poem's value as a poem depends on a transgression that comes, like incest or Eve's seduction, with our implied refusal to admit a difference between what is enunciated and what is put on view; hence the pleasure that comes when the parallel vectors of the narrative and enumeration are crisscrossed by other possible combinations borne by the disposition or the system of the poem. Once its layered form is evident, numbers are liable to be seen anywhere and everywhere, and without rhyme or reason:

> Un (1) Dictier (3) Joyeux
> Un [1] homme est pendu au gibet,
> Me dict ung [1] tres ort quodlibet.
> Qu'as tu ores, quoquin, quetis,
> Qui les brayes secs n'as toudis [10],
> Car [4] foire au cul as en septembre,

Octobre, novembre, decembre.
On se doit monstrer doux [2] et gent
Tre[3]s amiable a toute [∞] gent;
En purgatore seront mis
Quoquins et qui hait ses amis;
Toudis [∞] scet Dieu que jadis wit [o]
De sens [o] fut Adam et seduict [8]
D'Eve en paradis neuf, ou vint [20]
Sathan, par qui ce mal advint [20]

A chaos of letters and ciphers appears to inhabit the cardinal space of the text at the same time that an implied disorder is marked at a vanishing or dividing point. At the center, following the division of number and narration into two halves, a rebus surges forth embodying and summarizing the poem's system of differences. Because of the equivocation that homonyms formed by the uttered letters and numbers commands in the surrounding context, the banal homily "On se doit monstrer doux et gent" also summons, in a transverse direction, "Onze doi(g)t(s) monstré doux et gent(s)." Reference is made to the hand, the agent that counts the ciphers and that displays ("monstré") its ten digits. But when ten is passed at the numerical axis, after the eye moves from the seventh to the eighth line, a monstrous or demonic form appears in the visual register: Hands that count "eleven fingers" are shown at the vanishing center, as if the site were both the origin and the end of the picture being completed when, in the last line, "ce mal advint." "At twenty," "toward twenty," or "near twenty" becomes the Franco-Latin doublet that denies the abstraction of the Fall of Man. The end is spotted at the center, exactly where a compositional tactic inserts a negative or excessive form at the point of visible origin. Language and image are conflated in a pictogram where "eleven" fingers display an axis where a multiple order of progressions converge. The cipher of the demon, eleven, also initiates the digital activity of poetry by setting forth a difference posited within the identity of $1 = / \neq 1$.

With the coincidence of letters and ciphers comes a collapse of cause and effect or visible and enunciative dimensions. Emphasis on succession calls in question a guiding syntactic order. Confusion of images and written (or later, printed) characters bring into view a latent visual system that belies the narrative. A logic of spacing seems to ascribe equal or equipollent value to letters and the gaps between them. These and other indications evince a gridded or mapped text that plays on multiple surfaces of visible and lexical order and that can be traced with vectors and coordinates of valence equal to or greater than the poem's meaning. At the same time, the self-contained appearance of an ensemble of fourteen octosyllabic lines, framed in a rectangle, promises latent replication of itself, like the fiftieth story of *Les cent nouvelles nouvelles,* through its insistence on the differential order at its basis.

If "Un dictier joyeux" seems to be generated from paradoxes of clarity and confusion, it may be that a nascent cartographic sensibility is located in an area *between* the text and the reader. Because it is a manuscript, the text invites participation and marginal commentary that will help the reader pick his or her way through its vocables. Not yet under the late incunabular printer's controlling power of punctuation, the poem's ambiguity brings forth the reader's consciousness of navigating or finding one's bearings in the movement of back and forth from numerical to linguistic forms.[15] The Augustinian activity of reading understood as clarification of meaning is willfully sabotaged at the same time that diagrammatic activities of tracing and of mapping emerge.

Seen from one perspective, the poem becomes a sparkling surface of points that flash and then disappear when others, elsewhere, come into view before, in turn, also disappearing. An almost filmic surface of lexical and visual points suggests that a checkered grid would result if the major points of stress were connected by lines. Here and elsewhere, Molinet's verse invites the reader to attach rhumb lines to virtual "wind roses" or knots of meaning that would mark the points where language and image are condensed. These rhumb lines can emanate from the interior duplication of the fingers that count the ciphers at the vanishing point, as they also might be directed from the originary angles at the four cardinal points of the text. The invitation to retrace or draw furrows over the text belies its will to allow more to be made of it—to multiply its space at the same time that, like an ideogram, it contains expansion within itself—and its will to be confused with a general process of inscription. The latter, as recent criticism has demonstrated, implies an effacement of directionality that begins from a first point and leads to an end that confirms a pregiven, teleological order of things, an end that finalizes or "reveals" what was announced, like the coming of a god, in the beginning (Derrida 1972b: 388–89 and passim). The shared duties of reading, writing, commenting, and tracing in Molinet involve a "modern" sense of creation insofar as the poetry is in perpetual movement, of great permutative potential, self-inseminating, but also given to being variously mapped and navigated. However the eye constructs patterns through the verse, lexical units are coextensive with inscribed plot points, axes, or interstices between verbal and geometric figures. Because of the relation of space and of circuiting to the discourse, the poet's pen functions as a geometer's compass.

The dual role assigned to the writing serves to explain the erotic innuendo

of the circumstantial verse. Wherever Molinet seems obsessed by the erogenous zones of the female body or tends to delight in grime, a geometric impulse is made manifest. As in the *nouvelle,* delight in the nether regions of the
body is a function of the mapping of a paginal space and of a circuit that leads
the reader into areas *beyond* before the poem returns to a recognizable place.
Anatomy seems to derive from the mapping of the body on a grid or a window, such that points of coextension between the human figure and writing
mark the axes where language and image synthesize, disappear, and reappear.[16]
These points locate sites where a desire conflates the difference between two
orders—the visible or figurable and the utterable—and where, when they coincide or are isomorphic, they explode into wit that both reflects and confirms
the light of God. They produce a spark left on the page as dots that evince a
mystical contact between spirit and world. The site reveals points where discourse and space do not move away from each other (as will be the case in
literature in later ages of print culture), but where they collide or approach
identity of difference, as we have seen in the relation of language and figure
in Fouquet's paintings. In Molinet's tracings, these are also navigational loci in
the form of the poem's speech and writing.

They are seen as effects of a draftsman-poet's compass and protractor in one
of the poet's shortest *rondeaux*:

> Ceste fillette a qui le tetin point,
> Qui est tant gente et a les yeux si vers,
> Ne luy soyez ne rude ne parvers,
> Mais traictez la doulcement et a point.
>
> Despouillez vous et chemise et pourpoint
> Et la gectez sur un lit a l'envers,
> Ceste fillette . . .
>
> Aprés cela, si vous estes en point,
> Accollez la de long et de travers,
> Et si elle a les deux genouz ouverts,
> Donneés dedens et ne l'espargnez point,
> Ceste fillette . . .
>
> [This little lass with her firm breast
> Who with green eyes is so comely:
> Don't be perverse or treat her dumbly
> Treat her with tact, don't be a beast,
>
> Strip yourself of shirt and trouser
> On the bed, before you toss her,
> This little lass . . .

> After that, if with strength you're blessed
> On top and on the side embrace her,
> If her legs she will let you discover,
> Then stick it in, at her behest,
> This little lass . . .][17]

The *rondeau* is a fixed, circular form, but its contour, retraced with the incipit *ceste fillette a qui le tetin point,* indicates that the poem is testing a relation of the body to a retracing of circles. In the second line, the closed system of the poem opens with the amphibology of *tant gente* and *tangente.* The attractive shape of the maiden is due to a charm determined by the way the body is "compassed." The virtual nipple of the breast becomes both an axis and a tangent, the point where a straight and a curved line caress or graze one another.

Grammar, optics, and geometry are interwoven in the cliché. "Mais traictez la doulcement et a point" tells the reader to gaze upon the poem's condition of geometric abstraction. Given the homonym of the tangent, the imperative *traictez* also tells the reader to *trace* the line that configures the representation of a scene of desire in the style of a mapped landscape of an imaginary body. Poetic and geometric coordinates are literally placed upon the page visualized at the very axis of the poem, "sur un lit a l'envers."

The *rondeau* does not mediate only straight and curved lines. It also depicts the drawing of a conic section that opens from a point of origin. The poem describes a volumetric dimension gained through its narrative, but all the while the extended metaphor of a Euclidean and an erogenous *point* literally draws out the initial format that serves as a trellis, a base, or a ground for the projection. The *fillette,* in fact, seems to be a diminutive line, a little *fil,* a trait barely traced upon a paginal surface. The ideogrammatic figure of the body seems to be a signature of generation and geometry.[18] For a brief moment, the gaze it elicits is fixed and frozen, not as an elaboration of desire but merely as scientific evidence of the fact that the vision of the medieval subject (or here, the reader) moves into space as much as it receives rays from what comes toward it. At the end of the tenth line, then, an exchange of two active visibilities—or two angles that open onto each other—is registered.[19]

Using the mechanism of fixed and conventional forms such as the *rondeau,* the ballad, the *fatras,* or the *revid* (a poem given as a gift to a bride and groom at the time of their marriage), the poet establishes perspectives in which a topical depiction maps out a median area between the circumstance of writing, writing itself, and the inscription of the poet in the order of the world. Molinet assigns himself the position of a scribe who writes and pictures the universe before him, but at the same time he anticipates the very rivalry that sixteenth-century cosmographers will soon experience when they sign their works at a distance from themselves, their royal patrons, and the extension of the world being depicted. The "event" of Molinet's signature becomes the evidence of the construction of a map of social relations and of a drama of inscription in the organic world of language and things.

A glance at two poems can serve as a conclusion. In the "Lettre à Jehan de Ranchicourt," circumstance determines the placement of the writer's signature below the events that have been described, literally at the antipodes of the domain of the patron for whom the poem was composed. In the "Dictier pour Jehan de Tournay," read at a dinner party at the beginning of Lent in 1489, spatial counterpoint is used to develop, along the theme of travel, the figure of the conic section that was implicit in "Ceste fillette."

First, the "Lettre à Jehan de Ranchicourt" (Molinet 1933: 806–7) is a topical and circumstantial epistle written to a young nobleman; because of its wistful tones bemoaning the onset of senescence, it resembles a *complainte*. Weary, at the end of his career, the poet can no longer straddle a horse or any other animal; he is "au bout de ma roye" (at the end of my cord),

> Pouvre assés et mal atellés:
> Vieillesse m'assault a tous lés
>
> [Poor enough and badly bridled,
> With old age forever saddled],

needing a patron to give him employment and hard cash in exchange for wit. He looks to the good Magdeleine, Ranchicourt's wife. He bids them good will, ending with the couplet,

> Par vostre pouvre Molinet
> Qui n'a plus d'ancre en son cornet.
>
> [From your impoverished Molinet,
> With arid inkwell and nothing to say.]

The poet's name falls at the emphatic moment of the recitation, as the initial element of the ultimate rhyme that authenticates the letter. The conventional inscription of the signature at the lower corner of the text sets the poet in counterpoint to "Mon bon amy de Ranchicourt" addressed at the beginning. A space is established in which social distance is marked between the top and the bottom of the verse. The poet has the parting shot that calls attention to the divided nature of the verbal expression. When "Molinet" is uttered, the proper name calls into question its authority by underscoring its *graphic* relation defining the line of power extended between the poet and the receiver of the poem.

At the bottom, Molinet is inversely at the top. Set at the border, or *lisière,* of meaning, marked between the shape of the signature and its insertion as a key to the vault of the narrative design, Molinet here invokes linear hierarchies within verbal form. His signature becomes a function of a word aligned, a *mot liné* perhaps, not according to any abstract worth such as that of Ranchicourt's noble lineage but according to its own art of tracing itself. The empty inkwell of the last line carries the counterforce of a clearly drawn body, of a *corps* born (*né*) in the *cornet* of dissimulated misery. The name gains in analogical variety—hence worth—when it is associated with inscription and creation.

Multifarious figures emerge from Molinet's name when it occupies the position of a signature in the poem. That point identifies the area where the text becomes a virtual image of itself, or where the coextension of the two different orders within the same enunciation (or inscription) confirm the triumphant autonomy of the writer in either the best or worst of times. With the name comes a bonus of creative force that belongs to Molinet and to no one else.[20] In the "Lettre à Jehan de Ranchicourt," name and line are underscored in the context of ink and inkwell, which draw the eye to the material operation of writing and rhyming. A word is born of characters lined and cut into the world. In other poems, the product of writing will be likened to wheat ground into edible flour, bagged, and then properly stored in the windmill, which is, properly, the poet's atelier. (Editions of the work in fact emblematize the author's name in accord with the homonym of *moulin net/*molinet.

In poems that take up themes of travel, an implicit cartography of the self comes into view. Such is the effect of the strategy of counterpoint, developed along different lines in the "Dictier pour Jehan de Tournay" (Dupire 1933: 820–23), in which the poet welcomes the eponym's return from a voyage to the Holy Land:

> Joyeux suis de vostre retour
> Et grant lyesse au cueur en ay;
> Honneur a Dieu je fis ce jour,
> A touz perilz m'abandonnay;
> Nul ne scet le cruel destour
> De la mer, quand je cheminay
> En terre saincte et la enthour,
> En maint grant destroit me **tournay**.

[Joyous am I at your return,
Elated, that doubt would not allay,
Honor to God I would never spurn
And now and then, when I went away:
None would know the cruel turn
Destined when I took a journey,
En route to Jerusalem: Upon the way
Entered I did in a perilous **tourney**.]

Like the rest of the poem, the fixed form of the initial stanza tends to fill the "content" of the account of navigation with the same kind of clichés that marked "Un dictier joyeux." Invocation of God, mention of perils at sea, and description of the arduous voyage to the Holy Land are a function of the mapping or "compassing" along the horizontal and vertical axes defined by the acrostic. The *dictier* charts an itinerary through paginal space that, as the next stanza further illustrates, establishes a divided path or double set of "tracks" that invite the reader to find coordinate points where each converges upon the other. As it scans itself, the poem articulates a spatial rhetoric that implicitly compares the physical extension of the poem to a map or chart that represents the route between Burgundy and the Holy Land:

Grant chose est d'ouïr le recueil
Des chozes qui sont oultre mer;
Mais plus est de les veoir a l'oeil.

[Hear we must of things over the sea,
For much is said in those accounts,
But we do better to see what we see.]

Appeal to sight as the most sacred and infallible of senses betrays a keen visual sensibility, to be sure,[21] but in this poem reading becomes an art of navigation and travel. Textual space is mapped out by points that are both described in the narrative and indicated in rebuslike configurations incorporating the shape of the writing in the structure of the poetic itinerary. The second stanza literally tells how to decipher the configuration of an angle that opens the space of the textual world. Although the use of proper names in acrostics and in refrains is conventional (the practice dates to François Villon's ballads of the *Grant Testament*), the articulation of compassing and travel comes as a surprise. "Jehan de Tournay" is literally "turned" upon itself, in such a way that the itinerary of the *dictier* uses the proper name to bring the eye into the extension of space. In abstract terms, the poem is suggesting that the corners of each stanza open onto a navigable space to which the "compassed" proper name draws our attention:

J
E
H
A
N
D
E

tournay

An enumeration of places that follows in the third and fourth verses invites a haptic reading. A map of the Holy Land is scanned, its proper names and places are bundled together according to a visual rhyme that nestles the fourth and fifth lines (*b-b*)—which correspond to each other and to the middle lines of what precede and follow—between two sets of three-line units defined by an alternating rhyme scheme (*a-b-a* and *c-b-c*). The geometry of the verse allows the places, lifted either from Tournay's words or from the map accompanying Bernard von Breidenbach's recent *Voyage à la terre sainte* (1484), to be spatialized:

> Ce que le cueur devoit contemple,
> Le sainct Sepulchre, les saincts lieux,
> La saincte cité, le sainct temple,
> Les montaignes, forretz et rieux,
> Vous avez vu aux propres yeulx,
> La saincte terre digne et monde,
> En cui l'eternel roy des cieulx
> Conversa vivant en ce monde.
>
> Vous avez veu, comme j'entends,
> Le lieu ou la vierge enffanta,
> Le lieu ou dieu fit preschemens,
> Le lieu ou Sathan le tempta,
> Le lieu ou Judas le baisa,
> Le lieu ou souffrit passion,
> Le lieu ou son corps reposa,
> Et ou fut son assention.
> (Molinet 1933: 822, lines 17–32)

This third verse treats of geography, naming the physical terrain that Tournay saw, while its complement, the fourth, attributes sacred events to the site. At least two operations are evident. First, a language map sketches the salient traits of the Holy Land before motivating them with discourse. The visible features of the place (the Holy Sepulchre, the old city, the temple, mountains, forests, and rivers) do not begin to figure in the composition until, in the next verse, memorable events are attributed to the area. In these two verses, map and discourse are overlaid. Whereas the linear enumeration seems to offer a horizontal, serial mix of place names in the third stanza, the fourth rectifies the order through the vertical order of anaphora ("Le lieu ou," etc.), which fixes collective memory of mythic events to real places.

Second, if the effect obtained by the two verses can be compared to early printed maps that print place names without the support of relief or the inclusion of rivers and forests, we must wonder how the spatial treatment of language is tying self-authorization to print culture and cartography. These maps resemble calligraphic poems insofar as the reader must supply, in addition to the cardinal directions noted on each of the four sides of the page, the implied picture of the Holy Land.[22] An imaginary puzzle results, in which sites and names are pigeonholed or connected to each other. In the context of stanzas four through nine, in which description reviews the perils that pilgrims and merchants alike face in their travels to the east, Molinet exploits the conventions of the crusades to inspire a return to the Holy Land. Commerce, he implies, would be aided by conquest. Although the text bears none of the messianic trappings that characterize Columbus's *Libro de la prophécias,* in which the winning of the New World serves as a prelude to Christian victory over the infidels, it does bait the reader into seeing European lands from the point of view of the other (Molinet 1933: 823, lines 57–64). The world is turned topsy-turvy (65–80) in order to end with praise of Tournay's steadfast character. Confusion in Christian lands reigns supreme, whereas pagans and Muslims "tiennent mieulx leur fidelité, / Que ne font nos prochains voisins, / Suppos de la crestienneté" [adhere better to their fidelity / Than do our nearest kin / Raised in Christianity] (lines 57-60). The disparaging view suggests that, unlike others, only Tournay has been able to guide himself through troubled spaces and times. Encomium betrays a convention of exhortation that opens the lyric, but also, in the political dimension of its visibility, the relation of rivalry is left mute in order to emblazon the proper name that the poem is required to herald (lines 81–88).

The *dictier,* however, returns not simply to Tournay but to the collective group, seated around a dinner table and fireplace, that is pictured through the verse and in the art of its recitation. This means that all the travel of the poem circulates within the hero's proper name: Tournay succeeds by virtue of his *tournée,* his going and turning, which bring him to safety. The ultimate point of return is marked by Molinet's name. However much the poet mentions his name with affected modesty, the implied map of the *dictier* puts the signature at a point of value almost as great as Tournay's. To a configuration of

Mediterranean space is appended another, of social relations (between the nobleman and his chronicler), and still another, of social difference.

In this space, which displays the rungs of the social order in the disposition of the lines of poetry, we discover how the poet, like the future cartographer, will be obliged to recognize the contradictions that underpin the difference between the patron and the wordsmith or the engineer. The development of the self, when it is made as a map, moves toward a growing consciousness of the specialist's subaltern position in a social order that does not recognize the expertise needed to master new and growing technologies. In a very broad sense, we see in the figure of Molinet, like that of Fouquet, a figure of the artist and specialist who discovers how to articulate a new, almost scientific, sensibility of extension and language. Both seem to be aware of the role of the signature—of the self—which produces new articulations and new types of expression. In this material begins the story of the position of the writer and cartographer as author and political force in early modern literature. To see how it unfolds, we can now turn to Geoffroy Tory, a typographer and writer of the early sixteenth century who engages the labors of language and space that began in the revolutions of perspective and symbol in fifteenth-century France.

2

The Letter and the Grid: Geoffroy Tory

The writings of Geoffroy Tory, a printer and typographer from Bourges who lived and worked in Paris, are not generally associated with cartographic revolution. They pertain to the art of print culture and stand as handsome evidence of the dramatic changes that took place in printing ateliers from 1515 to the 1530s. Tory's most celebrated work, a manual for the design of letters that bears the prepossessing title *Champ fleury, Auquel est contenu lart & Science de la deue & vraye Proportion des Lettres Attiques, quon dit autrement lettres antiques, & vulgairement Lettres romaines proportionnees selon le Corps & visage humain* (Paris, 1529), is said to have utterly changed the face of the printed page in France during the humanist years (Catach 1968; Brun 1930, 1969; Butsch 1969).[1] His method for the construction of a classical, or "Attic," letter is the foundation of the aspect of typefaces that the Renaissance has bequeathed to us. Tory shifts print culture away from incunabular styles, which used a fairly standardized font, the *lettre de forme,* the *lettre bâtarde,* and the *lettre ronde.* He showed his readers how to design a font with a calm and classical measure, a font that marries the symmetrical ideal of the Vitruvian man, that is, the human being made in proportion to the world at large, to the geometer's circle, square, and triangle. He ushers in a graphic shape that characterizes the ferment in French letters during the 1530s. At the same time, he both sums up and praises shapes that had been current in France since the end of the fourteenth century (Saenger 1977).

In this chapter, I would like to argue that Tory's writings in general, and the

Champ fleury in particular, theorize the spatial imagination that had been nascently binding writing to geography, at least in the ways that the relation is
evinced in the vernacular poetry of Jean Molinet and in the form of *Les cent
nouvelles nouvelles*. Tory's work specifies much of what we have seen already
operating latently. The typographer further explores some of the implicit traits
of mapping and writing in his concerted effort to project the image of a
national and a historically founded space. Much of what he puts forward tells
of the climate in which grows the cartographic work of Oronce Finé. In its
broad strokes, Tory's graphic imagination emphasizes a strongly allegorical and
spatial sensibility of writing that will dominate much of the sixteenth century's
relations with language and extension.[2]

The *Champ fleury* deals with many topics, not the least of which is the synthesis of mythography, geography, and orthography. The way Tory goes about
describing a French heritage of writing and perspective determines not only
the project for a new "language map" of Gallia but also a spatial and volumetric poetics of printed writing. He correlates the graphic impulse, the literary
imagination, and the desire of plotting. Most important, Tory may be the first
humanist to offer a logical nomenclature for printed and manuscript types
that had become increasingly standardized with the advent of a growing liter-
ate class of students and of a nobility that, as of 1360, cultivated vernacular
texts copied in a Gothic cursive style. From this background, a specific vocabulary emerged, reflecting a growing uniformity of patterns of script. Tory's great
contribution to print culture, remarks Paul Saenger, "consists in the establishment of the canons of a vocabulary for gothic writings in books" and in the
correct reproduction of the proportions that accounted for both the height
and the width of their letters (1977: 498–99, 505).

Above all, Tory knew how to *name* what he saw. The ability to detect and
label different types and styles betrays the cartographic quality of Tory's innovations. For if Tory not only succeeds in distinguishing and classifying past
and present manuscript and printed styles, he also shows that a *perspectival
distance* exists between himself and the history of orthography. The nomenclature that is taken up in the final pages of the *Champ fleury* suggests that
Tory is in a position to see the range of the past forms of literacy from Greece
and Rome and that, because of this position, he is able to locate precisely how
typographic forms in aesthetic and political programs are anchored in recent
history. He allegorizes the past in terms of current ideological programs. Tory
thus becomes a major French exponent of a "Renaissance"—as opposed to a
re-nascence (Panofsky 1972)—of cultural materials. A reader quickly ascertains

that his program espouses the mapping of a French space and, beneath it, a specifically French history anchored in the authority of Greek myth.

The nomenclatures indicate that an objectifying perspective is brought to medieval and classical writing in such a way that a component of distance and point of view is visible throughout the treatise, both in the handling of its topic and in the very printed letters that convey it. All of a sudden, the printed page becomes a ground that can be subject to geometric operations; it can be gridded, fashioned into prototypes of pixels, coordinated, graphed, and even navigated.[3] What may strike a contemporary reader as charming but innocuously contrived allegories, *moralités,* or far-fetched memory images that correlate the square surround of the letter to the human body are important to programs that project writing into space and that chart new relations between the subject, the world, and modes of plotting. The author advocates at once a new "design" of the alphabet and the development of an apparatus of analysis that will map the ways readers and spectators can orient themselves—by way of imagination and perspective—within and outside of printed characters.

Three Allegories

The principal allegories are placed at the geometric center of the *Champ fleury,* in the second part (Book 2, fols. xi–xxx), which is flanked by an exhortation in defense of writing in French (Book 1, fols. i–x) and a practical review of the history, meaning, and geometric design of each of the twenty-three letters of the alphabet (Book 3, fols. xxxi–lxvi). In the table of contents, Tory announces that he has added "deux caietz à la fin" [two notebooks at the end] (fols. lxvii–lxxx), which name and reproduce thirteen styles of letters, along with "the instruction and manner of making ciphers of letters for golden rings, for tapestries, stained-glass windows, paintings, and other apparently worthy things" (fol. A.i v).[4] Although the bulk of the work is taken up in the fifty-eight folios that follow Book 2 and the lengthy appendixes, Tory makes it clear from the start that "Ce toutal oeuure / est divisé en Trois Livres" [this total work is divided into three books] in order to set the allegories at a mathematical vanishing point, or to have linguistic *history* and typographic *practice* turn about the axis of his *theory.* With an embedded configuration of this sort, a distance is gained, and it is this distance that inspires the content of the work.

Here Tory launches his reform. He corrects the proportions established by Luca Pacioli, Sigismundo de Fanti, and Lodovico Vincentino, and he modifies the alphabet of Albrecht Dürer (fol. xiii) by establishing a ten-point scale for

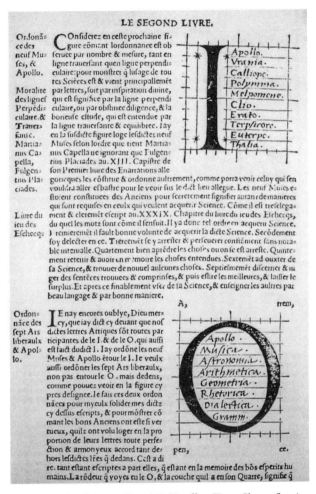

Figure 2.1. The allegorized I and O (Geoffroy Tory, *Champ fleury*)

Roman capitals. The square proportion of ten vertical and ten horizontal units lays out a grid whose area becomes what he calls the "body" of each letter. The initial allegory, which spatializes and leads the discourse to the configuration, is the upper-case *I* (Figure 2.1, top), which allots one "latitude" to each of the nine muses and one to their complement, Apollo, who is perched at the top. The second allegory, which draws out the capital *O*, inscribes Apollo on the topmost rung above an echelon of the seven liberal arts (with the trivium at the bottom), all contained within the periphery of the letter that occupies the top and bottom lines (Figure 2.1, bottom). He conceives of the *I* as Virgil's

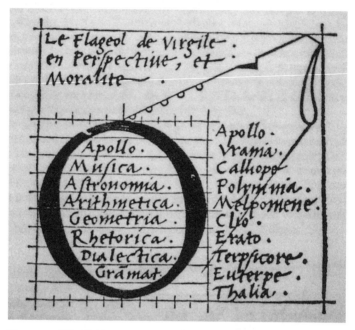

Figure 2.2. "Virgil's Flute in Perspective and Morality" (Geoffroy Tory, *Champ fleury*)

flute standing on its end, with either seven (representing the liberal arts) or nine (representing the muses) holes. The flute is then set on its side in order to synthesize the medieval curriculum and the classical muses of the sciences. The square has at each of its corners the four syllables of A-trem-pen-ce, or Tem-pe-ran-ce, the muse of good works, of clocks, and of moderation, who was an ideal for the ethic of the Protestant reform (Meiss 1974: 34–35). In the remarkable memory picture "Virgil's Flute in Perspective and Morality" (Figure 2.2), Tory sums up the first of his allegories: The *O* and *I* are seen together when the flute is placed on its side. The instrument moves into space and points to a new axis or a vanishing point at the upper corner. Implied is that the figure rolls about the axis, or that it can extend into space according to a cartographic logic of extension from a center (at the juncture of the line below Musica and the arc of the intrados of the *O*) to a corner, and then constitute a new axis that will extend new circumferences (Edgerton 1987: 10–14). Tory congratulates himself for his wit.[5] At the same time, he notes that the diagram is put forth unselfishly, "pour myeulx declarer l'intention, le segret, & la moralité des bons Anciens, & pour bailler enseignement & voye aux modernes & amateurs de vrayes, pures, & bonnes lettres" [to declare better the intention, secret, and morality of the good classics, and to provide information and a path for moderns and amateurs of true, pure, and good letters] (fol. xvi v). The *segret* of which he writes may be located in the distance that is implied to be held between the Attic *O,* and the older cursive style, the *lettre de forme* that names the device: The names of the medieval arts and the classical muses of the sciences are written in the incunabular style, in contrast to the new letter that conveys this memory. A sense of history is tipped into the graphic differences of typography and their respective referents. In this way, the *O* as flute is inspired by Virgil's verse, but it sings of the ingenuity of Tory, the printer's innovation being seen at the rim of the instrument and in the volumetric plan of the allegory. Hence, the past recedes into spaces along a diagonal axis while the present is foregrounded on the surface defined by the body of the *O.* Crucial to the design of this perspectival object is the correlation of a distance of time that is measured by a digitized treatment of space.

The third principal allegory, of the Vitruvian man inscribed in the gridded backdrop or body of the *O,* makes the extending, or cartographic, effect of the grid and perspectival view of the *I*-as-flute come forth by virtue of contiguity. Set on the opposite folio (fol. xvii), the figure immediately recalls the medieval, "moralized" configuration of world maps of the fourteenth century. In these creations, such as the Ebstorf map (Woodward and Harley 1987: 351), the cruciform image of Christ forms the cardinal directions of the world. In 1529, the reincarnation of the Vitruvian man could not fail to be laden with what was a moralized geography of space (Schulz 1978). Here, as we see in the coextension of classical and Gothic print in the figure to the left, the resemblance of Vitruvian man to the medieval *mappae mundi,* with their allegorical space, whose four cardinal directions are made by analogy with Christ's four bodily extremities, is no less evident. Two different modes of mapping are set forth in the same image. One is clearly of a "past" moment and the other, in the same image, heralds the here, the now, and the future of the typographer's innovations. The expansive quality of the "new" form is, of course, marked by the genitals at the axis of the circle and the interstices between the undrawn diagonals of the square. In Tory's system, it is not ironic that Clio, the muse of history, figures as part of the line that crosses the man's organ of perpetuation, nor that the text explaining the drawing proposes "ung Enigme, cest à dire un propos obscur" (an enigma, that is, an obscure statement), which makes the meaning of the three lines of Latin a function of the scansion of their digits.

Reading the text is tantamount to a mensuration of words, that is, of imagining them as equally sized units—like pixels—that are seen in a serial and discrete configuration. Conversely, if the enigma (which solves its own riddle within its formulation) is applied to the allegorical picture, the world (shaped in the image of a man) is lettered not in order to be moralized into abstraction but to be defined in quantifiable and reiterable (or movable) units. Thus, when Tory reduces the enigma to the cliché that "every natural thing is, and consists in, number, and this number is either even or odd" (fol. xvii v), by showing how the mouth, chin, head, navel and genitals are odd whereas the eyes, feet, hands, and ears are even, he underscores the facticity of his analogy. The remark indicates that the logic being presented cannot be trusted. He becomes, in a word, a trickster: For although the mouth (*bouche*) or the chin (*menton*) is odd because it has no complement, its name is still even because its name is composed of six letters. The arbitrary nature of the allegory comes to the surface, but nonetheless the correlation of the form of expression (the number of letters in the sign) to the shape of its referent (the single or double nature of the bodily part being referred to) suggests that a generativity and a possibility of growth or expansion into space is visible at the *divided basis* of the axis of the frame and figure of the Vitruvian man.

Another dimension becomes apparent when the opposing folios are scanned. The gigantic *O* on the left could quite possibly be fantasized as an extreme closeup of the navel of the Vitruvian man on the right; or the perspectival unit of both flat and rotund properties, and the erect flute as well, projected at a penile angle, could be a magnification of the genitals to the right. The carto-graphic virtue of expansion along a plan of center, circumference, and quin-cunx is matched by an erotic quality in which the absent lips that would pucker over the mouthpiece of the flute are at a point where the upper end touches and defines a triangle, below which there drips a drop of fluid in the shape of a flamboyant *soufflet,* the tracery pattern used in rose windows and on heraldic arches. The opening onto the moralized perspective of the flute from the upper left corner where the instrument touches the square is so erogenously underwritten that the name of its side, "trem" of "Atrempance," turns the figure for devout and chaste labor into an activity of giving and thrusting, of oscillating movement of male and female members of a self-perpetuating dyad. It could be said that the cartographic dimension of the two figures operates along a two-dimensional axis, and that the erotic side of the figure is cosmographic insofar as a complete universe is fashioned from a virtual model of infinite reproduction of volumes and of beings in three dimensions.

Other variants in the same allegory subscribe to the scheme that super-imposes components of mapping and generation from differences within and across each scheme. Seven figures elaborate the analogy of the body and the

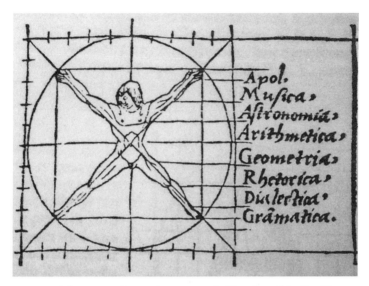

Figure 2.3. The quartered man who trains in the liberal arts (Geoffroy Tory, *Champ fleury*)

letter (fols. xvii v–xix v). They play, first, on the identity of the navel and sex organs as an axis for the circle and square surround. Noteworthy (in Figures 2.3 and 2.4) is how the figure is tortured by being constrained to obey medieval lines of form that bend the body according to its design (Baltrušaitis 1931) and how it is positioned as if chained on a rack, even though all the while it struggles against the outside forces that contain it. Its sex organ traces the meridian that Tory has likened to the Y axis of inspiration, in contrast to the X axis that is made of the equating lines associated with the long labors of study. The meridian bisects the navel in a manner that suggests a generative analogy in which

navel : travail/labor = penis : divine inspiration/calling

The eroticized geography is affirmed (as in Figure 2.3) where the sex organ bears attributes that could be qualified as *both* male and female. It coyly announces the coming of the *I-O* analogy (Figure 2.4), in which the body (the gridded square) of the letter contains both odd and even and male and female elements.

The allegory plays tricks in its ulterior manifestations. In Tory's explanation of the "chaste" character of the great initial *A* (Figure 2.5), the transverse bar below the median horizontal covers the man's pubis "in order to denote

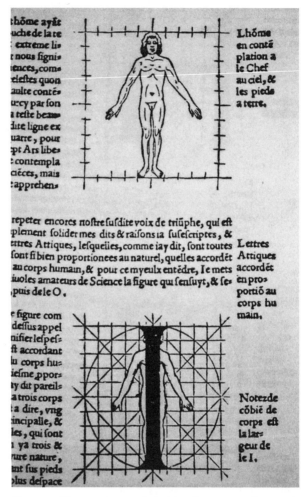

Figure 2.4. The man contemplating the nine muses and man as I and O (Geoffroy Tory, *Champ fleury*)

that Pudicity and Chastity above all else are required for those who demand access and entry into good letters, of which A is the opening and first of all abecedaria" (fol. xviii v). When the image bars access to the visual field, the text penetrates it. And as the genitals are effaced, so also are the eyes of the Vitruvian figure behind the *A*. Yet, in the medieval scheme that Tory puts forward, the picture nonetheless gazes at us. The moralized perspective of the *I-O* flute had brought a volumetric (or cosmographic) dimension to the printed letter. It could be said that the *A* constitutes an angle opening a

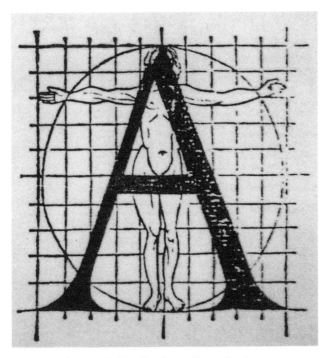

Figure 2.5. The letter A (Geoffroy Tory, *Champ fleury*)

monocular perspective from the Vitruvian man's "point of view" toward the viewer, and that the play of gazes correctly underlines the erotic association of the generative and visual faculties in the allegory that would otherwise erase them.

The two other letters that shroud and display the penal region, *H* and *K*, add two dissymmetrical—hence productive—elements to the analogy. The *H* (Figure 2.6) is compared to an architectural design in which the quadrature of the letter resembles buildings by "wishing to be erected solidly," with a house broader than the roof (fol. xix r). The implication is that the analogies of micro- and macrocosm, as well as letter/body and house/nation, require a method of gridding to obtain optimum balance. But also, the cruciform figure, which is at once behind and in front of the *H*, produces a depth of field in the configuration: The man's forearms rest in front of each trumeau and his belly is seen behind the transverse lintel; the organ of generation seems to be a fulcrum on which the whole is balanced.

The distance that the comparison of the *H* to the man gains from the comparison of the body to classical architecture can be noted through comparison

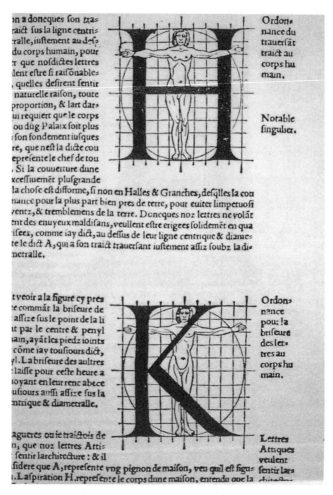

Figure 2.6. The letters H and K (Geoffroy Tory, *Champ fleury*)

with concurrent *Menschenalphabeten,* which contort carefully drawn bodies to conform to the shape of letters (e.g., Peter Flötner's 1534 alphabet, illustrated in Massin 1973: 72). The evident difference of man and letter endorses the play of androgeny and sexual difference that Tory has just projected through the perspectival treatment of the letters *I* and *O.* This may be why *K* (Figure 2.6) is a form presented as a totality in *briseure,* where the line of breakage unites the form along the central horizontal axis. That the *K* is a homonym of *cas,* the popular term designating the human sex organ, turns the example into a rebus that further proves the point. The bon mot contained in the letter subtends an Erasmian program that gathers a community of subjects together through appeal to both high and low levels of humor.[6]

A Fourth Allegory: Architecture, Letter, and Nation

The fourth allegory compares the letter to domestic architecture. Its first elements begin at the end of the third allegory. Here, the comparison brings into view one of the cartographic dimensions of the *Champ fleury*. In the margin to the left of a letter-figure ending the segment on the man in the letter (fol. xix v, the letter-figure immediately resembling the work of the Rabbi Maurus, illustrated in Massin 1973: 162–67), there is an indexical note that states, "montées et degres des Anciens" [stairways and steps of the classics] in order to reach a topic that in the 1520s was probably defining the differences in national styles or cultural visions of space and volume.[7] The *K*'s angular bars are likened to the ancients' longitudinal stairwells, which took a straight slope from one floor to the next. Suddenly, the text is turned into an ideogram that combines a perspectival view of the page (as a cruciform body, an abstract symbol, and a calligram of the Vitruvian man) and an ichnographic rendering of a French ecclesiastical building. From the former standpoint, the twenty-seven lines of text are bisected by the line beginning "on va tornant au tour du centre & noyau de la dictz viz le *I*, & le *O*, & le *S*" [we proceed turning about the center and core of the said stairwell of the *I*, the *O*, and the *S*], such that the axis and hub of the house being described also locate the vocables "center and core" at the center and core of the configuration. *I* and *O* seem to be situated at the penile area below the torso and outstretched arms of the calligram.

Tory is not merely being cute or self-conscious: He places the *S* in the *I-O* to designate a spiral staircase at the center of the architectural ground plan. As Jean Guillaume has shown (1985: 27), the spiral staircase at the center or the extremity of French buildings at the end of the flamboyant age (as at Châteauroux) stands as the consummate expression of a French design. The spiral staircase, he adds, in fact disappears from architectural idiolect at the very moment it reaches its greatest refinement. Could we be wrong in deducing that Tory is advancing a late-medieval, specifically *French* domestic plan of building in the very place where he discourses on the classical and synchronously imported Italian type of linear, or perspectival, stairway? Our brief excursion into architecture seems to confirm that he makes a case for recent French styles of manuscript and print just as he extols the "national" aspect of the late flamboyant mode that pertains both to domestic and ecclesiastical buildings.[8]

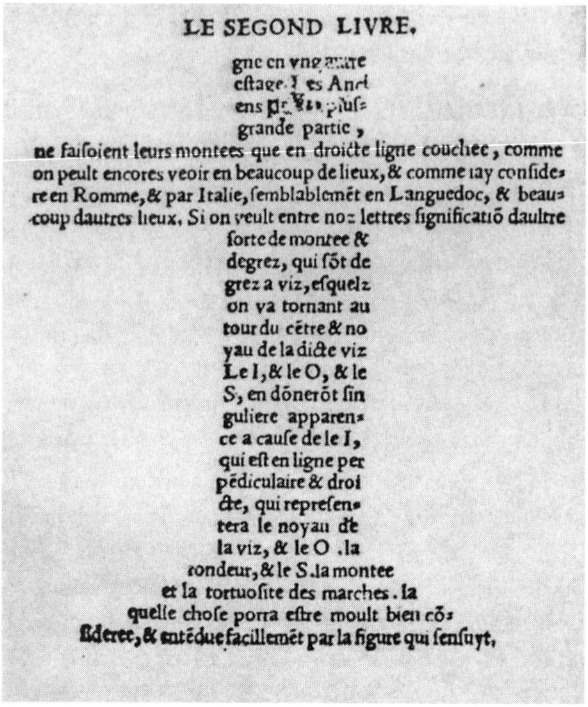

LE SEGOND LIVRE.

gne en vng ... re
estage. Les And
ens p... plus
grande partie,
ne faisoient leurs montees que en droicte ligne couchee, comme
on peult encores veoir en beaucoup de lieux, & comme iay conside-
re en Romme, & par Italie, semblablemēt en Languedoc, & beaucoup daultres lieux. Si on veult entre noz lettres significatiō daultre
sorte de montee &
degrez, qui sōt de
grez a viz, esquelz
on va tornant au
tour du cētre & no
yau de la dicte viz
Le I, & le O, & le
S, en dōnerōt sin
guliere apparen-
ce a cause de le I,
qui est en ligne per
pēdiculaire & droi
cte, qui represen-
tera le noyau de
la viz, & le O la
rondeur, & le S la montee
et la tortuosite des marches. la
quelle chose porra estre moult bien cō-
sideree, & entēdue facillemēt par la figure qui sensuyt.

Figure 2.7. An enigma: a cruciform ideogram (Geoffroy Tory, *Champ fleury*)

For the same reason, the identity of text and image, a dedifferentiated space where the unconscious motivations of the work are located, hinges on a paraph that is the cornerstone of the textual ideogram in the form of a ground plan for an ecclesiastical building. To see how, we can consider the figure as a function of the flamboyant style in domestic architecture. The calligrammatic figure resembles not a Gothic structure but, initially, a Romanesque structure: The transepts are extended as arms, whereas thirteenth century Ile-de-France buildings trimmed the collateral members, the arms of the body of the church, in favor of a compact whole with a polygonal apse at its eastern head; the east end (or the top of the page) is flat, *not* prismatically polygonal; the west end opens wide as if it were a narthex, the extension to the church that High Gothic had long since eliminated (Figure 2.7).

Why the seeming return to the older style? It may be because, first, Tory suggests that the origins of the Frenchness of Gothic and classical letters can be seen in Carolingian and Romanesque forms, in the works of scriptoria, which have an influence on the style of letters he is setting forward. Second, he implies that the spiral form that is at the axis of the diagram shares much with the flamboyant architectural style, an extensive idiom that defined itself in a dialectical relation with the Gothic by extending the transept, reviving the narthex, and flattening the east end, or the apse, of the church. That style goes hand in hand with his rehabilitation of the cursive forms that others had wished to reject (Saenger 1977: 499). A great French history of architectural space and of writing style appears to be extended into the diagram.

The homage to earlier and to recent types of letters and building programs is evident in the "signifier of demarcation" (Rosolato 1985: 63–82) that is set between the fixture of which it is a part and the domestic building that it heralds on the next folio. Tory has stated that the reader can see "between our letters" the signification of another design of stairwell and of steps, which are spirally placed, in such a way that the *I,* a central shaft, is set in an *O,* the containing cylinder. The *S* curves between the center and the circumference, "laquelle chose porra estre moult bien consideree, & entendue facilement par la figure qui s'ensuyt" [which is very worthy of attention, and can be understood by the figure that follows] (fol. xix v). What follows is an upper-case *S* that turns *s'ensuyt,* what follows, into the proof of what precedes, and vice versa. The very letter that is said to follow reappears in upper case at the originary angle or edge of the next page, prior to the diagram.[9]

This effect of trickery, of embedded images, riddles, or hidden agendas in the texture of the writing, in which the shape of the final word of the calligram and the first letter of the next paragraph translate each other into the figure of a spiral shape and the sibilance of an *S* into a vocable and a rebus, shows how a double reading also operates in the adjacent figure of the house of letters (Figure 2.8, top). Tory furnishes two diagrams at once. In the rectangle, he draws a house that is based on the classical font of the Attic capitals. The *A* is the slope of the roof, the *H* the sign of the two-level elevation, the *K* the extension of the same but also a classical stairway going from the ground floor to the second floor and attic, and the *O-I-S* constitutes the "French" solution to what *K* is offering. The parallelogram defining the outer area of the roof is so vertically sloped that a viewer sees a French, flamboyant domestic building but not a Roman basilica. The illustration conjoins the two styles to show that the French mode contains the classical past. A national program depending on fifteenth-century models at the cusp of "old" and "new" building programs (undertaken by Francis I in 1517) is visible. Tory retains elements of the "old" Gothic style—the French idiom—*as* the "new" design in both the angle of the

Figure 2.8. The house of letters, the textual L, and the cardinal I
(Geoffroy Tory, *Champ fleury*)

roof and the allegory of the spiral staircase. The flamboyant style is seen as co-extensive with the classical idiom. What follows,

> SI on deman-
> doit plates
> formes en nos
> dictes lettres At-
> tiques, on y en
> trouvera asses
> pour galeries,

begins with a heraldic *S*, two and one-half times as large as the typeface, an upper-case *I*, and a lower-case *o*, leaving

$$S\,I\,o$$

in descending order, in a line that gives perspective to the three components of the spiral staircase that are illustrated in the house below and to the right. The writing already embodies what it sets out to describe, thus conflating discourse and referent, tenor and vehicle, signifier and signified, and even cause and effect.

Betrayals of Diagram and Text

The second reading of the diagram is confirmed in the text itself, in areas where the text does *not* explain what abuts it to the right (lines 1–21) and what is above it (lines 22–31). Tory usually proceeds emblematically by placing an explanation just above ("la quelle chose iay cy faict en figure et desseing") or below ("La lettre . . . cy pres designee en son Quarre") an illustration. The announced allegory of the house of letters is, however, deferred. In its place he inserts a note on the difference in the naming of French and Roman buildings in France. In the French vernacular, classical theaters are called "arenas," which suggests that two kinds of nomenclature are also embedded in the unglossed image.[10] In place of a commentary in subscription, we read, first, a mapping of the letter. Tory endows the alphabetic unit with distinct cardinal traits that probably derive from the unmentioned analogy with the placement of High Gothic churches, which orient the apse eastward, toward the Holy Land. Now the four sides of the body of the letter are compassed, or endowed with cardinal directions. The point where the diagonals of the square meet is akin to the point where humanity finds itself in the world, and where a person can gain a sense of direction merely by contemplating the form of a letter.

The architectural metaphor enables Tory to develop a cosmography of writing. As a gallery, the *I* should face north or east. As a shape of a room, its long bar should face north, and its "paw" (*patte*) should look to the east,

> qui est la situation la plus sayne de toutes, a cause du dict dos quon tourne au Vent meridian, qui est pestilent tant aux corps humains que aux corps materielz & inanimez, & a cause de la face longue qui reçoit en elle le Vent de Byze qui est pur, nect, & agile, & a cause de la face courte qui est au dedans de la patte de la dicte lettre L, en laquelle le beau soleil levant regarde incontinent au point du jour, & y dure en y inspirant toute suavité, pour la plupart dudict jour.

> [which is the healthiest site of all, because the said back is turned to the south wind, which is as pestilent to humans as it is to material and inanimate bodies, and because of the long side that receives in its form the north wind, which is

pure, clean, and agile, and because of the short side that is inside the paw of the
said letter *L,* upon which the handsome rising sun freely gazes at daybreak, and
stays there, inspiring great sweetness throughout most of the said day.] (fol. xx r)

The environmental aspect of Tory's architecture is clearly inspired by Vitruvius
and Alberti, as he duly notes, but the innovation on the page is the graphic
block of text that suggests that the book can also be marked with cardinal
traits. The book as a spatial symbol, or compass, pertains to a Latin tradition
in the Middle Ages (Curtius 1963: 302–47), but it now gains new meaning in
that man is at the ostensive center of a letter seen as a compass in microcosm,
and in that the page conveying the image of the house faces south, toward the
book's gutter (and hence toward pestilence, as Ptolemaic wind maps had
shown in their lower corners); north to the margin on the right, what Molinet
had recently called the "border" or *lisière* of meaning; west to material above,
or to the top of the page; and east to the bottom edge, or to things below. Because the four points are correlated to the square of the page, it is also implied
that the book itself has other coordinates that relate to the cosmos. The spine
would point in one direction, the vellum cover in another, the colophon in the
opposite direction, and so on. The cardinal volume of the book is engaged
when Tory "cubes" his diagram of the man in the letter in order to make his
edifice resemble what Plato's *Timaeus* had equated with the world. In Plato's
work, the cube was likened to the earth, and here the same analogy is offered.

As Tory's discourse is always duplicitous, so, too, is the schematic design
that moves in the directions of surface and volume. When folios xx vi–xxi r are
scanned, the cardinal directions that were coordinated with the winds and the
path of the sun for the placement of buildings are projected onto a moralized
space that replaces the compass points with the four virtues of Justice, Prudence, Force, and Temperance. The inherited significance of their names is less
important than are their positions as figures of geometric calculation and, it is
implied, of navigation. Justice observes height and width; Prudence manages
the ruler and the geometer's compass; Force divides, measures, and apportions; Temperance masters the art of spacing and placement. The face "contained" by the personified corners of the square is an implicit map that can be
surveyed (Tory remarking that the "eyeline" is to be taken literally, as an equator that cuts between two pupils).

In the context of Tory's incipient and totalizing history of French language
and letters, the figure contained in the square would be an ideal subject of *Le
Roy très Catholique,* Francis I. By way of Ovid, Tory describes his man as he
who "ought to dominate over all . . . created things" except for the universal

creator. That a man can fit in the square area, and that his face fits the oval interior of the *O*, or that his seven orifices match the number of the liberal arts is only an epiphenomenal—patently Ficinian—praise of human beauty. In the greater context of state and nation, the comparison has at least three goals: It first suggests that a subject can be serialized according to Euclidean terms, hence *regulated* or replicated as an autonomous and infinitely reproducible form from a master-patron. What is wrought in the figure of the man-as-letter-as-grid-as-printed-diagram has decisive political implications for administrative officials who care to think through the elements of Tory's analogy. The gridding of space, body, and book can be correlated to produce a national body ascribed to an expansive space in which it is said to belong and to have a proper place, all the while the nude figure is dressed in the pious garb of Christian and humanist values.

The second goal, which seems to aim at what Descartes will make with his automata a century later, involves an extensive lettering of the body. By being named in terms of places, parts, figures, and seats of virtue, the body is mapped. Tory uses the same effects of nomenclature to link the body to space and serial reproduction in cartographic terms. His subject is ciphered, but it is also accompanied by a gazetteer that associates its notable places with figures of the arts and of the Greek sciences. The "lettered man" is rigged so that he is both explicated and determined according to alphabetic codes, and he is made to resemble a muscular puppet that can be operated by whoever can push and pull the letters of the alphabet (Figure 2.9).

The third goal undermines the first two and again shows how the trickster sabotages his most hermetic and symmetrical allegories. No sooner does the author put his man's face in the majuscule *O*, for the sake of the initial paradigm of the perfection of *I* and *O*, than he is obliged to bisect the circle with a vertical bar. But the shape reminds him of the Greek phi, and leads him toward jokes and rebuses that he is at first seduced into mentioning but that he then, in a return of reason, rejects.

> Les Grecs de ces deux lettres I. & O. ainsi logées l'une sus l'autre comme les voyez en la dicte figure, ont faict une autre lettre quilz appellent Phi. (L)a quelle Phi. vault autant ung P. & une aspiration, & laquelle Ilz ont en usage en lieu de F., qui n'ont pas entre leurs lettres. Il semble que nostre ditte figure soit ung Resbus & chose Hierogliphique, & que ie l'aye faicte pour faire resuer & muser les musards, mais tout bien consideré, non est.

> [The Greek form of these two letters *I* and *O* lodged thus one over the other as you see in the said figure, is made with another letter that they call phi, which amounts to a *P* and an aspiration, and which they use in place of *F,* a letter that

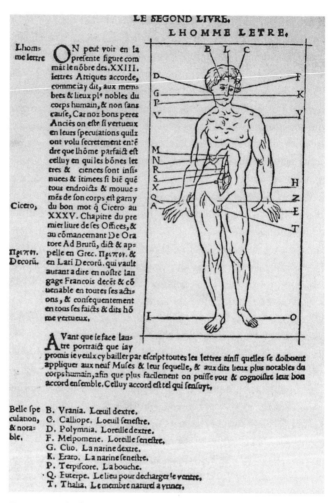

Figure 2.9. The lettered man, or "lhomme letre" (Geoffroy Tory, *Champ fleury*)

they do not have in their alphabet. It seems that our said figure may be a rebus and a hieroglyph, and that I have drawn it to inspire revery and to lead musing souls by the nose, but when everything is considered, that is not the case.] (fol. xxii r)

In going from phi to *F*, the reader follows the history of writing from the Greeks to the French. Each tradition is contemporary with the other in the gist of the sentence. But when the "said figure" is literally *spoken*, Tory is obliged to *name* the components of its vocal effect, "ung P. & une aspiration."

All of sudden, he abuts the unconscious that refuses to accept all of the limiting and controlling apparatuses that comprise the two goals noted above: A
P (a *pet* or a fart) and an aspiration (a good noseful of stench) mock the nobility of the Greek letter. The pun is too good for Tory to overlook in passing,
hence the logic of denial that follows a Freudian psychopathology to the spirit
(and explosive force) of the "essentially localized structure of the signifier." All
the humanist "aspirations" that are elsewhere being extolled now collapse in
the differential mechanism of the letter as a self-contained world and rebus
and as a unit set in a spoken discourse. Betrayed are the clichés that are the
basis of the first two goals:

> The *I*, which is a straight perpendicular line, placed thus between the two eyes,
> tells us that we must have our faces raised toward the sky in order to recognize
> our creator, and to contemplate the great gifts and sciences that he bestows upon
> us. And it may be true that God wishes us to aim our contemplation toward the
> heavens, as he gives us our head raised upward, and that of beasts lowered down-
> ward. (fol. xxi r)

Idealism of this kind is reduced to hilarious absurdity within the logic of
Tory's method.

The disruptive element—marked as intended in the author's disavowal,
which draws attention to his wit—carries over to the "lettered man" as mario-
nette. As a perfect figure, both a 10, as in *IO,* and a 23, a prime number, the
number of letters in the alphabet, which is the sum of nine (muses) + seven
(liberal arts) + four (cardinal virtues) + three (graces), the figure of the man is
a "house" (*logis*) of letters and of the muses and other personifications of virtue
and science. *P,* for Terpsichore, is at the mouth, suggesting that the world is
indeed both right side up and upside down. *Q* (a common pun and rebus on
cul) stands for Euterpe and is shafted into the man's anus, where the letter
becomes the thing itself by virtue of its placement in the right spot, "le lieu
pour descharger le ventre." *X,* the axial letter, likewise happens to be at the
navel. Tory hints that his motivation of the places by means of letters and
names is, paradoxically, both arbitrarily motivated and motivatedly arbitrary.
He has forsaken alphabetic logic ("tout à mon escient" that is, conscientiously)
to show that "their nature and virtue strive to be mixed one within the other,"
or that the system of mapping at the basis of his allegorical reasoning mixes
conventional signs with an artful design of his own signature.

A Well-Joined Marquetry

Evidence of the author as trickster is nowhere more apparent. His wit is shown
in an idiom that combines anamorphic projection, the art of perspective, and

the artisan craft dedicated to the intarsia. He chooses as the emblem of his book a marquetry and a mosaic. These are not just what he draws from Latin to describe his process (an "opus vermiculatum, opus tessellatum, & assarotum") or the flowered garden in spring ("la beaulté d'un pre & iardin est en la diversité & multitude assemblée de diverses belles herbes & fleurs" [the beauty of a field and a garden is in the assembled diversity and multitude of diversely handsome grasses and flowers] (fol. xxiii r), but also experiments in readings of three-dimensional figures on a flat plane. The marquetry refers specifically to the intarsia, cleverly inlaid woodcarvings that give the illusion of polygonal forms floating in a world of depth on a flat panel of wood.[11]

The figure of the garden as a marquetry reflects the title of the book, *Champ fleury*, but it also sums up the architectural component of the prevailing allegories in the second book. As in many writings of the early years of French humanism, the four components are tessellated, or "vermiculated," in the verbal style that describes the marquetry garden. The rest of the second book weaves the twenty-three letters, virtues, sciences, graces, and arts into allegories of the Homeric chain: a letter *I,* raised from the earth to the sky, that ties the earth to the heavens; the Virgilian branches of golden science and of ignorance that bear or shed the twenty-three leaves standing for the letters of the alphabet; the allegorized *O* as the Homeric chain wrought in a circle of the same number of links; a triumphal entry of Apollo that resembles those that the French king had known after his accession to the throne; a flaming fleur-de-lis made from Tory's *I* and *A*. All glorify dedication to and study of letters. They also convey a growing sense of the author's affiliation with the cartographer's identity as an artisan and a scientist who, by dint of discipline and meticulous labor, will become an autonomous subject of the nation represented by the vernacular idiom.

As he does elsewhere, Tory congratulates himself for the wit of his four moralized illustrations. It is the Homeric ladder, however (Figure 2.10) that spells out his relation to the cosmographer and the self-contained subject. Where Tory refers to Homer, he could also be referring to Giovanni Pico della Mirandola, whose famous ladder granted to the new individual, the self-made person, the means either to climb—aspire—to the heavens or to descend to the lower depths. The typographer wishes to take his reader skyward, but in a way that has been cleared by his own investment and self-realization in the work before our eyes. For this reason, we can hypothesize that Tory inaugurated the second book in cooperation with Charles de Bovelles (Carolus Bovillus) (fol. xi r), the French interpretor of Euclid. He had arranged the four elements according to a quasi-periodic scale of chemical and human activity.

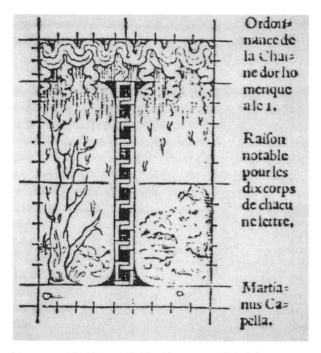

Figure 2.10. The Homeric ladder-I between earth and sky
(Geoffroy Tory, *Champ fleury*)

The rungs of his paradigmatic ladder went from *essere,* the earth, to *vivere,* or
water; from there to *sentire,* or air; and, finally, to *intelligere,* the empyreal rim
of fire. When Bovelles "makes the heavenly out of the earthly man, the actual
out of the political man, intellect out of nature, the wise man is imitating
Prometheus, who arose to take from the Gods the all-illuminating force,"
which ultimately means that the human can become his "own master creator"
who "acquires and possesses himself" (Cassirer 1979: 96). The itinerary is
cosmographic insofar as it will be equated, in Oronce Finé's drawings in the
Protomathesis (1532) and in his edition of Bovelles's geometry (1542), with experience and with a vertical movement from the center of the Ptolemaic universe to the outer reaches of the firmament. That same cosmography of self-
making is contained in silence, in secret (or as Tory would say, *en segret*), in
Tory's remarkable, flamboyant *O* that broadcasts the music of Apollo through
the fiery letters that burn on the rungs of the ladder turned into the shape of
the serpent of time (Figure 2.11). Tory may state that his musician is Apollo,
but since the typographer is a trickster, he also refers to himself as a new
Prometheus.

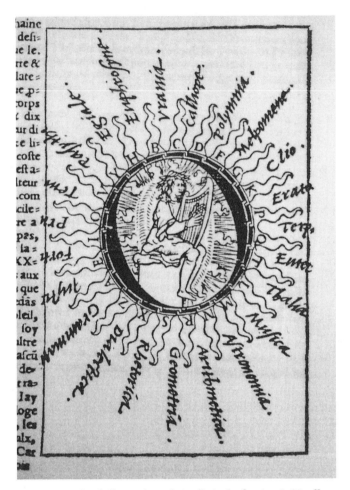

Figure 2.11. A "tresbelle conclusion": Apollo in the flaming O (Geoffroy Tory, *Champ fleury*)

The mention of Charles de Bovelles at the beginning of the second book is a key to another, alternate designation of the central figure of the god playing the harp in the final illustration, and this connection tells how the mapping impulse pertains to self-realization elsewhere in the book. We witness a desire to center oneself in order to disappear into the core of the material vision of letters. The presence of a selfless persona becomes equivalent to Bovelles's self-actualization in the graphic design of the *Champ fleury*, in its gridded form at the level of a totality found in each and every one of its individual units.

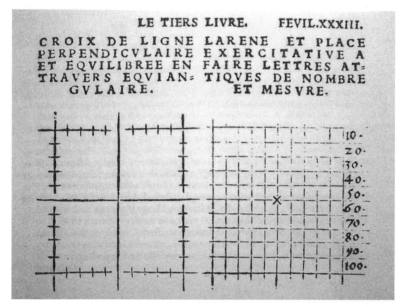

Figure 2.12. Grids for the background and body of the letter (Geoffroy Tory, *Champ fleury*)

A Cartography of the Letter

The proof of Tory's protocartographic sensibility, evinced in its most limpid form, without allegorical festoons, is located in the prefatory material to the third book. On folio xxxiii r (Figure 2.12), Tory illustrates the method he uses for drawing his letters. He inscribes a cross by marking first a perpendicular meridian and then its horizontal transversal, a line "diametrale & traversante equilibree, pour nous donner bon heur & commencement a entrer en noz lettres, & pour aider a les designer comme y leur est requis selon Reigle & Compas" [diametric and equilibrated crossing, to provide us with a felicitous beginning and entry into our letters, and to assist us in designing them as they require with a ruler and a compass] (fol. xxxii v).[12] Then a square is drawn about the equilateral cross. Five units of space are marked off above and below and to the left and to the right of each axis. A grid is filled in, with the result that eleven lines (5 + 1 + 5) are evident on each side of the square. The process is illustrated in the two contiguous squares: From the "cross of the perpendicular and equilibrated lines traversing the equiangular" to the left to the "arena and experimental place for making Attic letters in measure and number" on the right, we move from geometry to allegory, or to the site where the self's scaffold is created. Tory explains that the X at the axis of the graduated grid is the site of the "arena" where the essay, the exercise, or even the military operation (*place exercitative,* the arena, recalling the Latin *exercitus* with its military trappings) takes place. It is at the median point of one hundred pixels. Every letter must be generated from the same relation of the center to the equipollent configuration in general:

> Quant vous viendra a plaisir vouloir faire lettre Attique, debvez avant toute chose, constituer ung Quarre selon la haulteur que la pretendez faire, puis y signer une croix au mylieu, & consequemment les aultres lignes tant d'ung coste que d'aultre en equidistante mesure, en sorte que le dict Quarre soit esgallement divise.

> [When you will have the pleasure of making classical letters, above all else you will have to establish a square according to the height that you wish, then mark a cross in the middle, and then the other lines, as much from one side as from the other in an equal measure, so that the aforesaid square will be equally divided.] (fol. xxxii r)

As we have seen, the second book is set in place like the X in the grid of the surrounding material. A similar method of arbitrarily designating a motivated site, an X, also holds for the Ptolemaic system of topographical mapping that Tory's contemporaries, Pieter Apian and Oronce Finé, put forward in their practical manuals of mapping. Apian drew his map of Bavaria in a fashion resembling Tory's method in his 1523 *Cosmographicus Liber,* which was published in twenty-nine editions over the next eighty-nine years (Karrow 1993: 53). In 1532, Oronce Finé theorized the composition of a map of France that was also based on the designation of an axis, except that the square was shifted into a trapezoid in order to account for the rotundity of the earth's surface (see chapter 4). In each case, the common ground of cosmography, the drawing of letters, and the objective placement of a "self" at a crossing of a meridian and a median latitude are visible both in the printshop and on the cartographer's drawing table. The same method will hold for textual ensembles that grid their relations between the signature and the body of writing that follows or that are aimed at the author's secret mark. Printed writing becomes a function of spatial coordination and of perspectival drawing.

In order to see some of the consequences of the new relation between cartography and printed literature, we should now turn to Tory's two contemporaries, Rabelais and Finé. Before following Pantagruel's itinerary, we might wish to sum up the impact of Tory's work on cartographic writing. He composes a book that is a language map of French, codified according to the twenty-three letters of the alphabet and the nomenclature of other, earlier manuscript and typographic forms. These comprise a "flowered field" of what he underscores as a specifically French creation, whose roots are embedded more deeply in ancient Greece than in the world of Latin letters. The Greco-French mythography, which Jean Lemaire had recently mapped in his *Illustrations de Gaule et singularitez de Troie* (1511), serves to nationalize French objects to the degree that they mediate between local dialects, a great past, and a prescriptive model of the vernacular that is being heralded in Tory's own discourse. Like future maps, a national style of print, a standardized form that accounts for the historical variety of writing, gives coherence to French verbal geography. The style and explanation of the square-based letter argue for a particular history that would be, Tory hints, useful for military and political operations. At the same time, however, there emerges a *literary* persona that destabilizes programmatic issues by virtue of a system of inscription and spacing that runs contrary to the ideas being advocated. This intermediate area of play allows the author to contend with or to move about what would otherwise be an increasingly fixed or fixating space defined by perspectival grids. This persona becomes the *other*—the space, place, and person of alterity—who resides in and inspires the writer as a prototypical cartographer.

3

Oronce Finé: A Well-Rounded Signature

Oronce Finé (1494–1555) is a name that does not circulate widely in the world of literary history. But in mathematics, astrology, book illustration, typography, cartography, and cosmography of the first half of the sixteenth century, Finé's signature commands authority. No doubt because Ptolemaic cosmography quickly gave way to new information that called into question inherited ideas of space, and because new types of atlases developed at astonishing speed, his work is taken to exemplify the order that Copernican philosophy was soon to overthrow. If, however, Oronce Finé can be understood as a *rival* of the world he was presumed to be transcribing, then it seems premature to dismiss him. Like that of Rabelais, his work creates its own coordinates, its own extension and rotundity, which only later generations, such as our own, are positioned to rediscover. In any event, Finé's career and works have much to do with the mapping and making of a name, a nation, and a French subject.

In chapter 2, on Geoffroy Tory, we saw how gridding and spatial planning were aligned with the arts of typography and engraving. A French Dürer, Tory offers daring allegories that spatialize a language that aligns the human body with gridded space. In this chapter, to gain a perspective on the world shared by Rabelais, Tory, and the projection of space in early modern writing, I will first study how Oronce Finé's name is inscribed on world maps and topographical projections of France; then I will investigate what may be the broader consequence of how Oronce Finé accedes to the authority that his signature both heralds and contains. I will show in chapter 8 that the style and practice of his signature are not lost on writers of the next century. Descartes combines autobiography, mathematics, and engineering in his project of a universal *mathesis,* but we shall discover that Oronce Finé is partially responsible for what Descartes sets forth in his *Discours de la méthode* (1637). To see how, we must first scan the cartographer's life and times.

A Craftsman's Adolescence

Born at Le Champ-Rouët, an estate in the Dauphiné near Briançon, Oronce Finé embarked on a career that reflected his family's interests.[1] His father, François Finé, was an educated physician and astronomer. Two uncles, also of the Briançon region, were book illuminators who shared the same interest in astronomy. Not long after his father's death (between 1505 and 1510), Oronce pursued his career by moving to Paris and studying under a group of Spanish professors of mathematics that included Juan Martinez Guijarro.[2] He also worked with Jacques Lefèvre d'Etaples before earning an advanced degree sometime after 1515. Finé was already teaching at the Collège de Navarre when he began editing textbooks in the middle years of the decade. After publication of a map illustrating François Regnault's edition of Bernard von Breidenbach's *Voyage à la terre sainte* (1517), Finé's reputation as a mathematician and illustrator was launched.

In 1518, he was elected to the post of one of the four rectors of the University of Paris, and in the following year he completed his first great work, a single cordiform world map, now lost but revised and printed in 1534, which would soon be imitated and copied by three different engravers, in 1559, 1566, and 1586. In 1522, he earned a bachelor's degree in medicine and soon published an edition of his grandfather's essay on epidemics. He was incarcerated for a short time after 1523 for reasons that remain uncertain; he was an expert astrologer, and perhaps his prediction of French defeat at Pavia (in 1525) aroused the ire of the king. Or perhaps, as a strategist in charge of the fortifications in the battle of Milan, he foretold Francis's impending incarceration in Madrid. Representatives of the German nation at the University of Paris rescued him in 1525. He completed a map of France (now lost, but reported to have been published on six sheets by Simon de Colines). The map and its fortune have had a considerable history (Karrow 1993; 176–77; Dainville 1964a: 45–47) that is partially recounted in his great mathematical work (comprising arithmetic, geometry, cosmography, and dialing), the lavishly illustrated *Protomathesis* (Paris, 1532). This work came on the heels of Finé's nomination as the first Royal Professor of Mathematics at the king's newly founded Collège de France and precedes the updated, published version of the single cordiform map (1534), which was first drawn in 1519.

From the early 1530s until his death in 1555, Finé's career mirrors the fortunes of the French nation. In 1535, he married Denise Blanchet, who gave birth to numerous children, but he then encountered increased fiscal hardship. The generous salaries announced for the college were not readily paid. He undertook editing and proofreading, and he illustrated printed books that include various editions of Euclid; texts on alchemy, astrology, mechanics, and planetary theory; and even treatises on the quadrature of the circle. He translated scholarly materials from Latin to French, including his own *De mundi sphaera* (1551), which contained a printed version of a topographical view of the Dauphiné that had been completed eight years earlier. The prefatory materials to the Latin and French editions of this work portray a man burdened with debts, seeking a new patron after the death of Francis I, and trying to care for his family. He died on 6 October 1555 and was buried in the Carmelite convent at the Place Maubert. Summing up his life and works, Robert Karrow notes, "there is no gainsaying his very large influence, through almost forty years of teaching and especially some two dozen books issued in over seventy editions. And while his work was not on a par with the best being done, it was nonetheless the best being done in France" (1993: 190). Finé galvanized the teaching of mathematics and geography in Paris. His students, such as Etienne Forcadel, became renowned algebraists. Gerard Mercator owed much to Finé's projections, and even John Dee found in his works a font of inspiration.

The impression a reader gains from Finé's works, editions, and maps is of a writer, a draftsman, and an illustrator dedicated to exactitude, to professional commitment, and to craft. Whereas his work is not immediately innovative in the historical narrative on science, it fits squarely among late-medieval treatises on the cosmos and on astrology, conveying the present state of science and knowledge in France during the reign of Francis I.[3] In its breadth, copiousness, and fortune it parallels the works of Rabelais. A sense of excitement and eagerness—a joy over the marvels of the physical world—exudes from the materials written, drawn, and edited until the middle 1530s, before the labor of copying and translating took over. The work of his declining years reflects a will to meld science to what may be a growing sense of a national space. He translated works of the past into the vernacular and, even though as a translator and editor he was laboring to avoid penury, Finé's work still embodies the "struggle for the French language" (Longeon 1990), even before Joachim du Bellay's publication of his *Deffence et illustration de la langue françoyse* in 1549.

In its development, the work attests to the emergence—or even the psychogenesis—of a cartographic subject. Finé virtually grows out of a textual and scientific heritage; he acquires a signature of his own through mimicry and distortion of his masters, but he becomes a firm rival of the Valois realm that he describes and draws. Just as Rabelais evolves from a trickster under the name of Alcofribas Nasier to a doctor of medicine under his own signature, so also Finé develops from a composite, simulated image of Euclid, Astronomy, and Ptolemy to the person who creates the *Protomathesis,* the two great cordiform projections, and the first regional and national maps of France.[4] Finé also figures as an amphibious type, in the guise of serving the king, who strives to define a self and a space that remains between a body of works and a geography of French character.

The Finé Animal: A Face and a Strategy (*Voyage à la terre sainte*)

The earliest manifestation of the French cartographer's presence on a map may well be Oronce Finé's emblem in the lower right-hand corner of his rendition of the city of Jerusalem and its environs. Entitled *La cité de Jérusalem,* the map accompanied a 1517 reedition of Bernard von Breidenbach's late-fifteenth-century travel journal, *Peregrinatio in Terram Sanctum.* Published in Mainz in 1486, the work chronicles the author's adventures in the course of a pilgrimage made to the Holy Land in 1483 to redeem himself for having squandered his early life. Breidenbach commissioned the painter Erhard Reuwich to illustrate scenes he witnessed during the voyage. After Breidenbach returned to Venice in 1484, he, Reuwich, and Martin Roth began editing and translating notes for a Latin history of their travels. Figuring among Reuwich's city views and pictures of animals and human figures in exotic costumes is a panoramic view of Jerusalem (27 × 127 cm) "superimposed on a panoramic map covering the area from Damascus to Alexandria," in which "the view of Jerusalem as seen from the west, is at a scale many times larger than the rest of the Holy Land, which is oriented in the opposite direction, to the East"[5] (Nebenzahl 1986: 63; a foldout illustration of the map is on 64–68). The great size of the map allows the cartographer to depict many pilgrimage sites (e.g., the Temple of Solomon; the houses of Pilate, Caiaphas, and Herod; and the Church of the Holy Sepulture) and regions (e.g., the Coenaculum, Mount Zion, Golgotha) that pilgrims could visit. The work represents in striking detail the places that Reuwich and Breidenbach visited and tends to rely on other sources to include what had been seen.

The accompanying text, which includes an ample description of Palestine, a life of Mohammed, and tales of the Turks' sieges of Constantinople and

Figure 3.1. Detail of ship and port from Bernard von Breidenbach, *Voyage à la terre sainte* (1486)

Rhodes, along with notes on the customs, languages, and writing of the inhabitants of the Holy Land and excursuses on flora and fauna, no doubt contributed to the book's success, which led to the publication of thirteen editions by 1522. In 1488 in Lyon, Nicolas Le Huen completed a French adaptation that used copies of Reuwich's woodcuts. Xylographic images taken from the original version accompanied Jean de Hersin's revised translation of 1490.[6] The overall depiction was probably the most accurate information available to Europeans up to 1517, when the Turks, under Selim I, reconquered the Holy Land.

François Regnault's Parisian edition of the text and illustrations hardly matched the earlier versions in either size or detail. It appears to be a popular *edition de combat* with added material intended to inspire the French to launch a crusade to regain peace among Christian groups and to reform the church (Lecoq 1987: 259–65). Regnault hired Oronce Finé to draw two woodcuts and a map that would accompany the edition. Breidenbach's map of the Holy Land is no doubt the model that Finé used for the topographical plan of 1517 (Figure 3.1). The shoreline extends from Palestine to Egypt and displays an array of sites and place-names. But what Finé sets in place betrays the design of the original. In Reuwich's woodcut, an elaborate galley equipped with a

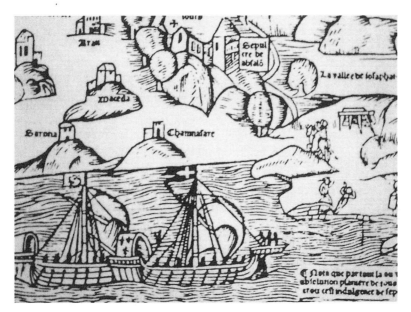

Figure 3.2. Detail of left side of *La terre sainte* (Oronce Finé, 1517 copy)

lateen sail is depicted nearing the harbor where pilgrims prepare to disembark. Their route is described as beginning at that point, which serves as an entry into the spatial narrative of sites and names studding the overall view of the city and environs. In Finé's version, however, two smaller, sea-going vessels move quickly toward the same point. Whereas Breidenbach's woodcut furnishes a technically detailed view of a galley (so accomplished, in fact, that it was used to represent Columbus in the New World), the French cartographer displays two rapidly moving vessels that approach the port (Nebenzahl 1986: 63; see plate 21, pp. 64–68).[7] The first ship flies the flag of the crusades from the main mast; its poop deck is covered with a canopy on which the fleur-de-lis of France is inscribed (Figure 3.2). Although the depiction of the ship is far less elaborate than Reuwich's model, a new, emblematic function of the map is underscored: What passes for a galley transporting pilgrims is, in fact, a new ship that carries soldiers who will disembark with the intent of winning back the Holy Land, which had only recently fallen to the Turks.

Finé adapts Breidenbach's woodcut to fit the narrative of a forthcoming crusade that had been planned shortly after the accession of Francis I to the throne. The cartographer also valorizes himself by a signature that fits congruently with the designs of the recently crowned king who had improved diplomatic relations with Rome. In the lower right-hand corner of Breidenbach's

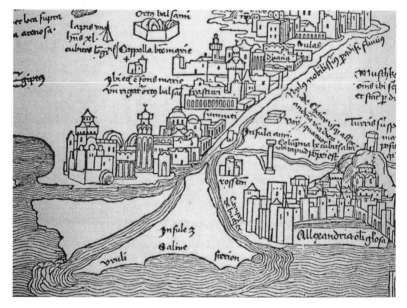

Figure 3.3. Detail of sea and rivers from Bernard von Breidenbach, *Voyage à la terre sainte*

map (Figure 3.3), groups of sinuous and finely carved lines represent the currents of the sea and whirls of rivers flowing into the southeast corner of the Mediterranean. Finé's rendition is much more approximate, except for the carefully executed device that appears to surge out of the waters and look upon the city, which the viewer beholds from an adjacent point of view (Figure 3.4). Looking up and to the left, a crowned dolphin has broken the surface of the water. Heralded is a signatory *festina lente*, the dolphin of the Dauphiné, Finé's birthplace, with the figure of France marked by the fleur-de-lis on the diadem perched on the mammal's head. The cartographer's signature is inscribed in a rebus that visualizes both the *dauphin*—the recently crowned king, Francis I—and Dauphiné, the birthplace of the cartographer. Yet, as the mammal shoots out of the Mediterranean, the maritime context also beckons the spectator to see and read an implied rebus of a *dauphin d'eau fine*, such that even a work "by" or "of" the author, *O. Finé* (*d'O. Finé*, Dauphiné), is a verbal identifier of the configuration. Since wit of this kind is part of an ideological program of the rebus that characterizes humanist literature (Demerson, 1981; 1994: 171–90; Jeanneret 1987: 252), we see evidence of a humanist calligraphy designed to illuminate or explode into knowledge through combinations of aural and graphic ingenuity.[8]

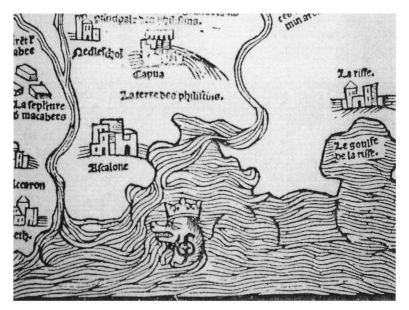

Figure 3.4. Detail of right side of *La terre sainte* (Oronce Finé, 1517 copy)

The perspectival plan of Finé's map offers two "French" points of view in the figures of the ships to the left and the dolphin to the right. When seen as sighting points in respect to the Temple of Jerusalem at the center, they appear as inscriptions establishing a logistics for invading armies. The city plan is set in a virtual cross fire superimposed on the presentation of the pilgrim's view of the Holy Land. Folded into Breidenbach's touristic representation is a tactical configuration that shows how the port might be approached from two angles.

Two other woodcuts that Finé drew for Regnault's edition show how the map deploys a tactic to valorize the heraldic signature in the greater plan of the volume. In a scene that represents the assembly of the council of Europe in preparation for the crusade (Figure 3.5), the Christian princes are clustered around the pope, who sits above, his face at the vanishing point of the perspective indicated by the tiled floor on which the figures are arranged. To the right, between two columns, Finé includes a ballad that exhorts its listeners to awaken and open their eyes to the Turkish menace:

> O chrestiens tant jeunes comme vieulx
> Roys ou barons, princes, marchans, bourgeois,
> Ouvrez voz cueurs et desbendez voz yeulx
> Ne soyez plus si tardifs que une fois
> Turcz et payens ne sentent voz exploitz

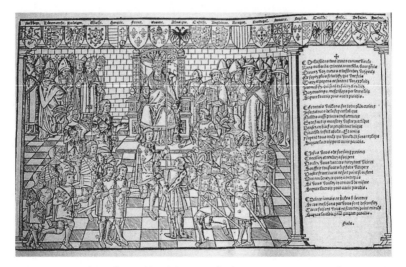

Figure 3.5. Woodcut of assembly of the council of Europe in preparation for a crusade to the Holy Land (Oronce Finé)

Irremissifs, qui sont en faictz et en ditz
Vos ennemys, mesprisans par leurs loix
Suyvre la croix pour avoir paradis.

François vaillans, sur tous plus curieux
Insectateurs de la foy catholique
Nobles aussi princes tresvertueux
En ce faict cy monstrez vostre practique
Pensez en brief ce peuple tant inique
Horrible, infect abolir. Et remis
Y soyent tous ceulx qui voudront sans replique
Suyvre la croix pour avoir paradis.

Jesus vous a de son sang precieux
Conciliez et renduz a son pere
Vouldrez vous donc ces turcs tant vicieux
Souffrir tousjours luy faire vitupere
Vostre franc cueur ne soit point si austere
Que nachevez ce quon a entrepris
Si vous voulez en ce monde de misere
Suyvre la croix pour avoir paradis.

Prince jamais ne fustes si heureux
Si ces meschans par vous sont desconfitz
Car ce faisant vous ne sauriez point mieulx
Suyvre la croix pour gaigner paradis.

Finis.[9]

The text of the poem and the adjacent woodcut constitute a divided or composite creation—a sequence of an image and an adjacent intertitle—that projects language into the space of the woodcut. And, like the rebus of the cartographer's signature, the discourse functions *within* the figure. The field of
tension in the woodcut derives from a flat, paginal appearance enhanced by
the brick wall of the background, by a frieze of eighteen coats-of-arms on the
upper cornice that serve as pictorial legends to the names of their nations,
which are printed immediately above, and by the three marginal columns that
frame the whole. The reader is invited to correlate the heraldic figures with the
insignia on the knights' heraldic garb and so to identify each of the sixteen
knights who cluster around the central axis, which is defined by a staff that is
held simultaneously in the right hand of the French emissary and the left hand
of the pope seated above. The rod serves as a vertical sight line that is parallel
to the columns of the frame.

The Latin cross at summit of the staff, adjacent to the baldachin over the
pope's head, reveals the sign of the crusade on the banner unfurling above the
pontiff's shoulder. The doubled crosses of the flag and staff mark the vanishing point guaranteeing the illusion of pictorial depth; their X also marks a horizontal sight line that is at the same latitude as the heraldic cross above the
poem to the right. The text and image of this creation are coded to indicate
that the reader must gloss the image and the text *exactly as* the refrain states,
that is, as the convention of the ballad dictates, four times: We must "suyvre la
croix pour avoir paradis." The crosses in the image bind the Catholic nations
to the papacy, whereas the cross above the poem marks an axis that rhymes
(again, as convention goes) with "Finis" below. Yet *finis* echoes the acrostic inscription of "Orontius Fine" in the first two stanzas of the poem, thus "crisscrossing" the visual marker of the image with the textual sign of the author.
The cartographer's name plays in a visual rhyme with the perspectival object
of the woodcut. The "croix" that we are asked to follow also figures on the
main mast of a galley at the vanishing point of the hypothetical battle that will
win back the Holy Land.

The same cross unfurls on the flag of the first galleon approaching the port
that offers access to Jerusalem. The movement evinced in the topographical
view compels the viewer—literally, in a haptic reading of the woodcut and
ballad—to "see and follow the cross toward Paradise." Indistinct shapes on the
enseign of the ship that follows the crusader's galley may indeed be the twisted
form of the royal salamander of Francis I. The map, ostensibly published for
the sake of knowledge and of tourism, is turned into military propaganda. Yet,
in both the map and the woodcut illustrations, the cartographer is free to

inscribe a signature that conveys its own autonomy. Finé moves almost amphibiously, like the dolphin or royal salamander of a *festina lente,* between the textual and visual material of his creation, achieving a position that rivals that of the leaders of state being represented in Regnault's reedition of Breidenbach's itinerary.

From Signature to Self-Portrait

Oronce Finé's signatory emblem soon evolves into a self-portrait. The cartographer initially seeks to inscribe an apothegm at an intermediary position between the cosmos and a world of his own figuring or drawing. In the first woodcut, known to be created by Finé, the title page to his edition of Georg von Peurbach's *Theoricarum nouarum textus,* Finé's signature accompanies a picture of the cartographer (Figure 3.6). It becomes a model that will evolve over the course of his career. At its beginning, the self-portrait shows how the cartographer literally inscribes his image in relation to the universe, and how the lines that connect the autograph, device, and image convey the impression of a process of self-actualization.

As in the reedition of Breidenbach's *Voyage,* in the 1515 *Theoricarum* Finé first portrays himself through the figures of others. He places himself in a median position; the artist appears to be a scribe of the world he is representing, but all the while he portrays himself in moderate control of the forces that determine his condition. The title page to von Peurbach's *Theoricarum nouarum textus* was partially inspired by a cut in a 1496 edition of Regiomontanus's *Epytoma in almagestum ptolomei,* in which the author and Ptolemy are placed under the celestial sphere.[10] Perhaps one of the most readily available of all images of an armillary sphere, the Regiomontanus woodcut could have offered something of a "drawing exercise."[11] For Finé, however, a filial relation to Ptolemy and to woodcutting has begun. In the *Epytoma,* the author (Johann Mueller) is seated next to a desk, on which are posed two closed books, adjacent to Ptolemy, who is seen in regal garb to the left, reading an open folio posed between his knees. The two personages are identified by phylacteries that unfurl in the border of the black passe-partout below. The arcs that constitute the celestial sphere are identified by names set in the white space of the greater field of the cut. In the border, Renaissance floral patterns alternate with the medieval interlace. On the upper half are scrolled the words *altior incubuit animus subimagine mundi,* which Finé will copy for his version prefacing Peurbach's text.

Finé's quarto-size woodcut (19 × 13 cm) complements the abundant illustra-

TEXTVS DE SPHÆ-

RA IOANNIS DE SACRO BOSCO:INTRODVCTORIA AD=
ditione(quantum neceſſarium eſt) cōmentarioq̃, ad vtilitatem ſtudentium
philoſophiæ Pariſienſis Academiæ illuſtratus . Cum compoſitione Annu=
li aſtronomici Boneti Latenſis:Et Geometria Euclidis Megarenſis.

PARISIIS.
⸿Vænit apud Simonem Colinæum/e regione ſcholæ Decretorum.
1521

Figure 3.6. Title page to Johannes de Sacro Bosco, *Textus de sphaera,* Oronce Finé,
copied from Finé's edition of Georg von Peurbach, *Novum theoricarum textus* (1515)

tions of Peurbach's manual of astronomy. The redrawn illustration establishes the commanding figure of the cartographer, but in drawing on Mueller, it brings into greater view the relation between the cartographer and Ptolemy, the avowed master of the science of mapping. Finé removes the interlace in favor of a more extensively uncoiling, floral design of grape vines that originate from the four corners, meet scrolls bearing inscriptions on the upper and side panels, and emanate from an escutcheon bearing the cartographer's device in the center of the lower edge. Between the two scrolls on the vertical panels is placed a pattern of grotesques that sets a fleur-de-lis in the center of a design that displays slight variation between the left and right sides. As in Regiomontanus, the inscription favors a clockwise reading of the image. Since the writing is divided into four scrolls and distributed evenly over the three upper sides of the frame, it brings into greater prominence the sign of the dolphin crowned below a fleur-de-lis on the front of a desk in the lower center.

The figure of the dolphin in the escutcheon connects the shaft of the armillary sphere within the frame to the shield set over the border, thus marking a point of passage between the outer and inner worlds *through* the heraldic figure of the cartographer. The fleur-de-lis decorating the desk appears to be an outgrowth of the center of the crown resting on the dolphin's head. Since the curvature of the lower edge of the heraldic shield matches that of the vines that push out to the left and right, the author's signature is aligned with the overall creation above: To the left, in the first bend of the ivy (or grape) branch, the tendril curls into an *F* that generates an *O* surrounding the space out of which its vertical line emerges. To the right, in a similar ploy, a unicorn grows out of the floral design. The *contrapposto* design recalls the royal salamander that figures in other decorations. The single horn of the unicorn seems to play the indexical role of leading the eye back up along a sight line that goes through the heraldic shield and up to the figure of Finé.

The two details indicate that the cartographer is likened to growing flora and fauna, and that he seems to move between vegetable and animal worlds. The signature is a rebus insofar as the letters *O* and *F* give birth to other forms in the overall design. The scribe's feet come over the ground and penetrate into the space, in a slight foreshortening effect that heightens the illusion of depth in the image. The humanist icon of the sleeping canine to the immediate right is poised so that its head arches back in a posture similar to the unicorn's twisted pose below, but so that its tail and paws give a depth of field to the image that moves between the foregrounded shield, the space relegated to the scribe's feet, and the decor behind. The rapport established between the border and the foregrounded materials displays the intermediary role of

Figure 3.7. Detail of lower edge and border of Figure 3.6

the cartographer, on the one hand, who is placed among natural things, beings, or growing forms while, on the other, the topographical world of real
space, objects, and historical personages is held within the space contained by
the frame.

Finé is seated on a bench shortened for perspectival relief, in a flowing cape
and in front of a book stand above whose diagonal line pages and the end of
a stylus can be seen. The form is held up by a perpendicular rod attached to a
pylon set in the desk. A belt hangs over its horizontal arm. The cartographer's
tools—a square, a compass, an inkwell, and a folio book (a copy of Ptolemy's
Geographia?)—adorn the secretary, on which is placed a great chalice that sup-
ports the armillary sphere above. He wears a humanist's cap and is shown, eyes
down, concentrating on his work. The ocular slits are cut with a razor-sharp,
Gothic-like edge that underscores an aquiline concentration on the material
that is being written and engraved. The underlying effect that is connoted
by the pose is that the sitter is designing or cutting the very image that we are
simultaneously seeing before our eyes (Figure 3.7).

Comparing Finé's piece to analogues and sources proves that the self-portrait figures in a greater evolution of forms. A Venetian source in a 1487 edition of Sacro Bosco shows Urania, Astronomia, and Ptolemy below the sun, moon, and stars and above flowers and small animals; and another, from Paris in 1487, but included in editions as late as 1531 (Figure 3.8), displays the three immortals in a triad in front of a bench; Finé may have made a composite creation to illustrate his own talent and character. One could argue that the title page to Peurbach copies the *Epytoma* in order to be in dialogue with recent Parisian editions of Sacro Bosco. Most likely, the Italian material is borrowed in order to launch a program that moves against the existing incunabula available at the University of Paris.

Where the 1487 Parisian woodcut places an alphabetic legend below the picture to designate the elements of the celestial sphere above (indicated by lower-case letters in *lettre bâtarde* adjacent to their figure), Finé pulls the script *into* the body of the design, thus making the gloss much more immediate and simultaneous than the "translation" that is encountered in the visual displacement from the script to the items seen in the image. The image and the writing are projected in a totalizing design that accelerates the transmission of names and things from the image to the spectator. We are asked to grasp the configuration and its language in a single sweep of the eye.

Just as the printed names are pulled into the image, so too are the zodiacal signs of the earlier ecliptic band. What appear as astrological symbols in the 1487 Parisian edition of Sacro Bosco are replaced with images that detail the traits of the twelve astrological signs. The starry horizon between the allegorical figures and the background is displaced, apparently for the sake of clarity, into the upper spandrels, which now contain the sun and moon. The terrestrial sphere, that appears as a black blob in the 1487 woodcut, has now become a carefully articulated global projection of the Eastern Hemisphere (typographically designated as Europe and Africa) seen from north to south as the eye moves up the meridian bar attached to the chalice below. Whereas the 1487 woodcut allows the sphere to float in an indiscriminate space, in Finé's rendition it is attached to the world and is suggested to be within human reach.

Further, the letters that describe the celestial sphere have a perspective or curvilinear design that enhances their spatial character. Unlike in Mueller's work or the Parisian edition of Sacro Bosco, the *polus zodiari* and *polus antarticus* on the upper arc now *bend* along the circumferential rib of the sphere, as do the descriptions of the Tropics of Cancer and Capricorn and the Arctic pole below. The designation of the *circulus eclyptica* in Finé's woodcut is dramatically abbreviated and broken into two units, *ecly-* and *-ptica,* on either side of the zodiacal band. The two major allegorical figures are named in ban-

VRANIA   ASTRONOMIA   PTOLEMÆVS

A f m g ʃphæra.
A punctus/polus arcticus.
A m linea/axis ʃphæræ.
B & c/circulus arcticus.
D e/circulus Cancri.
F g/circulus æquinoctialis.
H i/circulus Capricorni.
K l/circulus antarcticus
M punctus/polus antarcticus
N e h o/circularis ʃuperficies lata/zodiacus
P q circulus/eclyptica.

Figure 3.8. Woodcut of Urania and Ptolemy in Johannes de Sacro Bosco,
Textus de sphaera (1483), taken from 1487 edition (Paris)

deroles placed over their heads, within the design, in contrast to the earlier model, in which they are identified by letters below the figures and outside of the picture.

In sum, descriptive language is infused with spatial valence that contributes to the illusion of the circular and spherical dimension being promoted. The names lend a sense of depth similar to the depth provided by the rivet points on the right-hand colure that arches between the meridian to the left and the circumference to the right. The typical abbreviations of the names (*pol⁹*, *pol⁹ zo*, etc.) cipher the language with hermetic clarity. We see and record the words with increased rapidity and, too, find them in their appropriate place in the cosmos. The incunabular model is being respected and altered for what seem to be obvious ideological purposes, whereby the world will now be seen in a flash, its language transmitted in its proper place and in cosmic majesty.

Revealing shifts take place in the iconographic program. In the 1487 Parisian edition, Ptolemy is seen on the right, seated on a bench, wearing an Alexandrian cap (with horns, like a "capricorn"), an ermine collar, and a great toga, peering down at an open book that displays the spheres of the world above some lines of text. In the center, to his right, is a Christ-like Astronomia. She holds a sphere in her left hand and in front of her well-clad body; the astrolabe held up by her right hand also points to the nude and attractive Urania, the goddess of the firmament, who has long and flowing hair—like that of contemporary representations of Saint Mary the Egyptian—and a bending cloth that she drapes over her sex as she looks to her left hand, skyward, and to the sphere above. Finé changes the configuration by eliminating Astronomia and Urania. In the place of the latter, in an elegant dress and bonnet, Astrologia looks across to Ptolemy, on the right, who now holds the astrolabe that had belonged to Astronomia. Placed next to the scribe, who is named only by the ciphered material in the border just below, she metonymically "identifies" Finé by virtue of her placement behind him as the sign of the professional label that soon marked the cartographer.

Finé, who was soon to be known as an expert astrologer, valorizes himself as an interpreter of the arcane forces of the universe. Because he is noting what is about him, the scribe can be a functionary of *both* the sibylline goddess and the Alexandrian savant.[12] In any event, a human being now figures in the cosmic frame. He has pertinent, signatory traits that can be distinguished by the role he plays in the image, by his effects, and by the surrounding array of signs that liken him to human and celestial realms, to animal and vegetable worlds. In the attention it pays to elegant dress and by the enframing presence of the fleur-de-lis (unlike the 1487 model) the new woodcut shows allegiance to a French political iconography.

The background is developed with attention to what appear to be resolutely *French* shapes. In place of the Tuscan building in Mueller's woodcut, Finé places a Gothic agglomeration and a topographical view of the landscape behind the allegorical figures. In front of Ptolemy's right knee (which gently pushes beneath the toga) and to the left of the clasped book on the desk stands a bridge that carries a road from the foreground over a hill to a city on the horizon in the background. The bridge appears to be just that: a metaphor that goes from an allegorical to a "real" representation of a nation or region of the kind that will be seen in Finé's *Gallia* (1525) or the maps of southwestern France and northern Italy (1543 and 1551). A landscape is confused with the foregrounded scene that displays objects found in a scriptorium.

From Portrait to Self-Made Identity: The *Protomathesis*

The nascent self-portrait in the edition of Peurbach is placed adjacent to the topographical landscape and the figure of Astrologia. The cartographer gains greater autonomy with the publication of the *Protomathesis* (1532) (Figure 3.9). When he takes up the same pose on the following page of his great compendium of mathematics and cosmography, the nascent landscape of the 1515 model now becomes a rolling countryside of finely etched molehills that recede to a horizon against a stippled black sky of the firmament, in which hangs a celestial sphere (Figure 3.10). The perspectival articulation is underscored by the triangular quadrant between the author (to the right) and Urania (to the left); the quadrant points upward toward another bridge and the axis of the astrolabe that Finé holds with his right arm extended in the direction of the goddess (Figure 3.11).

The lunar landscape, without flora or fauna, brings forth the man-made objects that constitute the effects of Finé's life and works. The tools just noted are to his right, while the solar clock, his own invention, decorates the space to his left. He now holds Ptolemy's folio book in his left hand, his fingers curled over its spine, as if he were consulting its tables to determine the placement of sites for the topographical view before our eyes. Crucial to the new illustration is the absence of Ptolemy: The cartographer has arrogated the Alexandrian identity, now absorbing, if not *becoming*, the very figure whom he had adulated in the woodcut of the 1515 *Theoricarum* and its later reprintings. Ptolemy is now veiled in the garb of the individual who is seen surveying the lands that will be studied in the *Protomathesis*. What will follow about trigonometry, al-

Figure 3.9. Title page to Oronce Finé, *Protomathesis* (1532)

Figure 3.10. Frontispiece to Oronce Finé, *Protomathesis*

Figure 3.11. Detail of bottom of Figure 3.10

gebra, and mapping is allegorized here. The elision of identities underscores the oedipal character of the cartographer's relation to the received authority of the founding geographer of humanism.

The cartographer gains greater authority through a strategic placement of the signature. Whereas Finé had first designed the *O* bisected by the *F* in the earlier woodcut (as if heeding Tory's allegory that all writing is generated from the difference between straight and curved lines), he now recasts the apothegm with classical letters that are set in the rings that uphold the armillary sphere in the cosmos between the stele-like borders of the frontispiece (Figure 3.12). To the left, in the ring between the globe and the supporting statue, there is an upper-case *O*; in the right-hand ring, an *F*. The signature is almost invisible, but it is given a placement symbolically vital for the heavenly order of the cosmos. The representation of the world can be made, Finé implies, through the pivotal intermediary of the pertinent traits of his signature. At the same time,

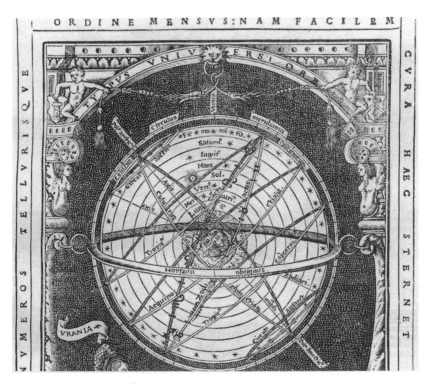

Figure 3.12. Detail of top of Figure 3.10

by introducing the classical font here, Finé marks a shift in style that corresponds to a change in iconographic programs: From the Gothic "look" of earlier works that he had edited (such as a 1534 treatise on the astrolabe [Figure 3.13], in which the allegorical personages of the seven liberal arts [plus Ptolemy or Geography] have a medieval aspect and are set against the stippled background beneath an interlace), we move to a more Italianate, classical style that is more heavily influenced by southern characteristics, including perspective and mannered shapes (as in the lettering and border of a 1542 edition of the works of Euclid [Figure 3.14]).

The cartographer's attributes, which were first seen in the 1515 title page to Peurbach's *Theoricarum,* are scattered through the decorative scheme—the borders and the letters—of the *Protomathesis.* Most pervasive, however, may be the effect left by the self-portrait in the historiated initial *O.* At the beginning of the fourth book (on cosmography) we encounter an ultimate view of the cartographer in his relation to writing, nascent autobiography, and mapping (Figure 3.15). The portrait initial shows a humanist in a three-quarter

Figure 3.13. Title page of Oronce Finé, *Quadrans astrolabicus*

view, set in a letter that, like a world, initiates the writing of cosmography. The letter seems to be an ambient mark that can roll and turn anywhere in the world. When seen in close view (Figure 3.16), the image could be that of *any* humanist. The figure sports a tricornered cap. The upper folds of the cape and the erect pose recall figures—Hans Holbein, Dürer, Erasmus—of the same stamp. A conventional look is achieved through the clothing, the position of the author's head, the intense gaze forward into the world, and the ambience of control and meditation in the light and shade of the surrounding space. Yet a miniature self-portrait is also evident in the traits that this figure has in common with the figure in the 1515 image and with the physiognomy in the title page to the volume: a slightly rounded, handsome, debonair, individual face.

In a way that recalls the archaic proxemic practice whereby individuals delineate a personal space by setting objects or attributes adjacent to their

Figure 3.14. Oronce Finé's title page to the 1542 edition of *De mundi sphaera* (taken from the 1536 edition of Euclid's *Geometry*)

❧LIBER QVARTVS❧

COSMOGRAPHIAE, SIVE MVN‑
di Sphæræ, De dierum & horarum tam æqualium,
quàm inæqualium,& umbrarum ratione : deĉg
singulorum accidentibus, iuxta ua‑
rium sphæræ situm obseruatis.

De Die naturali. Caput.I.

OMNES FERE, QVI DE COSMO‑
graphia, Geographiáue scripserunt, à diuersa tum
dierum & horarum, tū umbrarū, pro uario Sphæ‑
ræ situ contingente ratione : maximam intelligētiæ
partem, fructumue decerpere soliti sunt . Congru‑
um erit itacp, hoc quarto libro, ipsorum dierum,
& horarum , necnon umbrarum uniuersa percur‑
rere discrimina : & quæ singulis ipsius mundanæ
Sphæræ uidentur accidere dispositionibus , succin‑
ĉtè declarare. a Dierum igitur , alius naturalis,
alius artificialis dicitur . Naturalem solemus appellare diem, tempus quo cen‑
trum corporis solaris, ad regulatum Vniuersi motum , integram reuolutionem
circa Terram, ab ipso Meridiano supputatam adimplet. b Hæc autem reuolutio,
ex completa Aequatoris circunductione, & tanta eiusdem Aequatoris portiuncu‑
la resultat : quanta est ascensio recta partis Eclipticæ, quam Sol interea motu pro‑
prio, in contrarium ipsius primi motus absoluit. c Constat igitur dies naturales,
duplici de causa, esse adinuicē inæquales, nēpe ob irregularē motū Solis circa Mū‑
di centrum, & contingentem arcuum (etiam æqualium) ipsius Eclipticæ ascēsionis
diuersitatem : tametsi eiuscemodi uarietas, haud notandæ uideatur esse quātitatis.

CVM GENERALEM ASCENSIONVM ATQVE DESCENSIONVM, TAM
arcuum Eclipticæ, q̃ etiam syderum, capite secundo proximi libri describeremus imagi‑
nationem, euidens relinquimus, ipsum Aequatorem circulum temporis regulatam esse mensu
ram, atcp e diuerso, tempus ipsum regularem Aequatoris, uel potius uniuersi Orbis, ab oriente
per meridiem ad occasum metiri circunductionem. At cum uniuersa cœlestium orbium machi
na, una cum elementari regione (dempta ipsius Telluris & Aquæ congeriæ) eodem Aequa‑
toris, totiusue Vniuersi temperato motu circunducatur : non potuit ipsa mundana reuolutio a
quopiam circūductorum cum orbibus syderum notabilius designari, q̃ a Sole , hoc est, a Mun‑
di luminari, atcp inter errantia sydera, motu peculiari regulatissimo. ¶ a Placuit itacp primis
Dies naturalis. inuētoribus, completam centri solaris circa Mundi centrum reuolutionem, a uerticali aut sub‑
terraneo inchoatam Meridiano, id est, tempus quo centrum Solis, a dato Meridiani puncto, ad
idem Meridiani punctum, propter motum Vniuersi reuertitur, diem naturalem appellare : na
turalem quidem propterea, quoniam a naturali & regulato totius Vniuersi motu causetur, siue
cp naturalius ipsam dierum naturalium mensuram per Solem animaduertamus, q̃ si ab alio quo‑
piam sydere, uel dato quouis in Cœlo puncto notaretur. ¶ b At quoniam interea, hoc est,
dum

Figure 3.15. First page of the fourth book of Oronce Finé, *Protomathesis*

Figure 3.16. Close view of historiated O in Oronce Finé, *Protomathesis*

bodies, Finé encrypts himself amid the tools of his trade and the works of his signature.[13] The pattern of stippled dots that is found outside the letter, in the surround (two on the verticals and three on the upper horizontal), recalls the *fond criblé* that Finé may have designed for the device of Jehan Petit in the *Theoricarum* and that resurfaces in the dots on the book that he holds in the title page to the *Protomathesis*. At the same time, along with the four dots that mark the corners of a regular trapezoid within the circle, the design recalls Finé's attempts to accomplish the quadrature of the circle in his mathematical tracts and illustrations for other texts written by colleagues.[14] A cursory view of the letter and the order of dots shows that rapport between the square and the circle, the straight and the curvilinear line, and the body and the abstraction of symmetry are put forward as a dominant tension. Whereas Leonardo da Vinci and Geoffroy Tory had placed the entire human body in the square and circle, Finé inserts a self-portrait into a space that is rendered dynamic by virtue of the double frame (a macrocosm) and celestial dots (starry forms that both are microcosms and have cosmographic implications).

The self-portrait is placed within a graduated circle that refers to the cartographer's astrolabe. It hangs from a ring attached to a median globe below a heart placed just beneath the upper intrados of the *O*. The heart alludes to the single cordiform map executed for Francis I in 1519 and, possibly, to the contemporaneous double cordiform projection completed in 1531 and published in a work of Simon Grynaeus. Finé's specific contribution to the art of mapping is seen in the shift of pattern from the globe below to the heart above, all the while the two objects remain as miniature figures of the man's lifework. Following Platonic and scientific ideology, the heart is divided into nocturnal and diurnal sides. The same pattern of light and shadow gives depth and a sense of circularity to the self-portrait, which appears to emerge into the light from the striations denoting a world of shadow in the depths behind the face.

The play of light and shadow on the heart brings into view the play of the initials, *O* and *F,* that are placed on the left and right of the self-portrait. Like two extended earrings, the letters lend a bilateral symmetry to the picture at the same time that the *F,* couched in shadow, contrasts the bright background of the *O*. The image implies that the circle described by the astrolabe or globe turns on its axis, and that Finé's figure is inscribed in the center of a gyroscope. At the same time, the letter may roll—ambient mark that it is— over and through the text on a horizontal axis. It also turns about itself, connoting a sense of autonomy insofar as the world turns about the figure of the cartographer.

It is clear that the self-portrait in the letter *O,* a sort of résumé or curriculum vitae trademarked in a circle, is designed to set in counterpoint the figure of the celestial sphere that dominates the title page. Not only is there a resemblance between the two images of Finé, but also, the earth, at the center of the celestial sphere, is analogous to the image of Finé in the letter.[15] Since the role of the cartographer entails shifting energies away from the task of transcribing the order of the world toward another, which contends with it, the relation of the initials to the portrait signals that the humanist design of knowledge is built to convey an illumination of totality and immediacy. One aspect of the Erasmian or Rabelaisian vision entailed gaining a breath-taking view of a world of letters when scanning and absorbing them in one affective and intellectual sweep. To enhance rapid transmission of knowledge, scholars appealed to the pictogram and hieroglyph as a means of imparting to readers and spectators infinite vistas of knowledge.[16] It appears that in his circular self-portrait

Figure 3.17. Single cordiform projection of the world (Oronce Finé, 1519, redone and printed in 1534)

the cartographer "discovers" his ideal and universal site. The multiple and overdetermined configuration suggests that we behold a plethora of *O*s or, in other words, that we can say of the image, "O rond ce" or: "how round this is, this *O*," how perfect is the design congruent with the vocables of the author's name. Visual wit ties the signature to the letters, thus imparting an initial, Rabelaisian excess that marks a continuous beginning of an infinite play of language and form.

The Heart of the World: The Cordiform Maps

The valentine-like form that hangs above Finé's self-portrait in the letter *O* refers to the two single and double cordiform maps completed or being redrawn when the *Protomathesis* was being published. The single cordiform projection (Figure 3.17) combines scientific and mystical materials that had been circulating since the accession of Francis I to the throne in 1515. The map draws upon the specifically humanist themes saturating ideology and literary production of the first four years of the new king's reign. For that reason, a distinctly textual aspect of the map cannot be separated from the innovations it brings to the art of projection.

The map was printed from a woodcut on two sheets (510 × 570 mm) and subsequently colored by hand. The textual material in the left and right cartouches tells the "candid reader" that Finé had conceived the projection for the "great savant king of France . . . in the shape of a heart." Rodney W. Shirley notes that Finé incorporated more new information, reported from the courts of Europe, than had been printed in the double-cordiform map of 1531, three years earlier. "The whole eastern coastline of north, central and south America is, for the time relatively accurately shown" (1987: 77), and so are the outlines of the explorations of the conquistadores on the western shores of Central America. Conventional opinions are reflected about the Molucca (Spice) Islands being beyond the northwestern coast, about the lands of Mexico being inhabited by *canibales,* about the expanse of the single land of the *Terra Florida, Terra Francesca* (middle North America, as named by Giovanni da Verrazano when he sailed under Francis I's commission), and *Baccalear* (northern North America) extending westward from Marco Polo's Mangi, Tangut, and Cathay. Two ornate pillars flank the map on either side and support a portico on which swim four dolphins, whose fins are threaded into two fleurs-de-lis. Two putti look down on the map from the capitals on which they are perched. A printer's fleuron is placed before the title ("Recens . . .") over the banderole in the upper left spandrel, setting the shape of the map as a whole into a comparative relation with its miniature analogue (Figure 3.18).

The large expanse of the ocean is depicted in wavy lines and dotted by nine ocean-going vessels (three in the Pacific, six in the Atlantic). The map is uncommonly accurate and modern in its depiction of the Antarctic coastline and in the convergence of land masses around the North Pole. The polar meridian is set just to the west of the Canary Islands and encloses a scale of black and white rectangles. The intersection of diagonals extended from the four corners of the frame meet at the same point. More dramatically than do the *mappae mundi* at the beginning of contemporary editions of Ptolemy, the cordiform structure translates a desire to present in compact and immediately comprehensible shape all the prominent areas of the world. The meridian is equidistant from the North Pole, and its longest dimension is longitudinal (Kish 1965: 13).

The map becomes a model for other cordiform projections in the sixteenth century: the Haggi Ahmed Turkish world map, possibly of 1559 (Shirley 1987; 118, entry 103; Akerman et al. 1993: 11), a 1566 copperplate engraving by Giovanni Cimerlino (Shirley 1987: 136, entry 116 [Figure 3.19]), and Giacomo Franco's last copy of 1586–87 (Shirley 1987: 144, entry 152). The authority that

Figure 3.18. Detail of upper left border of Figure 3.17

Finé commanded was so great that in the 1566 copy the upper border between the frame and the two manneristic angels is inscribed, in italic letters, *Cosmographia universalis ab Orontio olim descripta,* the source being heralded rather than—as was sometimes the custom—erased. The association of the name with the projection is so pronounced that the Franco version of 1587 sets in the spandrels between the heart and the square surround four portraits, in circular frames, of immortal cartographers of the past and present: Ptolemy, Pomponius Mela, Strabo, and, in the upper-right corner, "Orontius" (who looks left over to Ptolemy, who simultaneously gazes back toward Finé).

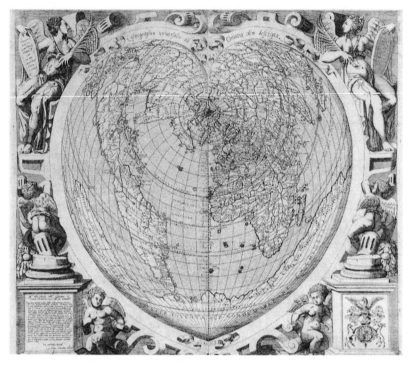

Figure 3.19. Giovanni Cimerlino's 1566 copperplate reproduction of Oronce Finé's single cordiform map of 1534

The technical innovations of the 1534 map are due no less to cartographic progress than to manifold relations of inherited models of projection, ideology, iconography, and the art of the signature. The dazzling view of the world seen as a single whole distinguishes the map from the first, "truncated" cordiform map in Bernardus Sylvanus's celebrated 1511 edition of Ptolemy. In Sylvanus's map, the concave design of the extreme north does not lead to an axial point from which the world seems to flow, and the meridian that cuts through the Caspian Sea, in a similar line of black and white squares, is not in the western Indian Sea adjacent to the *Barbericum Pelagus*. The Antarctic lands are not included, and the distribution of the European and Asian landmass is extensive, shaded in relief, and identified by place names (in red ink, in the only document of its kind) in an overall effect that tends to deemphasize the world's hydrographic mass.[17] Although the map departs from the Ptolemaic tradition by virtue of the swelling borders to the left and right, and although it includes a continent of South America (*Terra sanctae crucis*) below Cuba, Hispañola, and the *Terra labora*—which betrays new information about the western discoveries—the map remains allied with the Ptolemaic world-view; it is less totalizing and, in a glance, less balanced in its articulation of land and ocean masses. Sylvanus prints place names in red ink against a finely cut relief of mountains and rivers in horizontal lines of shading. Included are twelve wind heads and banners on the outside. The regional maps are executed in the same style, with ornate borders (ailerons, snails, elephants, birds, exotica) that abut the titles on the upper borders and that display a variety of designs in the corners of each rectangle (fleurs-de-lis for Gallia, a chalice and a helmet for Germania, etc.; see, e.g., Figure 4.1). Sylvanus's map figures in a carefully designed set of decorative motifs, whereas Finé's full cordiform projection calls attention to itself as a totality that can be grasped in an instant.

The model for Finé's projection is not a radical departure from Ptolemy. Johannes Werner, in his *Libellus de quatuor terrarum orbis in plano figurationibus* (Nuremberg, 1514), suggested how the map could be drawn (Kish 1965: 14). But Finé emphasizes the prevalence of landmasses in the Northern Hemisphere, and he provides, *in a single and commanding view,* a picture of all the world's continents, in the Northern Hemisphere, which counterbalance sea masses that make up much of the Southern Hemisphere. The equilibrating presence of Antarctica produces the image of a world in which land and sea are set in ideal proximity and balance. In accord with the humanist ideal calling for an immediate and effortless transmission of great masses of information without undue labor and gloss, the map constitutes a mystical, totalizing diagram of the names and places of the world.

What inspires the view may be grounded in the history of the politics and aesthetics of the first years of the reign of Francis I, when a "cordiform" iconography prevailed. When Francis I participated in the triumphal entries into the cities of Rouen (1517) and Poitiers (1520), and when the queen, Claude de France, walked through the allegorical pageant that Paris had prepared for her on 12 May 1517, the designers and artisans conveyed political messages through "textual diagrams" rendered in the shape of hearts and based on readings of Saint Paul (Corinthians) and the Song of Songs, two primary sources for the strain of evangelical humanism that the king's counselors wanted Francis to embody. In the triumphal entry into Poitiers (5 January 1520), one of the panels that faced the king bore the inscription "Inveni quem diliget anima mea" [I have found the one whom my heart adores] (Song 3:4). Appeal to this verse of the Song of Songs, contends Anne-Marie Lecoq (1987: 366), "was particularly in vogue in the time of Francis I," and took the form of a fiancée giving herself to the king who enters the city by opening her heart to her leader. When he enters the city, the king takes possession of the agglomeration as if it were his young spouse. The theme conveyed the metaphoric union of the king with the city, the province, and the nation (374) by infusing a domestic program with the aura of a union of love between king and queen (or country). Biblical proverbs allowed the king's *heart* to be held in God's hand, such that among the tableaux of the entries—following Pierre Gringore for that of Mary of England in Paris, 6 November 1514—divine providence would be seen acting upon a leader's heart ("cor regis in manu Domini," Proverbs 21:1, cited in Lecoq 1987: 377).

The most obvious appeal to the heart and to the divine marriage of king, family, and country was crafted, again by Pierre Gringore, in Queen Claude's arrival in Paris on Tuesday, 12 May 1517, three days after the coronation of the king at the basilica of Saint-Denis. Both events emphasized a *union* and *concord* by direct allusion to Corinthians 1:13. All the scaffoldings used themes playing on the union of the hearts of the king and queen, of the royal couple, of God, of the bond tying the French nation to its leader and to all Christian royalty:

> The mental image of the heart finally assumed a concrete and visual form. On the upper level (of the fifth station on the rue Saint-Denis) Gringore had placed a theatrical machine: one great heart that opened into three panels. In the center was "Divine love," and in the lateral panels were "National love" and "Conjugal love." The three types of love were not only illustrated with examples taken from Biblical and classical history, but also tied to contemporary reality. Above the core of God (in the center) was perched the French coat-of-arms, that is, of the King, and of Queen Claude above Conjugal love and above National love, that of Louise of Savoie. (Lecoq 1987: 386)

Complex treatments devolved from this order—in a fashion inspired by the Canticles—whereby the dialogue of the king and queen would insist on their adoration of wisdom over and above kingdoms and majestic castles. In this configuration, Sapience would be the king's spouse, and in her heart his generosity would find its source of inspiration. Gringore sought to imprint a feeling of mutual love between husband and wife that would extend to the politics of leadership. "At stake is no longer a poetic metaphor, in which the love of the city for the king, or of the populace for the queen, is staged through the image and discourse of amorous relations between man and woman, but of the invocation of a capital factor in the smooth workings of the ideally True Christian monarchy" (Lecoq 1987: 391).

Gringore and his assistants were asking Francis to bring a "kinder, gentler" embodiment of France to its growing population of subjects. The return to these biblical texts constitutes some of the mystical tenor of the reform associated with the king. Drawn and delivered to Francis, Finé's cordiform map frames the world in the terms that the monarch's patrons were advancing. To a great degree, the heart also recalls the spiritual milieu of "Réforme de Meaux" that developed in the correspondence between the king's sister, Marguerite de Navarre, and Guillaume Briçonnet and Charles de Bovelles.[18] Just as the fleur-de-lis was part of the French escutcheon, so thus could the Trinity be seen in its shape and number if it were projected along the two arcs that contain a world and a triangle within its area. The three corners of the heart would convey the mystery of divine creation and form.

If the map is read thus, the Trinity is also fixed in a cosmology derived from Ficino and the current political realities of the years 1519–1525. In a work entitled *Petit livre d'énigmes*, François Demoulins fashioned three sets of concentric circles, surrounding a heart in which are contained three additional hearts. One carries the totem of the eagle with its chicks, another of the swan, and a third of the rooster.[19] Lecoq determines that *L'aigle* carried the letter of Louise de Savoie, the swan (*cygne*) the sign (*signe*) of Marguerite, and the rooster (*le coq*), that of Francis. The cabalistic traits of the enigma underscore how much stress was placed on the recitation of prayers taken to be miraculous, "and of psalms in particular, accredited with a *quasi-mystical* 'virtue'" (Lecoq 1987: 410, emphasis added), that are related to Ficino's vision of God as the center of a planetary circle that is unique, indivisible, and immobile. The heart is also present in spherical form in the "triangle of eternity and divine glory" that the Ficinian vision seeks to locate, like a perspectival object, between the visible and invisible worlds.

At the same time that the mystical heart was used for political ends in the iconography of the early years of the reign of Francis I, the heart had already been associated with graphic conceptions of the world. In *El pelerinage de la vida humana* (Toulouse, 1490), the heart surrounds a mnemonic figure of the globe (which resembles a t-and-o map) (illustrated in Camille 1992: 285). Finé designs his *mappa mundi* to make the best of many worlds: Woodcuts are designed as memory images or as didactic schemes binding the earth to sacred forms; political programs are based on recent readings of the Song of Songs and the Psalms; recent projections come from northern European experiments with Ptolemy (Gallois 1890a). The latter seems to be an inspiration for the design that matches the scientific background visible in the cordiform maps of Sylvanus, Werner, and Pieter Apian.

The relation of the cartographer to the map is enhanced by the relation of the frame to the projection. Close inspection of the borders of the heart (Figure 3.20) shows that the viewer can move about and around the surface of

Figure 3.20. Single cordiform map of 1534, detail of Eastern areas
(Oronce Finé)

the globe and see the rotundity of the sphere from a point of view recalling, in
our age, that of video images taken from space shuttles. The viewer loses a
vertical grounding in respect to a picture seen at a distance, while the map is
held in a square surround. Since the inserted toponyms (in stereotype chiseled
into and flush with the wood surface) are not placed on a horizontal plane, the
eye is encouraged to follow multidirectional axes and to move with the curvature of the latitudinal and longitudinal arcs. *Terra Australis* tilts downward,
Terra Florida is set within and parallel to the peninsula of its name but moves

upward, while the names of the tropics follow the bend of their lines. Even though the squarish, almost maladroit, relation of the inset typeface seems to be at odds with the curvilinear grace of the ensemble—betraying a technical problem that woodcut images could not solve (Pastoureau 1992)—the fact that the place names do *not* fit in the curvature implies that the great form of the sphere exceeds the human language that names its parts.[20] An impression of a world with neither beginning nor end is felt in the contour of the projection.

Most apparent, the North Pole is thrust down into the body of the world, extending the meridian southward in order to yield the great curves to the left and right, in a way that resembles the site of a stem, a navel, an umbilicus, that is, the scar of a former connection with a greater body (see Figure 3.17). Physical and metaphysical attributes converge upon the North Pole. The latitudes radiate from it as an axis, while the longitudes follow a parabola of outward extension and descend to the southern tip. The origin of the map also resembles an apical meristem, or embryonic point from which the world's form is generated. In this sense, the map becomes a mobile structure that visibly grows and moves outward into a foreshortened space between the spectator and the plane surface of the surrounding square. It bears generative traits that meld the scientific project with the content of evangelical iconography.

The apical pole, seen from above, aligned with the center point of the Canary Islands (an archipelago that had been the threshold of lands known and unknown) at the vanishing point of the ensemble, indicates that the viewing subject is not far from the vantage point of a celestial being who is both out of the world and inside it. The viewer's eye seems to move up from the axis of the diagonal of the overall rectangle, the Canary Islands, which lay adjacent to the intersection of the Tropic of Cancer and the central meridian, to the North Pole, which is depressed to a position halfway between the upper edge of the frame and the Canaries. An almost Albertian model seems to prevail. But the putti look at the work from an oblique angle that suggests aberration and anamorphosis as the basis of the projection of a spherical body onto a flat plane. Their playfulness catches the eye. And so does Finé's rebus of the dolphin, which defines the upper border. Swimming toward the putti, the dolphin exhibits mobility in respect to the edge of the frame that it is simultaneously establishing. Finé's new device, the crowned dolphin (which replaced the *O* bisected by the Gothic *F* with which he had signed work prior to 1517), now figures in the frieze of the column. It occupies the liminary position of the trickster, but it also authors what projects an ideal and veracious image of the world. The signature effect in the corners opens onto a broader problem

of visibility and point of view at the same time that it underscores the relation
that the cartographer holds with the king.

In 1566, when Giovanni Cimerlino changes the map by adapting it to copperplate technology, he almost foretells the fate of the cordiform view. After copying the outlines to the letter of the original (probably by shellacking the map
to a sheet of copper and having engravers etch through to the metal surface
with burins), he designates the sea masses with dots instead of wavy lines. The
redrawn place names are cut along the implied curvature of the world and
produce an illusion of sphericity that the woodcut technique was unable to
attain. An entirely different emphasis is placed in the margins, where Cimerlino
seems to take his cue from the signature effect in the original. He places four
enlarged variants of Finé's putti next to two stylobates of broken columns on
the left and right vertical sides, on which sit precariously two more angelic
babies looking at the map. Energies that were only latent in Finé's version are
now released: The two upper putti balance their buttocks on the tilting columns as they hold their right (on the left) and left (on the right) arms to their
eyes as if to shield themselves from the dazzle of the map. But, seen from behind, their chubby bottoms outline in inverted form the overall shape of the
projection.

All of a sudden, what was Finé's emphasis on the locus of the mystical heart
in the cosmos moves downward. Heart and bottom are set in an implied correspondence between the decor and content. And the heroic female figures in
the upper spandrels to the left and right, executed in the Fontainebleau style,
exude a mix of masculine and feminine attributes. The woman on the left,
who carries a tablet displaying, from an oblique angle, Cimerlino's name, the
date, and the place of the drawing, has the athletic physique of a Diana, while
her counterpart is no less Amazonian. A multivalent, erogenous drive is associated with the generative qualities that characterize the original. It may be that
the design in the borders of Cimerlino's copy celebrates a degree of obliquity
and curvilinearity that the woodcut could not achieve. Nonetheless, a new
erotic charge is exuded within the scientific space of the cordiform projection.[21] The dividing line below the coccyx of each putto and between the
nipples of the androgynes' bare breasts makes the North Pole a zone whose
erogenous force elicits more than the effect of a world growing out of an Arctic
navel. The generative traits of the woodcut version of the cordiform project
are held in check; in Cimerlino's copperplate, the surrounding allegorical figures mobilize and eroticize the potential force that had been retained in a
more intellectual and mystical sense in the works of 1519 and 1534.

Comparison of the two versions shows that for Finé the body has a transcending, mystical, mathematical essence achieved by the relation of straight and curved lines—as allegorized in Tory—and in the corporal, Christological, and political resonance of the heart. Similar effects are achieved in the double cordiform projection (Figure 3.21) at the points of the meristems of the North and South Poles and in the divided aspect of the signature. This map obtains breadth by splitting the world along the line that runs through the Caspian Sea and the Persian Gulf en route to either axial point; but also, a novel connection between the author and work emerges from the central area. The escutcheon, a perspectival object that focuses the attention of the eye as it scans over the map, is squeezed in the spandrel at the center of the sheet and is marginal to the depiction of the world. The apothegm is located at the origin of a curvilinear angle, in other words, at a point of perception, the beginning of the map's field of visibility. In contrast to their appearance in the single cordiform world map, Finé's name and attributes are more central to the finished product. The signatory edge is more commandingly united to the scheme. A world divided into two parts enhances the generative features of a world that is multiplying through a kind of diagrammatic mitosis. Relations with the unknown are made prominent by the commanding view of the hypothetical continent of Antarctica, an area that balances the distribution of known masses of land and water.[22] It appears that the bodily and geometric features of the two cordiform maps belong to a long tradition, running from Romanesque sculpture and painting to cubism and modernism, that studies the relations between human and abstract shapes. In the context of early modern print culture, the relation is also visible in what Finé projects as the identity of and difference between figural and lexical shapes inflecting his own setting and being in the greater cosmos. That relation is made evident everywhere in the writing but is best focused in the map of France and in his first regional projection of its southeastern territories.

Gallia and the Topographical Map in *Le sphère du monde*

Oronce Finé's work in topography is not only unique in sixteenth-century France; it also internalizes many perspectival articulations of the self on the map and the world.[23] In 1525 he completed the map *Gallia* (680 × 950 mm, woodcut on four sheets) that was printed in 1538. "The map of France was quite influential and was copied" (Karrow 1993: 176), in simplified form, by Sebastian Münster before being engraved six more times in Italy by 1552. It is not as historically innovative as Sylvanus's projection of *Gallia* in his 1511 edition of Ptolemy (Broc 1987), but it does announce the liminary relation of the

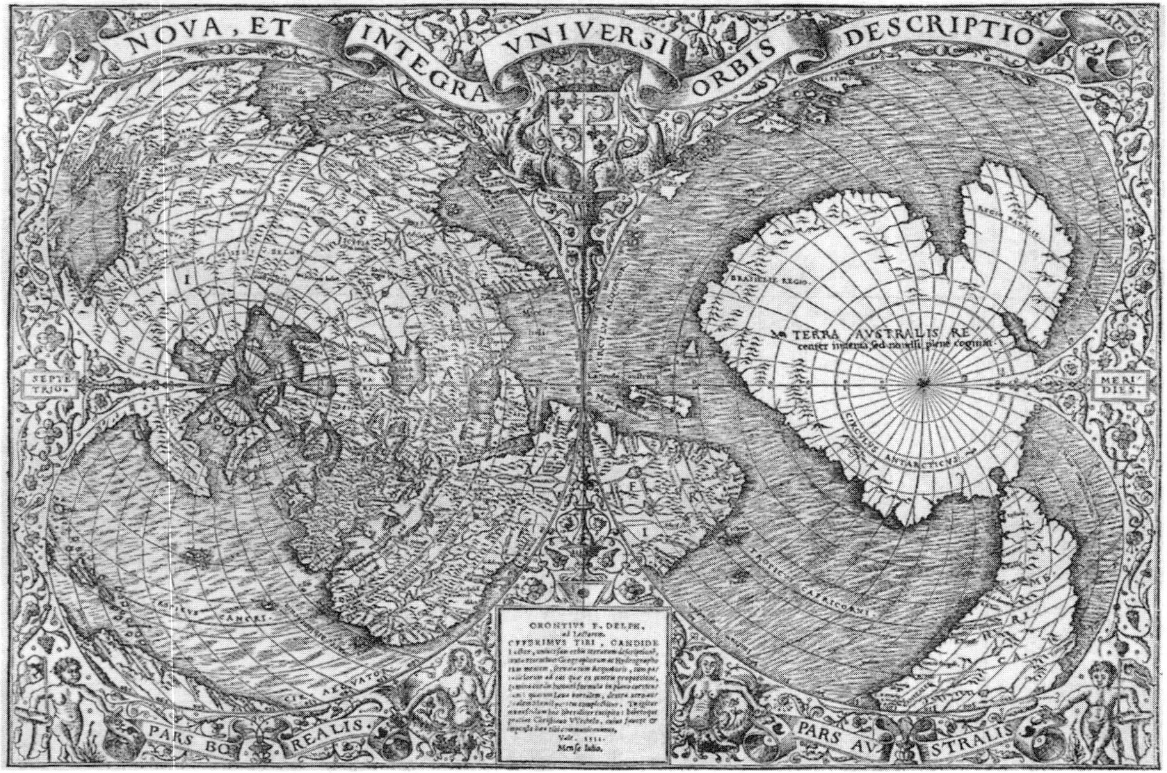

Figure 3.21. Double cordiform map of 1531 (Oronce Finé)

name to the mapping treated so masterfully in the cordiform projections. The title, *Nova totius Galliae descriptio, Orontius, F. Delphas, faciebat 1538*, encloses the view and again puts the author in a favored area along the entirety of the boundaries of the creation. At the same time, however, the explication in letterpress, set in a square cartouche placed over lands to the north and east of France, displays the almost unconscious textual character of the cartographic figures (illustrated in Dainville 1964b: X.3). In the letterpress, a compressed Gothic character defines the meanings of the symbols used to designate cities, towns, bailiwicks, castles, and other points of interest on the map. Following the stenography visible in the 1515 edition of Peurbach's *Theoricarum,* Finé puts the symbols into the lines of text *as if* they were words. There reigns a near-dedifferentiation between the cartographer's diagrammatic language and the French that describes the system of representation, the publisher, and the ten-year privilege above the map maker's device (*virescit vulnere virtus*). The graphic design indicates that no clear demarcation exists between discourse and figure, and that in fact, because the explanatory material is not in the more customary Latin, the "language" of his projection of *Gallia* is being promoted as French. A map of French space is conveyed through a synthesis of topographical signs and the vernacular idiom.

Finé's emerging Frenchness seems to increase over the duration of his career. The map of France in the *Protomathesis* appears accurate and instructive (Figure 3.22). The blendings of individual and national traits are strikingly visible in the topographical view of southeastern France, Switzerland, and northwestern Italy, which was printed in different editions of *De mundi sphaera* (Figure 3.23). The map was reputedly first drawn in order to be offered to Francis I in 1543. Its design was published in *Quadratura circuli* in the following year and later in *Le sphère du monde* (1551). The small map (Figure 3.24) is included to show how one goes about charting a region, as Finé had explained the method in paragraphs adjacent to the letterpress map of the contours of France in the 1532 *Protomathesis*.

How was it done? A mechanical process, like that of artificial perspective, is set forth. It shares much with the Albertian method, beginning with a horizontal line placed in a quadrant at the height of a viewer who would be of proportionate size in the frame. Finé states that an arbitrarily drawn vertical initiates the operation. In a description recalling Tory's creation of the perspective of the frame that houses the alphabetic letter (see chapter 2), it is stated that the line serves as a meridian that will be divided into ten equal units, and then paralleled (according to the curvature of the globe) by two lines on either side. Two extreme latitudes are chosen to complete the trapezoid, which is deter-

præmiſſum graduum numerum diſtributos : quorum occidentalior A C diſtat ab occidente ha
bitato 14 gradibus,orientalior uerò B D , gradibus 30.Circunſcribito tandem, proprios graduũ
tam longitudinis q̃ latitudinis numeros. Quibus abſolutis,imponenda ſunt loca ſingula,uel ſal,
tem inſigniora, pro ipſorum tum ab Aequatore, tum ab occidente habitato diſtantia : primũm
quidem urbes,oppida,caſtra, & pagi notabiliores,poſtea lacus & flumina, tandem montes pro,
montoria atq̃ littora. Vt Lugdunum emporium ſuper Rhodanum in puncto L , Lutetiam Pa,
riſiorum in puncto M ſupra Sequanam, Tholoſam metropolim in N : quorum longitudines
atq̃ latitudines, ex præmiſſa longitudinum atq̃ latitudinum deprehēdes tabula. Idē reſpõden
ter de cæteris locis intelligas : tũ ab ipſo Ptolemæo, tũ ab alijs,aut teipſo, uel à nobis obſeruatis.

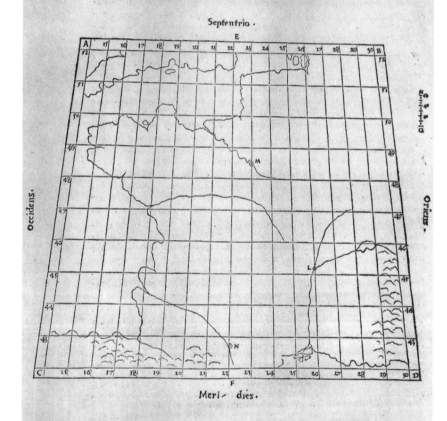

Chorographiæ ¶ b Apperiamus cõſequenter,qualiter faciẽda ſit Meridianorũ atq̃ parallelorũ cõtextura,quæ b
ex curuis lineis ſimilis exiſtat octauæ parti ſphæricæ cõuexitatis. Sit igitur circulus liberæ quãtitatis A B C : cu
cõtextæ figura ius circũferentia in tres partes æquas diuidatur,in ipſis quidē ſignis A,B,C . Impoſito deinde cir
tionis exẽplũ. cini pede in ſigno A,extende reliquũm in B,uel in C : & ducito arcũ B C. Rurſum inuariato cir
circino

Figure 3.22. Map of France in Oronce Finé, *Protomathesis*

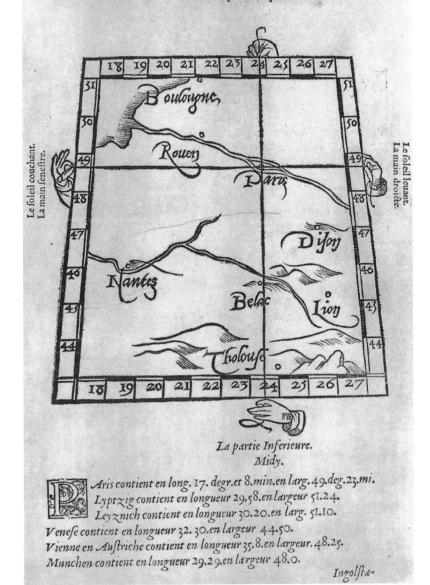

Figure 3.23. Pieter Apian's map of France reprinted in 1551 (Paris) edition of his *Cosmographie*

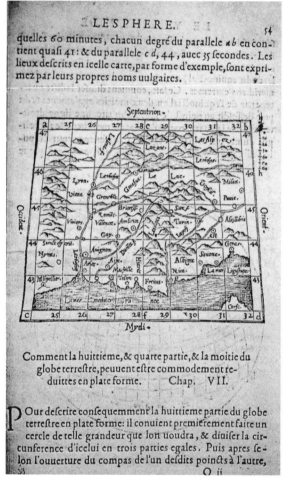

Figure 3.24. Topographical map of northern Italy and southeastern France (Oronce Finé, *Le sphère du monde*)

mined by a scale that divides one of the degrees (in tenths) into sixty parts,
corresponding to the sixty minutes of one degree of a circle, that gives a credible form to the frame. Finé draws on Nicolaus Germanus's trapezoidal projection to establish the model (Dainville 1970: 52). Once the graticule is formed,
Finé then places on the map, according to their distance from the equator and
in this order, the most important cities (*urbes*), smaller cities (*oppida*), castles,
and noteworthy villages (*emporia*) as they are determined by Ptolemy. Then
he adds lakes, rivers, mountains, capes, and coastlines. The perspectival grid is

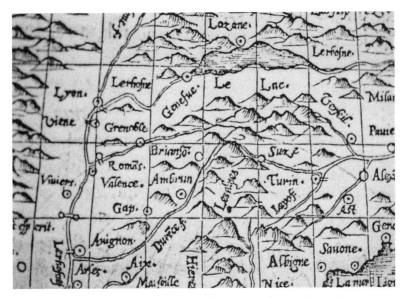

Figure 3.25. Detail of Figure 3.24: the city of Briançon at the vanishing point

established *before* the details are set in the image. The world, or "frame," is chosen and gridded according to calculations made using the astrolabe (illustrated in the frontispiece to the *Protomathesis*), while the remaining physical traits of the world are determined according to the mathematical calculations that pertain to the measurement of longitude by observation of the stars.

In the regional map printed in the *Le sphère du monde* (1551), the same procedure holds "by means of the longitudes and latitudes of places and by the itinerary distance between the same," a process that leads Père Dainville to conclude that Finé offers a mathematician's model for topographical mapping "in which the positions of places are more significant than rivers or coastlines" (1970: 55). Dainville adds that in the map of France in the *Protomathesis,* which was created following the method, Finé, unlike other cartographers of the time (such as Vidal de la Blache), does *not* include the town where he was born. Whereas many cartographers "sign" their works by an allusion to their birthplace, in the map of *Gallia* and in the text of 1532 Finé uses latitudes taken from Jean Fernel's *Cosmotheoria* (Paris: Simon de Colines, 1538) (Dainville 1970: 53). Yet Briançon *does* appear in the printed version of the regional map of 1543. In fact, if Albertian methods are applied to the map, the perspectival object is Briançon (Figure 3.25), placed at the vanishing point!

A spatial signature or a scientific rendering of the cartographer's umbilicus is obtained. The graphic point being marked is that of the emporium north of the bishopric of Ambrun, and south of Geneva. Finé writes his presence into the map by selecting as its point of projective identification the site of his birth, a navel, adjacent to his native city. Better than a written signature, the ciphered dot to the right of the name of Briançon marks the origin and the end of the picture. It is now Finé, not the king, who is the ideal viewer of the map. But the relation between the signature and the ground does not reflect an ironic or a self-congratulatory performance of cartographic rhetoric. Following the play of language and figuration that dominates Finé's writings and illustrations, the logic of the signature abides by the codes of a perspective of the selfless but self-constituted self—the servitor of the highest of the liberal arts—in the age of humanism.

The Analogical Style

In this little topographical map, Finé draws a spatial narrative of historical origins. The projection was ostensibly given to Francis I in 1543, yet its vanishing point happens to be Finé's point of attachment to—and distance from—his native Dauphiné. Inscribed is an arcane geometry of writing that also characterizes the cartographer's style and diction. We first noted that in the 1517 edition of Breidenbach's *Voyage à la terre sainte,* he composed an acrostic ballad of a tradition that reaches back to Villon and the Grands Rhétoriqueurs. Finé holds to the same type of writing in a ballad he composes in Latin at the end of the index to his edition of Peurbach's *Theoricarum.* Set at the end of the book, it denotes a spatial counterpoint to the title page. As it is subscribed by the paraph "finis" (fol. xci v), the work of the engraver blends with that of the writer. It becomes clear that from the beginning of Finé's career, spatial coordinates determine a cartographic form of writing. They do, however, undergo some modification. The style moves from the gridded, rectangular aspect that characterizes the space of fixed forms inherited from the fifteenth century, which we witnessed in *Les cent nouvelles* and in the verse of Jean Molinet, to a greater degree of circularity, in which cosmographic diagrams are cast in the newer, classical typography. The Ptolemaic view of the universe is invested into letters and, no less, into Finé's selection of poetic forms.

By 1532, Clément Marot was known as a master of *rondeaux* written according to a perspectival mode. When he built hermetic verse that enclosed its mode of generation at the center of its form, the axial point tended to be a point both inside and outside of language, a mark that welded graphic and diagrammatic forms to the field of meaning in the discourse (Conley 1992a: 36–38). It is not surprising that Finé identifies with this kind of creation, or that it persists in influencing his French, both poetry and descriptive writing, as late as the 1550s. The same tendency is seen in a *rondeau* that decorates the preface to his French translation of Charles de Bovelles's book of practical geometry:

> Rithmus circularis, Orontianus
> Sur tous les ars qui sont dictz liberaulx,
> Servans à tous, tant doctes que ruraulx:
> Le principal apres l'arithmetique
> Est le sçavoir appellé geometrique,
> Pour parvenir à ceux qui sont plus haultz.
>
> Tous artisans & gens mercuriaulx,
> Qui ont desir trouver secretz nouveaux,
> De mesurer fault qu'ayent la pratique
>   Sur tous les ars.
>
> Dieu a creé les corps, & animaulx
> Depuis le ciel iusques aux mineraux
> Par nombre, poix, & mesure harmonique:
> Heureux est donc qui de tel sçavoir explique,
> Et qui entend secretz si generaulx
>   Sur tous les ars.[24]

In this poem, the axial locution "trouver secretz" draws at the hub of the *rondeau* the very "secret" about which the whole is turning, as implied by the meaning of "to find" (*trouver*), in "to turn around or about" (*tourner autour*). The "truth" of the word is partially embedded in a spatial conception of language that allows the substantive to move to and from given coordinates. The poem is "mapped" to the degree that the roundness of Finé and his name are the secret, the cachet, of the composition. An implicit generativity of meaning—accomplished by recombining the shape, meaning, and placement of each vocable—results from an extension, or "prolation," of the practices of his formative years (1510–1520) into the humanist world. What we see happening in the discourse has an analogy in the world of maps in the mystical meristem of a polar point of the globe.

Of no less consequence are the inner workings of the descriptive prose in the textbooks and translations into the vernacular. At every point, the work grows copiously out of its own form. The latter is of course related to the maternal character of the curvilinear worldview, complemented by the (male) geometer's abstract and orthogonal line. In this sense, *terrae incognitae,* what we have taken from Rosolato's concept of the relation to the unknown, is already—always—located in the expansive form resulting from the diagrams and paratactic relation to adjacent typography. Thus, in *Le sphère du monde*, the new world, the very charter of the unknown, is not that new. It is not a great marvel, but rather, in conjunction with the schemes of cosmography and medieval science, a pregiven reality.

Apropos of the world's hydrography, he states modestly,

> Et convient noter, que l'eau n'environne point rondement & entierement toute la terre: ains est respandue par divers bras, traits, & conduits (que nous appellons mers) tant au dedans, que au tour d'icelle. Car il estoit nescessaire, que aucunes parties de la ditte terre fussent descouvertes, pour le salut et habitation des vivants: ainsi qu'il a plus au createur, prevoyant la commodité de toutes choses, Desquelz elemens, la figure est telle. . . .

> [It is worth noting that water does not surround so entirely and roundly the entire earth, but is spread forth in diverse arms, narrows, and channels (what we call seas) as much inside as all about itself. It was necessary that some parts of the world become discovered, for the salvation and inhabitation of living beings: Thus it pleased the creator, who foresaw the fitting character of all things, of whose elements the figure that follows is thus. . . .] (fol. 2 v)

In this and other formulations, the exposition turns about and toward itself centripetally and centrifugally, but always in directions that move toward and into *drawn figures*, and vice versa. As in the explanation in the cartouche adorning the 1538 copy of Finé's map of *Gallia*, writing and figuration are as fluid and as similar in space and texture as are the representations of land and water. The great amphibious mass of the globe is also an amphibological mass of figured writing.

From its sum emerges the full, well-rounded signature of the writer and cartographer. Finé is clearly a cosmographer in vision, but he becomes a topographer in the way his identity jells with the forms and fortunes of France after the end of the reign of Francis I. The consciousness of an empirical, self-made individual emerges and parallels, to a strong degree, what we witness in the late Rabelais and, differently, in the tradition of the *isolario*, or island book. Finé's world is isolated, but it disappears when a cordiform vision is abandoned in favor of topographical and planispheric views. His brand of cosmography gives way to the scientific modes that he may even have served to inaugurate with his regional map of southern France.[25] Finé and his work soon disappear with the advent of new science. It is perhaps fitting now to turn, first, to the world of Rabelais, Finé's contemporary, and then, later, to the island books or *isolario,* where we shall consider the relation that the new genre holds with the vanishing fortunes of cosmography.

4

Words à la Carte: A Rabelaisian Map

At the moment when Oronce Finé was revising his cordiform map of 1519, Geoffroy Tory, in his translation of Lucian's *Dialogues of the Dead,* which is appended to his *Table de Cèbes* (1529), describes a pedantic student of the liberal arts who abuses French in the worst of ways. The picture he paints of the affected, verbose, and inane character appears in a book, as handsomely designed as the *Champ fleury,* that marks an important moment in the history of typography. Decorated with ornate borders and floral designs that resemble the manual of letters published in the same year, *La Table de l'ancienne philosophe Cèbes . . . Avec Trente Dialogues moraulx de Lucien autheur iadis Grec . . .* launches a program of vernacular writing and of intellectual travel between sixteenth-century France and the Grecian past. The work is only one among a variety of the editor's projects, which include *itineraria* (cheap, practical pocket atlases) and a translation of Plutarch, but for the casual reader of sixteenth-century literature, Tory's opuscule is a source for one of the great episodes of *Pantagruel,* a work that François Rabelais would soon publish in Lyon (1532) and Paris (1533).

In the sixth chapter, Rabelais describes the itinerary of his hero's wanderings about Paris at the beginning of his studies in the Latin Quarter. The book had just begun with a flourish, with the description of the giant's momentous heritage and beginnings and an account of his earliest years. The initial chapters, which resemble chronicles common to universal histories of origins, lead from cosmic to human proportions. On a day, like any other day—the narrator

can't remember when—Pantagruel was taking a walk about the periphery of
the city:

> Quelque jour, je ne sçay quand, Pantagruel se pourmenoit après soupper avecques
> ses compaignons par la porte dont l'on va à Paris. Là rencontra un escholier tout
> jolliet qui venoit par icelluy chemin; et, après qu'ilz se furent saluéz, luy de-
> manda: "Mon amy, dont viens tu à ceste heure?"

> [One day, I don't know when, Pantagruel was taking a walk after supper with his
> companions, by the portal through which leads the road to Paris. There he met a
> very handsome student who was coming along the same path; and, after they sa-
> luted each other, he asked him, "My friend, where are you coming from at this
> moment?"][1]

The scene sets the frame for Pantagruel's meeting with the Limousin who mu-
tilates French by speaking an incomprehensibly pompous, Latinized French
that conveys reports of a lazy students' life in the local taverns. It signals a
program that, like Tory's *Champ fleury* and the *Table de Cèbes*, advocates speaking and writing in the vernacular language.

As we have seen in Tory's arguments for the square-defined letter, the episode
also has a complex cartographic dimension. The task before us in this chapter is
to study some of the elements of Rabelais's textual mappings in his two early
works, *Pantagruel* (1532–1533) and *Gargantua* (1533–1534), and some of their relations to contemporary works of cartography. And as we have also seen in the
world of Fouquet, the Grands Rhétoriqueurs, *Les cent nouvelles,* and Geoffroy
Tory, the writing of the work appears to be fashioned from a mapped design
that is held within its own form. But Rabelais, who subjects language to incredible torsions, also draws verbal chorographies and geographies of his own
imagination. These constitute some of the most extraordinary evidence of
language maps in the age of humanism.[2] Rabelais's language map comes into
view along the discursive and visual insterstices of *Pantagruel* and *Gargantua*.
The unalloyed appeal of these first two books owes much to the semblance of a
creation that discovers its form while it develops a sense of its own space and
coherence. Reading the two works in chronological order—*Pantagruel* before
Gargantua—reveals how the second volume happens upon itself, discovers and
extends its spaces, and how the first recrafts and refines, but also leads into new
directions, the forms that were initially essayed in the second.

Beginnings

In the two books taken together, we again witness something of what Henri
Focillon (1934) calls the "life of forms of art," a process both organic and serial

that, through experiment, seeks ways of changing a flaccid but exuberant chapbook, the *Grandes chroniques du grand et énorme géant Gargantua,* a narrative that serves as an initial paradigm for the comic epic of the deeds of good giants. A "classical" solution is found when the author builds a founding tale around a protagonist (Pantagruel) and antagonists taken from myth (the Dipsodes) or constructed as symbolic personages in recent history (Picrochole and his army) and includes adjudicating figures (Panurge and the Pantagruelic "compaignons") or mediating agents (Frère Jean) in order to mobilize, satirize, and rewrite scenes from the canon of Greek, Latin, and other sources. Rabelais has already refined his solution by the middle chapters of *Gargantua,* where the excesses of war are tempered by an abundance of language. The sum of the work nonetheless acquires a self-reflexive and self-contained world, what Focillon would call a "Baroque" turn, in the webbing of references that run through each of the two books and make the text fold upon itself.

At this juncture, we can see how the two books map themselves, and how they strive to become a verbal projection of a mythic world that contains the French nation and all the surfaces of the globe as it was then known. The work that seeks to solve its own formal problems tends, in the words of David Woodward (1990), toward a "route-enhancing" narrative projection: Characters are put forward; they act according to the psychologies assigned to them (Pantagruel learns to be wise, Panurge moves from the trickster to the comic butt, Frère Jean is a man of pure action who moves forward but never accedes to wisdom, etc.); the episodes relating their adventures move along a zigzag course to a deferred or nonexistent resolution. The unfinished work thus leaves space for sequels, new episodes, and the inclusion of *terrae incognitae,* or it merely refuses to capitulate to any predetermined scheme of containment or an allegorical goal. The promise of new adventures to come at the end of *Pantagruel* is made to be broken. There, the second book opens onto the reader's memory of Ptolemaic atlases and children's maps, such as that of the *Mer des histoires,* that place mythic figures and the rivers of Paradise in a t-and-o design inherited from Isidore de Seville and other sources:

> Vous aurez le reste de l'histoire à ces foires de Francfort prochainement venantes, et là vous verrez comment Panurge fut marié, et cocqu dès le premier mois de ses nopces; et comment Pantagruel trouva la pierre philosophale, et la maniere de la trouver et d'en user; et comment il passa les Mons Caspies, comment il naviga par la mer Athlanticque, et deffit les caniballes, et conquesta les isles de Perlas; comment il espousa la fille du roy d'Inde nommé Presthan; comment il combatit les diables et fit brusler cinq chambres d'enfer, et mit à sac la grande chambre noire, et getta Proserpine au feu, et rompit quatre dents à Lucifer et une corne au

cul; et comment il visita les régions de la lune pour sçavoir si, à la vérité, la lune n'estoit entière, mais que les femmes en avoient trois quartiers en la teste: et mille aultres petites joyeuseté toutes véritables.

[You'll hear the rest of the story at the forthcoming fair at Frankfurt, and there you'll see how Panurge was wedded and cuckolded after the first month of his marriage; and how Pantagruel found the philosopher's stone, and discovered how to use it; how he assailed the Caspian Mountains, how he sailed over the Atlantic Ocean, beat the Cannibals, and conquered the Perlas Islands; how he fought the devils and had five of hell's chambers put to fire; how he broke four of Lucifer's teeth, and a horn in his ass; and how he visited the lunar regions in order to see if in truth the moon was not full, but that women had three quarters of it in their heads; and a thousand other truly veritable delights.] (311–12)

Like a contemporary map that can be read in the direction of its relation to things unknown, the narrative retains alterity within its own form in order, perhaps, to enhance the character of its mendacity and open-ended composition. Likewise, in *Gargantua,* when all is said and done with the Picrocholine wars, and when the Thelemites' Abbey is erected, the book closes upon a "prophetic enigma" in order to exceed the imposing architectural limits of the silent utopia it has created.

Yet the narrative that unfolds in the direction of its relation with the unknown betrays an obsession with a form that it would like to offer as complete but that refuses, at the same time, to be led to a final or stationary equilibrium. At another level of its reading, the world being depicted has equipollent virtues, in that, at every moment of its itinerary, a totality can be seen in the moving articulation of its verbal and graphic parts. *Details* tend to reflect or to crystallize the general process of the book at any and every part of its composition. Unlike a classical narration of a voyage, which would stage each episode as a moment leading toward a denouement, Rabelais's oeuvre gives the sum of its construct at every point of its trajectory.[3] In this sense, the pictogrammar of the work becomes the hinge on which turn the detail and the whole. And, at the same time, certain vocables project the graticules of a verbal *mappa mundi* that extends out of itself all the while it folds upon its own form.[4]

In the introduction, I noted that the concept of the perspectival object is focused upon a presymbolic world where language, images, and sensations are mixed, where there holds no easy distinction between visual and aural forms, and that the art of analysis requires the subject to regress to this condition of nondistinction for the sake of moving ahead, over and again, to a line of demarcation between an illusion of narcissistic *plenum* and a disquieting void. When symbolic forms are introjected, or held in an imaginary buccal area, they are negotiated, even digested.[5] Now we can see if the cartographic consciousness of the first two books functions according to a mobile, dialogic scheme in which verbal and tactile qualities are apposed. Do their relations demarcate realms of symbolic form and of images that know *no* language? Do they make manifest a diagrammatic complexity that builds on the model of Tory's allegories in the *Champ fleury?* Do the ruptures of image and text produce enigmatic, imponderable areas where a multiplicative process—but not establishment—of meaning conveys the sense of flux and flow that exceeds the limits assigned by the gridding and the meaning of the text?

In response to these questions, it can be surmised that the dialogic process of the work seems to pertain to its cartographic latency, especially in those areas where the languages of the first two books acquire values relevant to mapping. The vast arrays of personal and place names are set in a ceaselessly flowing verbal medium.[6] For this reason, we can see if the apparently oppositional mode of the Rabelaisian narrative impugns the route-enhancing style of a smooth development of episodes that would be logical consequences of one another. When a *routine* is discerned in the story, a *via rupta* comes into view: Each component of the temporal map of events stands in opposition to a counterpart that is immediately adjacent or set in a scheme that has a gridded or checkered appearance, where alternating units or pairs, placed at calibrated distances, inform one another. This sense of a continually ruptured continuity, which proceeds by antithesis, masks episodes both *within* each of the first two books, at various intervals, and *across* the two works, such that one is a variant or a unit of another, whose sum makes up a hypothetical whole, until the ensemble of blocks of narrative in each book are seen pertaining *apart* from each other, when *Pantagruel* and *Gargantua* are witnessed growing out of or away from their own relations. Thus, what Erich Auerbach calls "the world in Pantagruel's mouth" (II, xxxii) (1956: 262–84) is seen in contrast to the story of the giant's malady and the curative pills he takes to have his intestines cleared (II, xxxiii).[7] The debate between Panurge and the English cleric (II, xviii–xix) seems to generate the satire of Janotus de Bragmardo (I, xviii–xix); the shift from tales of love's ruses to tales of war (II, xxi–xxxii) adjoins the movement from Gargantua's institution to his conscription in defense of the homeland (I, x–xxvi), to show two different versions of an awakening of national consciousness.

In each of these instances, we see how the dialogic mode of composition is of a multiply *paratactic* order. Logical relations that would hold between different episodes are eradicated in order, it seems, to allow their interpretations to multiply. Erasure of linkages promotes opposition, creative conflict, and a consequent development into imaginary space.[8] With parataxis comes the art of antithesis, what Victor Hugo called "la faculté souveraine de voir les deux côtés des choses" [the sovereign faculty of seeing the two sides of things] (1865: 215), but there also arises a new space that is included for the reader or spectator who remains, perforce, within the space of text as he or she also engages, follows, and reinvents it. What Hugo calls double reflexion informs Renaissance space: "L'esprit du séizième siècle etait aux miroirs; toute idée de la Renaissance est à double compartiment. . . . La double action est là partout. . . . Les contre-coups singuliers sont une des habitudes de ce grand art profond et cherché du séizième siècle." [The mind of the sixteenth century was made with mirrors; every idea of the Renaissance has twin compartments. . . . Doubled actions are everywhere. Unique reverberations are one of the habits of this great and concealed art of the sixteenth century] (293). Furthermore, the paratactic style of composition makes space, what Hugo calls its compartmental aspect, a paramount feature of discourse. What is being stated not only belongs to a prismatic construct of oppositions and of insular and singular units—monadic chapters—of episodes, tales, or encounters, but is also subject to shifts in visual and diagrammatic orders that apply spatial and volumetric configurations to printed characters. Parataxis has the added advantage of requiring the reader to invent the world in the gap between one unit and the next (Lyotard 1983: 110–20). Because no causal relation links sentences or clauses to each other, there is no reason to believe that letters naturally or necessarily follow one after the other.[9]

To determine how, we can now return to Pantagruel's meeting with the Limousin student on the outskirts of Paris. The preceding chapter, "Des faictz du noble Pantagruel en son jeune eage" (The deeds of noble Pantagruel in his youth) belongs to a nascent cartographic genre, the *itinerarium* (Lestringant 1993). Its stylistic impoverishment (Glauser 1966; Gray 1974) may, in fact, be due to its imitation of the serially placed toponyms that make up many of the lists of early printed guidebooks. The student proceeds along a unilateral narrative trajectory defined in terms of a succession of sites. The course that Pantagruel takes in his adolescence mirrors our own relation to the parataxis before our eyes: The sentences reinvent the same course, but with the reinvention comes a paucity of or minimal variation on the same anaphoric markers: *Puis, et un jour, et après, puis retourna, puis vint, ainsy vint*, and so on. Each is a phatic sign signaling a new stage of a single voyage. Pantagruel's father Gargantua

> puis l'envoya à l'eschole pour apprendre et passer son jeune eage. De faict vint à Poictiers pour estudier, et y profita beaucoup, auquel lieu voyant que les escholiers estoyent aulcunes fois de loysir et ne sçavoient à quoy passer temps, il en eut compassion; et, un jour print d'un grand rochier qu'on nomme Passelour-

din une grosse roche ayant environ de douze toizes en quarré et d'espaisseur qua-
torze pans, et la mist sur quatre pilliers au milieu d'un champ, bien à son ayse;
affin que lesdictz escoliers, quand ilz ne sçauroyent aultre chose faire, passassent
temps à monter sur ladicte pierre, et là bancqueter à force flaccons, jambons et
pastéz, et escripre leur noms dessus avec un cousteau, et, de présent, l'appelle-on
la *Pierre levée*. Et, en mémoire de ce, n'est aujourd'huy passé aulcun en la
matricule de ladicte université de Poictiers, sinon qu'il ait beu en la fontaine
caballine de Croustelles, passé à Passelourdin et monté sur la Pierre levée.

[then sent him to school to learn and pass his youth. In fact he came to Poitiers
to study, and profited much: In which place, seeing that the students enjoyed
their leisure, but did not know how to spend their time, he had compassion for
them. And one day he tore off, from a great boulder that is named Passelourdin,
a big rock, about twelve feet square, and of a thickness of fourteen yards, and he
put it on four piers in the middle of a field, where it was well situated; so that the
said students, when they were idle, could spend their time climbing on the said
stone, and there revel with wine, ham, and paté, and write their names on it with
a knife; and now, it is called the Raised Stone. In memory of this, no one today
can matriculate from the said university without having drunk from the Pegasian
fountain of Croustelles, gone by Passelourdin, and climbed on the Raised Stone.]
(186–87)

A voyage is rehearsed through its rebeginnings, but also by its propensity to
motivate a site through association with a myth. Names and descriptions of
events are attached to places for the purpose of making them recognizable
through the creation of mystery, that is, an element of invisibility that comes
when space and discourse are brought together, as is seen in the tale of
Pantagruel and the graffiti rock called Passelourdin. The mystification of a
place by means of a discourse inheres in the relation of anthroponyms and
toponyms to maps. A site acquires visual appeal because an event took place
at some time past and has since left a scar or trace that allows it to be seen.

Tourism

This chapter has the trappings of a secular hagiography, the story of a place
and a hero who is formed by it, except that the text seems to be seeking its
itinerary just as we, too, are looking for signs that will distinguish the text
from what, up to this point, it has been cribbing so abundantly from the
Chroniques gargantuines. The voyage that is virtually "jump-started" by
parataxis marks the beginning of a new cartographic style. The giant's adolescence is defined by places visited. His education consists in tourism, and a nascently military way of "seeing the world" ("voir et visiter le monde") prior to
committing himself to a site where the cosmos, like a book or a map, might

unfold before him. At the same time, the chapter plots a map of French university centers and thus becomes a scholarly chorography of Gallia perhaps as it was generally felt to be through the work of Ptolemy, perhaps as it was known through Bernardus Sylvanus's map in the great edition of the *Geographia* of 1511 (Figure 4.1). The chapter is also an early document of tourism, a "cultural production" that offers an idealized view of a regional and national space, a hypothetical melding of myth, place, and fact that legislates an imaginary consciousness of French soil and its urban centers.[10] The itinerary is predictable until, from the shores of the Rhône, Pantagruel "à trois pas et un saut vint à Angiers" (with a hop and a skip jumped to Angers) where, Alcofribas suggests, the stench idiomatically associated with the place name caused the hero to move to Bourges.[11] But a national space is depicted in a style that very much resembles the mix of myth and fact offered in contemporary *itineraria*, such as those of Jacques Signot (1515) and Charles Estienne (1558), in which the practical design—a paratactic list of towns, places, and rivers—is described by fables that historicize the place names listed, or at least give reasons to visit the areas. For example, in Symphorien Champier's *Cathalogue des villes et citez assises es troys Gaulles, avec ung trait des fleuves et fontaines, illustré de nouvelles figures* (Paris: Denys Janot, 1539), a miraculous fountain near Grenoble owes its virtues as much to the site as to the pun, the near-identity of "fertility" and "sterility," that eternalizes it: "Aussi on dit qu'après de Grenoble à la Sazonage . . . quand doit estre sterilité fertilité de biens, & famine, trois fines de pierre sont tousjours pleines: si c'est temps fertil, elles sont vuydes, & sans eau." [It is also said that near Grenoble in the Saxonage, during times of sterility and famine, three small transparent rocks are always full: in fertile times, they are empty, and lacking water] (fol. 125). The touristic appeal of the miraculous fountain is legendary, and is always noted in the second chapter of *Pantagruel* where, during a drought, "three fat drops of water" emerge from the ground as if, in response to the sky, "la terre suppléoit au defaut" [the earth made up for the lack]. The dynamics of forces that are placed in a relation of difference is due to the quasi identity in the graphic register of anagrams.

The Itinerary: Notable Places

In the guides and chronicles that Rabelais uses to display how the work is shifting from a fairly standard textual model to one under his own signature, several salient cartographic traits prevail. First, the manuals that were common to his age are rare today. *Itineraria* did not contain expensive map sheets. They were stuffed into pockets or purses and thumbed and tossed about the way

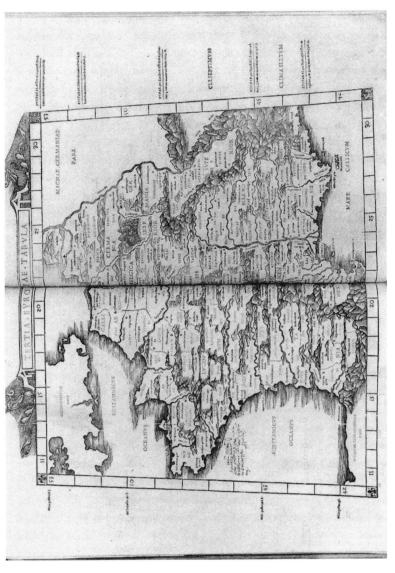

Figure 4.1. Map of Gallia in Bernardus Sylvanus's 1511 edition of Ptolemy, *Geographia*

road maps and tourist guides are today. Their function was evident in the reduced format of their editions; this reduced format also characterized *Pantagruel* and *Gargantua*. The articulation of imaginary space in these little books depends to a degree on the contrast between the format and the descriptions of great expanse contained within. The user supplied an imagination of distances in studying the toponyms and the points of interest listed or graphed in books that were no larger than four-by-three inches.

In the same way, *itineraria* constitute popular memory books that are not without resemblance to the Ciceronian pattern of organization, in which the rooms of a house or the points on a map are associated with components of discourse (Yates 1966). In the *itinerarium,* the place names that make up the nation offer a view of France as a restricted surface of memorable things and people and fabulous events. Frank Lestringant (1980c: 434) reminds us that Hondius, in his preface to Mercator's *Atlas universel* (1578–1595), whose map of France used Estienne's *Guide* (Bonnerot 1936: vol. 13), presents geography as "the artificial memory of history." He further notes that the compartmentalized and enumerative structure of the French guide manages, "in going from place-name to place-name while respecting a given order, [to create] *intervals of reading*" (435, emphasis added), in which excurses can be inserted, whether in popular etymology, historical points of interest, or analogies in the shape of witticisms that combine mnemonic art and popular etymology (*Poitiers* from *pois tiers; Bourgogne* from *bourg ongne,* etc.).[12] A discursive map emerges from the list of names that are presented as being of cardinal importance and annotated in blocks of discourse; these blocks of discourse attribute mythic status to what is given outside of the order of grammar. The mini-itinerary in the fifth chapter of *Pantagruel* is all that and more: There indeed we find a path that follows the French coastline to the west and south and east. We find an array of names and notable places and deeds, appended to the sites, that encode lore, autobiographical details from the author's own world (allusions to his course of study, and to colleagues and correspondents, such as André Tiraqueau), and elements of the novel that is being born (the first appearance of the Pantagruelic companion Epistémon, who will play a major role in the cosmography of the thirtieth chapter). We find a nascent tension between an enclosing design of *translatio studii*, a devout commitment to study, military duty, and the learning of geography. We find the shenanigans and trickery that foil the piety of lofty scholarly goals. Most of all, we find the furrows of a geographic novel of rural and urban tensions that leads to the later paradigm of French literature born of the middle classes (in Balzac and Flaubert), of a sentimental education that draws a gifted youth from the French countryside to the urbane and chaotic center.

Encounters of the First Kind

When Pantagruel meets the Limousin student on the road to Paris, the *itinerarium* ends and a new and more complex geographic novel begins. To see how, we can return to our point of departure: Pantagruel encounters this "escholier tout joliet" when—but we cannot be sure—he is en route to Paris and about to begin his studies. The end of the fourth chapter led us to believe that he is a pilgrim making progress, but the beginning of the sixth chapter relocates him in Orléans. The hesitations in the hero's adolescent behavior seem to be geographic markers of a sentimental itinerary. The new element being mobilized before our eyes, within the discourse of the novel, is a *dialogic map* in which the *escholier* resembles Panurge, introduced two chapters later, who will be Pantagruel's lifelong friend and alter ego. The Limousin, like John the Baptist, who was mercilessly martyred for his preachings, announces the coming of a more complex creation who will bear many of the same attributes. All of a sudden, the text affronts and represents its own heterology, its art of confronting the unknown. In the sixth and ninth chapters, two encounters are described; each is staged in a manner initially identical to the other:

> Quelque jour, je ne sçay quand, Pantagruel se pourmenoit après soupper avecques ses compaignons par la porte dont l'on va à Paris. Là rencontra un escholier tout jolliet qui venoit par icelluy chemin.

> [One day, I don't know when, Pantagruel was taking a walk after supper with his companions, by the portal through which leads the road to Paris. There he met a very handsome student who was coming along the same path.] (190)

> Un jour Pantagruel se pourmenant hors de la ville, vers l'abbaye sainct Antoine, devisant et philosophant avecques ses gens et aulcuns escholiers, rencontra un homme beau de stature et élégant en tous linéamens du corps, mais pityablement navré en divers lieux.

> [One day, Pantagruel, taking a walk outside of the city, toward Saint Anthony's Abbey, conversing and philosophizing with his friends and a few students, met a man of handsome stature and with an elegantly shaped body, but who was pitifully pocked in many places.] (207)

Each encounter takes place outside of the containing wall of the city, and each is announced, in a quasi-Proustian way, as a *singular* event that rises out of an unconscious passage of time.[13] Space is defined by a meeting with the unknown, which is defined through the presentation of an unintelligibility of language. The first, negative encounter with the Limousin appears to be the precondition for the positive encounter with Panurge. An archaic moment plots out a psychosocial space in the hero's shift from an initial *refusal* to entertain the other to a position in which he is more than ready to listen to or to mark an *acceptance* of the voice of the other. On each occasion, the protagonist is required to *invent the world before his eyes*, or to revive the experience of reiterated beginnings that define the problematic entry into symbolic forms or the passage from a state of closure to another of exchange.[14]

In the first episode, which is inspired by Tory, the Limousin's pig Latin bears meaning in the place names of the Parisian taverns that come into view, like islands, out of an ocean of verbiage. When the student responds to the question, "Dond viens-tu à ceste heure?" [Where are you from?], the toponym in the response, "les regions lemoviques," immediately recalls the spelling on Ptolemaic maps and allows the superposition of a projection and a narrative. "J'entens bien, dist Pantagruel; tu es Lymosin pour tout potaige" [I gather, said Pantagruel, that you're Limousin for all this soup] (193). The French national soup, which owes the origin of its own name, *potage*, to a French source (the national melting *pot*), serves as a popular map, against which one measure of transgression is deviation from national alimentary norms. The poor student, whom Pantagruel cuffs so hard that he soils his breeches (only to die, adds the faithful scribe Alcofribas, a few years later), is used to replicate Tory's program advocating a national space through a common use of French. The young Pantagruel is already a component of an ideology of space. It is summed up in the last words of the chapter, in an allusion to the sailor's *routier*, the book of the shoreline that is used for travel from port to port: "il faut eviter les mots espaves, en pareille diligence que les patrons de navires evient les rochiers de la mer" [flotsam words have to be avoided, with a diligence similar to the way ship captains avoid rocks in the sea] (193).[15]

That may be why the second episode inverts the spatial order of the first. When the Limousin was seen counterfeiting French, he was coming from the south central areas of the nation, while Panurge happens upon the Pantagruelists from the borders of Christendom.[16] His barrage of real and imaginary languages comprise verbal maps of countries surrounding France that recall the chorographic projections of contemporary editions of Ptolemy. What appears to be crucial for the genesis of the novel is above all that the meeting with alterity and history is increased thirteenfold, and that the definition of an *other* geographic space is conveyed in the discourse. Here, Panurge completes a European language map that is nonetheless gridded according to an axial plan. The center at which the chapter ends—the exchange of good French,

from the Touraine, where, according to myth, the language is best spoken—
is arrived at through the rearticulation of a recognizable Parisian dramatic
source, Pierre Pathelin's imitation of various French dialects that convince his
creditor of his insanity. In the difference between Pathelin's original and
Rabelais's new rendition, we witness, in contrast to the sixth chapter and to
the relevant sources in the fifteenth-century farce ("Il eut un oncle Lymosin, /
Qui fut frere de sa belle tante, / C'est ce qui le faict, je me vente / Gergonner
en Lymosinois." [He had an uncle who was Limousin, / Brother of his pretty
aunt, / That's what makes him rant / In Limogeois, a jargon of sin.] (II, v) the
borders of the known world and its idioms expanding as if on a curvilinear
surface. It works by way of paratactic installments of a panhandler's adjuration
in thirteen languages that eventually return to French. Flickers of meaning,
like the toponyms in the Limousin's speech, shine through the different idioms. Pantagruel addresses his interlocutor with a formal version of the same
query, "Dond venez vous?" elaborated with other questions that recall the biblical tale of the Samaritan: "Qui estes vous? Dont venez-vous? Où allez-vous?
Que quérez vous? Et quel est vostre nom?" [Who are you? Whence do you
come? Where are you going? What do you seek? And what is your name?]
(207), before the ensuing exchange recasts the phatic signs heard in chapter 5:
"adonc le compaignon respondit . . . Dont dist Panurge . . . Adonc dist
Panurge" [then the companion answered . . . then Panurge said . . . upon which
stated Panurge], suggesting that Panurge's "then" or "thus" (*dont*) is also, in the
paragrammar, the very *where* that Pantagruel uttered in the initial question.
These are stops that signal the sudden shift that moves us abruptly from one
language map to another and that sets in motion the representation of the rotundity of the world and its languages through expansion of a common gag or
mode of farce.[17] It might, as in the figure, be gridded by placing the two interlocutors at either end of a line through which, like a ray of light, languages are
prismatically refracted. The answers to Pantagruel's questions are developed in
a roundabout way that revolves around a given, almost mystical axis of understanding that is articulated only after the performance, not of interlocution
but of a literal act of *circumlocution*.[18] The enumeration does not quite follow
the order of Ptolemy's charts. If it seems to decline current and imaginary idioms on the European horizon, it also regresses to patois, to private or transitional languages that give perspective to Panurge's wit. No hierarchy is discernible; the utterances can be shuffled at will; yet a double axis is evident in
the listing of different variants on the same entreaty—hence, also evident is a
paradigm that constitutes an atlas of languages or a "language map" (Cave
1991, 1995) of the world in 1532–1533. A narrative vector, the metonymic axis

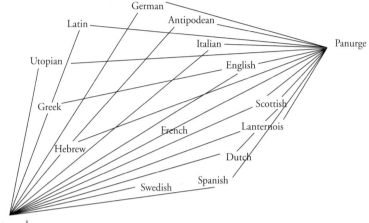

Pantagruel

that goes from a departure in French and back to its origin, also in French, is determined by the characters' (and readers') need to hear the languages of alterity. In an ethnographic perspective and in terms of heterology, the lesson that is gained, in contrast to the Limousin episode, entails *letting the other speak*. We see that Pantagruel allows a figure from the other world to talk because, in the distance covered between the sixth and ninth chapters, a geography of the world and of its alterities has been gained.[19]

Reprieve: Spaces to Listen

Thanks to parataxis and to spatial ordering of discourse, Rabelais appears to be inviting us to see why Pantagruel has become a prototypical ethnographer. In the space of time ("quelque espace de temps") elapsed between the two encounters, two vastly different chapters are intercalated to offer, as it were, geographic and rhetorical views of printed writing. The seventh chapter begins in the style of the itinerary recounted just before. A tourist, but not yet a committed French subject, Pantagruel "délibéra visiter la grande université de Paris" [considers visiting the great university of Paris] (194), where, after he decides to study the seven liberal arts, he happens upon the Saint Victor Library.

There follow columns listing a variety of concocted titles of Latin and vernacular books. Each entry is an explosive joke that satirizes almost every sector of learning and life in the 1530s. Some are directed toward a specific local end (*Decretum universitatis Parisiensis super gorgiasitate muliercularum ad placitum*), while others carry popular appeal (*Ars honeste petandi in societate, per M. Ortuinum*). Targets both high and low are the butts of the explosive pleasure of the enumeration (Bowen 1991: 169–70) and suggest a balanced range and equili-bration of wit (Demerson 1981: 77). A serial design prevails. The full list of 139 titles in the 1542 edition (expanded from 42 in the 1532 original) covers the whole gamut of knowledge, which is seen expanding in a geometric progres-sion at least as measured by holdings in libraries in the age of the manuscript (Zumthor 1987: 109–10). The chapter is a gazetteer of learned spaces, offering to the eye a stenographic view of real and imaginary realms of "knowledge." A cryptographic and tabular sensibility informs a will to spatialize intelligible things.

Furthermore, no teleological pattern emerges from the list when it is read according to the four cardinal directions. We cannot hypothesize that the first title, the anonymous *Bigua Salutis* [The perch of salvation] leads, like the alpha to the omega, to the last title, Merlinus Coccaius's *De patria diabolorum* [Of the country of devils]. Although the "list corresponds to a spatialization of meaning through language" (de Certeau 1987: 24), the explosion of discourse *into* space disseminates meaning along new trajectories. The page suddenly becomes a grid of relations that we, like spectators looking into a vitrine, dis-cover in following both what we see and what we hear in our fancy. In turn, the spatialization serves to show us how and why the list is being seen as it is. Viewers who allow themselves to watch how they scan the list let themselves, in the best tradition of medieval optics, see how they are moving about the paratactically ordered design.[20] We can see ourselves looking at the French ti-tles first, for they are more immediately recognizable for whoever digests Latin with difficulty; we can imagine a humanist or graduate of the Sorbonne look-ing at the list the other way round, valorizing the Latin at the expense of the vernacular; or we can even, for some of the greasier and macaronic entries, see ourselves moving indiscriminately from one linguistic boundary to another, as in *Du pois au lard, cum commento* [Of peas and bacon, topped with Latin sauce]. We might connect and disconnect titles among transversal or trans-columnar lines: "Du pois au lard" would be the weighty ammunition—with implicitly leaden "pois"—for the *Couillebarine des Preux,* the culverin that compares, in portmanteau designs, phallic cannons to their contiguous testi-cles. And so on: Meaning that is a crisscrossing or vectored sense of reading and seeing space is inaugurated when we allow ourselves to watch how we look at the tabular material beneath our eyes. Beyond the topical material of the chapter, the visual consciousness inspired in what it conveys as a new dy-namics of reading also brings a vital lesson in cartographic consciousness and in an implied science of heterology.

From an opposite approach, the next chapter imparts the same thing. Pantagruel receives an eloquent letter from Gargantua that lays out the curriculum that he is advised to follow. The title ensures that the letter is not only read, but that the scene of its transmission and transcription can also be imagined in a graphic way: "Comment Pantagruel estant a Paris, receut lettres de son père Gargantua, et la copie d'icelles" (How Pantagruel, living in Paris, received letters from his father Gargantua, and their copy). The "how" of the heading indicates that the hero receives the note as he was engaged in his studies, and that, like ourselves, he may hear, read, and see what was communicated, "comme assez entendez" [as you can hear or understand well enough] (202). A fantasy of a shrinkage of time and space is invoked through an allusion to the postal system that follows a nation of developing roads and reduced delays in the circulation of its decrees. A mix of modes of learning is implied. One, oral, involves dictation, while the other, visual and silent, entails the eye's aural faculties (and the inverse, the ear's propensity to see).

The style of the letter that follows "en la manière que s'ensuyt" [in the way that follows] (202) is anything but serial or paratactic. Written with Ciceronian eloquence, it contrasts the silence of the characters' and the readers' gaze cast upon the titles of the Saint Victor Library. Now we flow in the sway of rhetoric mediated by the letter, a printed form detached from but inserted into the body of the narrative, calling forth a totalizing image of a mirrored world (Brault 1966). All of a sudden, the broken, ruptured development of the preceding chapters—the *via rupta* of the hero's path to learning—takes on overwrought turns of phrase and gains Platonic sententiousness. The excess of space in the earlier chapter is now countered by a copious expression of received rhetoric. The paradox of its tone in the context of the seventh chapter suggests that an evangelical vision of the timeless world can come if the reader can allow its flash to occur. Within the labor of gloss or the patience of listening comes, suddenly and instantaneously, a ravishing accession to knowledge. The letters offer a microcosm of the world as it develops in time from one generation to another. When seen adjacent to the Saint Victor Library, the letter resembles what might be called a verbal *mappa mundi*.

Hence a geographic resonance: All knowledge that Pantagruel will gather through teaching and example, through the study of foreign languages (set in a prescribed order of Greek, Latin, Hebrew, Chaldaic, and Arabic) can be held in present memory, "à quoy te aidera la cosmographie de ceulx qui en ont escrit" [to which the cosmography of those who wrote of it will be helpful to you] (205). He is advised to learn the facts of nature by looking at the world from all cardinal points of view, by implied study of oceans, seas, and rivers ("qu'il n'y ait mer, rivière, ny fountaine, dont tu ne cognoisse les poissons" [so that there will be neither sea, river, nor fountain whose fishes will remain unknown to you]—a survey that recognizes all flora and chemical matter. The tone is borrowed from the Psalms, the source of evangelical writing that gives impetus to geography and to mapping in the years of humanism (Lecoq 1987; Dainville 1940; Skelton 1966a; Bagrow 1964). The world is seen, as in subsequent chapters, opening itself to the sight of individuals curious enough to look all over its surface.

The celebrated program of education is probably "new" only insofar as a cartographic sensibility informs the liberal arts. But the new speed of transmission that Gargantua perceives as an effect of print culture—"Je voy les brigans, les boureaulx, les avanturiers, les palefreniers de maintenant, plus doctes que les docteurs et prescheurs de mon temps" [I see brigands, hangmen, soldiers of fortune, stableboys of today more learned than the learned, the doctors and preachers of my time] (205)—is also shrinking the world, or making available reduced images of its totality. These are not specifically taken to be maps but are congealed in the "world-letters" that Tory had conceived, which Rabelais now seems to be citing by implicit allusion to the tables of alphabets in the appendixes of the *Champ fleury*, listed in the order that the typographer had assigned to their different degrees of virtue. "Maintenant toutes disciplines sont restituées, les langues instaurées: grecque, sans laquelle c'est honte qu'une personne se die sçavant, hébraïcque, caldaïcque, latine; les impressions tant élégantes et correctes en usance, qui ont esté inventées de mon eage par inspiration divine" [Now all disciplines are restored, and languages established: Greek, without which it would be shameful for anyone to be called learned; Hebrew, Chaldaic, Latin, the typographies in use, so elegant, that in my time have been invented by divine inspiration] (204). The world and the book are focused in the grid and form of the letter. The text suggests that a point of view is being gained on time and space at once, and that studious and virtuous souls can apprehend the world in a glance.

The globe thus becomes a perspectival object that serves as a function of space with respect to "la cognoissance des faictz de nature" [knowledge of the facts of nature] (205) and as a function of time with respect to the umbilical ties between Grandgousier, Gargantua, and Pantagruel. The content of the letter, when seen through the filter of the rhetoric that is tied to mapping, imparts a lesson of what might be called, if we keep heterology in mind, something like *ocular patience*: a measured, calm, receptive, but not aggressive view that looks to the world and time through the mystical glass of evangelism. It moves outward, it senses the infinite flux and flow of matter, and it allows itself to be illuminated by the myriad impressions offered by the sheer variety of things. In the narrative register of the letter, this is what, along with the spatial practices inspired by the Saint Victor Library, will soon allow the hero to listen to Panurge's volley of languages.

A City Named Parr rys

The opposition between the graphic and rhetorical styles in the seventh and eighth chapters generates much of the wit that follows in the rest of *Pantagruel* and in *Gargantua*.[21] The work now moves, not from point to point as in the *itinerarium* behind the fifth chapter, but by abrupt, sudden shifts, sallies, thrusts, and reversals. Yet a narrative geography emerges from an art of containment and spatial extension. Schematically, a diagram that generates the discourse might be drawn as a set of embedded oppositions (see p. 153).[22] Whereas meetings and engagements of characters are the topics in the sixth and ninth chapters, the seventh and eighth chapters are documents of silence, seen through the eyes of an intermediary who is the reader.

The narrative map of the first two books seems to develop from this overall process. A cartographic mode is born in the art of an episodic space and of dialogue. The specific language map and espousal of alterity of the ninth chapter throws the work out of the predictable line of development seen in the first five chapters.

The various foldings of global space elsewhere in *Pantagruel* have been studied at length (e.g., Auerbach 1956). Yet it must be emphasized that a thematic treatment of Rabelaisian plotting—where the characters go, how they travel, distortion of measured scales, the representation of national space (e.g., Lefranc 1905)—does injustice to the jostling effects of the letter, a spatial form, that continually erupts into the discourse. In fact, the work is reborn through the play of the letter that, both for Tory and Rabelais, might be termed a *cartogram* set within writing. Patient analysis shows that the spatial practices imagined in *Pantagruel* chapters vi-ix are varied or modified according to satirical or narrative contingency. To obtain a measure of the viability of the diagrammatic or spatial process of the discourse, we can turn to a moment in *Gargantua* that draws on the early pages of *Pantagruel* and that uses geography and letter to body forth new tensions.

The episode recounting Gargantua's theft of the bells of Notre Dame Cathedral recasts the spatio-hagiographic modes that motivated myth and place in chapter 5 and elsewhere.[23] An event in the comic novel strives to give aura to a place by attaching an originary fiction to the toponym. In the ideology of iconic forms that marks the reign of Francis I, the Song of Songs, the

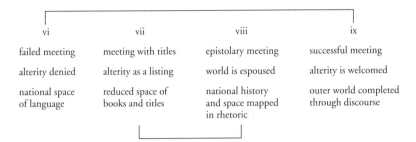

vi	vii	viii	ix
failed meeting	meeting with titles	epistolary meeting	successful meeting
alterity denied	alterity as a listing	world is espoused	alterity is welcomed
national space of language	reduced space of books and titles	national history and space mapped in rhetoric	outer world completed through discourse

Psalms, and the Letters to the Corinthians are integrated into the plastic and verbal arts. Goodness and kindness, gentility and generosity, faith and charity are elaborated in works that celebrate the king and his entourage. The glow of these texts serves as a lesson and council for the leader and his subjects, and it also projects over what is taken to be a unifying national space. Rabelais's and Tory's advocacy of "le langaige usité" seems to give reason to a broader design, as also do the fables binding mythic events to French place-names.

This is why the tale of Gargantua's theft of the bells from the Ile de la Cité exploits a spatial discourse to promote an evangelical lesson raising a "national" consciousness. After having crossed the Chartres plateau and having named Beauce for what he saw of a land razed by the switching of his horse's tail ("*Beau ce*," exclaims Gargantua, as every French citizen knows by heart), Gargantua "visits" Paris in the same touristic manner as had Pantagruel at the meeting with the Limousin:

Quelques jours après qu'ilz se feurent rafraichiz, il visita la ville, et fut veu de tout le monde en grande admiration, car le peuple de Paris est tant sot, tant badault, et tant inepte de nature, qu'un basteleur, un porteur de rogatons, un mulet avecques ses cymbales, un vielleuz au mylieu d'un carrefour, assemblera plus de gens que ne feroit un bon prescheur evangelique. Et tant molestement le poursuyvirent qu'il feut contrainct soy reposer suz les tours de l'eglise Nostre Dame. Auquel lieu estant, et voyant tant de gens à l'entour de soy, dist clerement: "Je croy que ces marroufles voulent que je leurs paye icy ma bien venue et mon *proficiat*. C'est raison. Je leur voys donner le vin, mais ce ne sera que par rys."

[A few days later, after they had rested, eaten, and drunk, he visited the city and was seen by all with great admiration. For the people of Paris are so sottish, so inane, and so naturally inept that a prankster, a bum, a mule with cymbals on its ears, or a hurdy-gurdy player will attract more people about them than a good evangelical preacher. And they hassled him so much in following him about that he could do no better than perch on the top of the towers of Notre Dame. Seated there, seeing so many people all around him, he uttered clearly: "I think these bullies want me to pay my entry and my *proficiat*. They're right. I'm going to give them some wine. But it'll be only *par rys*."] (53–54)

The joke expands on the touristic etymology playing on origin of Beauce, a place named by the closure of the space of a letter in *Beau* [ ] *ce*. Now the spatial conundrum inserts a narrative voiding into the same graphic void by splitting a letter (*r*) into two parts, and by implying the added presence of a bet (*pari*) that will be the stakes of a gargantuan micturition. The place-name becomes the site of its own vilification and new mythology.

The episode recalls the revenge that Panurge took upon the haughty lady who refused his amorous entreaties (II, xxii). Now, however, the name becomes the fulcrum and the pictogram of a narrative and of a fluvial comedy. A geography is set and then released in the site of the toponym (but not its referent) in order to exploit a narrative design that draws from the *itinerarium*. But it also reposes on the prismatic language map that Panurge had traced with the first speech he uttered to Pantagruel. When the victims of Gargantua's *pisserie,* "sweaty, coughing, spitting, out of breath," regain the hillock of the left bank, the text that records their epithets draws a map of popular dialects, patois, and names from the expanse of French territory and beyond:

> Commencèrent à renier et jurer, les ungs en cholère, les aultres par rys: les plagues Dieu! Je renye Dieu! Frandienne! Vez tu ben! La merde! Pro cab de bious! Das dich Gots leyden schend! Pote de Christo! Ventre sainct Quenet! Vertus guoy! Par sainct Fiacre de Brye! Sainct Treignant! Je foys veu à sainct Thibault! Pasques Dieu! Le bon jour Dieu! Le diable m'emport! Foy de gentilhomme! Par sainct Andouille! Par sainct Guodegrin qui feut martyrizé de pommes cuyttes! Par sainct Foutin l'apostre! Par sainct Vit! Par saincte Mamye, nous sommes baignés par rys! Dont fut depuis la ville nommée *Paris,* laquelle auparavant on appeloit *Leucèce,* comme dict Strabo, *lib.* iiij, c'est à dire, en grec, *Blanchette,* pour les blanches cuisses des dames dudict lieu. Et, par autant que à ceste nouvelle imposition du nom tous les assistans jurèrent chascun les saincts de sa paroisse, les Parisiens, qui sont faictz de toutes gens et toutes pièces, sont par nature et bons jureurs et bons juristes, et quelque peu oultrecuydéz, dont estime Joaninus de Barranco, *libro De copiositate reverentiarum,* que sont dictz *Parrhésiens* en grécisme, c'est-à-dire fiers en parler.

> [They began to renege and swear: God's scourge, I deny God, what da hell day-ouze want, y'all fuckallshit, ah forkass, Gotshimmelfarb, Christocuspidor, Oh-saintcuntn't, yervirtuesthere, my vows to Saint Thibault, the Lambs of God, howdydoodee if the devil and buffalo bill won't take me away, I swear on the Bible, oh saint Peckerhead who boiled in cooked apples, Oh Mayor Cock the Apostle, oh Saint dingleberry, oh sockcooking duckermother, we're all flooded in the pissyparis breeze! Henceforward was the city named Paris (that had formerly been named *Lucece,* acciding to Strabo, volume 4, that is, in Greek, a "little white one," for the white thighs of the ladies of the aforesaid site). And inasmuch as with this new imposition of the name all those present each swore by the saints of their Parish, the Parishians, who are made of all good people and things, are

naturally good epithetslingers, thus good jurists, a little overbearing, at least according to Joaninus de Barranco, in his *Copious Book of Expressions of Reverence*, who are said to be Parisians in the Greek idiom, that is, fierce in speech.] (54)

Each of the exclamations represents a region or a patois, all the while the sum of the episode is built over a project that nationalizes and evangelizes through toponymic wit determined by active speech—exclamation—in the place of place-names. It is also erected upon a plan that seeks to expand the imagination of national space through an encyclopedic register of language. Paris is a microcosm of an infinite variety of styles and articulations. The quasi-touristic model for the joke swings on a letter, a site, while an extraordinary deed appears to be endowing Paris with an aura of divine patrimony. The language map has become its own myth.

Words à la Carte

We have seen how Rabelais projects unilateral discourses into three dimensions. The enduring appeal of the text may be explained by its—and our—continuous reinvention of its world and space. The work is clearly held within an iconographic program of the time, but it exceeds its consciously ideological barriers by means of the new relations with the unknown. These are discovered in areas between language and space. One element of the cartographic writing that needs emphasis is its *mobile* mapping, or the construction of collages of mapping and discourse of a kind, perhaps, that our eyes might associate with cinematic experiments in montage or in computer graphics. The reader of *Gargantua* quickly discovers that the text encounters its own ploys of self-contained expansion, and that the ideal relation it proposes between the self and the world is located in the movement of the habitat—the textual volume itself—in which the imaginary characters acquire their identities. Beginning with the meeting of Panurge in *Pantagruel*, *Gargantua* proceeds to create the microcosm of Rabelais's birthplace, near Chinon, which is dotted with the names of Lerné, Chinon, Tours, Le Gué de Vede, and Thélème. As in the episode of the hero's inundation of Paris, to name a place is tantamount to discovering different fashions of surveying and, possibly, irrigating and arrogating it.

The autobiographical world is transformed into a cosmography. In the descriptions of the Picrocholine wars that make up a good part of *Gargantua*, European campaigns appear to be grandiose and epic, but also have the look of tempests in teapots. Great actions are produced in miniature, but with the effects that superimpose cosmographic and chorographic space comes a commentary on the relation of spatial expansion and nomination. When "Certains gouverneurs de Picrochole, par conseil précipité, le mirent au dernier péril" [Certain of Picrochole's generals, through precipitous counsel, put him at peril's end] (I, xxxiii), we see how the rhetorical mechanism of naming things means arrogating them. Rabelais impugns the rhetoric by distorting space through a verbal montage. The chapter begins when the warlord's advisers, Menuail, Spadassin, and Merdaille (that is, Duke Cheapskate, Count Assassin, and General Shitface), stage the beginning of an idiotic "Operation Desert Storm" that will lead their armies around the northern and southern parts of Europe and eastward to the Holy Land. Conferring together, the four men reproduce the cliché of "mapping and briefing." Each of their staccato volleys of place-names figures in an imaginary conquest of the world. Picrochole, listening to his counselors, mistakes words for real places. For Picrochole, "words become realities, transformed, bent away from their signifying possibilities: naming is tantamount to conquering" (Gray 1974: 99). The three noblemen name the world for the man who has no inkling of its extension. They set its notable regions in place, map out its perimeters, and flatter their leader by setting the sum under Picrochole's emblem.

The chapter is arguably as much a lesson in cartography as a rewriting of Lucian's *Dialogues of the Dead* among Scipio, Minos, Hannibal, and Alexander the Great.[24] Rabelais is said to invert a classical source (in which two dead heroes try to outdo each other's braggadocio), to turn it into a scene of comic ridicule, and to reshape the materials into a parable—the moral of the fable of the *pot-au-lait*—and an adventure of style. For M. A. Screech, the chapter represents a thorny but faithful rendering of French history. Rabelais projects current events of grand scale, negotiations between Francis I and Charles V, into the microcosm of the Touraine. "Ever since his release from captivity after the defeat of Pavia, Francis I's rivalry with Charles V took on a new dimension: Charles was convinced of French treachery; Francis was embittered by the crippling ransom imposed upon the kingdom and the obligation to send his two oldest children as hostages to the imperial court. The war in *Gargantua* contains overt allusions to these events and is partly conceived as propaganda" (Screech 1979: 65). An allegory results in which Picrochole, representing Charles V, is condemned for having ransomed Francis's children. The preparations laid for the conquest of the world narrated in the thirty-third chapter would thus superimpose Lucian's text on events taking place in 1534. "Mapping" contemporary time according to a classical paradigm, Rabelais would have Charles take Tunis from the hands of the Mulley Hassan and prepare to conquer Constantinople. The text alludes to Charles's emblem of the two columns bearing the device *plus oultre* through identity with Hercules's columns (that mark one stage of Picrochole's crusade from Chinon around western Europe and down to Africa before heading to the Holy Land). Thus, when he wants to conquer the world, Charles–Alexander the Great–Picrochole figures as an invincible monarch striking fear in the hearts of the French after the defeat at Pavia (1525) and the loss of Milan (1526). The allegory would prefer to invert the ill fortunes of France into an imaginary happy ending in which the good Gallic giants defeat the figure of pusillanimity.

The text begins from the dialogic matrix established in the meeting of Panurge. One voice listens—or punctuates—the discourse of the three others spoken in unison. With the same formula ("Je [dist Picrochole] . . . ," (which is marked ten times), Picrochole counterpoints the rhythm of the collective enumeration ("Nous [dirent-ilz] . . ." and its variants, which are printed eleven times) of place-names barked in staccato, mechanically, describing the first military movement (97–102). It moves forward in five textual blocks and resembles a chorographic rendering of "Gallia" that follows an itinerary leading first south to Spain and Portugal before crossing Gibraltar: "Vous passerez par l'estroict de Sibyle, et là érigerez deux colonnes plus magnificques que celles de Hercules à perpétuelle mémoire de vostre nom" [You will pass over the Sibylline Narrows, and there erect two columns more magnificent than those of Hercules for perpetual memory of your name] (98) (Figure 4.2). It then moves eastward, to western North Africa and Italy. They will proceed to the Mediterranean islands before reaching Asia Minor, crossing the Caspian Sea (la mer Hircane), Armenia, and arriving at the Euphrates. A second army will go north, through Gallia above the Loire, and move to Germany (including Lübeck), Scandinavia, Greenland, and the British Isles. It will proceed through Poland, the Baltic countries, Russia, and move southward through Hungary, Bulgaria, Turkey, and Constantinople. It will reach the Holy Land and there rejoin the other half of the Picrocholine expedition. The sum of the description makes up a world map of Europe, while each of the seven discursive units can be likened to conical projections in editions of Ptolemy's *Geographia* current since the 1480s.

Where *Pantagruel* and the early episodes of *Gargantua* fashioned a local space in the Touraine, this chapter superimposes various schemes of extension over the classical literary source. The projective route is broken by dialogic rhythms. Each paratactic unit conceivably recalls the disposition of names in space following the disposition of Ptolemy's atlas, as of 1490, that was apportioned into twenty-six regional projections following a world map. The text follows the movement (west to east) from Europe to the four sections of

Figure 4.2. Detail of Hercules' columns in the 1490 (Rome) edition of
Ptolemy, *Geographia*

Africa. (Figure 4.3).[25] Each discourse constitutes a chorographic "map" recalling the matrix and sequence of Ptolemy's atlas. The frieze of spatial verbal
units that results is animated through the literary interference of Lucian and
the tenor of the style being crafted.

    Coordination of the dialogue with the projections shows that the text is
mapping names in conjunction with Ptolemy, but that the names, because of
the analogical and verbal force invested in them, cannot themselves be fixed or
"inlaid" as they are in cartographic practices.[26] They figure among a mobile

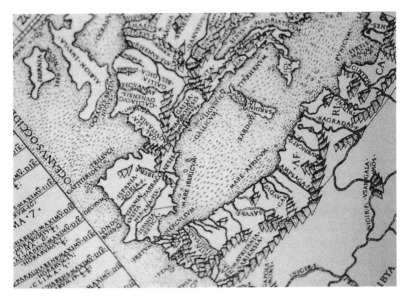

Figure 4.3. Detail of Africa from the 1490 (Rome) edition of Ptolemy, *Geographia*

network of divisible forms—letters—that scatter and mix across each dialogic unit in the chapter and through the entirety of *Gargantua* and *Pantagruel*. Nor does each reply-projection follow a law of center and periphery as a structuring agency common to maps and metaphors of the body and space (Edgerton 1987: 10–15). The names acquire a verbal life of their own by virtue of resemblances seen, as in other toponyms, in the letters and characters of other words. The place-names have an elasticity and contribute to the movement and measure of the volume by virtue of the montage that results from amphiboly and punning. They contain opposing forces in each other, and, by canceling each other's imaginary projection—like the greed of Spadassin, Merdaille, and Menuail—they work as a constructively organic process.

They offer a counterexample to the mechanistic style of those who utter them and hence bring the reader's eyes back from an abstract cosmographic scheme to a literal view of the words themselves (Demerson 1981). When the conference begins, they obsequiously announce, "Cyre, aujourd'hui nous vous rendons le plus heureux, plus chevalereux prince qui oncques feust depuis la mort de Alexandre Macedo" [Sire, today we shall make you happier than anyone since the death of Alexander the Great] (97). By marking the western or northern end of the chapter and recurring at the eastern or southern terminus, "Cyre" serves as an organizing vector, like a wind rose or a cardinal indication of latitude ("occidens" and "oriens"). *Cyre* is printed first as an oral sign that marks hierarchy, but it ends the chapter in an allusion to Cyrus the Great.[27] Its vocables literally generate variation through their presence in other toponyms. *Cyre* designates Picrochole in the fawning eyes of the three advisers, but it also bleeds into their mention of "Cypre" (99), "*C*élicie, L*y*die, Ph*r*ygie" (99), "Satal*ie*, Samaga*rie*" (99), "Siriace" (99), and "Surie" (101), all the more when the text generates spaces from the common noun by analogy: "Je vous donne," utters Picrochole about how he will award future spoils to his generals, "la Carmaigne, *Surie*, et toute Palestine. — Ha! (dirent-ilz) *Cyre*, c'est du bien de vous" [I give you Carmania, Syria, and all of Palestine. — Ha! Sire, that is generous of you] (101). Intentions and dreams are collapsed into the shape of the words. The place is verbalized as an outrageous desire to capture what is in the very form of the enunciation, that is, to encircle the very circle of the words, which are collapsed and self-canceling, as in the expression, "A Bayonne, à Saint-Jean-de-Luc et Fontarabie *sayzirez* toutes les naufz . . ." [At Bayonne, and Saint-Jean-de-Luz and Fontarabia you will take all the ships] (98), in which the *sire* is *seized* by the endless flow of language. The overweaning drive to reach the Holy Land or eastern region of the map is shown as a mirror image reproducing the *cirage* of the three sycophants' words. Two cardinal points form an axis from which other figures decline or arise. A schematic diagram of the chapter is similar to the diagram we saw earlier.

Cyre foretells the taking of the pot of gold that is Syria to the East, the endpoint long before it can be reached, but it also indicates where cartographic and common forms fold over each other. In their dreams, they have reached the Euphrates. But the leader remains a tourist rather than a commander: "—Voyrons-nous (dist Picrochole) Babylone et le Mont Sinay?" [Will we see, replied Picrochole, Babylon and Mount Sinai?] (99). *Sinay*, a crucial toponym in relief in maps of the Holy Land, can allude both to a variety of *itineraria* as well as to Picrochole himself, at once *niais* and childish, whose speech is *babil*. All of a sudden, the cartography elides qualities, characters, and places. On the one hand, an overriding allegory tends to control the direction that verbal recombination will take, since the staging promotes association of *babil* and *Babylone* and *niais* with *Sinay*. But on the other hand, the verbal process suggests that an unpredictable melding of space and language can take place when discourse and space are coextensive.

The model for these virtual recombinations extends and twists the borders of both the episode and the book. Two other words, *soubdain* and *transfrété*, follow a broader trajectory that replicates the same patterns of textual expansion through closed units beckoning or recalling new and other sites and problems. When Picrochole loses hold of his advisers' words, he drifts from the

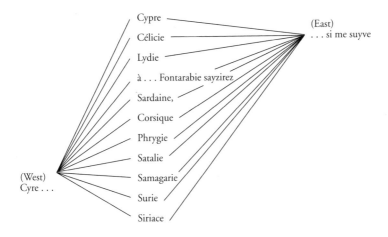

position of an active listener to a would-be tourist daydreaming about the aura of the place-names before him. He wonders if he will ever behold Babylon and Sinai. The generals bring him back to the business at hand: "—Il n'est (dirent-ilz) jà besoing pour ceste heure. N'est-ce pas assez tracassé dea avoir transfrété la mer Hircane, chevauché les deux Arménies et les troys Arabies?" [Now is not the time, they said, to think about that. Isn't it troublesome enough to have already crossed the Caspian Sea, ridden over the two Armenias and the three Arabias?] (99). The sites named are clearly based on Ptolemy's fourth and fifth projections of Asia, but their predicate, *transfrété*, takes up Rabelais's particular verbal cartography, recalling, in *Pantagruel*, the Limousin student's first words attempting to "map" the city of Paris through allusion to rectilinear city planning: "Nous transfretons la Sequane au diluscule et crépuscule; nous déambulons par les compites et quadrivies de l'urbe" [We cross the Sequana (Seine) at dawn and dusk; we amble through the streets and quarters of the city] (191). All of a sudden, in the words of Menuail, Spadassin, and Merdaille, space dilates through the force that vocables exercise on the space of memory obtained through our knowledge of the book-as-world. The initial meeting of Pantagruel and Panurge in chapter 9, we now recall, inaugurates the articulation of a global, curvilinear surface replacing the orthogonal plan of the giant's youth in the immediately preceding unit, which was analogous to the *itinerarium*. Remembrance of the spatial measure of France through *transfrété* serves to control the outrageous ambition of Picrochole's men.

Soubdain works analogously, but with different trappings. The adverb jumps off the page when it spins off the counselors' mention of Jerusalem, the Great Sultan of Egypt, and the Holy Land. As if they are looking at Oronce

Finé's map of the Holy Land drawn for the recent edition of Breidenbach's *Voyage à la terre sainte* (1517; see chapter 3), the advisers envisage the east under Picrochole's grasp: "Nous la tenons. Sainct Treignan, Dieu garde Hiérusalem, car le *Soubdan* n'est pas comparable à votre puissance!" [We have it now. Saint Treignan, may God keep Jerusalem, for the Sultan is not comparable to your power!] (99), but when he wishes to erect Solomon's temple on those lands, they retort, "—Non (dirent-ilz) encores, attendez un peu. Ne soyez jamais tant *soubdain* à vos entreprinses [No, they said, wait a little. Don't be so sudden in your undertakings] (99). The similarity of *Soubdan* to *soubdain* (both displaying mirrored letters in *b-d*) binds the movement of the discourse to a name marking a place. The sin of covetousness is parodied where we see mirages of things in words, but this word traces the crossing of textual and spatial vectors in both the episode and the book as a whole.

Soubdain-Soubdan becomes, in the combination that typography elicits, the very *festina lente* that the three generals incorrectly invoke to correct what they are projecting onto Picrochole. Elsewhere, *soubdain* generally marks a decisive shift in space, as in the beginning of the following chapter, where it spurs action: "En ceste mesme heure, Gargantua, qui estoyt yssu de Paris *soubdain* les lettres de son père leues" (102), announces retaliation where it coordinates the movement from one point to the next. A paratactic formula, it reflects the birth of the world of the book: "soubdain vindrent à tas sages femmes de tous coustés" [suddenly a pile of midwives sallied forth from every side] (22); "soubdain qu'il fut né" [suddenly as he was born] (23); and so on, indicating a shift from description to action. In the thirty-third chapter, *Soubdan* personifies the realm of the world beyond Christian—hence, for the ideology being advanced, rational—grounds of the world. Picrochole and his men always act suddenly, if not gratuitously, and always without heeding the emblem of the *festina lente* that goes with the king (Francis I's royal salamander that moves slowly but spits fire). Grandgousier wonders why Picrochole acts without temperance, which is the result of conflating speed and deliberation. "Adoncques . . . fut conclud qu'on envoirroit quelque homme prudent devers Picrochole sçavoir pourquoy ainsi *soubdainement* estoit party de son repous et envahy les terres ès quelles n'avoit droict quicquonques" [Then . . . it was concluded that they would send a prudent man to Picrochole in order to learn why he suddenly jumped out of himself and invaded the areas for which he had no right] (89). His action contrasts with that of Frère Jean. After having appealed to the nincompoop monks around him, unable to negotiate action, "Et *soubdain* . . . donnoit dronos" [he suddenly struck hard blows] (86). The word sums up the gratuitous cause of the dispute over locally baked pancakes (*fouaces*) in which, as in archaic scenes where different cultures encounter each other, the line between war and exchange is blurred with difficulty (Lévi-Strauss 1955: 346).

Quite possibly, when it dilates space through typographic means—as it does with these and other vocables—the text underscores the topos of a detail reflecting and reproducing a cosmos. Such *abîmes* are well known. But in the context of *Gargantua,* they indicate that mapmaking is limited by the absence of verbs, discourse, or fabulation. Maps lack the means to reproduce, impugn, or distort their form through iterative variation. Just as they cannot attain the illusion of extensive depth or perspective in their representation of masses of land and water, maps are unable to make space move. They lack interlocutors. To avoid becoming static accumulations of proper names, in order to be mobilized, they require animation from without. By animating spatial relations among its proper and common names, verbs, and adjectives, the margins of this chapter of *Gargantua* thus appear to show how maps produce ideology by an order that fixes words or human subjects to places.[28] The self-empowerment of the map that is achieved through the silence of its discourse is what the verbal labor of Gargantua calls into question. The text replots projected space through a montage that comes by way of inventive analogy.

Rabelais and the "Cordiform" Text

The chapter may also obtain a spherical contour by other means. If, in 1535, the text was disseminating evangelical materials[29] and allegorizing the wars of France and Spain, its display of new and extensive spaces can be linked with what humanists were drawing from the Psalms to encourage readers to find the presence of God in and through the expanse of nature. In that program, religious and cartographic missions coincide. Because the chapter bends up and around the northern coast of Europe as it also moves down and around southern Europe and over Africa, it implies how much its discourse wills to acquire the rotund shape of the globe. The reference to Greenland is significant. In standard versions of Ptolemy, Greenland is not included along the western periphery. Hibernia, England, and Scandinavia are at the edge of the extreme longitude that runs north and south from the Canary Islands. Why, if Ptolemy's conical projections seem to order the sequence of the counselors' units of speech, is an "absent" island included? Why do they advise Picrochole to lead his troops way off the mark, over "Lubek, Norwerge, Swedenrich, Dace, Gotthie, Engroneland, les Estrelins," all the way to "la mer Glaciale" (100), when they should merely skirt the northern shores before descending

Figure 4.4. Greenland, seen in 1513 hydrograph of Ptolemy

the plains to the east of Germany? Is the text making an ostentatious enumeration, telling the reader that it knows the names of the islands to the north and west? As we saw Gargantua writing to his son in *Pantagruel,* is it to insist that students of nature must be versed in hydrography no less than cartography?

If so, a common 1513 hydrograph of Ptolemy (Figure 4.4) answers part of the question. The text is arguably espousing not only Ptolemy but other projections, of more recent vintage and closer to home, associated with the humanist cause of experimental cartography and typography. Oronce Finé had recently drawn one of the more decisively spherical and organic world maps available. It figured in a project that set out simultaneously to represent and distort the globe through language and projection. In 1519 Finé, who would become the royal mathematician in the Collège de France, gave Francis I a cordiform projection of the world (see Figures 3.17 and 3.19).[30] Later, in 1531, he executed a double cordiform map that soon led to Mercator's projection of 1538.[31] Finé draws the meridian along the edge of the Canary Islands, down to Antarctica, and up through Greenland to the North Pole. In the double projection (Figure 3.21), Greenland radiates outward from the pole, whose meridian is now drawn from the eastern extremity of Madagascar down to Antarctica and up through the *Sinus Persicus* and the Caspian Sea.

In both maps, Greenland is located well beyond the European peninsula and is not, as it was in Ptolemy's earlier map, a Scandinavian peninsula, like modern Norway, extending from the upper reaches of the Asian continent. Its presence in the counselors' litany in *Gargantua* indicates that perhaps the Rabelaisian "vision" of the world moves with the innovations of Finé's stamp. Parallels can be established: Finé "signs" his work emblematically, with the escutcheon of dolphins adjacent to the fleur-de-lis, which marks his origin in Dauphiné, subtended by salamander-like dolphins spitting fire. The signature "Orontius F. Delph." in the cartouche of the 1531 projection sets the name on an axis, leading to his coat of arms, perpendicular to the meridian. Self and world are united and divided in a way that seems analogous to "Rabelais" and his anagrams melding into the toponyms of the Touraine, in which the author is in and of the world he plots in writing. Finé's cordiform projection retains a highly corporal, if not evangelical, relation to what it represents. The map is the world and the heart, the bodily center and totality, the pulse of creation, of a great body that is sensed to be beyond the mannered border to the left and right. The northern extremity curves inward and outward at once and appears virtually to generate the world's mass from its umbilicus. In terms that might be likened to botany, the North Pole is a point of embryonic growth, an apical meristem, that generates new surfaces but stands firm within its own point. Seen as a dynamic center, it works akin to the Rabelaisian letter that expands and extends in all cardinal directions all the while it is fixed in a grammatical montage.

It might be said that the overall plan of chapter 33 of *Gargantua*, when seen not from the points of view of the interlocutors or in relation to literary and historical sources, but in terms of the movement of style developing from montages of words and space, in fact generates a kind of "cordiform" text, a text whose mystical and rational orders extend and contain themselves, go beyond their means and yet hold to a bodily figure of mapping and writing, imply corporal orders within and without, and sustain a graphic means of binding the world, typography, and the body. These constitute miniature sums of both personal and collective signatures.

Seen from another angle, a comparison of chapter 33 and Finé's cordiform maps shows how an aura of humanism and Gallic evangelism is conveyed in a montage. It moves outward to *terrae incognitae* and to horizons that move from Greenland to the New World. Their mobilities also measure the globe in ways that, from the beginnings noted in the tradition of the *itinerarium,* disallow appropriation into centered units of "nation" or "self." The Rabelaisian text moves by means of its generosity: Its sense of being able to contain its own exuberance constitutes its lesson in view of the world that was being surveyed and conquered. To see how these same traits evolve, we must now turn to the relation that the novel will hold with the space of the *isolario.*

5

An Insular Moment:
From Cosmography to Ethnography

With the deaths of Rabelais (in 1553) and Oronce Finé (in 1555) also comes the end to an intellectual enterprise that explored the limits of language, space, the world, and the self for much of the first three decades of the Valois monarchy. When Finé was translating and downscaling his Latin editions of geometry and cosmography into French editions, Rabelais launched the fourth and (probably) last of his works, *Le quart livre des faicts et dicts héroïques du bon Pantagruel.* Three years earlier, at the moment when Finé was engineering a system of topographical mapping, Rabelais published the *Tiers livre,* a work, emerging after a gap of twelve years in the writer's career, announcing a design different from that of the first two books of *Pantagruel* and *Gargantua.* The earlier Rabelais, who fashioned himself as a prestidigitator, a *bonimonteur,* an alchemist, and a wordsmith in the person of Master Alcofribas Nasier, has now come to sign his works with authority and authenticity under a surname and professional title.

"M. François Rabelais, docteur en médicine" is placed below the title, conferring upon the writing an aura of truth. Readers are no longer transported to Dipsodia, or to an idealized representation of the French countryside, but they are now shown a sharply defined historical moment. We are told to respect the erudition and the learned substance of the dialogues that follow. Many readers in the industry of historical and critical investigation into the dramatic shift of focus and style ponder over what may have caused the work to change so radically. Why the sudden obsession with truth? What inspired the new turn toward irony and chiaroscuro? Why the presence of marine maps to navigate voyages about the shores of the river Loire around Tours and Chinon? What inspired the author to construct mysterious allegories that defy reduction to the characters, types, or forces that had been so evident in the propaganda of the 1530s?[1]

The parallels are even more obvious if one argues that Oronce Finé's last supplications to his ideal readers (Edward VI of England and Henry II of France) in the prefaces to different editions of *De mundi sphaera* displayed something of a cordiform humanism on the verge of thrombosis: A leading intellect and scholar of the preceding three decades, reduced to penury, begs for enough money to stave off his creditors. Times and attitudes have soured; enthusiasm and energy have withered under economic duress and divisions caused by reformed religious views. In their late phases, both authors' works display a tendency to abandon projects that would plot the perimeters of worlds without end. Now they pay increased attention to topographical views of contemporary space.

Prevailing signs in their creative work include involution, parcellation, increased atomization, and, above all, *insularity.* We witness Finé editing an astrological almanac and a treatise on the astrolabe; revising new editions of the works of Martin Borrhaus and Pieter Apian; and drafting a work entitled *De rebus mathematicis,* a guide to the planets, and a study of sundials. In short, he engages in limited projects that contribute to the comprehensive labors of the *Protomathesis* or the cordiform maps of the 1530s.

Rabelais's last two works also have an increasingly fragmentary aspect. The *Tiers livre* is constructed as a series of interviews between Panurge and representatives of most branches of knowledge, who inform the aging trickster of the fortunes and perils of marriage. Since the dilemma of the old rogue—now a coward and an object of ridicule—remains unsolved, the fourth book responds to the predictions made at the end of *Pantagruel* in order to continue the giants' quest for answers to the great enigmas of life.[2] They travel to foreign lands and plot an itinerary through imaginary spaces. A utopian and dystopian design accompanies the Pantagruelists' decision to take to the high seas.

So too, but now with new attention to detail, does a topographical plan and an appeal to a specific cartographic genre, prominent in the years 1528–1573: the island book, or *isolario.* Its presence in Rabelais has astounding effect and signals a vast change in the evolution of cartographic writing. When the *isolario* makes its way into midcentury literary creations, the cosmographic or universal view, shared by the analogical style and the world map, is attenuated.

In this chapter, I will argue that the impact of the *isolario* on cartographic writing precipitates a reshuffling of the taxonomies that order knowledge in the age of humanism. I will follow two different trajectories. First, in a brief treatment, Rabelais's relation to parataxis and the island book will be seen as a threshold to a new style of writing that moves between a diagrammatic impulse inherited from scientific procedure and sheer experiment with verbal space (Ong 1959; Fontaine 1984: 87ff.) The world in which symbols once prevailed now gives way to signs and diagrams that break away from the discourse that had been integral to them. Diagrammatic forms do not convey the analogies that once assured the presence of a divine plan; rather, they mark a far more perspectival view of a world that can be motivated as one chooses (Hallyn 1988; Knoespel 1987; Jacob 1992: 366). The perceiving subject whom we imagine living in the sixteenth century may sense that he or she has less and less reason for being alive, but nonetheless the individual has to invent some cause, a fiction, in order to maintain an illusion of continuity. As Lucien Febvre has shown (1968: 355–57, 384), increased emphasis is placed on doubt and skepticism in the form of reason. Emphasis on dialogue and on what marks the topographies of psychoanalysis (as outlined in the introduction) pertains to the historical parabola that I will trace in this chapter. From an inherited concept of a world mirror, we move to another, of subjective "singularities," that are fathomed in part by every individual's experience of the world. In the singularization of experience that affects cartographic writing, we discern the beginnings of ethnography, which in the 1550s seem to be the immediate effects of cosmography. The way that cosmography *fails* to explain the world gives rise to a productive fragmentation that momentarily allows various shapes of difference to be registered without yet being appropriated or allegorized. In other words, the waning of the symbolic efficacy of the earlier works of Finé and Rabelais signals a shift in practices of space and language.

Second, the displacement of the self that results from an increasing awareness of its entirely arbitrary presence in the world is evinced where authors depict carefully *spatialized* treatments of their own personas within their creations. The displacement is probed in the Rabelaisian voyages, but it is saliently drawn in the writing and cartography of André Thevet. In order to see how an insular and ethnographic moment of French writing takes place in the aftermath of Rabelais and the *isolario*, we can turn briefly to the *Tiers livre* before engaging the style of Thevet, the cosmographer of the generation that followed Oronce Finé's.

A Topography of the Face

In the twenty-eighth chapter of the *Tiers livre*, Frère Jean and Panurge return from a failed conference—one of many botched exchanges—with Herr Trippa (possibly Cornelius Agrippa, author of *De incertitudine et vanitate scientiarum*, 1530). They have come from the Bouchart Island where Trippa, a sort of mechanical monster, has just looked at the lines of Panurge's face and hands. After declining every available art of prediction, he deduces that "coqu sera" [he will be cuckolded]. Like the Sibyl of Panzoust, Raminagrobis, and others, the mad scientist is isolated in a world of his own. But the attention he brings to the details of Panurge's body signals the coming of an extended metaphor that compares the face of the aging hooligan to the portrait of the gentleman in Pieter Apian's famous emblem illustrating the first sentences of Ptolemy's *Geographia* (Figure 5.1):

> Geography is a representation in picture of the whole known world together with the phenomena which are contained therein. It differs from Chorography in that Chorography, selecting certain places from the whole, treats more fully the particulars of each by themselves—even dealing with the smallest conceivable localities, such as harbors, farms, villages, river courses, and such like. . . . The end of Chorography is to deal separately with a part of the whole, as if one were to paint only the eye or the ear by itself." (Ptolemy 1991: 25)

As the companions walk back to their point of departure, they speak about their recent encounter. The exchange of discourse moves over a space being traversed in a way that marks the displacement in discursive terms. Frère Jean comforts Panurge over his doubts about wearing horns on his head:

> Je t'entends (dist frère Jan), mais le temps matte toutes choses: il n'est le marbre ne le porphyre qui n'ayt sa vieillesse et décadence. Si tu ne en es là pour ceste heure, peu d'années après subséquentes je te oiray confessant que les couilles pendent à plusieurs par faulte de gibessière. Desjà voy-je ton poil grisonner en teste. Ta barbe par les distinctions du gris, du blanc, du tanné et du noir, me semble une mappemonde. Reguarde icy: voylà Asie; icy sont Tigris et Euphrates. Voylà Afrique; icy est la montaigne de la Lune. Voidz-tu les paluz du Nil? Deçà est Europe. Voydz-tu Thélème? Ce touppet icy tout blanc sont les mons Hyperborées. Par ma soif, mon amy, quand les neiges sont ès montaignes, je diz la teste et le menton, il n'y a pas grand chaleur par les vallées de la braguette!

> [I sympathize with you, said Frère Jean, but time kills all things. Neither marble nor porphyry escapes old age and decadence. If you're not with it for now, in a few years I'll hear you avowing that your balls flop all over because you didn't wear a gamebag. I already see your hair beginning to grey. Your beard, by the lines of grey, white, tan, and black, look to me like a world map. Look over here! There's Asia; here are the Tigris and Euphrates. There's Africa; here's the Moun-

*montaignes, fleuues, riuieres, mers, & autres chofes plus renommées, fans
auoir regard aux cercles celeftes de la Sphere. Et eft grandement prouffi-
table d'ceulx qui defirent parfaictement fçauoir les hiftoires & geftes des
Princes ou autres fables: car la painéture ou limitation de painéture facilement maine a memoire l'ordre & fituation des places & lieux, & par
ainfi la confummation & fin de la Geographie eft côftituée au regard de
toute la rondeur de la terre, a l'exemple de ceulx qui veulent entierement
paindre la tefte d'une perfonne auec fes proportions.*

La Geographie.   La fimilitude d'icelle.

ꝼ a Chorographie de la particuliere defcription d'vn lieu.

CHorographie (comme dićt Vernere) eft aufſi appellée Topographie,
elle confidere feulement aucuns lieux ou places particulieres en foy-
mefmes, fans auoir entre eulx quelque comparaifon ou femblance a l'en-
uironnement de la terre. Car elle demonftre toutes les chofes, & a peu pres
les moindres en iceulx lieux contenues, comme font villes, portz de mer,
peuples, pays, cours des riuieres, & plufieurs autres chofes, comme edifices,
maifons, tours, & autres chofes femblables, Et la fin d'icelle s'accomplit
en faifant la fimilitude d'aucuns lieux particuliers, comme fi vn painéfre
vouloit contrefaire, vn feul oeil, ou vne oreille.

La Chorographie.   La Similitude d'icelle.

A iiij

Figure 5.1. Illustration of initial figure of Ptolemy, *Geographia,* in Pieter Apian, *Cosmographie* of 1551 (Paris)

tains of the Moon. Do you see the marshes of the Nile? Europe is down there. Do
you see Theleme? This white tuft of hair is the Hyperborean mountain range. My
thirst tells me, my good friend, when the snows are in the mountains—I mean
the head and the chin—there's little left down there in the Valleys of the Balls!]
(428–29)

Panurge, of course, inverts the standard comparison, by retorting with a popular proverb that compares virility in old age to leeks ("though my pate is whit-
ened sheen, my stalk is forever green"), expressly omitting that in the source of
Frère Jean's description there remains an equivalence between the world and
the human face, an equivalence in which the face as a divine totality stands in
contrast to the detail that Ptolemy compares to a city-view. Frère Jean baits his
interlocutor merely by pursuing the logical consequence of the metaphor, an
ekphrastic description of a *mappa mundi*, but in doing so he shifts the reader's
perspective from a cosmographic perspective to a topographical perspective.[3]
A sum of the world is seen in chorographical details, which include the great
rivers and place-names of the Holy Land, and the nether region of the trickster's body. He perversely folds into his comparison the design of interpretation that Herr Trippa had first engaged in the exchange three chapters earlier.

Between one episode and the next is implied a change in focus, from whole
to detail, that carries with it a sign of the senescence of the world and the
author. In contrast to the generative, "cordiform" world picture seen in the
Chinonais of *Gargantua,* we are now obliged to envision implied, not real,
worlds from details, isolated units, or fragments detached from localities. The
cosmographic vision is giving way to an appreciation of knowledge and environment as a finite but indeterminable sum of insularities and disquieting
inversions: Asia is here, the Tigris there; Europe over here, Theleme there. The
toponyms, disconnected points or signs without analogical cohesion, are marshaled to compare white hair with sterility and senility. The very place-names
that echo from the Picrocholine briefing in *Gargantua,* thirty-third chapter,
now bring forth the signs of age that could not be seen in them before: The
Tigris redounds as a body part that is a "little gray." "*Là Asie*" signals an island
in anagram. The spleen of life, *la rate,* emerges from "Euphrates." As the description descends into the marshes that are the "cradle" of Western civiliza-
tion, "*les paluz du Nil,*" the river that runs through it is all that is *nihil.* Frère
Jean's "reading" of his companion's face crystallizes the relations of insularity
and irony that begin to further distance language from a desire to motivate the
space, figural designs, and shape of words used to name, in their own form,
multifarious resemblances of what is found in the world.

The map of Panurge's physiognomy is anchored between two paratactic lists that describe the attributes of the antagonist's testicles. As miniature globes—distant memories of the *couillebarines* in the Saint Victor Library— the body parts are the subject of a panegyric scatter, a diagrammatic treatment of the positive and negative traits of dessicated seminal glands. A paradoxical, antithetical treatment of adjectives, the listing appears as if it were preparatory notes for a blazon of the male body or a gazetteer to the map of Panurge's immortal parts, which stand in immediate contrast to the emblem of his face as an old, now useless *mappa mundi* of Ptolemaic origin.

It seems hardly by chance, in this diagrammatic moment of the *Tiers livre,* that the companion's discourse apposes the silence of agrammatical listings to the noise of dialogue. The narrative design of the episode in fact arches back to *Les cent nouvelles nouvelles.* The chapter self-consciously maps out the distance it takes from a folkloric, prehistoric, or merely prototypically gridded universe of language. Following his enumeration of 140 types of tired testicles, Frère Jean tells the tale of Hans Carvel, "lapidaire du Roy de Melinde," the celebrated jeweler who made a ring for Gargantua's wardrobe (30). Carvel never risked being cuckolded as long as he wore a certain ring (that is, in the dream being told, as long as he kept his auricular finger in his wife's vagina). The text explicitly recalls the eleventh tale of the Burgundian collection in order to turn a niggardly protagonist into a joyous one (Carvel was an "homme docte, expert, studieux, homme de bien, de bon sens, de bon jugement, débonaire, charitable, aulmosnier, philosophe, joyeux au reste, bon compagnon et raillart si oncques en feut" [a man of knowledge, expert, studious, a good man, of reason, good judgment, handsome, generous, a philosopher: furthermore, joyous, a great companion, as great a joker as there ever was] [432]). The rewriting also turns the grieved spouse of *Les cent nouvelles nouvelles* into a woman of wit, force, erotic drive, and of healthy feminism: She tells him to take his finger out and insert what really belongs in its rightful place. The narrator sums up the tale, noting, "icy feut fin et du propous et du chemin" [here was the end both of the dialogue and the road covered] (433). In the interstices between discourse and map, in the collage of the "negative" origin in *Les cent nouvelles nouvelles* and the "positive" reworking of the Carvel anecdote, we witness a diagrammatic or dialogic history of the ages being told to readers who know their literary folklore. But on another level, the paraph that ends the chapter snuffs out the continuity of an analogical space that might have belonged to the earlier tale. At the end of the road, a cartographic silence intervenes. The narrator's parting remark invokes—but also refuses to be associated with—the inner limit of Hans Carvel's wife's paradise, the *propous,* a word that formerly invoked verbal and corporal propulsion but that is now arrested at the end of the chapter.

The episode that follows begins as another island of dialogue. The characters tell the Pantagruel what had happened in the course of their brief travels. The insular qualities acquire stronger relief in the course of the narration. By now, the reader will have realized that the second attribute of Rabelais's name and qualities on the title page have much to do with the book as an *isolario* of words:

> Le tiers livre
> des faicts et dicts héroïques
> du bon Pantagruel
> composé
> par M. François Rabelais
> Docteur en medecine et calloier des isles hieres

"Calloier des isles hieres" refers specifically to Hiere Islands in Benedetto Bordone's *Libro. . . di tutte l'isole del mondo* (1528 and many subsequent editions). Bordone's book "foreshadowed the world atlases of the sixteenth century" (Skelton 1966a: v) by resembling both a traveler's guide and a summary of the world's islands. One, found in the Grecian archipelago, Hiere Island, soars vertically out of the Aegean Sea. On its crags, a forlorn monastic order has built a monastery accessible from the waters below only by a huge balance and pulley set on a fulcrum placed on a cliff above. The island is first shown in Bartolommeo dalli Sonetti's *Isolario* of 1484 (Figure 5.2), a principal source for Bordone's arrestingly illustrated—and uniquely detailed—image of the same site (Figure 5.3), drawn with such care, perhaps, because it was widely reputed for the singular qualities of its inhabitants, who were said to be aged but who also gave refuge to bellicose pirates.[4] Rabelais's title page cannot fail to refer to a woodcut from Bordone's composite work of maps and texts, a work that is the first of its kind in the sixteenth century to balance printed and illustrated material. The reader who scans the *isolario* is left with the effect of an ocean of writing that flows among islands of illustrations that seem to float on a calm verbal mass. Like flags, or like partial areas of firm ground where readers can regain their bearings, the illustrations queue memory images of strange places, oddities, and many foibles that make up the fragmentary infinity of the human condition.

From the outset, Rabelais casts his later creations into the form of episodic "islands" of discourse where there no longer reigns any necessary connection—no superseding allegory (Jeanneret 1982) that would tie the narrative to

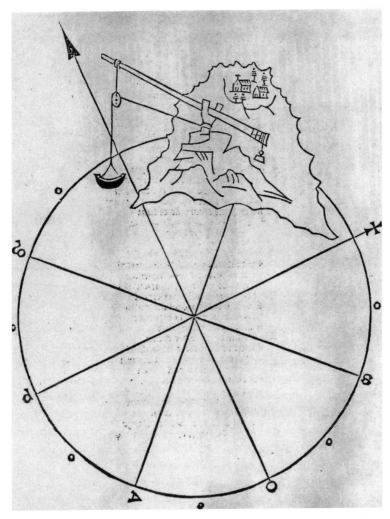

Figure 5.2. Woodcut of Hiere Island in Bartolommeo dalli Sonetti, *Isolario* (1484)

a totalizing moral design. The one (the discourse) floats in the other (the image), and vice versa, casting thus an aura of ambivalence all over the representation of the world and its islands. A floating, mobile creation results, in which, faithful to the Macrobian *mappa mundi* of the incunabular period (1485, Figure 5.4), landmasses are seen in the context of a thermodynamic system of energies transferred and circulated among torrid, temperate, and frigid zones.[5]

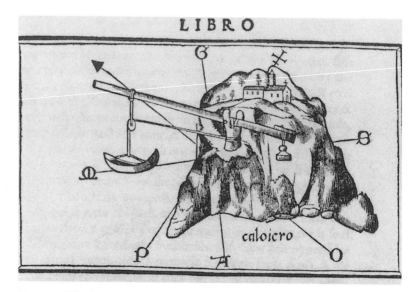

Figure 5.3. Woodcut of Hiere Island in Benedetto Bordone, *Isolario* (1528)

The *isolario* becomes a fitting ground for the caustic ironies and undecidable utterances that prevail in the last two books. As Panurge becomes increasingly infantile and cowardly, Pantagruel grows grandiloquent, stuffy, and sanctimonious. The surrounding characters resound like mouthpieces without bodies animating them. The Pantagruelists wander about the singularities of the world, and, overwhelmed by the variety of eccentricities and monstrosities before them, they become rubbernecking tourists who find not only that they have little reason for being where they are, but that they can also claim no origin to which they might return or use to identify a heritage.

The neutralizing tenor of the style, composition, and substance of the *isolario* is an important vehicle for the general disembodiment and effect of disaggregation that accrues in the material published after 1546. The deracination that comes through affiliation with this type of atlas may signal a second and powerfully ethnographic moment in the Rabelaisian enterprise. The first, as we saw in chapter 4, was held in the meeting of Pantagruel and Panurge; now it comes with a self-decentering gained by affiliation with the island book. What had intervened between the episodes, in the psychogenesis and "institution" of the benevolent giants—as well as of their faithful historian and scribe, Master Alcofribas—is scattered and pulverized. The reassuring center to which the personages return in the first two books, an umbilical area of family and nation, or even the "mother earth" of the French soil of the Touraine, no

L. .II.

breuitate cōtrah iſ. Deductio aūt latez lōgiıudie tropici ab utraq; pte
diſtēdıſ. Deniq; ueteres oēm habitabilē nɾam extētæ clamidi ſimilē eē
dixerūt. Ité qɜ oĩs terra in qua & occeanus ē: ad quéuis cæleſté circulū
quaſi cétron pūcti obtiet locū: neceſſario de occeano adiecit: Qui tñ tā
to noie q̄ ſit paruus uides. Nā licet apud nos athlāticū mare licet ma⁄
gnū uoceſ: de cælo tñ diſpiciétibus non pōt magnū uideri: cū ad cælū
terra ſignum ſit & pūctū: quod diuidi non poſſit in ptes. Ideo auté
terræ breuitas tam diligenter aſſerit: ut parui pédédū ambitū famæ

Figure 5.4. World map in Ambrosius Macrobius, *In somnium scipionis* (1485)

longer holds. A distance is gained; the view shifts from one of the microcosmic
self as the mirror of the macrocosmic world to one in which both the reader
and the characters discover that every figure counts as an insular entity among
thousands of others. Even the solid grounding of the islands on which events

take place are entirely fantastic projections of imaginary "meetings" with fic-
tive strangers. One critic calls the motif of island-hopping a voyage among
"îles mentales" (Glauser 1966), mental islands of obsessions, neuroses, or oddities, or material rich in fantasy for virtual case histories. The subjects who are
taken up in the third and fourth books owe their pertinent traits to detachment from identifying traits of language, nation, and origin. The perspectival
distance that goes with self-detachment becomes, thanks to the ethnographic
matrix offered by the island-book format, a space for an anthropology.

The *Isolario* and Cosmography

Along with Oronce Finé, André Thevet stood as the most visible cartographer-
cosmographer of sixteenth-century France. A resonant voice throughout most
of the century, born in Angoulême in 1516–1517, Thevet prided himself in the
position he held as royal cosmographer under three kings until his death in
Paris in 1592.[6] His writings, known to be overblown and excessively and obsessively mendacious, nonethelesss constitute the most complete sum of cartographic writing in Renaissance France. They retain a cosmographic vision
within the form of the *isolario* and accede, like the later work of Rabelais, to a
heightened, even acute ethnographic sensibility. Readers of his *Les singularitez
de la France antarctique* (1557) can see notable affinities with the ungrounded,
paratactic, or ambiguous discourse of the *Tiers livre* and *Quart livre*. Thevet
seems to extend the latent ethnographic dimension of the Rabelaisian relation
to the unknown into a world where fantasy and reality cannot be easily separated.

Recalling the principles adumbrated in the Introduction, we might say that
the backdrop of the *isolario* provides a *means to regain the "regressive moment"*
in the pictogrammatic dimension of cartographic writing, where reality and
fantasy are tested together, and where the subject continually invents his or
her relation to the unknown. Thevet's production of textual island books and
composite creations of images and prose confirms that singularization goes
hand in hand with heterology. But then, where and how do Rabelais and Thevet
happen upon an ethnographic view by means of the *isolario*? It may be that for
them and other readers of Bordone, imaginary travel to unknown lands and
beings comes by way of the production of "firsthand" evidence seen through
second- and third-hand sources. The fabled meeting with the non-European
"other" takes place *thanks to* the format offered by Bordone. His *Libro . . . de
tutte l'isole del mondo* has a firsthand "look" in its combination of rhumb lines
and wind roses inspired by portolano charts of the fifteenth century, but it also

has the feel of a "virtual" cartography of the type that Ptolemaic humanists had cultivated in academic centers. Bordone's creation taps into a medieval tradition that seems to inspire fantasies of originary travel.

The earliest extant manuscript of an island book, Cristoforo Buondelmonti's *Liber insularum arcipelagi* (1420), comprises an illustrated text of the Cyclades and surrounding islands, including accounts of their history from ancient to modern times. "A disorderly mixture of fact, fiction, and fantasy, compiled from personal observation, hearsay, and a variety of historical and poetic sources whose authors are frequently named" (Harvey 1987: 482), Buondelmonti becomes an early paradigm for the genre. The text represents the author striving to please his patrons with descriptions of the marvels of history and nature along with accounts of his own hardships at sea. P. D. A. Harvey reports that, in the Renaissance, new materials were added to the form, but "this was little more than an accretion" (482) about the medieval core. The geographic material is taken from Strabo and Ptolemy, who had each divided their topic into treatments of continents and islands. The latter are often a color different from the color of the former. In earlier maps that inspire the illustrations, such as in the Saint-Sever Apocalypse (eleventh century), green hues representing landmasses almost bleed into the bluish sea and its fish.[7] The end of the *isolarii*, which comes with Vicenzo Coronelli's *Isolario dell'Atlante Veneto* (two volumes, Venice, 1696) tells much about their beginnings.

With Bordone, however, the genre is as much a textual and literary creation as a stage in the development of the atlas or atlas concept.[8] Equal importance is ascribed to text and illustration. A sensible balance of verbal and visual material dictates the form of the book, each element intended to complement the other. The map offers a *spatial* order of figures that suspends the discursive itinerary. Comprehensive and encyclopedic, the *mappa mundi* and 108 smaller maps cannot disclose information without including substantial legends. The layout of language and image implies that the one may be unlike but is also a necessary part of the other; that, too, each can be figured as what defines its surrounding border or what it encompasses; that heterogeneity is the basis of the genre; that a system of alterity is literally "written" or "mapped" into the relation between the island and the sea, between the illustration and the text.

Its printed area holds or "incorporates" the illustrations in the flowing body of writing, yet the discursive material can only be navigated with the aid of plot points or "image roses" seen in the adjacent maps. Serving to produce totality and a mirror of matter familiar and bizarre, or an archipelago of things, places, and oddities, the *isolario* heralds a diagrammatic arrangement of knowledge. A sense of something "other" is held in its logic and execution

La gran citta di Temistitan.

TERRA di sancta Croce ouer mondo nouo,fu la prima di tutte queste isole, che trouata fusse,& benche alcuni hebbeno ferma openione,che al nostro cōti-nete cōgiunta fusse,nōdimeno al presente possono esser certi,esser gradissima iso la,percio,che da uno capitano del re de spagna,una & laltra parte e stata uedu-ta,cio e la costa,che uerso tramotana e posta,& laltra, che allostro giace, alla qle per giorni sei passando mōti,ualle,& fiumi cō lo esercito suo puenne,Hor dūque noi sciamo certi esser isola & nō col nostro cōtinente contenuta,& il principio suo hauere uerso l'oriēte,laquale ha forma di angulo,& uerso ostro &garbino in chlina,& laltra parte,che al settetrione siede,uerso ponente si stēde miglia tre mi la,& doppo uerso tramotana piega,& cō terra del laboratore(sopradetta)fanno

Figure 5.5. Woodcut of Temistitan (Mexico City) in Benedetto Bordone, *Isolario* (1528)

and reveals its latent attraction to ethnography.[9] The *isolario* makes a "famil-iar" alterity the effect of its appeal; in other words, the format becomes that which conditions a reader's invention of the experience of discovery. The para-digm of the genre fashions a shape and range of life before the hypothetical traveler ever lives through it.

The paradox of a familiar alterity is salient in Bordone's city-view of Temistitan (Mexico City) (Figure 5.5). Bordone attests to the novelty of his version of the genre, to the actuality of its contents, and, especially, to the allure of its timelessness. The system of the allegorical landscape inherited from late-medieval traditions applies to the juxtaposed views of Venice at the beginning of the volume and of Temistitan near the end. Presumably based on a figural view of reality, the composition suggests that views of landmasses in the New World are in accord with models that make the "old" versions of representation a necessary part of a "new" variant. Diacritical comparison of the former to the latter provides a model for what can be assimilated in the Venetian terms of the world-archipelago. The earlier one is not abandoned in order to give way to a more authentic truth or to affirm an ideology of progress, but to show that permanence is inscribed into repetition and variation of history. Temistitan complements Venice in order to offer a sense of closure to the infinity of islands on the globe.

The city-view of Temistitan is copied from the famous Cortez map (Nuremberg, 1524) (Figure 5.6), taken from a Meso-American original. The figural context of the *isolario* makes Mexico City a complement to Venice: The square center of the plan is surrounded by agglomerations of houses whose bases move around the map. The viewer can circulate around the view in the directions indicated by the dark figures paddling canoes on Lake Texcoco, which surrounds the center. At the axis is the sacrificial temple of Teocalli. Bordone's copy, entitled "La gran citta di Temistitan," reverses the plan, sets the perspective straight so as to simultaneously provide both an ichnographic and a scenographic view, excludes the adjacent representation of the coastline of the Gulf of Mexico (from the Yucatan to Florida), and encloses the ensemble in a surrounding landmass that also mediates the circular plan and the square surround. The map is adjusted to appear as an element in a book. Letterpress place-names and descriptive legends are included. Most important, the city is depicted as an island in which the usual centering device of the wind rose and compass, if applied to the city-view, would cross at the navel of the miniature "man in a square." Converging lines lead to an integral and triumphant human figure at the center.

Bordone does more than alter the copy of the Mexican original by an appeal to Albertian perspective: He removes both the textual legend that denotes the place of the sacrificial altar and the adjacent ideogrammatic material. Detail is cleared away in order to balance the torso in the space of the square. He reattaches the head, seen between the twin towers of the pyramid in the original, to the torso of the ritual victim. Thus "recapitulating" the central area of the Cortez map (Figure 5.7), Bordone removes the narrative of excess from its axis. The Cortez map placed a religious foundation of violence at the topographical center of Aztec society; Bordone does not. Ostensive confusion of Christian and Aztec religious customs, a detail that would endow the map

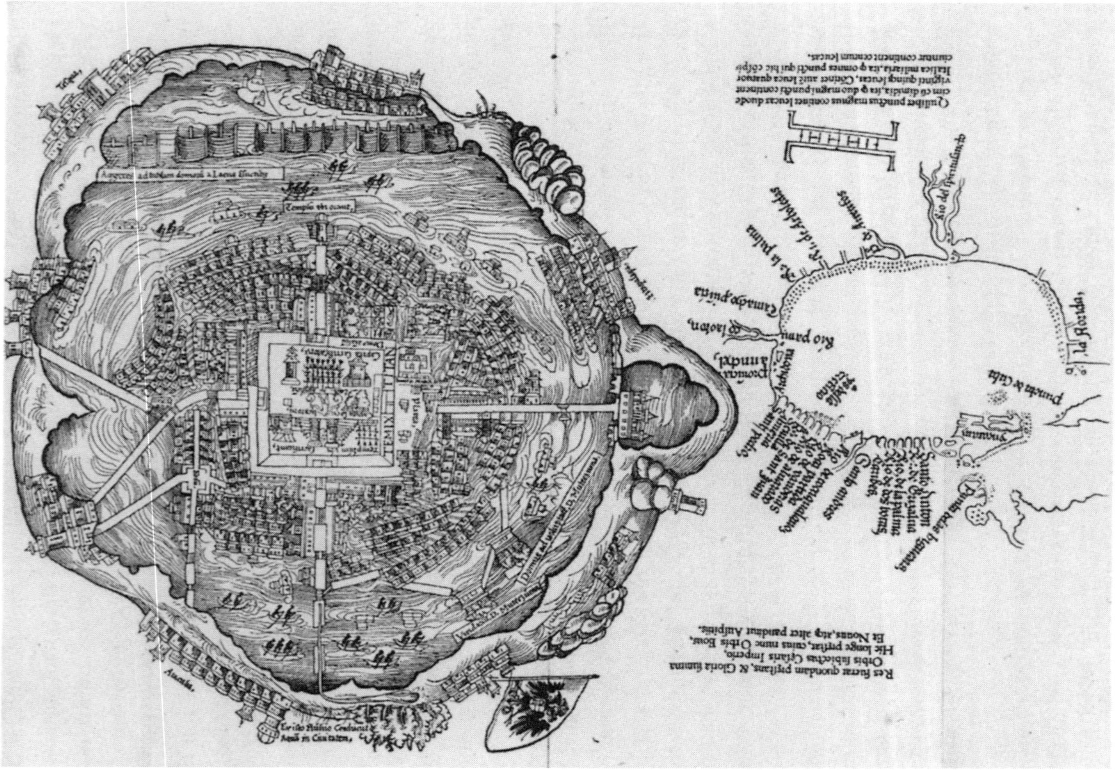

Figure 5.6. Cortez Map, view of Temistitan (1524)

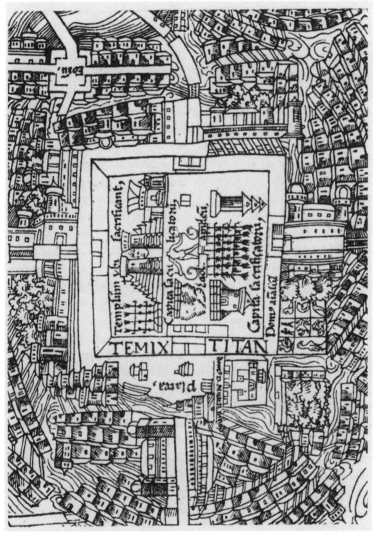

Figure 5.7. Cortez map, Temistitan, detail

with chronicle and narrative, is omitted. Where the Cortez map schematizes a theory and practice of religion, Bordone stresses the integral and central presence of *man* at the axis and origin of the world. Elsewhere in the map, alterations of the city-view ratify the overall design of Bordone's *isolario* that generally neutralizes universal differences through the presentation of a homogeneity taken to be greater than the sum of its particulars. The minuscule change that Bordone's copy brings to the plan of Temistitan is decisive for the volume. Man is everywhere at the axis, in the city-view, in the cardinal design, and in the declarative style of the text.

The maps of the islands appeal to recent discovery while providing a veneer of real-life experience of the kind that also animates portolano and navigational charts. In both Bartolommeo dalli Sonetti (the Dromi Islands, Figure 5.8) and Bordone (the Island of Psara, Figure 5.9), the jagged tracing of the shorelines of the island-views intimates that the coasts have been seen and are now transcribed as they have really been observed; or, if not, the outline appeals to a fantasy of things and events that are jagged, unpredictable, or literally accidental. Addition of rhumb lines that extend to the four cardinal compass points complement the quadrant of the four prevailing winds. The map is given a nautical aura at the same time that its design assures the viewer that a central point is charting—thus determining—the character of the island. A vertical axis is drawn by the line connecting the north (*tramontana*) to the south (*ostro*); it is bisected by the horizontal axis running from west (*ponente*) to east (*levante*). Intersecting the axes are the two opposing winds, Maestro and Sirocco, between the northeast and southeast, and the Greco and Garbino, between the northwest and southwest. Islands are schematized to resemble others and to assure a narrative that moves from one to the other. The format appeals to a technical code in order to lead the viewer to a familiar center whence all travel can follow a trajectory of departure and return.

The addition of rhumb lines to the oval world map in the preface to the 1528 and later editions produces the effect of the world quartered, but it also serves a purpose analogous to printed letters' reference to the names in the gazetteer. Cartographic and discursive orders work together to relate the text to the image and to cause the world's form to be remembered through *a spatial arrangement of linguistic signs*. Thus, the content of the world map and the island-views that follow seems less important than its taxonomical scheme. The world and its fragments are seen floating on an ocean that is open at the polar regions. Unlike its model, Francesco Rosselli's first oval projection of the world (1508),[10] Bordone's map excludes the Antarctic landmass and the ring of islands around the North Pole. Since the islands are coded by letters and num-

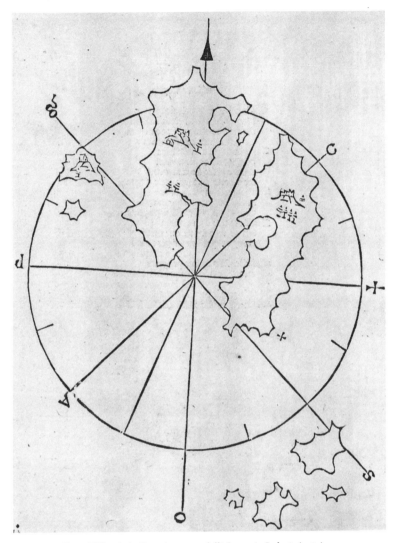

Figure 5.8. Dromi Islands in Bartolommeo dalli Sonetti, *Isolario* (1484)

bers, an overriding scriptural process holds the mass in place. The prevailing impression of control, seen in the system of reference, indexing, and design, is matched in areas of style. By and large, the descriptive text is presented as factual and informational. Classical sources are cited, history and chronicles are summarized to yield a balanced report. Autobiographical intrusions do not overly jostle the order of inherited facts.

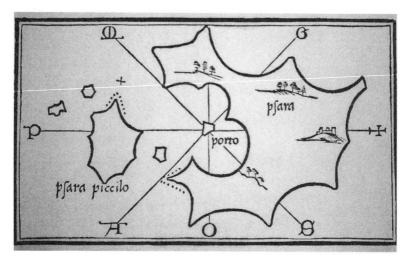

Figure 5.9. Island of Psara in Benedetto Bordone, *Isolario* (1528)

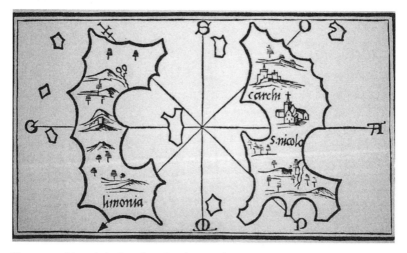

Figure 5.10. Limonia in Benedetto Bordone, *Isolario* (1528)

Yet for all the control that is evident in the design of the book, it is implied that the islands share an animistic force and are capable of replicating themselves. Images beget themselves and may supersede their legends. In the islands of Limonia (Figure 5.10) and its complement, in Psara and Piccolo Psara, and Dromo and Sarachino, the landmasses resemble protoplasm, amoebic shapes that extend pseudopodia in order to engulf particles in their midst. Or else the shorelines recall jaws that will clasp the smaller prey that lies just beyond them. With Dromo and Sarachino, the islands appear either to be about to copulate (the peninsula of the former ready to penetrate the lagoon of the latter) or to be separating after having undergone mitosis. A sense of biological genesis, of embryonic growth, and even of atomism lends to the depiction of the islands a sense of a world that is in congress, multiplication, and dispersion.

If the numbers of its reeditions are taken as evidence, Bordone's work must have had a fairly extensive influence. The same order of text and illustration is used in 1534, 1537, and 1547. In his *L'isole piu famose del mondo* (1572), Tommasso Porcacchi uses the same format. Porcacchi enjoys a similar popularity, his book being reprinted in 1576, 1590, 1604, 1605, 1686, and 1713.[11] The island-city as a model for the world continues to be held, despite the many discoveries made since the heyday of its publication. "An archipelago of 138 islets, the insular space of Venice remains the paradigm," notes Frank Lestringant (1980b: 431). While islands reclaim the virtue of their singularity of different flora, fauna, and human custom, Venice "owes its glory and fortune uniquely to human invention that has graced the city with the artifice of all of the singularities of Creation" (472). Thus is characterized the "constitutive law" of the *isolario* by Venice, a city that symbolizes an originary totality being "recreated instantaneously," in opposition to the *heterogeneity* of things discovered in the infinity of the world's islands. Bordone's and Porcacchi's efforts to produce an anthropocentric unity are split by the pairing of Venice and Temistitan. The implicit typology of the arrangement allows one axis to be displaced by the other. Because combinations of text and image are based on parataxis, the connection that ties the originary city to its counterpart is only implied. The spatial trope turns a narrative of islands into a serial creation that can begin and end anywhere. The order that the genre proclaims appears to be both enhanced and undermined by its own format.

André Thevet's Staging of Alterity

No doubt the appeal of scatter, jagged coastlines, protoplasmic islands, and a virtual infinity of forms inspired Rabelais's and Thevet's variations on the model. André Thevet, especially, folds much of the text and many of the island-views into his cosmographic writings, which include *La cosmographie de Levant* (Lyon, 1554), *Les singularitez de la France antarctique* (Paris and Anvers, 1557 and 1558), *La cosmographie universelle* (Paris, 1575), and the *Grand insulaire et pilotage* (unpublished manuscript, 1586–1587). Paradoxically, as he moves ahead in his career as the official cosmographer of France from almost the middle to the last decade of the century, Thevet draws more and more from Bartolommeo dalli Sonetti's *Isolario*, but, paradoxically, at the very moment its veracity is called in question by documentary evidence and more accurate modes of mapping the Western Hemisphere.[12]

We are obliged to ponder why, and to ask what the consequences have been both for the future ordering of knowledge and for the beginning of ethnography. It is a commonplace that Thevet's material is erroneous. On cursory impression, his travels to the east and to Brazil borrow so much that they seem to be exercises in copying. Yet for all of his mythomania, Claude Lévi-Strauss ranks his work as the "ethnographer's breviary" (1955: 44).[13] Fact and fiction are so confused that the barriers between things real and imaginary are eroded. Both *Les singularitez* and *La cosmographie universelle* turn descriptive language into its own object, simultaneously as a subject of study—a style—and a monumental physical object of its own mass. The mix tends to pull the world of fact and real forms into the flow and rhythm of its constant textual recreation. Through its distortion of the *isolario,* the work becomes a legacy of utopian discovery and, too, a site of singularization and of dialogism.

Much of Thevet's first journal of discovery, *Les singularitez,* are transposed in *La cosmographie universelle.* In the later work, the narrative gains an especially composite appearance. The two volumes—of over a thousand folio pages each—resembles an ocean of text copied and culled from diverse classical and modern sources. Chapters are studded with illustrations designed to verify the "facts"—both common and monstrous—presented in the descriptive text. Like an *isolario,* the plan aims at collecting and arranging the sum of the world's mosaic pieces. But unlike François de Belleforest's rival work of the same name (Paris, also 1575), which builds on the model of Sebastian Münster by adding new text to many new cityscapes of France, Thevet's book contains few cartographic references serving as points of reference or comparison. Two maps, one of Africa and another of Asia, are guides for each of the volumes. A wealth of detail is taken from Bordone and recopied, but in a way that seems inversely proportional to the direction in which the genre otherwise appears to evolve in its approximation of an atlas structure.

Thevet's cosmography seems to be what the literary anatomist Northrop Frye calls a "menippean satire," a genre in which the author shows "his exuberance in intellectual ways, by piling up an enormous mass of erudition about his theme or in overwhelming his pedantic targets with an avalanche of their own jargon" and has a "magpie instinct to collect facts" (1969: 311), resulting in a collection of objects amassed pell-mell, from the four corners of the world, and left in disarray. *La cosmographie* is an *isolario* that refuses to concede to an atlas structure. It would draw extensively on the information supplied in the Venetian models, depend on insularity to include and organize an infinity of facts, syncopate images and discourse of different provenance and style, and develop a supple and encyclopedic form that bears everywhere a prevailing signature. A "self-made" creation of Thevet's hand—since no other work quite resembles it—*La cosmographie* not only represents the real world but also encapsulates its infinite variety. As it compiles and copies things through the filter of a self-encompassing style, Thevet's ambitious work becomes a world or insular space of its own, distant from the real world, but also an island-sum that resides within it. This commanding paradox of form is adduced in the areas where Thevet seeks to *deny* the presence of the *isolario*. He rejects the tradition most vehemently in his introduction to his chapters devoted to the New World. Taking up Vespucci's naming of the American continent, Thevet exhorts,

Plus s'abusent ceux, qui pensent que ladicte quatriesme partie du monde soit une Isle, pour ce que certains Italiens, Allemans & François, faiseurs de faulses Cartes, tant marines que autres, se sont trompez si lourdement. . . . Car si c'eust esté une Isle (Comme Munster faulcement dict en sa cosmographie) de mesme qu'est la Taprobane, Madagascar, & autres qui sont des plus belles, ne l'eussent-ils pas environné, d'une part & d'autre, pour y trouver quelque destroit? A quoy ils ont travaillé par l'espace de quinze ou seize ans, sans aucun profit: & toutesfois ils avoient la mer libre, & aucun ne leur donnoit un seul empeschement, si ce n'estoit la mesme nature. Ce qui se peult conjecturer les voyages de Magellan, lequel ayant bien couru & au long & au large, & plus que jamais homme ne feit, comme m'en ont fait le recit le grand deluge d'eau, qu'ils disent estre advenu en leur terre, & duquel je parleray poursuivant ce discours.

[Those who think that the so-called fourth part of the world is an island are entirely wrong, because certain Italians, Germans, and Frenchmen, who drew incorrect maps, whether marine or other types of charts, were stumped so foolishly. . . . For if it were an island (as Sebastian Münster states wrongly in his cosmography), in the same way as we find Taprobana, Madagascar, and other islands of the finest beauty, would they not have enclosed the New World from one end to the other in order to locate some kind of narrows? They labored at this in utter futility over the space of some fifteen or sixteen years: And nonetheless the open sea was there, and nothing impeded them in their labors, if it were not the very world itself. The truth can be drawn from the travels of Magellan, having sailed both far and wide more than any man had ever done before, in evidence also confirmed by the tale that natives tell about the great watery deluge that they say covered their lands, and of which I will speak as I follow this discourse.] (Thevet 1575: II, fols. 911–914 r)[14]

Thevet argues against the view that calls continents islands, but in a context where commentary flows in such tidal waves over and about the controversy that the event itself bobs like flotsam in a great swell of words. Thevet, as he admits, *follows* his own discourse: He seems to delight in watching the words that spill from his pen. An ocean of verbiage is written to surround or introject the debate on continents and islands. Here, Thevet identifies Ferdinand Magellan as the discoverer of a continent that, he underscores, Amerindians had already known in the adventures of their imagination. The drift of the text indicates that myth and observation are of equal worth, and that the apparent totality of a world of both insular and greater masses of land and sea had been known in the New World long before European experience was ready to confirm the fact.

He builds his ethnographic fiction on Bordone's model by describing the Western Hemisphere in a style characteristic of earlier cosmographies. Adumbrated are the location, the coordinates of longitude and latitude of Antarctic France, its approximate extension, and its relation to the fabled Anian (Bering) straits. Yet as he amplifies the original sources by means of his narrative, an autobiographical persona emerges from the field of description. Thevet loosens the ideology of natural or received fact that the *isolario* had conveyed in the focused treatment of the world's oddities. The material is subject to distortion by virtue of a mobile point of view that the text forces the reader to use. The "zero-degree" focalization that reports the facts is now called into question at the very locus of its authority.[15]

The inscription of a mobile point of view into the static form of description inherited from Bordone assures both an omniscience ("I, André Thevet, royal cosmographer, have seen and experienced what intellectual geographers—except yourselves, deserving and discerning readers—will never know.") and fluidity of inquiry ("Before moving into these matters and discourses, I ask great philosophers to solve this riddle: How is it possible that thousands of islands were forever uninhabited, and that now they are populated with infinite varieties of plants and animals . . . , now that, as I was saying," etc.). By virtue of a prototypically free indirect discourse (anticipating that of Gustave Flaubert), Thevet can share the point of view of others at the same time that he remains outside of their purview. The oceanic flow of the writing seeps into the world of the figures being described at the same time that it is isolated from them. This freewheeling technique allows the author to discuss anything and to pass in and through his topics as he wishes; to digress; to go beyond proper limits, to *extravagate*; and, no less, to move inward, to *intravagate*.[16] Thevet takes pains to reject the worldview advanced by the Venetian writers of *isolarii* on the basis of their frame and the material he can crib from them. The substitution of zero-degree focalization, by the subjective tenor of his experience, transforms the genre. In the passage cited above, Thevet's adamant defense of seeing North and South America as continents is connected to the "transformative" style that allows the indirect discourse to both conflate and respect different points of view or of speech.

The manner of argument develops from differences that are given in the patterns of text and illustration. Woodcuts and engravings give definition and a virtually nautical bearing for the reader, who navigates through the text. Like objects or relics brought back from voyages, they attest to the narrator's visual experience and the truth of the account. But the closed relation of image and discourse makes the writing a literal image of itself, a truth based on a narcissistic mechanism of self-defense. The island-views and portraits of illustrious men begin to acquire verbal traits that liken them to emblems or rebuses that hold hidden relations to the verbal material.[17] The discursive mode is liable to fold into that of the maps and images, and vice versa. The format of *La cosmographie universelle* thus undergoes the metamorphoses that the narrator reports in both physical and cultural geography.

This transformational mechanism of *La cosmographie* defines certain features of its ethnography. To give credence to his opinions about the consequences of Magellan's travels, Thevet looks to Tupinamba mythology for evidence about the origins of the new continent. European discovery is verified by preexisting American fiction: Braids of Tupinamba myth that stem from a deluge explain what is seen and recorded by European circumnavigators. Because of their deity's deeds, the Amerindians take pains to impose upon the idol "le nom de Mairé-Monan," which means prestidigitator, "d'autant que cestoy-cy estoit fort adextre à transformer aucunes choses en d'autres" [since the latter was very adept at changing certain things into others] (fol. 914 r).

Now, because the form of the printed cosmography tests the barriers between water and land or objects and language, Thevet's narrative persona tends to blur into the deity of the Amerindians. What he says of the Tupinamba pertains to himself as writer and to the distortions he brings to the *isolario*. The Tupinamba god is characterized

> estans sans comencement & sans fin: & c'est luy, ainsi qu'ils disent, qui ordonne toutes choses selon son bon plaisir, les formant en plusieurs manieres, & puis les convertissant & changeant en diverses figures, & formes de bestes, oyseaux, poissons, & serpens, selon leur païs & habitation, changeant l'homme en beste, pour le plaisir de sa meschanceté, comme bon luy semble.

> [with neither beginning nor end: And it is he, as they say, who commands over all things according to his whims, forming them in several fashions, and then converting and changing them into diverse figures and forms of beasts, birds,

fish, and snakes, in accord with their worlds and their environment, and changing men into beasts, for the pleasure of his mischief and delight.] (II, fol. 914 r)

These remarks become a site where the figures of the Tupinamba god and
Thevet begin to focalize into the same imaginary or perspectival object.[18]

In the myths reported, a great deluge has divided the world into continents.
There follows the study of imperfect doubling, or of the splitting of single deities into twins both identical and different from each other. The resulting tensions of identity and diversity, which generate an infinite number of variants
and recombinations of myth, also inform the relation of *La cosmographie* to
the island books. Thevet's effort at including all of the world's facts and
features in printed and illustrated form begets a sort of "continent of archi-
pelagoes," a narrative mass that is at once unified and scattered. Fragments can
be both autonomous and part of a process of forms in perpetual flux. If, too,
the figures of the "self" and the "other" are seen in the same matrix of change
and difference, the beginnings of ethnography emerge visibly from the *passage*
or, as we have seen in the work of Rabelais, the *montage* of words and observations. If there exists in the writing a nascent ethnology, it comes in the comparative study of the different forms of evidence adduced within the work
itself (Panofsky 1955: 32).

The figure of the cosmographer in the service of the ethnographer is projected through two types of report. One involves the form and rhythm of the
writing in its relation to the material evidence it displays, and the other is
concretized in the typographic substance of the text that is offered as a kind
of firsthand evidence of its own. With respect to form and rhythm, it can be
said that the work builds its mass in order to shape an enclosed and self-
referential universe. Now and again observations about the New World in the
second volume are compared to observations in the first volume about the
Mediterranean or the Holy Lands or Africa, but the self-confirming format
(that is, of Mexico City as an analogue of Venice) that had marked Bordone's
work does not take hold in this ocean of writing. Rather, association works by
chance and a fairly free play of analogy. The narrator appears to remember or
compile data according to the logic of free attention; if the authorial persona
does not recall what literally "jumps off the page" or is ciphered into the play
of illustration and description, the readers—who have navigated through
the whole—are asked to discover the order on their own. Thus the order of
the world mirror is now made up of reflective, mosaic fragments, typographic
units, pictograms, or other signatures that impel the "author" and the "other"
(*l'autre*, who can be the reader, the subject of study, and our imagination of

Thevet) to organize the work together. The dialogic scheme refuses the impo-
sition of a single sum or totality of fact.

The unfinished appearance serves to inspire an ethnographic process of
description. In this way, *La cosmographie* invites myriad route-enhanced mappings through its weave of image and text. When discussing matters of idolatry and fetishism, Thevet requires his readers to rove about the many island-
fragments before their eyes. In chapter 11 of book 11, Thevet takes up the
temple and idol worshiped by the inhabitants of *Japart*. Idolatry and insularity
are so confused that the one becomes a quasi identity of the other. Yet, at the
same time, the elements of the description of Japart are extended, thirty folios
later, to the study of cult objects on *Palimbotre*. The signifier *ebene* (ebony)
becomes the link—like a piece of debris, lost on one realm, and washing up
on the shores of another—between remarks on the aspect of the island, the
daily life of its inhabitants, and their elementary religious structures. An oceanic
mass of words conveys the observation

> En outre, nous sçavons que c'est la seule Inde, qui porte & nourrit le bon Ebene,
> bois tant estimé: mais sur tout autre païs c'est en ceste isle, que se cueille le plus
> beau, noir, & plus fin. De cest arbre ils font leurs images: & voyla pourquoy j'ay
> dit ailleurs, que leurs Idoles estoient la plus part noires. Davantage, je vous
> ay aussi discouru des meurs & façons de vivre des trois provinces principales,
> ausquelles sont contenus trente & quatre Royaumes, tous idolatres qui ne recog-
> noissent Iesus Christ, Moyse, & moins le faulx Prophete Arabe, hormis cinq qui
> en ont quelque opinion, entre lesquels aucuns Iudaisent. Parquoy il ne fault que
> le lecteur prenne en mauvaise part, si je me suis attaqué en plusieurs endroits
> contre ce peuple idolatre, qui ayme plustost vivre en quelque opinion de religion,
> que ne fait le peuple Sauvage de l'Antarctique, & libertin, qui n'a ne loy ne foy. Je
> dy cecy, pource qu'*en ceste isle la plus part des Insulaires idolatrent, & tiennent leur
> Idoles*, qui sont faites de bel bois d'Ebene, au lieu que leurs voisins de terre conti-
> nente les font de marbre, pierre, sandal, & autre matiere. Et n'est pas tout: car
> d'autant qu'ils sont pauvres en estoffes, & n'ont commodité d'eriger de beaux
> temples, ils mettent ces gentils Dieux de bois dans des grotesques: d'autres les
> posent en lieu public & eminent, où chacun peult venir faire la priere, ainsi que
> l'esprit maling le conduit, comme vous pouvez voir par la precedente figure, en-
> semble le produit de l'isle, & comme elle se comporte. Au reste, les Rois en por-
> tent leurs bastons royaux, & les plus grands d'entre eux *boivent dans des hanaps,
> & tasses d'Ebene, pource qu'il ont ferme foy, que le venin ne sçauroit nuire* à celuy qui
> boit dans ces vases, & que ce bois a force contre les poisons. J'en acheptay deux
> d'un Indien en un cazal pres la mer Rouge, nommé Bochri; de l'une desquelles je
> feis present à feu d'heureuse memoire M. Pierre Thevet, mon frere & amy, &
> l'autre me fut prinse par un Capitaine Provençal, auprès de Carcassonne, au re-
> tour de mon second voyage. En somme l'Ebene est fort semblable au Gaiac, sauf
> que . . .

[Furthermore, we know that only in India is this great and esteemed ebony worn and valued: But above all other countries it is here, at this island, where the most handsome, blackest, and finest wood is gathered. From its tree they fashion their images, and that is why I stated elsewhere that their idols were mostly black. And too, I have also told you of their ways and customs of living in their three principal provinces, in which are contained thirty-four kings, all idolatrous, that neither recognize Jesus Christ, Moses, nor, to a lesser degree, the false Arab prophet, except for five who have some kind of opinion, among those some of whom are of Judaic faith. For this reason the reader must not be alarmed if, here and there, I have taken this idolatrous nation to task, that rather prefers to live in some opinion of religion than do the Savage populations of Antarctic regions, that are libertine and lack both law and faith. I say this because *in this island most of the inhabitants idolize and respect their idols,* which are made of decorous ebony, where their neighbors of the continent fashion them from marble, stone, sandalwood, and other materials. And that's not all: For inasmuch as they are lacking in clothing, they place these lovely wooden gods in grottoes; others they place in open public spaces, where everyone can assemble to pray, just as the evil spirit leads them, as you can see in the preceding illustration, at once the product of the island and the way it looks. Finally, the kings carry their royal staffs of ebony, and most of them *drink from ebony goblets and cups, because they have the firm belief that poison could never blacken* whoever drinks from these containers, and that this wood can counteract toxins. I once bought two cups from an Indian, at a small village named Bochri, near the Red Sea. One of them I offered as a gift to the late and happily remembered Pierre Thevet, my brother and friend; the other a Provençal captain stole from me near Carcassonne, when I returned from my second voyage. In short, ebony is quite like *pockewood,* except that . . .] (I, fol. 409 r, emphasis added)

Thevet describes the properties of ebony by encompassing it within a great verbal flux.[19] The description appears to link native beliefs to fetish objects at the same time that the figure of the "*Idoles*" caps a graphic alliteration that binds "*idolatries,*" the activities that cement a group into place and make their identities cohere, to *insulaires,* the circumscribed sites on which they take place. The black color of the wood cannot be dissociated from the color of the printed letters that convey the depiction. So strong is the motivation to bind insularity and religious curiosity that the black hue of the vases and cups from which the natives drink will prevent them from being poisoned (from *nuire,* literally "to blacken") by noxious fluids or spirits. The wood itself (*bois*) has a further analogy with what predicates the drinking of its contents (*boit*), thus folding cause and effect into the signifying surface that the reader animates through observation of the printed page.

The appended account of the purchase of two vases also serves to double the figure of the author. It may be that the textual representation of Pierre Thevet (Thevet's brother) shares affinities with the twinned traits of Tupi deities. No matter how alluring the connection may be, literary and historical evidence cannot be disentangled: A textual replication of ebony vases and of figures named Thevet—which are idols, insofar as they might be likened to stone (*pierre*, which is reported as being blackened when idols are erected on Japart, I, fol. 383 r–v)—binds the mythic and factual registers of the text to the image of its typographic reproduction. Yet the protective virtue of the sacred objects is denied by the brother's death, which occurred—if historical evidence is correct—in the same year as the publication of *La cosmographie universelle*. The gift has the traits of an object of archaic exchange, a *Gifte* and a poison, which takes the life of the brother at the same time that its powers bring the cosmography into the world.[20]

The analogies that hold on the surface of the text bind the narrator to the Tupi myths of the creation of the New World. Over and over again, Thevet underscores how much the discovery of strange objects, flora, fauna, or myths pertains to "singularity." The disparity that seems to reign in the order of things finds a cohering force in the proportional relations established between the idea of an American continent and archipelago. In order to assure that the new lands will be associated with his own name, Thevet takes care to reject the *isolarii* and the historical accounts that he used to produce his fiction. *But the visible language of the arguments tells more than their content.* Setting straight the form of Antarctic France, in order to plant a French name in South American soil, he soon appeals to a webbing of figures that confuses the shape and fabric of his representation:

> Et ne sçay ou ceste excellent personnage (Adrien) Turnebus est allé pescher ce songe, de dire, que avant que Americ Vespuce descouvrit ceste terre, celle estoit desja cogneuë, & elle avoit quelque nom, & que c'estoit une *Isle*. En quoy certes *il se* trompe, mesme aussi de l'appeller *Isle*, *s'il ne* vouloit quant & quant nommer tout *l'*uni*vers Isle*, d'autant qu'*il est* entouré d'eau. Et en ce mesme endroit s'est trompé *le Sei*gneur Thomas Porcachi, Aretin, Ita*lien*, dans *un livre des Isles*, nouvellement imprimé à Venise. (Emphasis added)

> [And I can't tell where this great character Adrien Turnebus went fishing for this dream by saying that before Amerigo Vespucci discovered these lands, it was already known, and that it had some kind of name, and that it was an island. Here he is clearly mistaken; even by calling it an island, he wanted to call the whole universe an island since it is surrounded by water. And in this same place Tommasso Porcacchi, an Aretino and Italian, is also mistaken, in an *isolario* recently published in Venice.] (II, fol. 907 v)

Typography dissolves the island into the greater mass of vocables. The proponents of the island theory become the very shifters that signify islands. The "others," *l'autres,* whom Thevet impugns, are also part of the creation of the *author.* So prevalent are the surface tensions of printed writing, that a reader cannot entirely distinguish objects and figures described *in* the text from the graphic mass that conveys them or pulls them off its signifying surface. The writing self is scattered all over the verbal map that he is reproducing.

Perhaps the most visible evidence of the book's existence as a mythic continent and island-world of words can be found at the terminus, the very point where thousands of pages of description must be assigned a provisional finality. The printer ends *La cosmographie universelle* in a conventional typographic flourish, in a *cul-de-lampe* design that leads the margins of the text toward a verbal vanishing point. A last island off the coast of China, Quinsay, is being described before the text comes to an arbitrary end:

Quinsay, reste encor à descouvrir, je n'ay peu vous mesurer l'Asie du coste du Nort:
tant y a qu'elle est de telle & si grande estendue, que si l'on mesuroit le monde selon le partage mal fait des Anciens, il y en auroit de mal partis. Aussi devez
vous sçavoir, que ce qu'ils en ont fait, & de ce peu qu'ils ont eu cognoissance, a esté plus pour exprimer ce qui est monde, que pour l'ega-
lité des terres, veu les proportions observees par la contemplation des degrez; mais encor y ont-ils failli, à cause
de ce, qu'il ont estimé inhabitable, & de la terre, qui depuis a esté descouverte, que eux
& les Modernes ont pensé, que ce
fust une certaine & perpe-
tuelle course de
l'Ocean.

The text funnels down to a last word, *Ocean* with an upper-case *O,* a figure that both contains and is contained by the verbal flow of the work. Every printed letter that precedes is taken as an "insular singularity" held in a map of infinite verbal mass. But "Ocean" is also *O ceans,* or an "O inside" that conflates space (*O,* ocean) and time (*O,* the annular sign of this year, this *an*). A *mappa mundi* of words and figures, the cosmography completes, renews, and stages other renewals of the island book. Its two final points, the *O* juxtaposed to the period, constitute two scales of infinite containment and a proportional difference. The word vanishes into its own infinity.

Some Fortunes of *La cosmographie universelle* and Its Ethnography

Because the representation of the New World is intimately tied to the figural and textual design of *La cosmographie,* it is legitimate for us to wonder about

the directions its transitional and indeterminate form might take in later development. The ever changing aspect of the discourse—like the content of
Tupi myths—cannot become objective or stable enough to be the subject of
science. The information contained in the work is at once so novel, so far-
fetched—indeed, so global and *insular*—that its basis in fact can only be that
of an anamorphic imagination. From the historian's standpoint, the cosmography may indeed mark both the crisis and the end of a tradition that began
with printed editions of Ptolemy and *isolarii* and ends with the advent of the
atlases of Ortelius and Mercator.[21] But from the standpoint of the ethnographer and the adept of cartographic writing, for whom imaginary productions
are a reliable measure of ideology, the *isolarii* and *cosmographies* do not vanish
into oblivion.

   In their evolution toward a predominately pictorial form, atlases tend to jet-
tison their textual baggage. Verbal decoration is reduced, set on verso pages, or
suppressed. Like the repressed, the verbiage that flows from the cornucopia of
cosmography does not simply evaporate. It returns in different forms. One of
these, of course, is the encyclopedia, which will channel information according to artificial organizational schemes—as, for example, did Diderot's great
eighteenth-century creation—in ways that aim at reviving the energetic virtue
of Thevet.[22] A second is the novel of travel, which uses the seriality of the *isolario* to assemble discrete episodic units that are studied from multiple points
of view. Such would be the narrative and the map-legend of Béroalde de
Verville's *Le voyage des princes fortunez* (Figure 5.11), or even the itinerary of
Don Quixote. A third variant would be the early modern "Who's Who," which
skims from the cosmography the many descriptions and engravings of "illustrious figures" that complement the views of islands. Thevet's own two volumes of *Les vrais pourtraits et vies des hommes illustres grecz, latins, et payens,
recueilliz de leur tableaux . . .* (1584) mark the convergence of copperplate
engraving of portraits and material taken from the cosmographic project.
Fourth, and no less important, is Thevet's own unfinished work, *Le grand insulaire et pilotage,* also in two volumes (in manuscript), which includes eighty-
four original engraved maps of islands in a total of 263 illustrated chapters
(Lestringant in Pastoureau 1984: 487–95; Karrow 1993: 536), a work that would
otherwise give a new identity to the tradition of the *isolario.*[23] Last, *La cosmographie* grounds the work of natural history, ethnography, and ethnology.

   We now can ask not how *La cosmographie* splinters into different genres,
but why, as a mendacious and overwrought fiction, it remains a founding
document for the science of man. In his recent *Histoire de lynx,* Claude Lévi-
Strauss argues that a vast and syncretic structure of myths extended from

Figure 5.11. Map in Béroalde de Verville, *Le voyage des princes fortunez*

northwestern North America to southeastern Brazil, and that careful study of the inversions and variations of their forms reveals much about the cultural geographies of the populations that lived in the New World long before the Columbian encounter. In a delicate and powerful analysis of Montaigne's *Essais,* he shows that throughout much of the Renaissance, the New World did not make much of an impact on the European mind (1991: 277–97). The New World merely confirmed what was discovered in recent forays through the classical and biblical canon: "Too many novelties at the same time dizzied the minds of scholars and thinkers. What they expected from exotic cultures were the proofs—confirmed by contemporary witnesses—of what classical letters were beginning to teach: not only reality of the devil and his works, but also that of strange races of humans . . . and *singular encounters* in which, even if by way of analogy, they would not fail to recognize the biblical Eden, the classical Golden Age, the garden of the Hesperides, Atlantis, the Fountain of Youth, and the Fortunate Islands" (1991: 290–91 emphasis added).

He adds that Thevet and Montaigne complicate this perception when evidence from recent travels impugns the authority of science and reason. For Thevet, the myth of Monan, which is recounted at the end of *La cosmographie universelle,* tells of a god who produced a world whose thankless inhabitants caused the deity to burn them in a universal fire. The conflagration gave relief to a world that had been flat and endless, without either sea or rain. The one man who survived, whom the god Monan lifted to the sky, begged the deity to cool the earth. The god extinguished the fire under a diluvial rain that accounted for the "origin of the sea" (Lévi-Strauss 1991: 66) and the world's hydrography. The decor of the world in which the remainder of the story unwinds—which involves a question of twinning and of rival brothers—confirms the very form of the book, its illustrations, and its plotting of maps and texts. As a figure who stages a universal creation of singular things, Monan resembles Thevet. He also bears a likeness, the reader of Lévi-Strauss is led to believe, to the persona of the Montaigne who wrote the "Apologie de Raimond Sebond," a monstrous essay—and cosmography within the frame of the *Essais*—that utterly demolishes rational thinking.

Lévi-Strauss observes that the essayist's radical skepticism defies the pleasure drawn from empirical observation. Affirming what psychoanalysts have stated about traumas at the origin of every individual's existence, humans can thus "cultivate affective satisfactions, as if life had a meaning, although intellectual sincerity attests that such is not the case" (1991: 286–87). The unassailable gap between the absurdity of life and the simple pleasures that one cultivates to produce fictions of meaning is found not only, as I suggested in the Introduction, in the venture of retrieving our own fabled psychogenesis, but also, and no less, in differences that stem from the perception of large and small forms, of liquid and solid shapes, or of continents and islands moving about each other. The contradiction of logic and affect that assigns meaning and absurdity to life, fundamental to Montaigne's fideism, is inspired by a view of the oceans and landmasses discovered in the west. Montaigne writes:

> Ptolemeus, qui a esté un grand personnage, avoit estably les bornes de nostre monde; tous les philosophes anciens ont pensé en tenir la mesure, sauf quelques Isles escartées qui pouvoient eschapper à leur cognoissance: c'eust esté Pyrrhoniser, il y a mille ans, que de mettre en doute la science de la Cosmographie, et les opinions qui en estoit receuës d'un chacun; c'estoit heresie d'avouer des Antipodes; voilà de nostre siecle une grandeur infinie de terre ferme, non pas une isle ou une contrée particuliere, mais une partie esgale à peu pres en grandeur à celle que nous cognoissions, qui vient d'estre descouverte.

> [Ptolemy, who was a great figure, had established the limits of our world; all the ancient philosophers felt that its measure was under control, except for a few scattered islands that were just beyond the reach of their grasp: It would have amounted to Pyrrhonism, some thousand years ago, to call into question the science of cosmography, and the opinions that had been received from its practitioners. It was a heresy to avow the existence of the Antipodes: Now in our century we see an infinite breadth of *terra firma*, but not of an island or a particular

country, but a part almost equal in size to what we used to know, that has just been discovered.] (Montaigne 1962: 555)[24]

A paradox of intellectual nihilism and sensuous fiction is built over debates concerning the proportions of islands and continents. For Montaigne, the difference proves that identity and contradiction go together and that ultimately we can never relate to being: "nous n'avons aucune communication à l'estre" [we have no way of relating with being] (Montaigne 1962: 586). For Lévi-Strauss, Montaigne's remark shows that contradiction and difference form the basis of all certitude. Intellectual and sensual life depend on the cultivation of a geographic paradox.

Likewise, Lévi-Strauss continues, as he had shown in his analysis of Thevet's account of Mairé-Monan in *La cosmographie,* Amerindian myths are constructed in a twinned, or "gemeled" fashion, except that the two identities (brothers, gods, tricksters, etc.) always carry within them elements of diversity. These points of contradiction are set in the mythology in a "solidly organized" way, "as if, in its initial state, it set in place empty areas voids or lacunae: in expectation, so to speak, of things coming to fill them from without, and by virtue of which its structure would take final form" (292). Thus, in the mythology that Thevet transcribes, the native was prepared to greet the arrival of the other because his or her mental structure had reserved a place for the other's coming.

The bitter consequence was, of course, that the other who came to fill that area had refused to allow contradiction to inhabit its own definition of gemelarity. The other was the identity of the self; self-made and self-symmetrical, Europeans conquered the New World exactly where the indigenous population had either predicted or welcomed their arrival. The network of Amerindian myths had accounted for the future of history long before Europeans, obsessed with their accounts of themselves, sailed westward. Through Lévi-Strauss's return to *La cosmographie universelle,* we begin to see how the paradox of a world of island-continents and oceans grounds French ethnography. Thevet's representation of Tupinamba myths is entwined in the fictions of transformation, of doubling and difference, and of movement to and from unification and disaggregation.

Thevet's persona who rewrites the *isolario* by mixing the myth of experience with fact and who extols his own sense of observation is also the one who isolates himself from the other through the creation of his own oxymoronic mythology—"une cosmographie universelle"—that welcomes, on his side of the world, the arrival of native Americans in the body of its textual contradictions. The work takes its view of the other into its own process of antithesis and paradox.[25] The ethic of distance that ensues is rooted in the transformation of the island book, in the sensuous creation of a world-object, and the adventure that identifies *insularities* as *singularities*. From Rabelais, Bordone, Thevet, and Montaigne we learn a lesson of tact, pleasure, and art that sows seeds of ethnography in the furrows of cosmography. To see better the wealth of that tradition, we can now, before encountering Montaigne, turn to another composite creation of map and text, the first atlas of the French nation: *Le théâtre françoys.*

6

An Atlas Evolves:
Maurice Bouguereau, Le théâtre françoys

In 1575 André Thevet's *La cosmographie universelle* was matched by François de Belleforest's counterpart of the same name. Drawing on the success of the French translation of Sebastian Münster's *Cosmographia universalis* (1544), Belleforest practices a mode of compilation that departs from the intellectual and theoretical enterprise of cosmography examined in chapters 4 and 5. Belleforest does not just contemplate an oceanic world of infinite volume and grandeur that expands with new information brought by travelers returning from overseas; he takes special care in collecting and digesting information, which he solicits and gathers from reliable sources around him.

Münster had led the way. Among other works, the cartographer in Basel had edited and redrawn a commanding edition of Ptolemy's *Geographia* (1540). His *Cosmographia universalis* attempted to summarize all classical and medieval sources about the world, incorporated information gathered since the turn of the sixteenth century, and, no less, solicited individuals for items pertaining to all the local areas of Europe and other continents. Its initial size, 659 pages and 520 woodcuts (Karrow 1993: 427) qualified the project as ency-clopedic. It expanded progressively (1545, 1546, 1548, and 1550) to a bulk of over 1,200 pages. Twenty-seven editions were published from 1553 to 1628. Its success did not go unnoticed among French compilers and authors.

In this chapter, I should like to see how its influence leads to a dramatic shift in the form of cartographic literature, and how it also provides a negative model for a composite work, Maurice Bouguereau's *Le théâtre françoys* (1594), the first French atlas by a Frenchman. In juxtaposing the works of Münster, Belleforest, and Thevet to that of Bouguereau, I do not want to retrace an evolution that moves from an encyclopedia or a "menippean satire" to a full-fledged atlas but, rather, to continue the study of the birth and growth of a mix of dialogic and diagrammatic sensibilities that was begun in the preceding chapters. I would also like to see how these sensibilities take firm hold in cartographic writing of Protestant leanings. Bouguereau's work becomes affiliated with an ideology of nationhood—a common and collective land of French origin—and with plotting a military and touristic literature (gathered from cosmographies) that mix myth and strategic thinking. Even if it did not have the impact of Münster's *Cosmographia universalis* or Ortelius's *Theatrum orbis terrarum,* Bouguereau's atlas furnishes a decisive plan for statecraft that will develop during much of the seventeeth century. Before examining how Bouguereau's atlas comes about, we will do well to look at the context of cosmography in view of Thevet, Belleforest, and their sources.

Belleforest's *La cosmographie universelle* (1575) signals innovation in the ways that knowledge is compiled, categorized, retrieved, and disseminated. Unlike Thevet, for whom the discipline projected an image of the cosmographer sailing about both real and imaginary oceans and gathering singularities of fact and fiction, Belleforest strives to fashion a more strongly inflected ideological object: In one of the volumes, his cosmography will be comprehensive; unlike Münster's, it will stress *French* history, *French* regions, and *French* leaders and magistrates. It will underscore their strong affiliation with the Catholic church and the enduring power of the kingdom in relation to the surrounding world.

Contrary to his reputation, Belleforest is more than a compiler. He adds sixty maps to the first volume of *La cosmographie universelle,* devoted to France, that more than supplement Münster's four illustrations of the nation (two maps of *Gallia,* a city-view of Paris, and a scene of the siege of Nancy). Belleforest prefers to use maps from Abraham Ortelius's recent *Theatrum orbis terrarum* (1570) to give a modern luster to his endeavor (Pastoureau 1980: 52–54). In contrast to Thevet, who aspires to the production of a truly universal work of cosmography gathered from an infinite number of islands, people, and earthly oddities, Belleforest stresses French regions and their history. The intention and vision of the compilation are strategic. A network of communication dictates what will be said, how illustrations will be sought, and what will result in the shape of an extensive historiographical encomium of France.[1] Like Thevet, Belleforest includes significant material from the New World, but his treatment does not "invent" the Western Hemisphere through verbal imitation of pictorial sources or through distortions of documents as had the

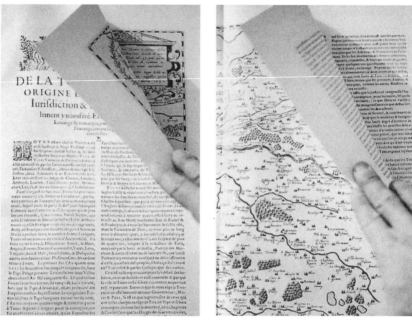

Figure 6.1. Map and text from Maurice Bouguereau, *Le théâtre françoys* (1594): an equal distribution of text and maps

royal cosmographer's (Lestringant 1990: 201).[2] The order of a compilation is clear, and no less evident are his efforts to use verbal effusion, or *copia* (Cave 1979), for the purpose of publishing a monument of writing and illustration. Only when there is roughly the same quantity of diagrammatic and discursive material—when they are of the same approximate extension—does the structure of the atlas emerge (Figures 6.1a and 6.1b). When the copious discourse of the cosmography is challenged by the dense and increasingly authenticating presence of city-views and maps, the atlas structure is born.

Ortelius's publication of the *Theatrum orbis terrarum* in 1570 appears to turn both Thevet and Belleforest into representatives of an old-fashioned, if not archaic, mode of composition. In the Dutch publisher's work, the folio map is printed on one side of the page and columns of text are printed on the reverse. Instead of placing maps and figures within the flux of discourse, the material process of production accords equal but separate space to image and to text. Of primary interest are the maps—each printed on a single sheet, which is folded and mounted on an *onglet*. The full folio page displays the map. On its reverse side is printed the descriptive text pertaining to the map. On the upper side, then, is the image of the area, while on the inverse side is situated the quasi-ekphrastic material that animates, follows, or diverges from the map. Textual limits are imposed by the format of the atlas. In the first edition, Ortelius furnishes a brief description of the area to be seen following and leaves the opposite page blank. The accompanying text cannot be copious. Restricted by the physical plan of the book, the discourse of analogy cannot compete with the cartographic evidence printed on the reverse side of the page.[3]

When Ortelius commissions individuals to procure material that he can edit into a single work, he produces a serial creation, a book of others, that acquires an identity less through an innate design than in the way it fashions received information. An ordering in which an individual authors his or her creation gives way to another order, in which there reigns a system of variation that serves to distinguish different areas of the enterprise.[4] The residually mystical universal of Thevet, in which the subject floats amid images of islands and people, is now established according to discrete cartographic units, each of which is the result of topographical survey. Ortelius's innovation in the science of cartography is that he attends less to the "big picture" of the world than to putting together an illustrated summary of a possibly infinite number of fragmentary parts.

Yet the shift from the technology of cosmography to that of the atlas does not happen without mediation, confusion, or paradox. In the broader history of the birth of the atlas, Maurice Bouguereau's *Le théâtre françoys* appears to be an intermediary work that shares much of its visual material with the Ortelian vision at the same time that it draws much of its discourse from the French cosmographic tradition of the 1570s. The atlas betrays the image of an editor searching for a method and a design that cannot quite be formulated or synthesized in explicitly textual or diagrammatic terms. A transitional condition is made manifest. A unique document of cartographic writing is captured in the contradictions of its form. A project is staged to unify information gathered about the nation, to catalog heterogeneous material, and to explore the potential effects of different mixes of discursive and cartographic processes. The maps arrange in profile a new authority of verisimilitude through schematic and geographic views of French territories, but the writing holds to an older logic of analogy. The archaic mode of discourse furnishes the maps with ideology and propaganda that will create a new image of the nation, while the maps themselves will be used for strategic ends in the long-range planning of the state.

Two different modes of conceiving and of "working through" the world coexist.[5] Neither is quite defined or solved in Bouguereau's modest work, but the adventure that a reader follows in reconstructing—or "inventing"—the atlas shows how each works in conjunction with the other. The new system, based on Ortelius while drawing amply from Belleforest, does not simply fall in place or get installed as might a machine. A dialogue is opened, and different orders are exchanged and coexist within each other. In this intermediate area or confusion, the concept of an "atlas structure" (Akerman 1991) comes into existence.

Also changed is the notion of the self with respect to mapping, at least insofar as the intellectual and quasi-ethnographic project of the earlier cosmographies now acquires a new sense of mission in the service of a nation that is defining its borders and its languages. The evolution that bears on these questions is dramatic and, for patient readers and viewers, startling. First, the format of the atlas comes into view when schematic representations of space surpass—and eventually suppress—the textual material that had been an integral part of the composition. Second, the "self," like the signature of Oronce Finé or François Rabelais, which had gained agency and identity through the technical mastery of engraving and mensuration or a style of vision, now gives way to a more entrepreneurial type that fashions identity by virtue of the labors of others. Finally, the atlas seems to discover its political and strategic efficacy less by design than almost fortuitously, within the process of its physical elaboration, in its display of conditions of possibility. Such are the effects one sees in moving from Münster and Belleforest to Bouguereau and, later, as we shall see, to Jean Leclerc. The history of Bouguereau's atlas tells much about these shifts.

The Idea of a National Atlas

The atlas, as it were, "takes place" in Tours, at the rue de Scellerie, in 1594. In a remarkable study of the book's sources and place in the history of French cartography, Père François de Dainville (1985: 295–342) shows that Bouguereau, a Protestant, was affiliated with the publication of the anti-Catholic pamphlet *La satire ménippée*, printed and engraved in Tours at the same time.[6] Following earlier findings of Ludovic Drapeyron (1889), he surmises that "if the *Satire* paved the way for the defeat of the Catholic Holy League, the *Théâtre françoys* is the erudite expression of this defeat" (311). The duc de Guise had recently been assassinated. The new king of France, Henry IV of Navarre, took up residence in Tours because of revolts occurring in Orléans and Paris. "His presence brought with him a crowd of prelates, magistrates, men of letters, artisans, especially faithful Parisian printers, and booksellers who were cutting down the 'guysards'" (312). In their midst was Gabriel Tavernier, a Flemish engraver of Protestant inclination whom Bouguereau, a Protestant printer, hired to execute a copperplate version of Guillaume Postel's map of France in exchange for the promise to lodge Tavernier "and furnish him with a bed and wood enough to last him well and honestly" (letter of 23 April 1590, cited by Dainville 1985: 312). Lacking knowledge of the art of mapping, Bouguereau then wrote to the king in quest of information from "des hommes entendus éz Mathématicques et Geographie" in order to obtain regional projections. The dedicatory letter to Henry betrays his design:

> Or de c'est amas, mon dessein à touiours esté de dresser le Theatre des Provinces particulieres de vostre Royaume, tant pour le plaisir qu'il y à de voir les particularitez & choses remarquables d'icelles, que pour l'utilité des hommes Martiaux, soit pour les departemens des logis des gens de vos ordonnances, que pour vos Receveurs & Thresoriers, qui peuvent asseoir leur iugement pour les Paroisses, journées & conduicte de vos deniers és Provinces establies à la recepte de vos finances, qu'aussi pour servir d'adresse à tous vos subjects pour le commerce exercé en vostre Royaume.

> [Now out of this pile of things my design has always been that of erecting the theater of the particular provinces of your kingdom, no less for the pleasure of seeing the particularities and remarkable things that remain within, than for its utility for military men, for men administering your orders, and for your treasurers and ministers of revenue who can base their judgment for parishes, days, and the circulation of your monies in the provinces established for the receipt of your finances, and also to serve and help all your subjects for whatever business is conducted in your kingdom.] (7)

A new utility is perceived. Not only will the atlas be a handsome object and a view of the world about which a princely architecture will be crafted, but it will also have strategic virtue in matters of warfare, commerce, and taxation.

The work was begun in 1590 and, as the dating of the maps proves, the folio sheets were executed over the next four years, the last map (of the Limousin) bearing the date 13 February 1594. The atlas was, however, published unfinished because history caught up with it. In 1594, at the end of March, Paris opened its portals to Henry IV, who then claimed the city as his capital. The printer of *La satire ménippée*, Jamet Mettayer, moved to Paris with the Protestant entourage, but he sold Bouguereau printing items—castings, letters, *lettrines*—that would allow him to finish the atlas. Bouguereau needed to finish the work before other employees also departed for the new seat of power. He labored over the summer of 1594 before printing the first copy, on 15 October as indicated on the dedicatory letter to the "benevolent readers" (2). On this page, opposite the frontispiece, which lists the areas to be depicted, evidence shows that Bouguereau sent the atlas to press without maps of Normandy, the Ile-de-France, or detailed views of the southwest or the Midi. The editor needed to get the work to the public of Tours and to the king before its concept could be superseded by new events. The way that the publication develops indicates that Bouguereau no doubt sensed the timeliness—not the cosmographic timelessness—of his *Théâtre* and that he intuited its utility as an instrument vital to logistics and statehood at a critical moment during the Wars of Religion. Unfolding, then, is a mix of speculation and of dialogue with materials, inherited from other contexts displaced into the specific historical moment of Henry IV's battles to gain Paris and the lands to the north and west.

Iconography: The Title Page and Opening Pages

The title page indicates much about the strategic design of the atlas (Figure 6.2). The arcade of a triumphal archway surrounds the title, which is set at the level of the structure's cornice. The title is placed under the vault below a cartouche bearing the coats of arms of France and Navarre under a diadem and the crowned *H* (a letter that Henry used as of 1594). An *atlante* and a caryatid are perched on the two edges of the pedestal above, holding decorative horns of fruits and leaves that serve to draw the eyes to two allegorical figures standing in front of the two fluted columns behind: to the left, Geographia, and to the right, Geometria. Each appears to be modeled from Cesare Ripa's *Iconologia*, but with significant differences. In her right hand, Geometria holds a measure and a square; her left arm, drawn with much-less-exact shading and with more-approximate contour hatching, descends over the square plinth of the column against which she stands with her right knee thrust forward. She uses a pair of dividers to indicate Bouguereau's name and the place where the work is printed. She is bathed in daylight and displays a robust body and even a pubis unveiled by the opening folds of her toga.

By contrast, the figure to the left is not so easily identified by what she grasps; she appears to be designed to confound Ripa's standard distinction between *Geographia* and *Corographia:* the former is usually shown pointing a compass skyward, whereas the latter aims the same instrument downward toward the physical world. The figure on the left in Bouguereau's picture, whom Dainville (1985: 288–89) identifies as Geographia, holds not a compass but a quadrant in one arm; with the other she braces a map printed on a tablet against her ample thigh. Contrary to Ripa's description of Geographia, she bears attributes and a demeanor that render her enigmatic. Ripa had called

Figure 6.2. Title page to Maurice Bouguereau, *Le théâtre françoys*

Geographia a "donna vecchia, vestita del colore della terra, a piè della quale vi sia un globo terrestre, con la destra mano tenghi un compasso, con il quale mostri di mesurare detto globo, & con la sinistra un quadrante geometrico" [an old lady, dressed in earthen colors, at whose feet is a terrestrial globe, whose right hand holds a compass, with which she shows how to measure the world, and with her left a geometrical quadrant] (1624: 2, 274). Chorography is represented as a young woman in contrast to the wiser and more wizened Geography. But the copperplate displays a seductive woman who looks down toward the map at the same time that she casts the spell of her vision upon us

Figure 6.3. Figure of Geographia (detail of Figure 6.2)

(Figure 6.3). The darkened eyelids depict a woman who looks in two directions at once, casting a Medusa's stare toward the viewer at the same time that she looks down at the map on the booklike tablet that extends from her midsection. A figure ostensibly endowed with sibylline powers, she figures as an odd sister to Geometria. Where Geometria lets the billowing folds of her toga reveal her sex, Geographia, her body covered, draws attention to the omnipotent power of her gaze. Geographia looks down and outward at once, to the world and to the future, it seems, to predict the course of history—if not to control it—by the means at her disposal. It is implied that the king, the fore-

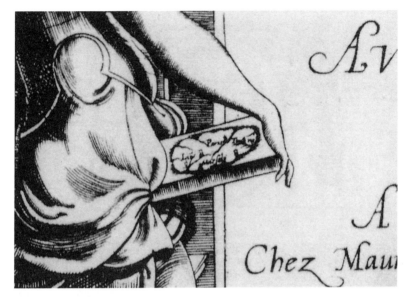

Figure 6.4. Detail of map in Figure 6.2

most recipient of the atlas, should follow Geographia's mystical counsel by using the new art to gain control of his nation.[7]

The map that Geographia is holding can be read, like her eyes, from two points of view at once (Figure 6.4). A cursory glance might recall a vague remnant of a t-and-o projection, with its dark border of the watery "ocean river" or *écoumene* about the land mass. A closer view reveals a map of the French nation from an oblique view, as adduced by the place-names of Paris, Marseilles, and two other cities, possibly Tours and "Lisl," but they are not located in a way that would put them on a recognizable map of France. The landmass seems to resemble—or elicits our fantasms to produce—a map in the figure of the portrait of a king. There can be discerned at the bottom the outline of a nose and at the top a mass that resembles a head of hair. As the miniature detail of the engraving tends to resemble a face, a nation, and a black surround, the equivocation prompts the reader to look ahead for resolution. An anamorphic process is coordinated with the figure of Geographia in order, perhaps, to identify the art of mapping with strategies of illusion, wit, and deception. The design of complementarity in gender and eros is already suggested by the receptive traits of Geometria in contrast to the figure of the commanding phallic female who is Geographia.

The verso page varies in design from copy to copy but extends much of the

Figure 6.5. Verso of title page in Maurice Bouguereau, *Le théâtre françoys*

equivocation seen on the title page. Of the seven extant copies of *Le théâtre*, the edition in the British Library (copy 22) displays Thomas de Leu's portrait of Henry IV of Navarre hinged over an anonymous map of France. The copy in the Bibliothèque Nationale has the portrait pasted over a sonnet, printed just below the map, that emblazons the king through an acrostic design (in which *Henry de Bourbon* is spelled out by the fourteen letters beginning each of the fourteen lines) (Figure 6.5). Other copies print the map in place of the portrait and leave the sonnet below (Paris, Sorbonne). One hinges the map over the sonnet and leaves the portrait above (Paris, Mazarine); another glues the map over the sonnet below the portrait (London, British Library, copy 22); a third omits the picture altogether (London British Library, copy 23), while yet another prints the map in place of the portrait above, with the sonnet remaining below (Loches, collection of Boulay de la Meurthe) (Dainville 1961: 307).

It may be that a *mobile allegory* of text and image is put forward, with the portrait (*Roy*) at play with the sonnet (*Loy*), and the nation (*Foy*). Faith is directed toward the king, who is a physical manifestation of God in a political theology (Kantorowicz 1956) but who is also synonymous with the body politic represented by the geographic view of the French nation.[8] The indeterminacy of the placement of each of the terms underscores the force that is invested in—or that emanates from—the allegory seen as a montage or collage of a picture, a text, and a map. The arbitrary quality of the placement paradoxically confirms the motivations of Bouguereau's encomium as a layered or manifold mechanism.

In the British Library copy (copy 22, also the facsimile), a specific allegory of the king and his nation is underscored when readers are induced to establish coordinates between the portrait and the map below. In order to relate the face to the map, we are required to view the two pictures from a skewed angle (Figure 6.7), much like the one that is opened between the gaze of Geographia, the map on her tablet, and the reader's eyes in view of the title page. When it is hinged *over* the map, in the geography of the king's face, the most arresting features of the portrait are virtually matched by toponyms just below. The left eye sits over Pont-Audemer, the right eye over Mantes; the tip of the nose is adjacent to Dreux; and so on. From the standpoint of the desire to shape the future that is at the basis of many of the allegories of the time that carry "a more than visual meaning" (Panofsky 1955: 167–68), the connection of sites on the face and the places below becomes a writing seeking both to reflect and to shape the course of contemporary events. In the years 1593–1594, after Henry officially abjured the Protestant faith (25 July 1593), northern towns that had been against the king were now obliged to "declare, or rather sell, their loyalty" to him (Buisseret 1984: 46). Among them were Honfleur, Rouen, Pontoise, Noyon, Meaux, and other agglomerations all the way up to Amiens, Cambrai, and Montreuil and as far east as Vitry-le-François. These very places are aggregated in the region of Henry's face on the map below de Leu's portrait. In the world of allegory, where relations multiply both to confirm and scatter an ideology (Benjamin 1977: 165–66), Henry's eyes, ears, and nose are set forth both as *desiring* those locations and as charismatically *conquering* them. Further-

Figure 6.6. Detail of face of Henry IV (Maurice Bouguereau, *Le théâtre françoys*)

more, as anamorphosis remains the privileged expression of the realm of desire, the placement of the portrait melds projective identification, ideology, and history.[9]

The gaze of the king is designed to be ubiquitous (Figure 6.6). When placed over the map and above the sonnet, his gaze reaches out in all directions to capture the eyes of all viewers. Patterned along the lines of van Eyck's *Man in the Red Turban* (Panofsky 1971: 2, plate 133), in which the position of the eyes of the turbaned official make him seem to be gazing directly at the spectator,

Figure 6.7. Detail of portrait of Henry IV over map of France (Maurice Bouguereau, *Le Théâtre françoys*)

no matter what the spectator's position may be in relation to the portrait, de Leu's rendering of Henry aims the gaze all about the area both in front of and behind the map beneath. The portrait's position on the verso of the title page, above the sonnet or below the map (no matter which), confirms that the construction is one of a *visual theater*. Henry's gaze constitutes a point that initiates a visual reading of the material. A free mobility of the gaze is associated with the art of viewing *as* reading. The superimposed map and portrait generate the idea of a three-dimensional, ordered space that the king is seen giving to his subjects through the generosity of his gaze. It might be schematized in a cardinal fashion (as shown on p. 216).

The spectator can be situated (or seated) anywhere around the page; he or she will be in direct contact with the king, *who speaks with his eyes*. We thus find ourselves in a dramatic space that is both a text and a geographic representation, in which a play of spaces determines movement between visual, lexical, and cartographic registers.[10] As the engraving gazes upon us, we are induced to move—hence to gain a common sense of position, through displacement, that will allow us to be in dialogue with the image—about the picture.

North

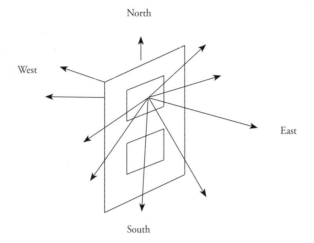

West

East

South

We accede to a mode of reading that is not determined by exclusively discursive means (mostly left to right) or by coded directions in painting (which would move from bottom to top or in other directions) established by iconography (e.g., van Eyck's *Annunciation,* in Panofsky (1953: 2, plate III), or what Francastel (1967: 245) also notes of van Eyck, when light as a symbol becomes multidirectional in the eyes of the viewer). The configuration of the portrait, the map, and the sonnet tells us that where power seems to be imposed by the figure of an absolute monarch, the opposite is also the case. We are common, communicating subjects in the relation we establish with the gaze.

It may be that Bouguereau unwittingly uses fifteenth-century models to establish a double relation of monarchic and democratic power. The picture would be the former, and the discourse, as we shall note, will give agency to the latter. The multidirectional quality of the portrait and its placement create a text that becomes an image thwarting the unilateral direction of history set forth by surrounding panegyric. Because of the proximity of the topographical projections that follow and the presence of the anamorphic map on the title page that precedes, we suddenly realize that when we modify our point of view, the book of maps is also "subject to proportional anamorphoses in the successive places" (de Certeau 1987: 18) we occupy. In, for example, the middle years of the sixteenth century, maps—such as those of the Dieppe School, including Pierre Desceliers's 1550 world map and Jean Rotz's *Boke of Idrography* (Wallis 1981)—were often "designed to be laid flat on a table and examined from each side in turn" (Buisseret 1992a: 103). The Ortelian atlas changes the way maps are to be viewed. Formerly, world maps and large sheets required a princely space in order to be viewed from all directions. With Ortelius's portable folio atlas comes a miniaturization of the reading and viewing, which can be accomplished from any angle and from a distance that can be changed according to the way one walks around the book.[11] Hence, the attention that the title page and the verso page draw to the mobility of the viewing subject confirms an intention to craft a "theater of operations" that can be imagined from all cardinal points, especially when the book is seen from the four sides of a table on which it rests.

Henry's face does not just gaze at us. It also seems to look backward, quasi-panoptically, confirming that when we look through the folio and the portrait imposed upon the map, the king's mouth is placed at a position that is identical to that of the crown over the escutcheons of Navarre and France in front of the arch on the title page. (In fact, the heart, barely reminiscent of Oronce Finé's iconography of world and nation, that surrounds the coat of arms of the king and his lands, seems to float over the fronton of the archway. The effect of suspension may indeed be related to the mobile design of the portrait on top of the map or the sonnet.) And as the oval portrait uses an ellipse as the containing frame, the geometry of the portrait bears an allegorical connection to the suspended heart on the opposite side of the folio. Henry's face and bust are figured by the double axis of the oval, implying that the axial points signify the head and heart, generating the image of a grandeur that surges forth and even dwarfs the personifications of France and Navarre (to the left and right, respectively).[12] If the portrait (16.6 × 15.5 cm) is placed over the sonnet (as it is in the Mazarine copy and the British Library copy 8), which is of approximately the same proportions (15.2 × 12.7 cm), then the king's body spatializes the encomium that is dedicated to him. His gaze is equated with Mars and Charlemagne (line 2) and the lower part of his bust with the force that will defeat the Spanish, the "Maran" (line 13), or the infidel, what Randle Cotgrave (1611) called the "circumcised Christian" population.

The sonnet also appears to be spatially conceived. Like the face and map above, its vocables are coordinated to fit in the general allegorical configuration. It is squared off, compassed, and endowed with cardinal virtue. Announced and gridded as

SONNET ACROSTICHE
de la renommee.
AU ROY

H eroique Monarque, Allexandre puissant,
E xercité en Mars: & second Charle-Maigne,
N oble en faits & en dits, le premier Henry-Maigne,

R ace de Sainct Loys par qui tu vas croissant.
Y ssu du sang Bourbon, tes ayeuls surpassant,
D iscret, bening, vaillant sur tout à la Compaigne,
E ntre les Martiaux, Vertu qui t'accompaigne
B urine en mon Autel ton Renom florissant.
O nc un tel Pardonneur ne fut n'y peut estre
V ers les siens rebellez, ausquels il tend sa dextre,
R enversant l'Orgueilleux & honorant le bon.
B eny de l'Eternel, recouvriras Navarre
O bstant ce vieil Maran, y planteras ton Phare,
N arrant par l'univers le nompareil BOURBON.

      M. Bouguereau.

[H eroic Monarch, an Alexander exceeding,
E qual of Mars, and second to Charlemagne
N oble in act and deed, the first Henry-magne,
R ace of Saint Louis by whom you go not conceding
I n any Bourbon blood, to your kin not receding,
D iscreet, kind, valiant over all the countryside
E ngaged with warriors, virtue by your side,
B ring to my awl your renown, ever etching,
O n high what no Pardoner could ever afford,
U nder your might, and under your sword,
R eward as you do the good with your crown.
B lessed with Eternity, you will win Navarre
O 'er the savage infidel shall be sent off and afar,
N arrating over the world the name of BOURBON.

      M. Bouguereau.]

The poem is drawn or "etched" onto a copperplate as if it were also a map ("*Burine* en mon Autel ton Renom florissant," line 8), its design depending on the coincidence between the fourteen letters of the king's name and the number of lines that constitute the sonnet. The editor has recourse to the spatialized practice of heraldic poetry. Here, it also allows discourse to locate a perspectival object that embodies all the contradictions of the poem.

It is just as likely that the printer is making an obvious appeal to acrostics and anagram to underscore the divinatory power of the atlas. Throughout the sixteenth century, the shuffling of letters was associated with the art of prediction. The sonnet conjures up an imaginary power that will influence the course of future events.[13] The appeal to earlier modes of composition underscores the persisting analogy that printed characters hold with the gridding of space. The monumental, squarish form of the poem is emphasized by the historiated initial. Vertical scansion traces an axis perpendicular to the axis marked by "Bourbon" as the cornerstone of the sonnet's architecture. The bombast is matched by the arched shape of Henry's cuirass in the lower part of the portrait, which projects outward toward the viewer, and the latitudinal graticules of the map (parallels 40, 46, and 50, visible in the lower-left corner of Figure 6.7), which pull the outline of France outward and toward the viewer, as if the curvilinear surface of the globe were a convex mirror.

Yet it is the pictorial aspect of the text that, as it strives to motivate the allegory that was initiated on the title page, also *demotivates* or neutralizes the rhetorical configuration. The space that grounds the poem seems *not* to share analogy with the encomium, the bombast countered by the empty areas that call into question the authority of the lexical material. The poem collapses at the very point that it brings the textual and visual registers together. In the eighth line, close to the poem's vanishing point, "B urine en mon Autel ton Renom florissant," "*ton* re*nom*" underlines the seriality of the poem in the mirrored visual rhyme, as does "B uri*ne en* mon Autel" as the eye moves back to the first hemistich. Mirrored space makes equivalent the art of engraving and, when the acrostic letters are detached from the initial words of each line, the act of micturition emerges (the poet asks the king to urinate in the workshop!). Where Bouguereau draws attention to the signature of his creation, a work that owes its form to the art of engraving, he also emphasizes the merely conventional traits of what he is magnifying.

The logic implies that the *renommée* of the king is a function of "renaming" that can be easily performed through a spatial play of alphabetic units. By means of acrostics, anagram, and amphiboly, the king will be *re-nommé* to the point that *Henry* could also be shifted into nothing (*rien*), into something to deny (*nier*); elsewhere, Henry IV could be cross-dressed as what is "four times risible," according to the surrounding quadrature of the work, *en ris quatre*. The precariousness of the circumstantial rhetoric is made evident through the figural quality of the discourse that disrupts its pomp and circumstance. Simultaneously, the schematic logic of the anagram is aligned with the spatial tactics of places and names that are fixed together on the maps: The double acrostic set in the sonnet duplicates the fluid rigidity obtained by the collage of the map and the portrait above the verse. Henry's picture is subject to a visual and verbal scansion that moves in all directions. When the upper border of the portrait is glued to that of the map of France, the overwrought relation of body parts to toponyms (in which analogies—such as left eye = Pont-Audemer, right eye = Mantes, nose = Dreux, lips = Chartres, left ear = Picardy, dimple = Paris, etc.—can be multiplied at will, producing a memory map of France based on the facial anatomy of the king) is shown to be contrived.[14]

The spectator's desire to see the mouth at *Meaux,* or the eye in the *oeil* of the Ile de la Cité, and so forth, is both served and denied. The metaphor that seeks to make king and country identical to each other becomes admittedly risible, just as the poem sprinkles aspersions over the king in the very words that intend to praise him. The editor betrays an increasing distance between the visual shape of language—what assures its power of analogy, as we have seen in Geoffroy Tory—and meaning. In the words of Montaigne, in an essay printed just two years before the publication of *Le théâtre françoys,* anthronyms and toponyms comprise "une piece estrangere joincte à la chose" [a foreign piece joined to the thing] (*Essais,* II, xvi: 601).

Bouguereau's stratagem might be read to be saying that, indeed, Henry's face is *not* equivalent to the map, and that the artificial binding of one to the other traces a line of desire, like an unfinished allegory, folded into the editorial rhetoric. Henry is *not* the king of the lands below his portrait, but the effect of the imaginary identity of the face and the map merely promotes the idea of the synthesis and, in doing so, uses a ploy of visual design to promote another, of factitious conquest. Hence, the picture and map are *not* real or virtual places; the monarch's body has no relation to the space, region, or idiolect with which it is associated; the rapport of the king to his country is, from the beginning, completely fortuitous. Just where the image is motivating the relation of word and name to a place and a national body, it is also implying that none exists. An art of *demotivation* in Bouguereau's allegory saturates the encomium.

Bouguereau's Maps

The title page and its verso page of *Le théâtre* appeal to the magical arts in order to convey to the king and the reader an idea of the arcane power of geography. We have seen that the creation splinters in at least three different ways. Most obvious, the addressee, or implied interlocutor, can be both the king and the commoner. Henry IV becomes the mirror and the perspectival object of the picture, poem, and triumphal arch. The composite praise attests to the monarch's deeds but also deploys its form to shape the order of events to come. The rhetoric magnifies the virtues of the king as it also neutralizes and conventionalizes them. An imponderable opposite seems to inhere in each instance of discourse: in the entrepreneur's self-interested description of Henry's magnanimity; in a concave or reducing mirror in the convex shape of the bulbous portrait; in an avowal that the king is identical to his country only where the strip of mucilage glues the upper edge of the portrait to that of the map.

Finally, the appeal made to formerly mystical and sibylline powers of language and figuration—the gaze of the king, the acrostics, anagram, heraldic letters that cast their spell on the viewer, anamorphic imagery—indicates that the maps that follow also carry a double inflection. On the one hand, they are presented as belonging to a mystical and humanist heritage, and as such they afford the viewer an instantaneous vision, the blitz of landscapes made up of infinite positions and points of view, or an impossible gaze on a regional totality that can only be seen magically, as if the spectator were above the world. From this standpoint, the maps are reminiscent of a heavenly voyage soaring over the French nation, and their form confirms the truth in the abstraction and analogical form of their evidence. The aura of the maps, like the traits of Geographia who looks in all directions at once and who holds an anamorphic object that contains a history of cartographic types (what de Leu's portrait and the map strive to do on the following page), appeals to a hidden vein of nonreason within a body of reason.

On the other hand, in the *advertissement aux benevoles lecteurs*, in the figure of Geometria, in the firm line of de Leu's hand, in the letter *AU ROY,* in the preface to "the mayor, the magistrates, the body, and community of the city of Tours," and in the other prefatory matter, the work shows how deeply embedded it is in the political and ideological struggles of the early 1590s. The book has a mission of informing the king about the practical value of an atlas, not just as an image that broadcasts the king's name over the world ("Narrant par l'univers le nompareil BOURBON") by containing it in a microcosm of a "new" Ptolemaic project of Ortelian design, but as a mode of specific counsel. It will diagram the new perimeters of the nation; show how cartography can be used for fortification, warfare, and national defense; present the picture of a country of infinite variety and charm within a finite space, thus fostering the growth of secular pilgrimage or tourism; and offer a new view of the fluvial resources—a potamography—of France.[15] And it will, no less, emblazon the Touraine, the birthplace both of Bouguereau and the atlas, to coordinate the expression of faith in one's identity, soil, language, heritage, and "tradition" in relation to the leader and his capital: It will schematize a new topos of "king and country" or the dialogue between the provincial subject and the administrative center.

It will also use the confines of the Ortelian atlas to program new relations to language and space. By offering a compact national alternative to Thevet's and, in particular, to Belleforest's cosmographies, Bouguereau counters his Catholic enemies with a model taken from Abraham Ortelius, an entrepreneur and amateur of maps and antiquities and also an editor who came from a family inclined to favor the Reformation (Karrow 1993: 1). The new economy of the atlas, especially its mercantile virtue, owes to parsimony of both space and language.[16] Bouguereau will take this in the most literal of ways, not only by printing a number of maps lifted directly from Ortelius but, moreover, by cribbing and then slashing the text of the Catholic Belleforest for the purpose of defending his enterprise to Henry IV. In order to see how Bouguereau goes about his task, we can now compare some of the regional maps to their textual complements.

Maps and Texts Compared: Nicolaï and Symeone

The atlas opens with four maps of France. The first folio map, by Plancius (48 × 39 cm), follows the *privilège* (license) and is placed over Jean Jolivet's *Gallia* (41 × 34.2 cm; this map appeared in Ortelius and is missing from the British Library copy 23) (see Dainville 1964b) but without text on either verso. Guillaume Postel's recent *Gallia* (50 × 34 cm) is sandwiched between pages on the history of the French monarchy and an acrostic quintain, of Bouguereau's apothegm, dedicated to "the city of Paris."[17] There follows Jean Surhom's map of Picardy (40 × 35 cm); Nicolaï's map of Boulogne and Surhom's of Vermandois; Dauphiné, Languedoc, Gascony, Provence, and the Saintonge by Mercator (45 × 34 cm); Mercator's Burgundy (44.5 × 32 cm); Mercator's northern Lorraine (45.5 × 35.8 cm) and Lorraine to the south (47.5 × 63 cm); two maps on one folio, of the Berry and the Auvergne (46.5 × 34 cm), copied from Jean Chaumeau and Gabriele Symeone; Jean Fayen's Limousin (which included an inserted city-view of Limoges in the upper-right corner [47 × 35.5 cm]); Jean du Temps's region around Blois (33 × 47.5 cm); the Touraine by Isaac François (45 × 36 cm); an anonymous map of the Maine (which Cornelius de Jode would soon copy in his *Speculum orbis terrae* [Antwerp, 1593]).[18] The atlas is rounded out by Licimo Guyeto's view of Anjou (46 × 34 cm) and an anonymous map of Brittany (47.5 × 36 cm), taken from a history of Armorica (1588) (Dainville 1985: 327–31).

In sum, seventeen folios of eighteen maps, and fourteen folios dedicated to all of France—except for Normandy and the Ile-de-France—offer a changing perspective on the nation at large. It is seen from afar, that is, in general terms (Mercator's view of the Languedoc); in concise detail of coastlines and forests (Nicolaï's Boulogne); with striking, original views of rivers and the "garden of France" (the Blésois, Maine, Touraine, and Anjou); and with a keen view of coastlines (Brittany). And Postel's map *Gallia*, a work that held its authority well into the 1630s, heralds a sense of detail and totality that neither Ortelius nor de Jode showed in their maps of France.

The drama of the work unfolds in its labor of transformation and trans-valuation. Just as the art of copying engages creative and historical processes in painting and literature, so also does the preparation of Bouguereau's local views and their accompanying texts. In the projection of Boulogne drawn from a previous map by Nicolas de Nicolaï, we follow a line of creation that stretches from France to the Netherlands and then returns to France by way of Ortelius. The map displays its itinerary all over its surface. Born in the Dauphiné, Nicolaï had been a spy, an engineer, and an appointed geographer under Henry II. He first drew navigational maps of Europe and the Mediterranean (1544), soon worked at the fortification of Le Havre after the fall of Boulogne to Henry VIII of England, and later traveled to the British Isles. There, with Lord Dudley, who was then the grand admiral of England, he went north to survey the environs of Scotland, but only to release his findings to Odet de Selvé, the French ambassador to Britain (Hervé 1955: 224–42).[19] In 1548 he was probably at work fortifying the cities of Calais and Guines. That same year, when the duc de Guise expelled the English from Calais, Guines, and Ham, Nicolaï printed a general map of the area (94.6 × 79 cm, on four sheets) (Karrow 1993: 435). In 1570, Ortelius printed a reduced version of the projection (33.6 × 23.9 cm) next to Jean Surhom's view of the Vermandois, with a round cartouche in the lower-left corner and, to the right, the attribution that names the author and the date of execution and includes mention of the *privilège* in the lower-right corner (Figure 6.8).

Gabriel Tavernier redraws both maps for *Le théâtre*. The very slight changes and omissions indicate that the map was respected as authoritative, but that the pressing need to publish the atlas dictated economy in the preparation of new copperplates. In the lower-right-hand corner of Ortelius's version, the name and date are recorded in the vacant space of the town of Montreuil (Monstreul), traced with a flourish, and placed adjacent to the *privilège*. The mountains of Neufchâtel and Dannes are represented as finely hatched *taupinières* ("molehills"), indicating a shift in composition that is caused by the way the engraver handles his burin (Figure 6.9).[20] The English channel is stippled with fine dots, the shorelines shaded by clearly articulated parallel lines of 8–10 mm width. The trees representing forests are done in a specific style, as rounded tufts about a trunk with branches of dots occasionally placed at the edge. The walled cities of Etaples and Montreuil are schematic but detailed in form, just as the River Canche is shown widening its flow with short, wavy, broken lines that accrue near its mouth.

By contrast, Tavernier's drawing (Figure 6.10) is more schematic, if not more vacant. The stipples are less numerous, and the lines defining the molehills

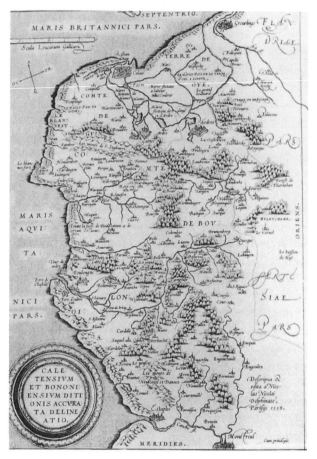

Figure 6.8. Map of Boulogne copied from Nicolas de Nicolaï
(Abraham Ortelius, *Theatrum orbis terrarum*, 1570)

blend into dark blotches south of the mouth of the Canches, or else, to the
north of Etaples, they are omitted. The lines of the river are straighter and prone
to mix, as are the hatchings defining the coastline. The calligraphy of place-
names is finer, the representation of the cities is less compressed (Montreuil)
or squarish (Etaples), while the shape of the trees is clearly more compact,
with broader trunks and horizontal figures of branches (Figure 6.11). In the
copy in Ortelius (Figure 6.12), by contrast, the trees are rounder and in a
denser and fuller agglomeration below Le boÿs Labbé. Nicolaï's careful rendering of the Bollemberg fortress is missing. The date of Nicolaï's rendering and
the sign of the *privilège* are erased. The map looks more "modern" in 1594

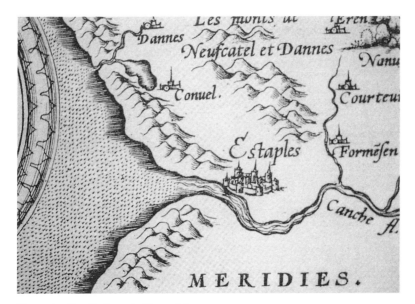

Figure 6.9. Detail of map in Figure 6.8

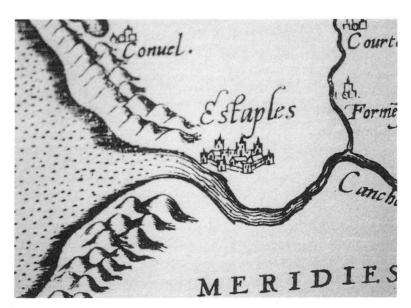

Figure 6.10. Detail of Gabriel Tavernier's redrawn version of Ortelius's map (Maurice Bouguereau, *Le théâtre françoys*)

Figure 6.11. Detail of Gabriel Tavernier's redrawn version of Ortelius's map, Boulogne area (Maurice Bouguereau, *Le théâtre françoys*)

without the date 1558, a year that would not have been overly distant for Ortelius in 1570. The plate acquires a signature in the way Tavernier *copies the copy* and, in doing so, partially erases the history of its composition.

The decoration along the shores and in the northern region of both maps is brought forth by the text on the back of Bouguereau's folio. Of all the maps in *Le théâtre,* only Nicolaï's pays close heed to fortification where, in the Boulogne, three fortresses—La Tour d'Ordre, Le Fort de Chastillon, and the Fort d'Oultre eau—sit between the city and the channel. The same holds

Figure 6.12. Boulogne (middle left; Abraham Ortelius, *Theatrum orbis terrarum*)

for Guines, Ardres, and Calais, whose representations display their system of moats and waterways. (Ardres and its environs in Ortelius are shown in Figure 6.13.) Attention is brought to this feature of the map in the text, it seems, by coincidence. Bouguereau finishes his description of the Boulogne with praise of the fortification in 1560 (see the end of his text in Table 6.1). His text sketches an itinerary in accord with the place-names on the map verso.

It appears that the Tourangeau editor has looked closely at the map and has taken care to bring forth Nicolaï's rendition of the region's defensive network.

Figure 6.13. Ardres and environs (Abraham Ortelius, *Theatrum orbis terrarum*)

The text follows the map in a haptic description that moves from Blannes ("Les blancnes fort") on the coast, eastward along the Saint Inglevert mountains ("S. Inglenert" on both maps), to Guines, which indeed shows a fort separated from the town by a marsh, with the chateau on solid ground, "chose imprenable selon les hommes" (a reputedly impenetrable retreat). The description continues along the same axis to Ardres, passing by the floating swamplands of Bellingen and Ardres ("on voit les marests flottans"), as shown on Tavernier's copy in Bouguereau (Figure 6.14). The description turns north and west along the channel separating the cantons of Guines and Oye (marked in upper-case letters on the map). The prose follows the same course to the sea by the port of Nieullet ("pont" on the map) and Calais, "d'où se void à descouvert le fort de Ribant le long de mer." Calais is described as it is seen on the map, "in quadrangular form." Since its walls have recently been fortified to protect against the English, the site has become one of the "most powerful cities of Europe."

Text and map confirm each other so clearly that Bouguereau's description seems to follow an itinerary across Nicolaï's projection, to dwell on its salient details, to historicize the space in parentheses, and ultimately—albeit indirectly—to suggest that he is underscoring the logistic value of his atlas. These details, to which attention is drawn in ocular terms, would show that the en-

Figure 6.14. Ardres and environs (Maurice Bouguereau, *Le théâtre françoys*)

trepreneur has grasped a practical dimension of the atlas by emphasizing in writing what Nicolaï has also underscored in imagistic detail.

But at the same time, the persisting tradition of cosmography and *copia* shows that, although Bouguereau is indeed cribbing Belleforest's description of the area, he is also adjusting it slightly to correlate it with the map, which in turn renders superfluous the tidal waves of Belleforest's prose. The map obviates recourse to *copia* and compilation at the same time that it gives reason and authenticity—the firsthandedness of a visitor's account of real travel—to Bouguereau's creation. Comparison of the text and its source—as in Table 6.1—shows that the atlas project is born of an economy based on religious considerations, which are transmuted into a style that mediates *copia* and *brevitas* (italicized portions show what Bouguereau cribbed from Belleforest).[21] The text of 1594 is compiled to appear to be a function of the map, or a spur prodding the reader to follow a history that is congealed in the space of the map. Drawing on Belleforest's formulas evoking an ongoing itinerary ("vous entrez . . . de là on vient à . . . ," etc.), Bouguereau fabricates a description that follows the map at the same time that the words come by way of another compiler. The new textual form discovered its mobility by an art of selection, excision, and juxtaposition. Citations are tailored to fit the map, but also to rewrite the local history and to give more immediacy to the impression of carto-

Table 6.1. Comparison of Texts of Bouguereau and Belleforest

Bouguereau	Belleforest
Passé Boloigne & la fosse d'icelle, qui contient vingt et six lieues de circuit: vous entrez au Comté de Guisnes, auquel sont les places de Blannes, qui est un fort, la place & monts S. Inglevert, puis la ville & fort de Guisnes separé en deux, comme le voyez de l'autre part, l'une partie estant dans le marest & pallus maritimes, & l'autre sur terre ferme: chose imprenable selon les hommes. Entre Guisnes & Ardres, forte ville (ou se feist l'entreveue des Roys de France et d'Angleterre, François premier & Henry huictiesme) on voit les marests flotans de Bellingen, d'Ardres, & le canal de la mer qui passe à Guisnes, separe les Comtez de Guisnes & d'Oye, rendans le païs presque inaccessible, puis on vient au port de Nieullet & à Calais forte ville, d'ou se voit à descouvert le fort de Ribant le long de la Mer. Calais est en forme quadrangulaire au Comté d'Oye, place forte, regaignée sur les Angloys par le Roy Henry deuxiesme, au plus fort de l'hyver, au grand estonnement de toute l'Europe, veu l'assiette et force d'icelle, comme aussi Guisnes: Nous avons traitté cy dessus, de son Antiquité & nom, elle fut fermée & ceincte de muraille du temps du roy Saint Loys, que Philippe Comte de Boulogne oncle du Roy ceignit de mu-	*Passé Boloigne, & la fosse d'icelle, qui a quelque 16. lieues de circuit, vous entrez au comté de Guisnes,* lequel vous avez veu cy dessus, comme fut desmembré de Flandres, *auquel sont les places de Blānes qui est un fort,* puis *la place de S. Inglevert* & les monts portans mesme nom, & soudain s'offre la ville, & *fort de Guisnes separé en deux, l'une partie* assise *dans les palus maritimes, & l'autre en terre ferme,* & si fort qu'il semble impossible qu'on y puisse donner attainte. *Entre Guismes, & Ardres,* qui est aussi une belle ville, & puissante forteresse, & en laquelle fut *l'entreveuë des Roys de France, & d'Angleterre François Premier, & Henry huistiesme on voit des marests flottants,* qu'on appelle Marests *de Belingen, & d'Ardres; & le canal de la mer qui passe à Guisnes separe les comtés de Guisnes, & d'Oye, rendans le pays presque inaccessible,* & de là *on vient* à Hames, & au haut païs de Guisnes, à Hartincourt, Peuplingue & Conquelle, & *puis à* ce fameux *port de Nieullet* gaigné par les françois en l'an mille cinq cens cinquante huit, conduits par le Duc de Guise François de Lorraine, lequel aussi conquist la puissante, & presque invincible ville de *Calais,* de laquelle je vous ay mis un dessein, & figure selon l'enceinte, & assiette d'icelle *en forme quadrangulaire,* la faisant paroistre effroyable de tous costez. En tant que de la part Septentionale on voit le Risban sur la pointe de la terre entrant en mer, puis la chaussee du pont de Nieullet à l'Occident, au Midy les marests flottants de Hames du costé de Saint-Pierre. Et au Levant luy est le reste de la terre d'Oye, & les Dunes d'icelles s'estendans iusques à Gravelingues: estant ce pays renommé d'Oye d'une petite ville no(m)mée ainsi, avoisinée d'une place nommée Hosterbecke, qui est la haute terre à labeur du pays d'Oye. Or quant

raille, & y dressa & fortifia le port, pour servir de rempart contre l'Anglois, qui l'a toutesfois depuis fortifiée, mieux flanquée, & rendue des plus puissantes villes de France.

à la ville de Calais, on sçait de quelle consequence elle est, & combien les Roys de France ont travaillé à la rescouvrer depuis les Angloys la prindrent sur Philippe de Valois, apres la malheureuse journée de Cressy en l'an trois cens quarante sept, de sorte qu'il ne leur a esté possible de la ravoir iusque'à ce que *Henry second* y mist la diligence, & que François de Lorraine Duc de Guise y alla a main armée, *au plus fort de l'hiver,* & non sans *esbahissement de toute l'Europe veu la forte assiete* de cette place, & le haut coeur de ceux qui la deffendoyent. Et *autant* en feist il *a Guisnes,* qu'on estimoit aussi estre imprenable. Quant à *l'antiquité* de Calais, *nous en avons parlé cy dessus, &* monstré le discord qui est entre les auteurs touchant *son nom:* car quant a son estre, tous confessent que du temps des Romains ce fut un port, & par consequent qu'il estoit habité, & y avoit des maisons, edifices, & clostures pour se deffendre. Neantmoins ne fut elle un fort long temps qu'un simple bourg champestre, iusqu'au *temps du Roy Saint Loys, que Philippe Comte de Bouloigne oncle du Roy ceignit ce lieu de muraille, & y dressa, & fortifia le port, a fin que servit de rempart contre l'Anglois,* & que aisément on peut là dresser une armée de mer, lors que la necessité viendroit le requerir. *Depuis* les Anglois l'ont de mieux en *mieux* remparee, munie, *flanquee, & rendue des plus puissantes villes de* l'Europe. (II, 1 fol. 387)

graphic ekphrasis. Belleforest adorns his sentences with long enumerations of toponyms that the map is better able to display in diagrammatic form. Bouguereau lifts the reference to the duc de Guise in order to downplay Catholic military presence in the chronicle. Belleforest calls Calais one of the strongest cities of Europe, while Bouguereau extols its virtue in respect to France. A brief, salient style of description—describing only what is considered to be historically and topographically worthy—is born on the grounds of paginal economy, yet it includes the suavely drawn conceits that Belleforest gathered from earlier sources.

Bouguereau takes care to define the borders and to use the chart as a point of reference.

> Au levant . . . toute ceste estendue de pays comprend plusieurs villes & infinité de bourgs, chasteaux, villages, Rivieres & forests comme la Charte vous demontre, & descripte par Nicolas Daulphinois. . . . La longueur du Boulonnois comprend depuis les monts Saint Inglevert, iusques à la riviere de Canche: & sa longueur depuis la Mer Occidentale iusques à la forest de Tournehan, ou l'on voit infinité de belles maisons & places dignes de remarque, comme le verrez en ceste Charte, mesmes le pont de bricque & le fort d'oultre l'eau, & celuy de Chastillon.

> [To the east . . . the entire stretch of country includes several cities and an infinity of towns, castles, villages, rivers, and forests, as the map shows you, as done by Nicolas Dauphinois. . . . the length of Boulogne goes from the Saint Inglevert mountains to the River Canche: and its width from the sea to the west as far as the Tournehan Forest, where are seen an infinity of handsome houses and things worth being remarked, as you will notice in this map, including the brick bridge and Châtillon, the fortress beyond the water.]

The process of cross-referencing or of footnoting within the text was common to cosmography; for example, the text here figures the redoubtable wall of Calais and demonstrates the strength of the duc de Guise ("who also conquered the powerful and almost invincible city of Calais, whose view I offer to you in a drawing"). But in *Le théâtre,* the correlations become manifest, evident, and *immediately* discernible, even if they are made in passing or without intention. A prose that is haptic, historiographical, touristic, and ostensibly neutral is attached to the map and is coextensive with it. The discourse gains its signature through a latent system of correspondences to the map.

A remarkable evolution of text and writing emerges from the small map of "La Limaigne d'Auvergne" (Figure 6.15). Tavernier copies the map from Ortelius just as he redrew Nicolaï's Boulogne from the 1570 *Theatrum orbis terrarum.* Once again, the copy is drawn hastily. Yet Tavernier's hand is evident in the removal of the flourishes at the beginnings and ends of place-names (e.g., Moson and Liarium). Ortelius's designer gives the upper edge a perspectival effect that is due to the mountains to the left and right of *septentrio* by the upper edge of the frame, whereas Tavernier lets one mountain cross the upper line (to the left) and sets other mountains (to the right) in front of the margin. The cartouche that acknowledges the map's origin in Symeone is sketchy. Ortelius remarks on the verso page of the map, "Sic Auctor in Dialogo pio &

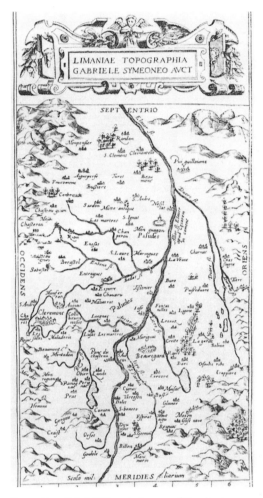

Figure 6.15. Gabriel Tavernier's copy of Ortelius's "Limaigne d'Auvergne" (Maurice Bouguereau, *Le théâtre françoys*)

speculativo (ut inscriptio habet) Italicè à se scripto, ubi haec tabula videri licet": He refers to Symeone's original woodcut (dating from 1560), which accompanied a book of emblems that form part of a philosophical dialogue published by Guillaume Roville.[22]

Published by one of the most avid printers of images, emblems, and memorabilia, the map, imprese, and dialogue seem to reflect the midcentury taste for antiquities and singularities, which localities used to valorize the rooted-

Figure 6.16. Gabriele Symeone's "La Limania d'Overnia"

ness of their "national origins" (Figure 6.16). Symeone plots and draws the
map for the Bishop of Clermont in exchange for the protection he receives. In
the original woodcut, two textual features are apparent. First, the spandrel-
like spaces between the oval frame and the edges of the rectangular sheets are
filled with four festooned coats of arms: Catherine of Medici (upper left),
Guillaume du Prat, Bishop of Clermont (upper right), the City of Clermont
(lower left), and Symeone's own, of his own invention (lower left). Sites are
indicated by alphabetic signs that refer to moments in an accompanying dialogue, held between a student and a master, that unfolds the history of Julius
Caesar's conquest of Gergovia in the seventh book of the *Gallic War* (Julius

Caesar 1917: 380-85). Each inscription on the chart refers to an event in a text that animates the map. Symeone has crafted a narrative, historical, and even "talking" map that includes figures in the landscape not only for decorative or perspectival reasons, but also for the sake of mobilizing the speech (or authority) of a chronicle that is being reenacted. An archaeological value is conferred upon the place in order to reestablish the oldest evidence of French tradition. Symeone gives to the region a tradition and, most important, a *voice*. He conflates its cause and finality into a figure of a cartographer and his apparatus on the foregrounding mountain that establishes the bird's-eye view. The map stands as the first depiction of a specific region of France at the same time that its dialogic reconstruction of Caesar's battle remains authoritative (Renucci 1943: ix; 1944). Like an emblem, however, the map is drawn to be written in the form of what might be called a mute speaker, or a picture that camouflages its silence with imaginary discourse, confirming that "emblematic compositions of the Renaissance speak to the dream of transparency that inhabits the imagination of the time in its *desire to make the world speak*, to restore the mute language of signs" (Mathieu-Castellani 1988a: 29, emphasis added).[23] With Symeone's map, too, we see that the "uncanny silence" of the emblematic map, that is, its "insignificance" (29), is literally what the cartographer strives to repress. Such is its relation to the unknown: It attempts to give voice to a relation of difference between discourse and diagram. In a broad way, Symeone's design appears symptomatic of the fear of the mute authority that the language of maps—including his own—will gain in the future.

The fear that underlies the will to give voice to "La Limaigne d'Auvergne" may be confirmed in the redrawn version in Ortelius's *Orbis theatrum* and Bouguereau's *Le théâtre*. In fact, when Belleforest plagiarizes Symeone's map in *La cosmographie universelle*, he continues to make the diagram speak, but he does so through the garrulous tone of his own *copia*, which literally *frame* the oval projection. In Belleforest's design, the original dialogue is not silenced, but it is rendered unintelligible under the cosmographer's amplification in the accompanying columns of text. The alphabetic markers and the historical images (such as the rows of troops preparing for battle) remain but go unmentioned. Although the heraldic material is kept in the frame to enhance the chapter of the *Cosmographie* on the Auvergne, the decorations above and below are cropped away. Belleforest chooses to reproduce the Gallic campaign through the war he declares on Symeone in the dialogic register. It affirms its own veracity through the archaic analogies of names and places that had marked Rabelais and the *itineraria*:

Le bas pays d'Auvergne est appellée Limaigne, sur le nom duquel les opinions sont diverses, car les uns pensent qu'il soit dict ainsi du limon, & terre boüeuse, tant pour estre les vallons humides, & arrousez d'eaux, que pour la gresse de la terre: d'autres le prennent du mot Latin Alimonia, nourriture pour ce que le pays est gras, fertil, & tresabondant de toutes sortes de vivres. Et suis d'une opinion contraire, & pense que l'un des fleuves outre l'Allier, qui passent par cette contrée, produit iadis le nom de Limaine, à quoy me fait condescendre un passage de Gregoire de Tours.

[The lower region of Auvergne is called Limaigne, about whose name opinions are divided, for some think that it is said thus as much because of the silt, and muddy ground, or the wet valleys that are sprinkled with water, as for the fat of the earth: Others derive it from the Latin word *alimonia*, nourishment, because the country is fleshy, fertile, and abounding with all kinds of foods. And I am of a contrary opinion, and believe that one of the rivers beyond the Allier, that go through this country, used to carry the name of Limaine, which reminds me of a passage of Gregory of Tours that flows down to me.] (II, 1 fol. 222)

Belleforest admits that the river of the map carries its name, just as our knowledge of the area flows downward from historical origins in a passage from Gregory of Tours. The flow of fertile and sterile names grounds a noisy dispute with the map being plagiarized:

Le Liman se desborda tellement qu'il esmpescha plusieurs d'ensemencer leurs terres: voire les fleuves de Loire, & l'Alier, & autres torrens s'escoulans en iceluy, s'enflurent de sortes, qu'ils outrepasserent les limites, que iamais ils n'avoyent passé. Voyez la façon de parler de cest auteur [Symeone], & remarquez les mots de prez, & je suis seur que me confesseray qu'il parle non de la province de la Limaigne, ains d'un fleuve, estant en icelle, & duquel tout ce pays porte a present ce nom. Aussi ay-je sceu que la riviere dicte la Lymone ou la Lymonne, descend des montaignes en la Limaigne, & à son coure vers saint Fleuret, Nochers, & Saint Amans, & Saint Saturnin, Talende Martyre de Vaire, & va se joindre a l'Alier, & est sans autre celle qui a donné le nom au pays de la Limaigne. Que si quelqu'un a des raisons meilleures, qu'il les ameine, car (comme tousiours i'ay dit) ie ne suis homme qui refuse de m'humilier soubz l'equité de ceux qui parlent, & raisonablement, & avec verité.

[The Liman overflowed such that it impeded other rivers from fertilizing their lands: Indeed the Rivers Loire and Allier, and other torrents flowing in this one, swelled up so much that they exceeded every limit that they had formerly passed. Look at the way this author [Symeone] speaks, and study his words closely, and I am sure that everyone will avow that he is speaking not of the Limaigne province, but of a river located within, and from which the entire country now carries this name. Thus I know that the so-called Limone or Lymonne River descends from the mountains in Limaigne, and flows toward Saint Fleuret, Nochers, Saint Amans, Saint Saturnin, Talende the Martyr of Vaire, and proceeds to be joined with the Allier, and is none other than the one that has brought the name to the

province of Limaigne. If anyone has a stronger reason, may that person bring it
to me, for (as I have always said), I am a man who does not refuse to be humbled
under the equity of those who speak and reason with truth.] (II, 1 fol. 223)

The author shunts the dialogue between the map and Symeone's text—a vital
part of the creation of 1560—into one between names and of self-reproducing
artifacts in his own verbiage. Like Thevet, he produces evidence in the flow of
the discourse, the words flowing *like* the rivers being described, with the point
that Belleforest is making proven in the way that the *Limaine* leads him to the
site of his dispute, the cause and effect of the toponym in the paragrammar
visible in the verbal flow: "Que si quelqu'un a des *raisons meilleures*, qu'il *les
ameine*."

Bouguereau works differently. With a dry style reminiscent of Tavernier's
burin, the text seeks a matte description that would be closer to the Protestant
Charles Estienne's itineraries and descriptions of rivers than to Belleforest's rivers of words.[24] Fancifully motivated etymons are replaced by the description of
the limits of the area and its chateaus, its bailiwicks, its presidial court, and its
county seat; other towns, natural resources, *singularitez en ce pays,* and points
of interest are enumerated: fountains, subterranean rivers, windmills and
paper mills; limestone formations and mineral waters (alum, sulphur, cal-
cium), "having a taste of wine, but unpleasant to drink"; ruins, silver mines,
mountains and pasturelands; natural drugs; even, in Rochedagou, a rock that
splinters into diamondlike pieces, or golden silt in a lake that can be used to
approximate the gilt-edges of expensive books. The description follows an itinerary (Rore to Puy-de-Dôme to Cherre to River Ordonne to Besse to Vichy)
that is *not* coordinated with the map. A touristic and informational, *denotative*
prose is set in place. The evolution from Symeone, Belleforest, and Ortelius
shows how the truth effects of the atlas structure begin to fall in place.

An Atlas of Rivers: Chorography, Potamography, and the Image of a Nation

Belleforest's description of the River Allier next to the woodcut version of
Symeone's "La Limaigne d'Auvergne" pushes words along a tortuous verbal
flow. His style corresponds to a potamographic map: It pulls the reader into its
current, swirls about, crests, and washes over a vast paginal area. Bouguereau
attempts to channel or control that flood without sacrificing its content and
flow. He deploys rivers to disseminate to the commonwealth the shape of an
idealized national geography. The trick involves, first, building an encomium
of the *fleuves* of France in the style inherited from Estienne and Belleforest,

but without letting tributary information disappear under the flow of words that describe their course. Second, the river's appeal to the imagination is retained in order to keep the idea of the cohering nation associated with the network of fluvial passages. Belleforest had already celebrated the Seine, which flows through the heart of the nation, in terms that linked the health of the body politic to the freedom of its waterways.[25]

Throughout *Le théâtre françoys,* a descriptive potamography celebrates the author's native Touraine. The most striking maps in the atlas are the richly veined portrayals, executed by virtually unknown local cartographers, of the Limousin, Poitou, the areas around Blois and Tours, the Maine, Anjou, and the mouth of the Loire beyond Nantes. The succession of maps—from the juxtaposition of Chaumeau's and Symeone's maps on the same folio—seems to follow the course of the Loire from its juncture with the Allier at Nevers. There begins a fluvial narrative winding through the second half of the volume (seven maps).

The Loire becomes Bouguereau's perspectival object. It is represented as a nourishing mother of rivers to which the author owes his identity. Serene and generous clichés abound along the way. Amboise has before it "toute ceste belle plaine . . . decorée de ce beau fleuve de Loyre qui la lave & d'où l'on voit les batteaux monter & descendre" [this whole handsome plain . . . decorated with this beautiful Loire river that washes it and on which boats are seen continually moving upstream and down] (fol. xi r). Tours is "situated on the Loire, which embraces the city when the river rises on its sides" (fol. xii r) and provides for its citizens a view from the central bridge, "whence are seen the boats that move along, upstream and down, for over a distance of twelve leagues" (fol. xii v). In the description of the Maine which responds directly to the form of the map it is appended to, the area is said to be "embellished with several forests, flatlands, and pastures, better suited for hunting and cattle grazing than farming, in addition to the adornment of forests of high trees, vineyards, rivers, and ponds"; in its climate "great minds abound," and a literary geography, lists, as if they were famous sites, the poets Arnoul and Simon Gréban, the du Bellay brothers, Lazar and Jean-Antoine de Baïf, Ronsard, Jean and Jacques Peletier, Nicolas Denisot, Jacques Tahureau. . . .

The descriptive process finds its most exhilarating synthesis of maps, history, and ideology in the folio dedicated to the Anjou (Figure 6.17). Licimo Guyeto's fluvial map of the area, resembling an anatomical depiction of a pulmonary system of arteries and veins, is synthesized in a prose that indiscriminately mixes geography and genealogy.[26] The analogies are lifted directly from Estienne and Belleforest. "La principale des rivieres qui lavent le pays est ce

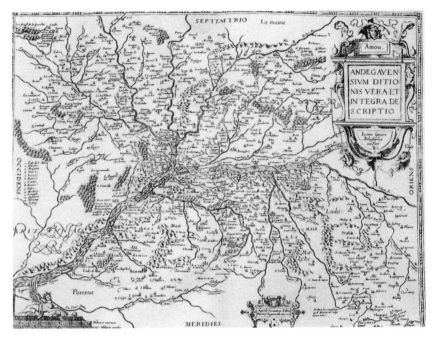

Figure 6.17. Licimo Guyeto's Anjou (Maurice Bouguereau, *Le théâtre françoys*)

Loire qu'on nomme tout ainsi le pere des fleuves de Gaule" [the main river that washes the country is this Loire, which is thus named the father of waterways in Gaul], wrote Belleforest (vol. 2, 175). One must see, he adds, "les fleuves qui arrousent l'Anjou" [the rivers irrigating the Anjou] from all cardinal directions (vol. 2, 177). But, in contrast to the cosmographer's inflated enumerations, Bouguereau conflates two registers in an arid prose in which a confusion of history and geography emerges from the expanse of a descriptive landscape. The historical, geographic, and genealogical background needs to be seen in the expansive virtue of its fluvial style:

> Ce pays est lavé de plusieurs rivieres, à sçavoir, du Loyre Pere des fleuves Gaulois, entrant en iceluy Vienne (qui vient du Lymosin) à Candes Limitrophe de Touraine & Anjou, au dessus de Saulmur Ancien Siege Presidial. Y entre aussi au dessoubs de Mon soreau, le ruisseau des fontaines de Fonte-vrault, Abbaye de filles autant honorable qu'autre de ce Royaume, par le bon & sainct gouvernement des Abbesses qui y ont esté en ces derniers temps, mesmes de louable & heureuse memoire deffuncte Loyse de Bourbon Dame Saincte & vertueuse, ne luy degenerant en rien Madame Eleonor de Bourbon sa niepce, auiourd'huy Abbesse dudit lieu, vray miroyr de Saincteté & Tyge de ce bon Roy Sainct Loys, lumiere des Bourbons. La se voyent les Tombeaux des Roys & Roynes

d'Angleterre, comme aussi la susdite Eleonor, pour l'amour qu'elle portoit à Madame Loyse sa Tante & predecesseure, & sçachant qu'il la faut suivre. A fait dresser tant pour la deffuncte que pour elle, un Tombeau excellent eslevé sur pilliers de Cuivre richement elabouré, au milieu du coeur de l'Eglise dudict lieu: & outre amplifié ceste maison de tresbeaux bastiments, à sçavoir de l'Hotel de Bourbon avec sa Chapelle tres-somptueuse & l'Enfermerie ou sont les mallades.

Revenans à nos fleuves nous dirons que la Dive venant de Montcontour & passant par le Poictou entre en icelle la Losse Poictevine & passant pres Brezay, S. Just & S. Cir se joint dans le Thoüet pres Chassé, lequel Thoüet passe à S. Generoux, Pontorson, Montroeil-le-Bellay, se joignant à celle d'Argenton tombe en Loyre au dessoubs de Saumur, au pied de l'Abbaye S. Florent. Suit apres le Layon dans lequel entrent, le Lys, Lyronne, & Ligne, qui sourd entre la Tour Landry, (renommée de ce Maire du Palais, qui feist mourir le Roy Chilperic, à la sollicitation de sa femme Fredegonde) passe par Chemillé, qui recevant le ruisseau creux & large nommé Ieu, qui entre au Layon & eux deux se font joindre en Loyre au dessus de Chalonne. Le Leure se joint aussi à Loyre au dessous du pont S. Florent, comme aussi la Guygnate au dessoubs de Ghantoceaux, & la Sevre et Maine vers les marches d'Anjou & de Poictou s'assemblent au Loire. L'Authyon & le Loyr, est du costé du levant, & la riviere de Latan se trouve entre les deux, laquelle vient de l'Estang de Rillé au haut Anjou, à costé de Bourgueil, qui se va joindre à l'Authion au dessus de Rille. En ce mesme fleuve, entre le Couaisnon, lequel passe par Baugé, & Beaufort, puis se vient joindre à l'Authion au dessoubs d'Angers pres l'Isle de la Merdiere. Le Loyr semblablement venant d'au dessus du Lude arrouse ladite ville. Dans iceluy entrent les fleuves de Mareil & Torcé, puis à Lucé à la Flesche, Duretal, le Verger, Matefelon, Sechet & Corzé, au dessoubs duquel il reçoit le fleuve d'Ouste, puis va à Briolay & au dessoubs se joinct à la riviere de Sarte qui vient de Normandie, & coulant le long du Mayne vient au Pont de Parcé, de la à Sablé, Chasteau-neuf, Chesses, puis passant à costé de Briolay rase Escouflans, & la, le Loyr & Sarte confluent ensemble, & au dessoubs de l'Isle S. Aulbin tombent en la Mayne, & y perdent leur nom. La Mayne ou Mayenne vient du Mont S. Cir & de Mayne, deux lieux au dessoubs d'Alençon, prenant accroissement de la belle fontaine Mevite, passe par Mayenne dont elle porte le nom & venant à Antrames reçoit le fleuve d'Ionne, & est enflée par le ruisseau de Villiers-Charlemaigne d'ou fut natif Guillaume de l'Esrat, President à Angers & duquel sont sortis deux enfans qui ont esté tous deux Presidents, tant à Angers, qu'au Parlement de Rennes. Mayne s'en vient de la, passer à Chasteau-gontier, & entre Mesnil & Daon le Maine reçoit le fleuve Beron, & à Grez y entre Oudon, au pont d'Espinar, & de la à Angers rasans le Chasteau & se vient rendre à deux lieües au dessoubs dans Loyre audict lieu Bouchemaine. (L)a riviere d'Oudon sort du Craonnois, recevant les rivieres de Cossé et Crosmes au dessus de Craon, au dessoubs du Pont de laquelle entre en l'Oudon, le Charrans pres de la forest ancienne de Nioyseau ou jadis philosophoient les Saronides, puis y entrent Uresée, Argos & Omée, & passant par Segré tombe en Mayne au dessoubs du pont du Lyon d'Angers ou il perd son nom. Loyre enflé de tous les fleuves prend encor la losse Angevine & Erdret, venant de l'Abbaye du Loroux. Oultre les singularitez que dessus, se treuve pres d'Angers d'excellent marbre tant blanc que noir, puis les excellentes perrieres de fine ardoise, qui fait admirer ceux qui les vont voir, pour la grande profondité d'icelles & fraiz qui s'y font, mesmes que les hommes travaillants au fons des-dictes Ardoisieres semblent comme petits nains, tant la profondeur est basse. Voila Lecteur ce qu'au plus abregé nous t'en pouvons dire.

[This country is washed by several rivers, that is, from the Loire, Father of Gaul's rivers, into which enters the Vienne (originating in the Limousin) at Candes, at the line between the Touraine and the Anjou, above Saumur, a former presidial seat. Also entering, below Monsoreau, is the rivulet from the springs of Fontevrault, the abbey of ladies as honorable as any in the kingdom, under the good and saintly leadership of the abbesses who have been there of late, even of the happy and praiseworthy memory of the late Louise de Bourbon, a saintly and virtuous lady, not at all diminishing that of her niece, Madame Eleanor de Bourbon, today the abbess of the said place, a true mirror of sanctity and the stock of this good king Saint Louis, the beacon of the Bourbons. There are seen the tombs of the king and queen of England, as also the aforementioned Eleanor, for the love she carried for Madame Louise her aunt and predecessor, and in knowing that it must follow her. As much for the deceased as for her is erected an excellent tomb raised on richly decorated copper piers, in the middle of the choir of the church of that site, the house further extended with handsome buildings, notably the Hotel de Bourbon with its sumptuous chapel and infirmary in which its patients are held.

Returning to our rivers, we must state that into the Dive, coming from Montcontour and passing through Poitou, enters the Poitevine Losse. The Dive passes near Brezay, Saint Just, and Saint Cyr, is joined by the Thouët near Chassé, and then passes to Saint Generoux, Pontorson, Montroeil-le-Bellay, being met by that of Argenton, then emptying into the Loire below Saumur, at the foot of the Saint-Florent Abbey. Then follows the Layon River, into which enter the Loys, Lyronne, and Ligne, that erupts from the ground by the Tour Landry (renowned for the mayor of the castle, who had the king Chilperic put to death at the command of his wife Fredegonde), passing by Chemillé, which receives the deep and wide river named Jeu, that enters into the Layon. The two join the Loire above Chalonne. The Leure is also connected to the Loire below the Saint Florent Bridge, like the Guygnate below Ghantoceaux, and the Sèvre and Maine toward the threshold of Anjou and Poitou flowing into the Loire. The Authion and the Loir are to the west, and the Latan River is located between the two, and comes from the Rillé pond in upper Anjou, next to Bourgueil, which then joins the Authion above Rillé. The Couaisnon flows into this very river, which passes near Baugé and Beaufort, then connects with the Authion below Angers near the Merdière Island. Likewise, coming from above Lude, the Loir washes the city of Angers. Into it empty the Mareil and Torcé Rivers, then, at Lucé at La Flèche, Duretal, the Orchard, Matefelon, Sechet, and Corzé, below which it receives the Ouste River, than goes to Briosay and below is joined to the Sarthe River that comes from Normandy, and flows through the Maine in coming to the Parcé Bridge, grazes Escoulfans, and there joins the Loir and Sarthe, and below the

Saint Aubin Island they empty into the Maine where they lose their name. The Maine or Mayenne originates at Mont-Saint-Cyr and the Maine, two places below Alençon, growing from the Mevite spring, going by Mayenne, whose name it carries, and comes to Antrames, receiving the Ionne River, and is swollen by the Villiers-Charlemaigne creek whence came William of Erat, president of Angers and from whom issued two children who both were presidents, at Angers and at the Parliament of Rennes. The Maine bends by, passsing next to Château-Gontier, and between Mesnil and Daon the Maine receives the Beron River, and at Grez the Oudon enters into it, at the Spinach Bridge, and from there to Angers grazes the Château and empties into the Loire two leagues below the place named Bouchemaine. The Oudon river goes out the Craonnais, receiving the Cossé and Crômes Rivers above Craon, below the bridge from which the Charrance dumps into the Oudon, near the old Nioyseau Forest where the Saronides formerly philosophized, where then enter the Uresée, Argos and Omée, and flowing by Segré, falls into the Maine below the Lyon bridge at Angers, where it loses its name. The Loire, swollen from all these rivers, then picks up the Angevine and Erdret creeks coming from the Loroux Abbey. In addition to the singularities above, at Angers is found excellent marble, no less white than black, and then the quarries of delicate slate that everyone who visits them cannot fail to admire, both for their great and cool depths, so much in fact that the miners working at the bottom of these slate quarries look like dwarfs since the mine is so deep. There, dear Reader, is what in a few words we can tell you about the region.] (fol. xiii r-v)

Bouguereau follows the river as it is drawn on the map, dotting his survey with architectural and historical sites remembered by the proper names attached to the toponyms. Like a logo, each anthroponym and toponym gives the area an effect of legitimacy.

As the stem of the Bourbon family is planted at the beginning of the itinerary, the map confirms the chronicle and genealogy listed in the preface to the atlas. And in writing "revenans à nos fleuves," Bouguereau's guide admits of an oblivion that the text must retrieve or motivate through heroic enumerations that mix family names with sites noted along the Loire. The junctures of tributaries are depicted in clichés of the bodily congress and copulation that assure the genealogical transfer. Both Fredegonde and the river "receive" the hollow and wide rivulet named Leu, which penetrates Layon, and together ("eux deux") they assemble the whole. The Loir does likewise, following down to the Loire, and at the juncture, in congress, of the various bodies "y perdent leur nom" [therein they lose their name]. The Villiers-Charlemaigne creek that meets or enters the Maine at Antrames, in the fantasy of the late William of Erat, is virtually born of the waters swollen like a pregnant belly. A detailed survey accompanies the map, the writing miming the unification of the river as if it were that of the entire nation. The tributaries lose their names in order to be-

Figure 6.18. Detail of Figure 6.17: tributaries of the Loire (Maurice Bouguereau, *Le théâtre françoys*)

come the great trunk of a genealogical tree that moves from leaves and branches to the Atlantic Ocean.[27] A regional and national allegory is fused through the conflation of the text and design of the map and its details (e.g., Figures 6.18–6.20, which go from La Flèche to Anjou). The prose is so closely related to the style and form of the map that it achieves what is proposed in the relation of the figure of the king to the nation set forth in the preface to the atlas.

The Signature: Bouguereau's Vanishing Point

The style of the editor's description of the Anjou reverts to the copious mode that identifies the major sources for the atlas, but it does so for both covert and overt political and ideological reasons. The Loire blends into a great, wide trunk likened to the single *Loy, Roy,* and *Foy* of the French nation. From the beginning of the atlas, with the anamorphic presentation of France in the hands of the sibylline Geographia, Bouguereau puts together a coherent totality that will soon exercise a strong influence over the cartography of the first half of the seventeenth century. Just as Guyeto's map will be used as a model for Christophe Tassin's classical epitome of 1640 (Figure 6.21), so also will Postel's *Gallia* and other topographic views from *Le théâtre* figure in successive editions of Jean Leclerc's atlas (1619–1632) (Dainville 1985).

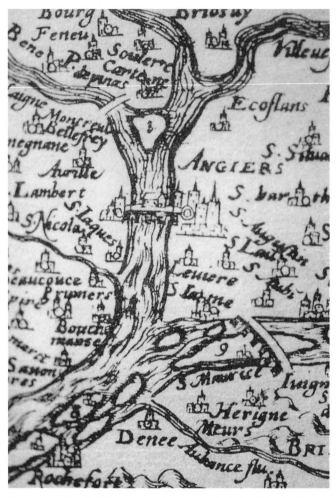

Figure 6.19. Detail of Figure 6.17: Angers and the Loire (Maurice Bouguereau, *Le théâtre françoys*)

Probably the most unifying and patent trait of the volume is its expanded and
pervasive sense of a signature. Père Dainville remarks that Gabriel Tavernier,
the Flemish engraver hired to engrave the atlas, remains a principal "actor" in
Le théâtre. Because he copies all of the various maps with the same hand, many
different styles are brought together under the name of the same engraver.
Even if the maps resemble those of Ortelius and are copied hastily, muddied
with adjoining prose, or altered to accommodate recent history, in the *style* of
the work a new and fresh creation is born. A single and collective trait prevails,

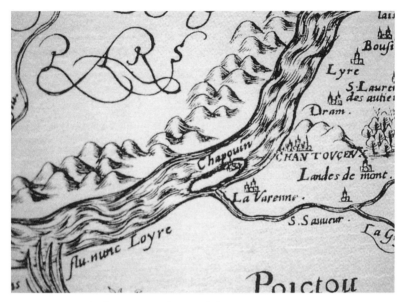

Figure 6.20. Detail of Figure 6.17: the Loire below Angers (Maurice Bouguereau, *Le théâtre françoys*)

first, in the Flemish calligraphic manner that draws the French toponyms on the maps and, second, in Bouguereau's particular way of copying, which distills pages of chronicle and cosmography that had been accumulating over the past century in a growing body of French history.

Here, if one of Jacques Derrida's celebrated formulas may be adapted, Bouguereau's signature is "an event that is being staged." It is an "effective intervention in the historical field" that is being constituted (1972a: 393). A coherence is gained by a single artist redrawing a motley group of maps, in tandem with an editor using the confines of the folio format to produce a controlled, attractive, often haptic, but always varied description that reproduces French topography to unify the diversity of its history. The map produces a nation of different subjects under the banner of cartographic variety. Like the Loire, the nation comes to unity when it reaches the Atlantic to the south of Brittany (Figure 6.22). The impression that Bouguereau leaves is one of a collective self created by a conflation of sources in a single, at once familiar and foreign signature. Its identity is also colored by its investment in what it perceives to be its relation to recent history and to the unknown, in other words, the uncertainty of the future. That relation is concretized in the allegorical figures of the title page, who entice us to look at the atlas as if we were part of the

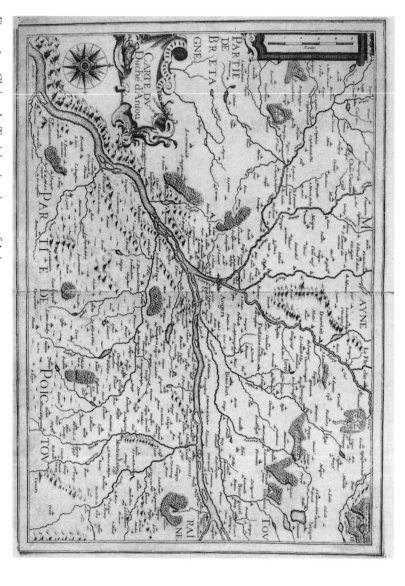

Figure 6.21. Christophe Tassin's epitomic map of Anjou

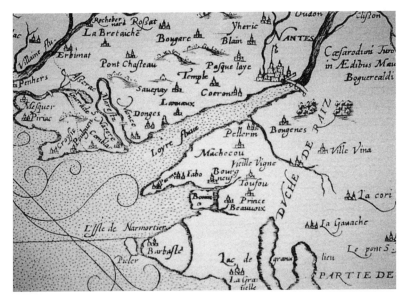

Figure 6.22. Anonymous map of Brittany, detail of the mouth of the Loire (Maurice Bouguereau, *Le théâtre françoys*)

royal family. Bouguereau unites his nation and projects the nascent idea of a commonwealth of citizens, like himself, who hail from different centers. A new and visible chorography is seen opposite the rewriting of national chronicle.[28] To see how the literary maps are fashioned from the relation of an author to a province and to local history, we can now turn south, to Gascony, *un païs à l'écart*, to see the role that Montaigne plays in a textual chorography of the French historical and literary theater.

7

Montaigne: A Political Geography of the Self

In the middle of his rhapsody on love and eros in "Sur des vers de Virgile" [On some lines of Virgil] (*Essais,* III, v), Montaigne responds to the would-be critic who castigates the author for using a heavy-handed, provincial style offending the ears of urbane readers. "'Tu es trop espais en figures. Voilà un mot du creu de Gascoingne. Voilà une frase dangereuse'" [Your figures are too dense. Here's a raw word from Gascony. There's a dangerous sentence].[1] Montaigne is writing about how he sees himself projected onto a surface of printed characters. Like his predecessors Tory and Rabelais, Montaigne pauses to wonder about the strange spatial relations that are born of the material shape of writing, words, and meaning being transcribed. Who is the I in print? Is there a reader other than that of an ideal construct, a "moitié," or a dead friend, who can be fathomed to be looking at the book? How does the space of the essay relate to the urgent political issues at stake in the Wars of Religion? In these reflections on the distance that printed writing inserts between a subject and an interlocutor, Montaigne does not adhere to the idea that printed writing has a merely substitutive function: Writing does not simply transmit meaning through graphemes representing phonemes. To a great degree, the medium of the essay is spatial, riddled with plastic, ideographic signs that inhere in reported speech. In their printed shape, the *Essais* engage the "form" and "matter" of expression through their play of logic, rhetoric, and meaning.[2]

An increasing estrangement of the shape and form of print from meaning—brought about by the settling of typographic experiments in the early part of the sixteenth century (Martin 1994: 207–32)—gives to French books published after 1580 an increasingly stable and recognizable character. The settling of print seems to accompany that of grammar and, to a degree, geography. The nation is defined in part by the triumph of a vernacular idiom, French, which moves between local speech and the official administrative language, Latin, which had been losing authority since the Ordonnances of Villers-Cotterets in 1539.[3] But the circulation, meaning, and reception of French cannot, the essayist avows, be easily located. Because it partakes of weakened deixis (Godzich and Kittay 1987; Metz 1991: 36), the essay erases the points defining the subject-positions of the author, interlocutor, and reader.

The doubt that printed writing inspires is matched by that of the skeptical philosophers who inhabit Montaigne's library. To allay their effects, the writer produces a world of his own, a textual geography that mimics and supplants the national space in which the *Essais* are circulating. The sheer bulk, "cet amas," of reflections piled and ordered together makes up a verbal region that the author can survey, map out, and traverse as he likes. He knows exactly where he is at every point in his textual travels. His trick, of course, entails the art of writing and composing a work that can extend itself in mental directions that will move long enough and far enough to yield a verbal geography that can be experienced through both intellectual and physical means. For Montaigne, a writer who seeks the help of topographers—"il nous faudroit des topographes qui nous fissent narration particuliere des endroits où ils ont esté" [we need topographers to provide specific accounts of the places they have been] (203)—the task is complicated by a desire *not* to follow the lead of a Thevet, Belleforest, or other cosmographers who would produce an indifferent mass of verbiage lacking any recognizable attachment to given places. In other words, Montaigne does not want to fall into the cosmographer's trap, in which the signature gained by the copyist dissolves into a sea of bizarre marvels.

On the other hand, the essayist has to compass his work so that the effect of a doubly weakened deixis—first, of the printed work and, second, of the highly abstract idea of the French nation, the "public" who reads the memorial writing in a dominant vernacular idiom—will be attenuated. From the chaos of fragments, singularities, borrowed citations, and translations, but also from individually chosen and reformulated comparisons, there must emerge markers that designate both an individual and a collective subject, a French author, Michel de Montaigne, and a national space in which his signature can circulate freely. The book has to approximate the history and geography of a French sensibility at a highly problematic moment in the nation's being. The essays must circulate a collection of national views, as well as reflections by a subject who is both one and many individuals. The book has to be written from a point of view that both stands *above* the French nation and its jagged lines of division and, no less, remains *within* its perimeters. The book must mimic the old cosmological scheme of a microcosm and a macrocosm at the same time that it embraces a protoscientific, chorographic method of self-presentation.

In a context of cartographic writing, the book must strive to be cosmographic in its universal appeal and in its relation to a long span of time, but also quasi-Ortelian in an exact representation of local spaces and history. Hence, the project of the *Essais* engages plotting and mapping by virtue of where it stands in an ineluctable context of history and structure: history, to the degree that the essays are in a dialogue both with events and with the emerging rapport of an autobiographical self; structure, insofar as the author is found in the midst of quickly changing views that determine new and conflicting articulations of the world, of national space, and of those areas where the writer can stand in order to negotiate these changes. The project of self-mapping is complicated further by the ideology of authorship and authority that marks the nascent writer of literature: Montaigne is obliged to create an analogical, self-conceived, self-perpetuating, citational book that will change according to changes in context. A work written, like Bouguereau's allegory of Geographia, to offer sibylline counsel to a reader who can be located anywhere and at any time in history, it must be of a logical category high enough to work with total social facts—the subject of ethnography—as it also perpetuates its own immortality as a specific, *local* political creation that will forever renew its symbolic efficacy.

The essays appear to be written as a part both of the moment in which they are read and of the broad rhythms of universal history. They give veiled advice to whoever seeks informed views about any of the subjects indicated by the titles crowning the 107 chapters. And because the author writes in a climate even more volatile than that of the surveyors who contributed to Bouguereau's *Théâtre,* he must compose the work delicately, with extreme finesse, with the care and exactitude of a royal engineer, an *ingénieur du roi.* As Montaigne expresses the dilemma in the opening sentence of the third volume, "Personne n'est exempt de dire des fadaises. Le malheur est de les dire curieusement" [No one is exempt from uttering banalities. The ill fortune is in uttering them in an overly mannered style] (767).

The task in this chapter is to study the both cosmographic and chorographic projection of Montaigne's "self." How does it move through both diagrammatic and discursive expression? Do we witness or reinvent the creation of a verbal world being surveyed before our eyes? Do two heterogeneous systems work together in the same textual space? Cast in terms of the reader who is drawn into dialogue with the *Essais,* we can also wonder how memory systems of discourse are mapped out to locate the readers and the author in the skeins of historical and autobiographical figures. Following the example of *Le théâtre françois,* we can ask, in turn, how a cartographic practice aids the cause of a sibylline—but also rational—writing that both summarizes and changes the status of the world that until then had been thought to be senescent and approaching its demise.

Legions of critics have approached these questions by diverse means. As do other writers of his time, Montaigne inherits an increasingly visible sense of language (Ong 1983: 93), but he also uses chorography to inspire the art of composition. The essays are divided into discursive and diagrammatic components in which the abstraction of "meaning" or philosophical reflection in the shape of concepts is countermanded by a hieroglyphic and graphic organization that supplants and confirms, but also contradicts the register of meaning. A cartographic practice plots the text; it maps itself as it advances; it allegorizes itself; but it also undoes the controlling schemes that are being plotted.

A Book Engineered

Montaigne's coy remarks about the ways he has crafted his writing are especially visible in the material printed as of 1588, when the publication of the third book brings forward, on top of the circumstantial essays written in the 1570s, an increased authorial self-consciousness. A veneer of self-congratulatory or defensive narcissism draws attention to the form—indeed, the surface tensions—of the chapters. They also bring into view a topographical consciousness that gives an illusion of extension to the writer's sense of subjectivity. Montaigne has to appear as if his persona were entirely self-made, tangling the causes that inspire the writing into a vast array of stylistic and plastic effects. Thus, he can attest both to an autonomy of a book-machine that writes him as it takes over ("Qui ne voit que j'ay pris une route par laquelle, sans cesse et sans travail, j'iray autant qu'il y aura d'ancre et de papier au monde" [No one will fail to see that I have taken a road by which, endlessly and without effort, I will go as long as there are ink and paper in the world] [922]), and to his identity as a member of a national and linguistic body ("Je ne veux pas oublier cecy, que je ne me mutine jamais tant contre la France que je ne regarde Paris de bon oeil: elle a mon cueur dès mon enfance" [I don't want to forget this, that I am never divided against France so much as I gaze on Paris in admiration: since my childhood the city has held my heart] [950]). To see how he mediates the paradox, it suffices for us to return to the mock encomium of his topographic design in "Sur des vers de Virgile":

> Pour ce mien dessein, il me vient aussi à propos d'escrire chez moy, en pays sauvage, où personne ne m'ayde ny me releve, où je ne hante communéement homme qui entende le latin de son patenostre, et de françois un peu moins. Je l'eusse faict meilleur ailleurs, mais l'ouvrage eust esté moins mien; et sa fin principale et perfection, c'est d'estre exactement mien. Je corrigerois bien une erreur accidentale, dequoy je suis plain, ainsi que je cours inadvertemment; mais les imperfections qui sont en moy ordinaires et constantes, ce seroit trahison de les oster. Quand on m'a dit ou que moy-mesme me suis dict: "Tu es trop espais en figures. Voilà un mot du creu de Gascoingne. Voilà une frase dangereuse (je n'en refuis aucune de celles qui s'usent emmy les rues françoises; ceux qui veulent combatre l'usage par la grammaire se moquent). Voilà un discours ignorant. Voilà un discours paradoxe. En voilà un trop fol. Tu te joues souvent; on estimera que tu dies à droit ce que tu dis à feinte.—Oui, fais-je; mais je corrige les fautes d'inadvertence, non celles de coustume. Est-ce pas ainsi que je parle par tout? me represente-je pas vivement? suffit! J'ay faict ce que j'ay voulu: tout le monde me reconnoit en mon livre, et mon livre en moy." Or j'ay une condition singeresse et imitatrice: quand je me meslois de faire des vers (et n'en fis jamais que des Latins), ils accusoient evidemment le poëte que je venois dernierement de lire; et, de mes premiers essays, aucuns puent un peu à l'estranger. A Paris, je parle un langage aucunement autre qu'à Montaigne.

[For this design of mine, it expressly happens that I write at home, in a wild country, where no one either helps or edits me, where I rarely associate with anyone who understands the Latin of their paternoster, French even less. In another place I would have executed it better, but the work would not have been so much my own. I will surely correct an accidental error, and I am full of those, given that I skim over the work inadvertently; but for the imperfections that are ordinary and constant in myself, it would be treason to remove them. When someone or even myself will say: "Your figures are too dense." "Here's a raw word from Gascony." "There's a dangerous sentence" (I never avoid any of those that are in use in French streets; those who want to battle usage with grammar are fooling themselves). "There's an ignorant discourse." "Now here's a paradoxical discourse." "There's one that's too crazy." "You often play with yourself; people will think that you are uttering directly what you state coyly."—"Oh, sure," I say, but I correct errors of inattention, not those of custom and habit. Doesn't it suffice that I am speaking everywhere? Am I representing myself naturally, as I am? Enough! I've done what I wanted: The world recognizes me in my book, and my book in me. Now I am born with an imitative, simian condition: When I got mixed up with writing poetry (and only wrote my lines in Latin), they obviously smelled of the poet I had just been reading; and, among my earlier essays, some have a strange odor. In Paris, I speak a language somewhat other than in Montaigne.] (853)

It is implied that Gascony is an origin. Latin has no meaning in the sylvan region around his chateau. French is barely understood. The conundrum is that the essays are nonetheless in French and are sprinkled with Latin but are drafted in a place where they cannot easily be deciphered.

For that reason they have to travel. All the blemishes of the book would have been reduced, he implies, if it had been written *ailleurs,* possibly in Paris, but at the axis of France in the northwest its local signature would have made the writer's character much fuzzier. Appeal is made to a dialogue of at least three voices in the text: an eccentric Montaigne always *ailleurs;* the credulous reader who upbraids the author; and the *other* Montaigne, the Gascon bumpkin, who writes with dense figures, who responds to the effect that he always writes "everywhere" and is impelled to portray visible signs of the oxymoron of his "universal self-portrait." The picture of the essayist becomes, like Bouguereau's design of Thomas de Leu's portrait of Henry IV affixed to the map of France (see Figure 6.7), a composite identity, a diagram but also a discourse. The spatiality of the *dessein,* a figural design and a map, is erected in the amphiboly in the would-be critic's statement, "Tu es trop *espais* en figures": You are too regional, too provincial (*ès païs,* in the country) in your writing. The "mot de creu"—"crude, raw, unripe, over-new; imperfect; also, unsavorie" (Cotgrave 1611)—of "Gascoingne" contains in the place-name the corner (*coin*) into which the author's rough vocables will be stuffed. To gain an identity, the style must be a regional form projecting onto a national body.

Elsewhere Montaigne argues that his French is altered by "la barbarie de mon creu," in contrast to other localities—Périgord, Poitou, Saintonge, Angoumois, Limousin, Auvergne—that are "flaccid, dragging, tepid," whereas "il y a bien au-dessus de nous, vers les montaignes, un Gascon que je treuve singulierement beau, sec, bref, signifiant, et à la verité un langage masle et militaire plus qu'autre que j'entende; autant nerveux, puissant et pertinent, comme le François est gratieus, delicat et abondant" [there is just above us, toward the mountains, a Gascon that I find singularly handsome, dry, concise, on the mark, and truly a more masculine and military language than any I hear; as nervous, powerful, and pertinent as French is gracious, delicate, and abundant] (622). A national identity is engendered by the copulation of the male region, *Gascoingne,* with the French body, the feminine countryside, and the graciously refined style to the north and in the Ile-de-France. The perspectival object of the essays marks a congress of differences within the lexical and chorographic overlappings of the text. It is tantamount to the "picture" that the essayist projects in the hatched verbal strokes translated and engraved in printed type.

The picture being constructed bears strong affinity with the chorographic method that Geoffroy Tory initiated in his design of capital letters, and with the topographical method that Oronce Finé theorized in the *Protomathesis* and *Le sphère du monde*. Like the Dauphiné cartographer, Montaigne chooses a site, draws the limits of the projection with its meridian and parallels, but only as a function of an initial vertical trait that crosses a center from which minutes and degrees of longitude and latitude will be marked. Close to the spatial and geometric center, the vanishing point of the first book, Montaigne tenders the famous comparison of the *Essais* to a Mannerist painting:

> Considérant la conduite de la besongne d'un peintre que j'ay, il m'a pris envie de l'ensuivre. Il choisit le plus bel endroit et milieu de chaque paroy, pour y loger un tableau élabouré de toute sa suffisance; et, le vuide tout au tour, il le remplit de crotesques, qui sont peintures fantasques, n'ayant grace qu'en la varieté et estrangeté. Que sont-ce icy aussi, à la verité, que crotesques et corps monstrueux, rappiecez de divers membres, sans certaine figure, n'ayants ordre, suite ny proportion que fortuite?

> [Considering the way that a painter of mine happens to work, I took a fancy to follow him. He chooses the most beautiful spot at the middle of each wall in order to set upon it a picture that is richly developed; and the empty areas all around, well, he fills them with grotesques, that are fantasized paintings, their grace belonging only to their variety and strangeness. What are these, too, in truth, if not grotesques and monstrous bodies sewn together from diverse members, without a clear figure, having neither order, design, nor proportion other than by chance?] (181)

To which the reader responds, no, the monstrous bodies are a function of a practice quite common to painters, surveyors, and cartographers. The vanishing point is also a site reserved for an origin diagrammatically evident in the verbal register. Although Montaigne "lodges" the memory picture of Etienne de la Boëtie at the apparent center of the verbal cartouche, it is Montaigne who implicitly becomes the subject and the end of the chapter's frame. The text suggests that a spatial logic is required for the reader to survey the verbal material. The process recalls the polar or center-enhancing perspective that had been drawn by Pieter Apian (Shirley 1987: 57) (Figure 7.1; see also Figure 3.23) since the first quarter of the century. The self is designed to be centered, but to move about in relation to a plot point that is marked at a strategic axis in each volume.[4] If the essays are designed to be center-enhancing, they must also engage a movement away from their site of origin. The discourse allows the essayist to divagate, to adventure, indeed, to err or wander away from the text that fills the space of a confining grid of associations.

quil y aura aultant de degrez du meridien , comptant du Cercle equino-
ctial iufques au zenith de l'homme, comme il y aura de l'arcq dudict me
ridiain, entre le Pole du monde & le cercle de l'horizon.

Corrollaire ou addition.

L E Zenith de la tefte eft toufiours egallement diftant de tous coftez
du horizon, ceft a dire. 90. degrez ou vng quadrant. Pource eft ap-
pellé le pole du horizon. Et en quelque lieu ou place que la perfonne foit,
toufiours la moicié du ciel ou Hemyfphere(ofte tous les aultres empef-
chemés)luy appert. Et dautāt que la perfonne fe elongue de lequinoctial,
allant vers le Septentrion ou midy , dautant fe rebaiffe & cache le horizon d'une part deffoubz le pole, & d'aultre part fe eflieue d'aultāt fur
le Pole oppofite.

Lefquelles chofes à plus plain vous verres en ceft inftrument.

Figure 7.1. Volvelle from Pieter Apian, *Cosmographie*

The route-enhancing traits of the essay are most evident in "De la vanité" [Of vanity], a chapter that treats of travel over space and time. In it we see how the writing is plotted. An emblematic tactic disseminates in the body of the writing the particles of the title and number of the essay. The letters of the title, like the motto at the top of an emblem, are reprinted in different combinations in order to be seen embedded, like freeze-frames in a film, in the gist of the moving narrative of travel. The text is built over a neutral set of graphemes,

d - e - l - a - v - a - n - i - t - é,

that circulate and recombine variously. The adventure of the essay is congealed in the often uttered formula "par aventure" (which occurs over twenty times in the chapter, more than anywhere else in the *Essais*) that draws on

-a v a n-

and circulates the winds of change (*vents*) that send the essayist all over the world. So does "avant," or what constitutes the "before" and "after" of the historical allegory of the essay; and, too, the economy of liquids that are drawn, sucked off, or blown forth (*vantés, ventousés*) just as the "coprographic" quality of the printed page (Mathieu-Castellani 1988b: 198–220) depends on a *veine* or a *vene* (turd), which is contained in the establishing and vanishing term. So obsessive is the relation of the text to the title that the profusion of visible graphemes of the inverted identities of the letters

-A-V-

suggest that an illusion of volume is obtained through their "compassed" aspect. Each opens a point of view at the juncture of their bars, and their movement in space recalls the art of conic sections and projections that belong to mapping. Numerous historiated initials, such as those from Apian's print shop, had already depicted the cosmographer using a pair of dividers to measure the proportions of the globe or to prepare a conic projection of a given region. Entire views of the world are established by the angle of the letters when the two shafts open a perspective that contains both terrestrial and celestial globes. The letters convey what Tory and other writer-artists had allegorized for political ends.[5] The particles of the title, and even the shape of the letters, determine a navigational plan. As we tend to get lost in the long and fugal meditation on war, time, travel, politics, economy, eros, feminism, and writing, the gridded quality of the text always tells us where we are (Conley 1992d). The resulting "auto-geography" allows for a plot-enhancing projection to work in conjunction with the center-enhancing mode that places, at a vanishing point, Montaigne's remarks pertaining to the figure of his work: "Mon livre est tousjours un" [My book is always one] (941) and its mobile composition as an "ill-joined marquetry," a kind of optical intarsia associated with cartographic and anamorphic practices (Tormey and Tormey 1982). Montaigne seems to construct an obsessively supple form, at once closed and open, in which he can both locate himself and get lost. There also reigns a closed, labyrinthine, and equipollent design from which no exit is possible.[6]

The apparently self-enclosing design of this chapter and of the *Essais* as a whole would pertain to a form of pure autobiography and commemorative discourse if it were not deeply anchored, like maps, in the politics of the time. The plotting is not just accomplished to please the eye of the author or to precipitate the admiration of a reader. It is also engaged in order to inflect history, to deploy both common and unique, both collective and monomaniacal, qualities of an author within and above history. The compositional tactics of form that are made manifest in "De la vanité" become exceptionally visible in the movement resulting from the author's avowed attraction to novelty. Where we find novelty and things new, we also discover the writer's desire to cope with the new geography that came with the information from the New World. The new geography is couched in older schemes, such as in Jean Bodin's writings, a storehouse of the spatial views that identify Montaigne's sense of the New World. We will turn to these before we examine how the essayist casts his gaze to the west.

The Book as a Cardinal Form

Montaigne's compositional tactics, as he underscores in both "Virgil" and "Vanity," possess cardinal and geographic virtues that bear on national policy.[7] The relation between history and allegory shares much with the worldview of man and his climates that Bodin takes up in the fifth book of *The Republic* (*De la république* [Paris, 1577]). Bodin theorizes a realm of space and history in order, it appears, to cope with the effects wrought by the Columbian discoveries and the recent Religious Wars on French soil since 1562. He maps the world by superimposing the four humors over the four cardinal directions: northerners are phlegmatic, heavy, dull, and of fair complexion, while southerners are constant, grave, and of darker hue, signaling a melancholic bent. Those to the east tend to be nimble and courteous, and of yellow—Chinese— skin, signaling choleric origins. Brazilians, to the west, are as sanguine as the wood of their name: strong, cruel, and savage. Bodin apportions the two hemispheres into three units of thirty degrees each from the equator to the North Pole and, likewise, to the South Pole. "The difference of manners and dispositions of people, is much more notorious betwixt the North and the

South, than betwixt the East and West" (Bodin 1962: 562). Northern and southern nations "can never concur together for the contrarietie of manners and humors" (552) between them.

Projecting an immortal dynamic order beyond history, his cosmography appears to emerge from the recent events it schematizes. Populations of the median regions (France and Italy, located between the thirtieth and sixtieth parallels) enjoy a moderation of opposites. Gallic souls have more temperate ways than do their German or Iberian neighbors, and for that reason they are given to democratic rule. Northerners govern themselves "by force of arms," while southerners elect to follow the laws of religion. The Germans find their patrons in *Reiter*, the knights, whose might makes right; the French abound in reason and judgment; the Spanish "in craft and subtilitie, like unto foxes; or unto Religion: for eloquent discourses agree not with the grosse wits of the Northern people" (559). Most crucially,

> It is not mervail then if the people of the south are better governed by religion, than by force or reason, and which is a point verie considerable to draw the people, when as neither force nor reason can prevaile: as we reade in the historie of the Indies, that *Christopher Columbus* when he could not draw the people of the West Indies into humanitie by any flatterie or fair meanes, he showed them the Moone the which they did worship, giving them to understand that she should soone lose her light: three days after seeing the Moone eclipsed, they were so amazed, as they did what he commanded them. (560)

The feats of Columbus are put forth to show that a mild dose of constancy in religion might eventually cure a France sickened by its civil wars. Yet France serves as a corrective to the bloody events that the Spanish precipitated in the New World: Following Aristotle's observations, Bodin remarks that southerners are prone to lust and lechery, like hares by virtue of "spondious melancholie" (557). Moderate peoples cannot see or hear of northern or southern cruelties. He implies that a likeness attracts the Spanish to South America, where Brazilians "are not contented to eat the flesh of their enemies, but will bathe their children in their blood" (559), in punishments no less horrifying than those the ancient Egyptians were wont to practice. The model appears to be used, on the one hand, to account for and react to the Treaty of Câteau-Cambresis (1559), by which Spain craftily acquired the Savoy province, which Francis I had gained in his Milanese campaigns earlier in the century; on the other, it argues for a course of reason or less "interior heat" that should be followed to avoid repeating what took place in the West Indies.

In Bodin's scheme, moderation of extremes through analogy triggers an event that can allow for their perpetual revision. By charting the four humors as corresponding to the four cardinal points, Bodin manages to combine a ruse of analogy with the forces of history. The contingency of battles between Charles V and Francis I colors his worldview, but its aura of timelessness owes much to its quasi-Aristotelian form taken from the *Politics*. In one way, the book is supple—it can move with the current history of the West Indies—while in another, it is clad in its own allegorical chain mail. Bodin offers a prototypical semiotic grid for the sake of a French cause, but all the while the coordinates of human and geographic space tend to distance the writer, keeping him from identifying with his synthetic design.

Montaigne, who may have contemplated the same analogy of religion, leadership, and fear in the discussion of Mexican religion that concludes "Des coches," no doubt shared with Bodin a critical view of Franco-Iberian relations as they had developed over the course of the sixteenth century. Nonetheless, writing against overly schematic logic, he remarks, "Il ne faut pas se clouër si fort à ses humeurs et complexions" [We must not nail ourselves so forthrightly here to our humors and complexions] (796). The opening sentence of "De trois commerces" (III, iii), set in the third chapter of the third volume, appears to criticize the rigidity of designs that combine geometry and the elements of humors.[8] The *Essais* share the same principles evident in Bodin's *De la république*—in their view of Spanish history and in their dynamic form—but they embody a far more serpentine movement. What they have in common is *moderation* in their inflections of meteorology, mood, space, and political conduct. The political ground plan of the essays is drawn to yield a dynamic moderation that will assure a future climate of bodily and international equilibrium. Following an ideology of apparent political conservatism intended to guide the national vessel through its time of turbulence, the allegory indicates that moderation results from a constant balancing of multifarious forces at play in the cosmos. Examples are similarly incised into the marquetry of the *Essais*. Like the shifting shores of the Dordogne described in "Des cannibales" (201), recent news from the West Indies moves over time and betrays a more urgent consternation about the efficacy of the universalizing heritage of history.[9] Cartography claims to be more reliable than naturalistic or cosmographic versions of history, and thus the Western Hemisphere of the *Essais,* like the perplexities of the New World, accrues increasing structural importance between 1580, the date of the first two volumes, and 1588, the date of the third. "Des cannibales," a showcase chapter of the first edition, corresponds to "Des coches" of the third. Each is situated next to the center of their respective volumes; each takes up a specific historical issue and then digests it into smaller units (sentences, syntagms, words, letters, and graphemes) that describe a circle in which moderating forces are put to play.

The Politics of "Des cannibales"

As in the most carefully crafted chapters, "Des cannibales" (I, xxxi) begins not after its title but in the last lines of the essay that precedes it. In that essay, "De la moderation" (I, xxx), the author takes up what Bodin and other political thinkers had wished their French compatriots would heed. "J'ayme les natures temperées et moyennes" [I like median and temperate natures] (195), he writes, as if to show that extremities, whether in virtue, philosophy, marriage, theology, or even books can harm the world's order: An archer who overshoots a butt is no less immoderate than one who can't reach the target. Discourse leads to accounts from the New World that abound with massacre and homicide, two extremes, alas, "universally embraced by all religions" (199). There, living idols drink human blood. Young subjects are burned alive, half roasted and withdrawn from pyres only to have their hearts and entrails ripped out and collectively consumed. For other gods, women are skinned alive, their hides used to clothe and mask tribal fetishes. The display of extreme religious practice is taken directly from the French translation of Francisco López de Gómara's *Histoire generalle des Indes* (II, 4) but appears, however, to have a spatial role in prefacing another passage taken from an Italian translation of the same author's *Istoria di don Fernando Cortés* (Venice, 1576), in which the Spaniards' Tlaxcalan enemy, having been defeated at the hands of Cortez, Montaigne reports, offers the conqueror a choice of gifts:

> Je diray encore ce compte. Aucuns de ces peuples, ayants esté batuz par luy, envoyerent le recognoistre et rechercher d'amitié; les messagers luy presenterent trois sortes de presens, en cette maniere: "Seigneur, voylà cinq esclaves; si tu es un dieu fier, qui te paisses de chair et de sang, mange les, et nous t'en amerrons d'avantage; si tu es un Dieu debonnaire, voylà de l'encens et des plumes; si tu es homme, prens les oiseaux et les fruicts que voyci."

> [I will still relate this account. After being beaten, some of these peoples sent envoys to acknowledge him and seek friendship; the messengers offered him three kinds of presents, in this manner: "Lord, here are five slaves; if you are a fierce god who lives on flesh and blood, eat them, and we shall bring you more; if you are a worldly god, then take our perfume and feathers; if you are a man, please accept the birds and fruits we offer you."] (199–200)

Thus ends the essay, without resolve, turning Gómara's description into a riddle and suspending it above "Des cannibales" in the shape of an emblematic superscription or enigma to the essay that follows. The question prompts readers to ponder the choice that the account refuses to resolve: What kind of man did he turn out to be? What did Cortez do? Is *he* the barbarian described in the next chapter?

In Montaigne's textual geography, the Spanish account is turned against itself. In Gómara's original, Cortez tells the Mexicans that he is mortal, as they are, but that he is truthful, as opposed to them, with their penchant to lie; that he is friendly but forced to engage in battles that they had begun. The envoys are dismissed; the Indians attack and are again beaten. On a second mission, the Mexicans return with gifts but, the historian notes, with the intent to spy. Cortez learns of (or conceives) the stratagem and in consequence has the hands of each of the fifty envoys cut off before he sends them back to their people.[10] The abridged sequel is juxtaposed to the exemplum of Pyrrhus in the sentences, directly following, that inaugurate "Des cannibales." Pyrrhus, too, is an awesome leader but, unlike Cortez, he realizes that his Roman enemies are hardly as savage as popular Greek belief had taught him. Along the divide of the two essays, Cortez is opposed to Pyrrhus and, likewise, so are the tenets of "De la moderation" to "Des cannibales." Given the friendly motives that the Tlaxcalans personify, "De la moderation" has thematic strands leading back to "De l'amitié." At its end, the Mexicans are seen seeking the bond of friendship that had been at the center of the former chapter. Montaigne thus *rewrites* Gómara's account of Cortez by leaving aside the details of the Spaniards' pillage and by adding, in a clause that does not figure in the original account, which is otherwise transcribed verbatim from the biography, "(ils) *envoyerent le recognoistre et rechercher d'amitié*" (199, emphasis added). Gómara does not portray the Indians in search of friendship. *Amitié*, the trait unmarked in the Spanish chronicler's history, is situated precisely at the other cardinal end of the chapter on moderation. In its quest for a median demeanor in human action, the text puts the Spanish conqueror at the *extremity*, the southern, or, following Bodin's map, barbarous end of the composition. The more familiar and temperate end of the chapter is contained in the essay in homage to Etienne de la Boëtie. The essay "moderates" a course between cultural and geographic extremes by staging the scene of civility that his forthcoming cannibals will personify in ways no less compelling than those of the Mexican Indians.

The design appears to draw its course from two vectors that are part of the reigning plan of the *Essais*. One traces the axial schema of center and circumference that shapes the allegory of Destiny or ambivalence at the hub of each volume. The first and last chapters are at the periphery of the axis, located between chapters 28 and 29, which demarcates the world into two halves, or

Extremity ←	Axis	→ Extremity
I, i	I, xxviii-ix	I, lvii
"Par divers moyens on arrive à pareille fin	"De l'amitié" and "Vingt et neuf sonnets d'Estienne de la Boëtie"	"De l'aage"

"moitiés" (akin to two friends or, in the logic of an archaic political organization, two groups that share an identity through the nominal differences they impose upon each other).[11]

On another level, as these chapters are placed at the center of the first book of *Essais*, a similar division bisects the axis itself. The twenty-nine sonnets, congruent with the twenty-ninth chapter, are set between friendship and moderation, two virtues that will color the picture of the cannibals adjacent to (or just to the east of) the immediate center.

"L'aage" is the end of the wandering announced in "Par divers moyens on arrive à pareille fin" (By diverse means we arrive at the same end) (I, i), while the median ground, the double center (or ellipsis) of the friendship of two different souls, Montaigne and la Boëtie, concretizes the bond that holds the essayist to the cultural "other," that is, his dead companion and the Indians of "De la moderation" and "Des cannibales." Each unit tends to temper the other and to move, as in astronomical drawings of the Renaissance describing the play of micro- and macrocosm, back and forth from an unconscious humanity of Indians, recently born into history, to the essayist and his readers. A nascent parabola is visible, in which equal values are accorded to all points on the surface of the essays. The multiple ellipses that can be drawn between and among different chapters have the effect of drawing schemes that engage relations with the unknown or with worlds that are other.

"Des cannibales" acquires a historical specificity immediately manifest in spatial and graphic terms.[12] The praise of Amerindians virtually counters Gómara's orthodox view of conquest. The essay appears to develop from a series of visible inversions contained in words, in the representation of Spanish and French accounts, and in the focal properties of point of view. One of the favored terms is "*barbarie*," a word recurring at several nodal points, which reveals how the expansionist and self-centering policies of European culture exceed all reports of barbarity in the New World. The aphorism that crowns the first half of the chapter, "chacun appelle barbarie ce qui n'est pas de son usage" [we call barbarity whatever is not of our custom] (203), foreshadows the more direct allusion to the Black Legend when it is used again, five pages below, to impugn European reason. The Indians are barbarous, but in no way are they so loathsome as their conquerors: "Nous les pouvons donq bien appeler barbares, eu esgard aux regles de la raison, mais non pas eu esgard à nous, qui les surpassons en toute sorte de barbarie" [We can therefore surely call them barbarous in respect to the rules of reason, but not in respect to ourselves, we who exceed them in every kind of barbarity] (208). With *barbarie* valorized as a sign of culture, the cannibals become ciphers or, like the doubled shape of the word itself, shifters that locate how and where the west surpasses its own geographic dominion. *We* are slaves to an expansionist economy, while *they* are not. The anti-Iberian moment of the early essay coincides with an oblique praise of the self-moderating order of the pre-Columbian cultures. It probably harmonizes with the tone of Bouguereau's anti-Iberian remarks at the outset of *Le théâtre françoys,* where the king is enjoined to quash the infidel maran (Cotgrave 1611: 12: "An Infidell, Miscreant, Apostate, Renegade . . .") to the South. Unlike the Spanish, Montaigne implies, Amerindians are not expansionist:

Ils ne sont pas en debat de la conqueste de nouvelles terres, car ils jouyssent encore de cette uberté naturelle qui les fournit sans travail et sans peine de toutes choses necessaires, en telle abondance qu' *ils n'ont que faire d'agrandir leur limites.* Ils sont encore en cet heureux point, de ne desirer qu'autant que leurs necessitez naturelles leur ordonnent; tout ce qui est au delà est superflu pour eux.

[*They are not debating the conquest of new lands,* for they still enjoy this natural fecundity that provides them, without labor or difficulty, with all necessities, in such abundance that *they do not have to expand their limits.* They are still at this happy point of only desiring as much as their natural needs provide; for them everything beyond that is superfluous.] (208, emphasis added)

Debat underscores the recent fortunes of Spanish policy—perhaps by alluding to the Valladolid debates of 1550–1551—while the praise of self-containment does not come as the residue of edenic myths or utopian belief. Rather, the cultural model of their symbolic ecosystem is aimed against European nations (including France, as "Coches" will emphasize below) and their policies of economic expansion.

For most of the sixteenth century, the French had directed their principal commerce toward the Mediterranean. Trade went west for dyes taken from Brazilwood on the eastern coast of South America and for fish in the northwestern Atlantic. The nation did not stand to profit by imitating the massive colonial programs that their Spanish neighbors had launched. A byproduct of economic history and the counterpart to the Black Legend, the myth of the

French *génie colonial* depended on exchange only with riparian and coastal cultures. The failed Protestant expeditions to Villegagnon and Florida had shown that any move to settle or to convert indigenous populations was unlikely to succeed. Possibly for these reasons, the text immediately qualifies its initially serene view of a steady-state culture by noting that they are like any culture insofar as they engage in war. But their battles are matters of equilibration, that is, of balancing or, like the text itself, of *essaying*, rather than of expanding. When the cannibals do transgress their borders, they cross only natural limits (*montaignes*, a toponym that through its rapport with the author's name indicates an unswerving and self-containing locus moving back to the printed page) that separate one culture from another:

> Si leurs voisins passent les montaignes pour les venir assaillir, et qu'ils emportent la victoire sur eux, l'acquest du victorieux, c'est la gloire, et l'avantage d'estre demeuré maistre en valeur et en vertu; car autrement ils n'ont que faire des biens des vaincus, et s'en retournent à leur pays, où ils n'ont faute de aucune chose necessaire, ny faute encore de cette grande partie, de sçavoir heureusement jouyr de leur condition et s'en contenter.

> [If their neighbors cross over the mountains to attack them, and if they win over them, the victor's spoil is glory and the advantage of being supreme in value and virtue; for otherwise they can live without the booty of the vanquished, and then return to their homeland where they lack none of life's necessities nor, what is more important, knowing how to take pleasure in their condition and be happy with it.] (208–9)

These "extreme" conditions nonetheless attest to policies that accord glory not to goods or to lands gained but to symbolic abstractions. Physical waste of prisoners and dead bodies are not worth being managed. Subsequent description of captives "neutralizing" their enemies by offering themselves to be eaten, "invention qui ne sent aucunement la *barbarie*" [a stratagem hardly smacking of barbarity] (211), folds a merely apparent horror of anthropophagia into a dynamic balance of physical and cultural economy. The cannibals show that a "triumphal loss," where valor and skill superseded the untimely results of battle, took place when Ischolas fought against the Arcadians. In topographical terms that justify placing "cannibales" adjacent to "moderation," Ischolas "print entre ces deux extremitez un moyen parti" [opted for a middle choice between these extremes] (210). His enemy won, but only, like the Spaniards who lurk in the margins of the example, at the price of being seen as butchers who put their victims to a senseless death.

Wherever it falls in the essay, the term "*barbarie*" becomes associated with cultural moderation. Each of Montaigne's intermediaries, another visible inversion in the text, also figures in dialogue with Spanish reports of the New World. His first interpreter is a simpleton, a prototypical topographer, who, unlike many a recent historian, does not "incline or mask" what he sees "according to the countenance that they had" of the Indians (202). His information, which comes from a regional cartographer, is truer than "what cosmographers say of them" (203). The words are ostensibly aimed at his source, Thevet's *Les singularitez de la France antarctique* (1557), which had drawn much from Gómara's *Historia general de las Indias* (first Spanish edition printed in Zaragoza, 1552). The description of the cannibals comes not from the go-between's voice of experience, which could provide the visual evidence of having "seen" the Indians in their true habitat, but from the mediation of the woodcuts that illustrated Thevet's *Singularitez.* The 1580 material depicting the cannibals' wars and weapons, the decapitated heads of their enemies placed over the entrances to their homes, the ways they placed prisoners in bondage, and the dietary fashion of eating the enemy communally (211) are taken from six woodcuts that are set in Thevet's middle chapters on South America (Figures 7.2 and 7.3).[13] The personified intermediary whom Montaigne evokes also happens to be the ensemble of images that grounds these descriptions. The Amerindians that were thought to be found without mediation of others, the text reveals, are already filtered through pictures; they happen to be as much a familiar product of Fontainebleau style as of reported alterity; they are represented only through the combination of text and image, which conspires to produce an effect of authentic immediacy. Here, the descriptions make their fiction of veracity the ground of truth.

The principal "horrors" of the Amerindians—nudity, cannibalism, and idolatry—were already conventions that Italian artists in France had been depicting in their renditions of classical myths.[14] Their drawings of masses of contorted bodies function according to the laws of vanishing points that organize the mythologies they depict. Montaigne's description flattens the pictorial aberrations of the models and in turn reduces the accompanying rhetorical amplification of the written sources. The text mediates the images and hence incorporates its concept of "experience" through its own visual patterning of expression. The style is far more optical than the French translation of Gómara's Spanish, a narrative written in a moralizing tenor, and it is less inclined to supply commentary than the original. In the folds of his own words, but not in direct experience, Montaigne engages what Thevet had announced at the conclusion of *Les singularitez*: "Il est malaisé, voire impossible, de pouvoir justement representer les lieux et les places notables, leurs situations et distance, senz les avoir veuës à l'oeil: qui est la plus certaine cognoissance entre toutes,

ueilleux, non par l'eſpace de trois ou quatre iours, mais d
quatre ou cinq moys. Et le plus grand dueil, eſt aux qua
tre ou cinq premiers iours. Vous les entendrez faire re
bruit & harmonie comme de chiens & chats : vous ver
rez tant hómes que femmes couchez ſur leurs couchet
tes penſiles, les autres le cul contre terre ſ'embraſſans l'v
l'autre, comme pourrez voir par la preſente figure : diſan
en leur langue, Noſtre pere & amy eſtoit tant homme d

bien, ſi vaillant à la guerre, qui auoit tant fait mourir de
ſes ennemis. Il eſtoit fort & puiſſant, il labouroit tant bien
noz iardins, il prenoit beſtes & poiſſon pour nous nour-
rir, helas il eſt treſpaſſé, nous ne le verrons plus, ſinon a-
pres la mort auec noz amis aux païs, que noz *Pagés* nous
diſent auoir veux, & pluſieurs autres ſemblables parolles

Figure 7.2. Woodcut of Indian burial ritual (André Thevet, *Les Singularitez de la
France antarctique*)

chement eſtoffée de diuers plumages. Et tant plus le
riſonnier verra faire les preparatiues pour mourir, &
lus il monſtrera ſignes de ioye. Il ſera donc mené, bien
é & garroté de cordes de cotton en la place publique,
ccompagné de dix ou douze mil Sauuages du païs, ſes
nnemis, & la ſera aſſommé cóme vn porceau, apres plu-
ieurs cerimonies. Le priſonnier mort, ſa femme, qui luy
uoit eſté donnée, fera quelque petit dueil. Incontinent
e corps eſtant mis en pieces, ils en prennent le ſang & en
auent leurs petis enfans maſles, pour les rendre plus har-
is, comme ils diſent, leur remonſtrans, que quand ils ſe-
ont venuz à leur aage, ils facent ainſi à leurs ennemis.

ont faut penſer, qu'on leur en fait autant de lautre part,
uand ils ſont pris en guerre. Ce corps ainſi mis par pie-
es, & cuit à leur mode, ſera diſtribué à tous, quelque nó-

v

Figure 7.3. Woodcut depicting cannibalism (André Thevet, *Les Singularitez de la France antarctique*)

comme un chacun peut juger et bien entendre" [It is difficult, indeed (*voire*) impossible, to be able (*pouvoir*) to represent correctly the remarkable sites and places, their situations and distance, without having seen them with the naked eye: which is the most certain of all knowledge, as everyone can judge and well understand] (fol. 161 v). The essay conflates the imaginary and objective sides of Thevet's report along the very crease of the highly visible writing that divides them. In its distance, his tertiary account appears more real, more balanced, and far more veracious than that of either Thevet or Gómara.[15]

Nonetheless, the experience of recent history, Montaigne implies, is a better foundation than Aristotle. The Greek authority is mentioned in "Des cannibales," it appears, in order to be dismissed: "Cette narration d'Aristote [on explorations dating to Carthage] n'a non plus d'accord avec nos terres neufves" [Aristotle's story is not in accord with our new lands] (202), Montaigne concludes, effectively rejecting the very authority that papal authorities had marshaled to adduce the cultural inferiority of the Amerindians. The essayist opts for an intermediate form of *experience,* that is, a combination of observation, analogy, writing, and language, to move toward a mapped view of the New World that is inseparable from the textual coordinates of the *Essais.* The effect of concomitance of world and essay prompts the voice to move back and forth, from one world to the other, over and over again.[16]

Here, a third axis of inversion is manifest, one that focalizes Montaigne and the Amerindians at the center of a mystical projection. Two shapes of alterity, Montaigne and his subject, are combined into a single viewpoint, but like the two foci of an ellipse, they remain independent of each other.[17] The process duplicates the movement toward and away from center and circumference in the overall plan of the *Essais,* but now the effect approaches the subject along the axis (or sight line) of the very alterity it describes. In this light, Montaigne does not merely observe the "noble savage," nor does the chapter mark a step on a path toward an enlightenment that would move from marvel to deeper understanding of the foreign world. The other, the cannibal with whom Montaigne identifies, is both himself and other.[18]

The end of the essay stages the same inversion. Using his unreliable memory as a lens through which he can discern their fate, Montaigne recalls that, recently, three Amerindians met King Charles IX (in fact, in 1562, when the adolescent monarch ruled under the regency of Catherine de Medici) in Rouen. The French asked them what they found most admirable about the nation. "Ils respondirent trois choses, d'où j'ay perdu la troisiesme, et en suis bien marry; mais j'en ay encore deux en memoire" [They answered three things, but I've lost the third and am quite ashamed; but I still recall two of them] (212). Failure of memory authenticates the encounter; it also demonstrates a play of doubling in which Montaigne's distance from the cannibals affords an uncannily common proximity. Montaigne enables his words to speak *through* the Amerindians and to gain a perspective on the state of his nation simultaneously from within and without its borders.[19] The text reports that he met three of the natives, and that they could not understand how grown, strong men—"perhaps the Swiss guard," Montaigne qualifies in a protective measure—could submit themselves to a child. In a move that cannot fail to be read as calling into question the sorry state of the national budget of the post-1550 years, the text tells how, for all its wealth and pomp, the nation insulated the elite from a mass of homeless subjects: "Secondement (ils ont une façon de leur langage telle, qu'ils nomment les hommes moitié les uns des autres) . . . ilz avoyent aperçeu qu'il y avoit parmy nous des hommes pleins et gorgez de toutes sortes de commoditez, et que leurs moitiez estoient mendians à leurs portes, décharnez de faim et de pauvreté" [Secondly (they have a way of speaking such that they name men half the one and the other) . . . they noticed that among us there were men stuffed and filled with all kinds of fine things, and that their other halves, shriveled by hunger and poverty, were begging at their doors] (212–13).

Critique of French economic policies is done through the other, who amounts to the "half," which contains the self ("*moy*-tié") but doubles it in a way that recalls his friendship with la Boëtie, when it was "un assez grand miracle de se doubler" [a rather great miracle to be doubled] (190) and where "nous estions à moitié de tout" [we were entirely halved] (192). Through the filter of uncommon friendship, Montaigne reports that "I spoke to one of them for a long time," but in such a way that the syntax makes *one* of them *two*: "Je parlay à *l'un* (1) *d'eux* (2) fort long temps" (213), or a double of himself and his position. Two points of view are held within the narrational perspective.[20]

The three modes of inversion (the focal or vanishing term, "*barbarie*"; the presence of intermediary images, reports, or reporters; and the elliptical axis of self and Amerindian) utterly change the status of the historical sources that inform the writing. The immediate political views that argue for self-contained and self-regulating domestic and international policies and a more even distribution of wealth bring forth elements unknown to Gómara or Thevet. Furthermore, the essay dismantles the authority of Aristotle, which had been used to favor policies encouraging conquest of the New World. To test the strength of these views, we can look again to "Des coches" (III, vi), an essay placed next to the axis of the third volume, which itself forms a point of a double axis with "Des cannibales."

Fumée's Gómara and "Des coches"

"Des coches" (III, vi) projects the optical structure of "Des cannibales" into a mirrored duplication *en abîme*, or a self-reflective labyrinth. The ostensive topic—regal coaches, signs of munificence in the European aristocracy—is apposed to the litters on which Amerindians display their monarchs. The title, "Des coches," equivocates with the second person singular of the verb *descocher* (*descoches*), which tells its interlocutor or viewer to "release," "let an arrow fly," or "fire!" The verb is laden with amorous connotations developed in poetry of the Pléiade, but here it is imbued with military history in the discussion that compares harquebuses to longbows (879) and that leads to a consideration of guns on mobile wagons and their effects on cavalry and infantry (the Hungarians beat the Turks when they "les *descochoient* dans leurs escadrons pour les rompre et y faire jour" [released their fire on them in their squadrons to break them and clear a way] [879]). Like the entire essay, the word forms its own abyss. At its center is the letter *O*, a sign of the axis and circumference of the *Essais*; of the wheel that is the metaphor of metaphor or of representation in general; the origin of mechanical printing; the figure of European weapons aimed at those looking directly at armed European conquerors readying to kill them; the circle of Time and Saturn; a Ptolemaic conception of the world surrounded by concentric spheres.[21] Discursively, the *O* of the chariot wheels evokes the open mouth of subjects aghast at the view of extravagant public display or at the impact of a projectile as it splatters into their bodies. The figure ramifies into reflections on economy, by which the *O* signifies the shape of golden coins; Spanish plunder; mercantilism; and deficit spending. The essay is the nexus of a geography that marks the intersections of the Old and New Worlds; north and south; antiquity and present time; France at its center and its periphery.

Gómara's accounts of Mexico and Peru play a crucial role in the overall design. The Spanish West Indies offset the Old World by opening a space where contemporary France can be studied from without and within. At the fulcrum of the essay, the text turns about-face to the New World in order to develop the convention of Europe beginning its decline upon contact with the West Indies; it underscores how the static condition of lavish wealth has equaled whatever Europe has displayed to its populace. The descriptions are lifted almost verbatim from Martin Fumée's translation of *La historia general de las Indias,* which appeared in Paris in 1569. No doubt it was sold in France to make the public take note of the accounts of the fourth book, the translator remarks, which "discourses amply on the civil wars, that came about among

the Spaniards for the domination of the Peruvian king," and offers comparative examples that might help give perspective to "such calamitous times" of
French civil strife: "Il convenoit au temps turbulent, auquel pour lors nous
estions" [It was fitting for the turbulent times in which we were living]. Fumée
adds that Thevet's *Singularitez,* one of the principal French sources for depictions of the New World, is "filled with lies, not only forged by the author but
also the sailors who told them to him so that he could pass them on." "Vous y
verrez de beaux comptes des Amazones, des faultes en la situation des lieux, et
des abuz en l'interpretation de beaucoup de choses" [You will see exaggerated
accounts of the Amazons, errors in the designation of places, and abuses in the
interpretation of many things] (fol. ix).

Cosmographers, historians, warriors, and philosophers, he adds, stand to
gain from Gómara. Fumée's translation will correct French perceptions of the
New World, and its example will buffer the horrors of the Wars of Religion
that resemble what recently occurred in Peru. Montaigne's motives for using
the source are not far from Fumée's, yet with it, he elaborates a different
textual geography and a cultural critique arching back to the first volume.
An icon of a world past and another freshly discovered, the coach figures in
Gómara's relation. The Peruvians, Gómara notes, were a population led by the
rich: "Ces seigneurs n'estoient pas egaux à s'asseoir, ny és autres honneurs,
parce qu'aucuns procedoient les autres, autres se faisoient porter en lictière,
autres en portoires, autres alloient à pied. Autres se seoient sur des sieges hauts
et grands, autres sur des sieges plus bas, autres à terre" [These lords were not
equal on their thrones, nor in other honors because some came ahead of others, while others were carried on litters, and others by porters, while still others
went on foot. Others were seated on high and great seats, others being not so
high, while others walked on the ground] (López de Gómara 1569: fol. 140a).
Gómara offers a discursive emblem to the title "Des coches." And, like the images used to produce descriptions in "Des cannibales," the text ostensibly sets
forth what contemporary illustrations had used to figure the New World: su-
pine Indians in hammocks, longhouses, human members roasted on skewers
over fires, nude maidens, in sum the paraphernalia that had illustrated *Les
singularitez,* that was part of Oviedo and Benzoni, and that would soon be
recast in Théodore de Bry's *Greater Voyages,* in whose third volume, *Americae
tertia pars, Navigatio in Brasiliam Americae* (Frankfurt, 1592), the scenes of violence are reproduced.[22] It appears that the observer of 1588 has obtained more
information in the eight years since "Des cannibales," or that information
about the Black Legend and the excesses found in Gómara's descriptions were

already impetus enough to argue further against the colonial policies they had developed.

Contrasted once again to European barbarity are the Amerindians. Attabalipa signifies one mode of courage, and the king of Mexico another. When comparing Mexican cosmology to that of Christianity, the text draws on Gómara, verbatim again, to describe the five ages and five consecutive suns of human time.[23] The first perished when all humans and animals were drowned in diluvial waters; the second came with the fall of the sky; the third by a fire that burned and consumed everything; the fourth, "through a commotion of air and wind that razed everything as far as several mountains; men were not killed but changed into *magots*" (a species of monkey). After fifteen years of darkness, a man and a woman were created to refashion the human species. The chapter follows Gómara quite closely except for a slight—but crucial and astonishing—change in wording. In Fumée's translation, the text reads:

> Quant au tiers soleil, ils disent icelui avoir esté consumé par le feu, ce monde bruslant par longues années, et durant lesquelles tout le genre humain, et tous les animaux furent enflambez: et que le quatriesme print fin par l'air, estant le vent si fort, et si violent, que tous les edifices, antres et rochers tomberent par terre: mais que les hommes ne moururent poinct, et qu'ils furent seulement convertis en singes.

> [As for the third sun, they say that this was consumed by fire, the earth burning for many years, and during which the whole human race and all animals were immolated; and that the fourth came to an end through air, the wind being so strong and violent that all buildings, lairs, and rocks fell to the ground; but that men no longer died, and that they were only transformed into monkeys.] (Fumée/López de Gómara 1587: fol. 158b)

Montaigne appears merely to abbreviate his model, tightening the description of the third and fourth cataclysms:

> Le troisiesme, par feu qui embrasa et consuma tout; le quatriesme, par *une émotion d'air* et de vent qui abbatit jusques à plusieurs montaignes; les hommes n'en moururent poinct, mais *ilz furent changez en magots* (quelles impressions ne souffre la lácheté de l'humaine creance!).

> [The third, by fire that burned and consumed everything; the fourth, through *a commotion of air* and wind which razed as far as several mountains; men no longer died, but *they were turned into magots* (from what impressions suffers the cowardice of human belief!] (893, emphasis added)

Two changes are obvious. First, Montaigne replaces the "quatriesme print fin par l'air" by "une émotion d'air"; then, "les hommes ne moururent poinct ..., ils furent seulement convertis en singes," is altered quite extensively into "les hommes n'en moururent poinct, mais ilz furent changez en *magots*" prior to the interjection in parentheses. *Magots* replaces *singes*, while a sigh about the risible condition of humanity infuses Gómara's model with sardonic irony. *Lâcheté* is printed, it appears, to reflect on the motif of chairs (*la cheze, la chaise*, suggested by *lâcheté*, along with release, as *lascher* is triggered from the synonym of *descocher*). The spatial and allegorical frame of the context might explain why *magots* replaces *singes*. A synonym of *singe* (or a monkey without a tail, of the "mazacques" family), *magot* appears to duplicate the cardinal design of the chapter, since it also refers to *sacoche*, or a pouch that contains money. According to Littré, "the *magot* must have been a money bag; it would have to be written *magaut*, and hence confused and assimilated as *magot*, or monkey." The philologist traces it back to provincial usage, in which *magaut* also means "old coins found in the ground."

The word is hence a corruption of the old Latin *imago*. Not only does *magot* mean a genre of monkey and a "sum of round money usually hidden in a secret place," but it is also an image or a visual figure of the kind used to construct the chronicle of authenticity. As is the case for other terms in "Des coches," the substantive is self-perpetuating in its play among its referent, its own visible form, and its place in the moving skein of plotted figures. Allusion to a simian confirms Montaigne's avowedly mimetic tendency, his "condition singeresse et imitatrice" [monkey-like and imitative condition] (853), and all the more in respect to Gómara's text that he apes. In contemporary iconography, the monkey was an animal that signified the sin of copying and parodied the curious souls who looked vainly for worth in secret places.

But *magot* also ramifies into nominal and theological issues. As an allegorical landscape, the essay is striated by lines demarcating worlds old and new; by apposed cosmologies that explain in different languages the beginnings and endings of man; by the sight of one world in decline and another in rebirth. At its center, foretelling the end of Europe and the growth of the west, the essay states, "L'univers tombera en paralisie; l'un membre sera perclus, l'autre en vigueur" [The universe will fall into paralysis; one member will be withered, the other in vigor] (887). It cannot fail to be inflected by at least two theories of apocalypse that had attempted to explain the origins of "man" that news of Columbian discoveries had unearthed. They are related to the beginning of "Des Cannibales" (200–201). On the one hand, an argument for polygenesis superseded the belief that the Amerindians were born of the sons of Noah. According to the teachings of the Apostolic church, the discovery of a New Jerusalem would usher in a new world to replace the old. In this millenarian view, which was current at the end of the sixteenth century, the books of Genesis and Apocalypse figured prominently in the interpretations of the origins of the Amerindian.[24]

The *magot* would certainly point allusively to Gog and *Magog,* the two characters in the terror of a second coming who embody the millenarian moment that Gómara draws out of Mexican cosmology and that figure on many Ptolemiac maps of Asia. *Magot/Magog* would refer, to be sure, to the book of Ezekiel (chapters 38–39), in which God tells his son to warn Gog, king of Magog, that all creatures will quake in his presence, and that mountains will be leveled. Biblical wrath is aimed against the avatars of Gog's peoples, but in ways that identify Montaigne with a hidden, common god of his own letter. In Persian, "Gog" signified a mountain, such that "Magog" meant a "great gog," high mountains, a high plateau or, following a common gloss, it would result that Gog and Magog were a collective name for barbarians coming to conquer inhabited lands. In the eyes of the natives, the Spaniards would be a sign of what was revealed in their cosmology. In the concomitantly political dimension of "Des coches," where Montaigne's critique of munificence and endorsement of thrift are invested in the density of his words, *magot* becomes a substantive, like the letter *O,* or the title, through which pass all the themes of the chapter. It becomes a miniature meridian, a word-coin struck with poetic thrift countering the *lâcheté* of the Spanish legend and its official historians.

Montaigne's rewriting of Fumée's translation of Gómara changes a descriptive account into a specular machinery that conflates time, legend, and figure according to coordinates located both at the cardinal extremities of the essay and in the analogical configuration of words and letters that mark and mirror those same points. Such is *magot,* in the parenthetical "(quelles impressions ne souffre la lâcheté de l'humaine creance!)," where the opening of the parenthesis is akin to that of a textual body farting an "émotion d'air et de vent qui abbatit jusques à plusieurs montaignes." Montaigne replaces Gómara's image of land leveled ("rochers tomberent par terre") with the toponym of his signature in the common plural, thus inserting in his own writing the signs of a second coming. But now, in the overall geography, it remains to be seen how the "commotion of air and wind" reflects the initial figure, placed at the beginning of the essay, that asks why we bless those who sneeze. Aristotle, rejected in the discussion of geography in "Des cannibales," is now invoked for his clever reasoning that can adduce specious origins to be the cause of common effects. Sly rationale allows truth to be bent for the end or elegance of those who fashion their arguments as they do:

Me demandez-vous d'où vient cette coustume de benire ceux qui estrenuent? Nous produisons trois sortes de vent: celuy qui sort par embas est trop sale; celuy qui sort par la bouche porte quelque reproche de gourmandise; le troisiesme est *l'estrenuement*; et, parce qu'il vient de la teste et est sans blasme, nous luy faisons cet honneste recueil. Ne vous moquez pas de cette subtilité; elle est (dict-on) d'Aristote. (Emphasis added)

[Do you ask me whence originates this custom of blessing those who sneeze? We produce three kinds of wind: What goes out of the bottom is too dirty; What goes out of the mouth carries some reproach of gluttony; the third is sneezing; and, because it comes from the head and is blameless, we accord it this honest reception. Don't laugh at this subtlety; it belongs (they say) to Aristotle.] (876)

The implicit geography of the body and its orifices is reminiscent of Bodin's map of the humors and climates, a moderate body conceivably balancing its expulsive forces according to cardinal virtues. But the origins, or *maistresse cause* (899), given to bless the sneezer come from without or from a space, if the idiolect of cinema can be used, *off camera*, that remains undesignated except by passing reference to Aristotle. Whence come not only the custom of blessing but its very agency? Who has the right to *benire*? In the portmanteau style of the *Essais*, Montaigne cannot but refer, in the figure of those who *bless*, to dominant powers of religious authority.[25] But those who sneeze (*estrenuent*) can also allude to those who traffic in naked beings (*estres nues*), that is, in the context of the greater part of "Des coches," to Iberian slavers. Those who bless could only be the authorities, from Aristotle to Pope Alexander VI, who give Spain reason enough to conquer the West Indies.[26] Furthermore, the conquistadores are those who "sneeze" or, in the gridding of the chapter, popes and armed soldiers who are prone to fire (*descocher*) figuratively or literally on the Amerindians. They sneeze "at" the very beings they plunder, incarcerate, torture, enchain, and sell. At the same time, when the text ironically compares the empyreal regions of the head to goodness, it also inflects the standard picture of the political body with naggingly historical innuendo. The head is not just a source of abstraction, for it is attached to what it seeks *in its own name*.

Now it stands to reason how and why the figure of wind is plotted in the cardinal configuration of the essay. The sneeze at the beginning rhymes spatially and geographically with what Montaigne visibly alters from Gómara's original description of the Mexican ages of man. The "émotion d'air" in the cosmology described at the end responds to this passage on the other side of its textual line of demarcation. The Mexicans have as much right, as long as their economy is not expansionist in policy, to believe in an age when man is swept away (as far as some *montaignes*) in an "émotion d'air." The sneeze on one side of the chapter gives political and economic cause to the effect of windy cataclysm on the other. It wipes out everything, including a number of *montaignes*.

Montaigne's parenthetical exclamations about why men were turned into monkeys and from what impressions suffers the cowardice of human belief do not refer solely to Mexican Indians. "Impressions" implies the effect of printing, an agency of power that divides and conquers the indigenous tribes no less efficiently than gunpowder.[27] And what suffers (*souffre*) is homonymically what "sulphers" from the effect of harquebus fire in the same connections: "Nous nous escriïons du miracle de l'invention de nostre artillerie, de nostre impression" [We were exclaiming about the miracle of the invention of our artillery and of our printing] (886). The *lâcheté* of human belief happens to weigh upon its "coachness," or its will to accept authority because authority, like a pope or a king, gains its effect of power while sitting on a throne, in a coach, or on a palanquin. The pun had already marked his choice of Alcibiades' tale of Socrates' courage next to *Lachez* (877, taken from the *Symposium*), which plays on cowardice (*lâcheté*) and chairs (i.e., *la chaise*). Here it recurs in the network of figures denoting authorities as well as those of release, as the verb *descocher* had implied. It associates whoever "releases" a bull, that is, the popes aligned with Spanish foreign policy, with those who are cowards. Both conquistadores and the Roman church bless those who sneeze or shoot and those who pillage the Americas.

The essay is so arcanely drawn that its allusions encircle the effect of its discourse into its verbal (visual, syntactic, graphic) causes. When seen juxtaposed to its Spanish sources, its apparent "difficulty," a convention of the official canon of Montaigne studies, becomes clear and resonant. Montaigne crafts a dense, parsimonious style whose worth contrasts with the deflated value of the gold flooding the European market; the words display a firm resolution to counter the strife-ridden France of the Wars of Religion with its own image of itself—the monkey business of its (i)*mago*(t)—in its very discourse. It continues to argue obliquely against colonial development by insisting that European nations would do well to curtail deficit spending, to arrest the plunder of the New World, and to regain a balanced economy that distributes wealth more evenly among its subjects. The example of what the text prescribes is found in the scriptural economy of the essay itself, in its delimited perimeters, and in its ecological relation to its sources and to its own discourse. From another standpoint, the text also shows exactly where and how far Montaigne's views of the colonial ventures had come in the eight years that had passed since he wrote "Des cannibales."

The 1588 essay is written guardedly, amid civil war, and happens to be congruent with Bartolomé de las Casas's view of the New World in the wake of his debates in Valladolid with Juan Ginès de Sepúlveda.[28] It turns the sources of Spain's official history against itself for the sake of advancing positions against intervention and expansion. For the purpose of the implicit cartography of the new world in the *Essais*, the issue of Montaigne and las Casas is not irrelevant. In its overlap of spatial and discursive areas, the *Essais* appear to respond to the earlier debates. Sepúlveda, following Gonzalo Fernández de Oviedo's biased accounts of the Indies, argued the inferiority of the Amerindians by way of Aristotle and Saint Augustine. Aristotle stated that indigenous groups function effectively in mechanical, but not in rational, ways: They have no apparent form of governance, and they need order imposed upon them from without. Las Casas argued that the Amerindians had a right to their lands and that the Spaniards had no business taking them over.[29] Las Casas's work had been known since midcentury and had reached France by the time Montaigne was rewriting his essays.[30] In strictly historical terms, he may neither have read las Casas's reports from the New World nor have had much inkling of the events of Valladolid.

But in more pervasive and unconscious ways, the relation may have been far more intimate. At the end of "De la vanité," in one of his typically Freudian gestures, Montaigne states that his first, living impressions of Rome (captured during his voyage on 30 November 1580)[31] and first related in the *Journal de voyage en Italie*) were more immediate in his childhood than in the experience of later life (in the *Journal de voyage*, 1212–13). In the essay he writes,

> Le soing des morts nous est en recommandation. Or j'ay esté nourry dès mon enfance avec ceux icy; j'ay eu connoissance des affaires de Romme, long temps avant que je l'aye eue de ceux de ma maison: je sçavois le Capitole et son plant avant que je sceusse le Louvre, et le Tibre avant la Seine.
>
> [We are advised to take care for the dead. Now, I have been nourished by them since my infancy; I have known of the affairs of Rome for a long time before those of my own house: I knew the Capitol and its map before I knew of the Louvre, and I knew the Tiber before the Seine.] (975)

The scene recounts how a stronger bonding is gained through the passage of death and life—that is, the experience of writing—than through the contingencies of history, which, at a cursory glance, have less immediate impact. In the moving, mystical element of a loosely diagrammatic writing that creates a present past of living relations through its own means, "De la moderation," "Des cannibales," and "Des coches" appear to bond an unconscious rapport with the ethnography associated with las Casas through an absolute identity of viewpoint.

Montaigne and las Casas meld in their study of slavery and excess. Textually, both challenge the currency of Aristotle in modern times, and both reject political appropriations of his work for conquest. The intimacy they gain across these issues makes their rapport, like the concept and practice of friendship in "De l'amitié," all the more compelling in both human and political spheres. Where las Casas's appeal to human rights is based on observation, Montaigne fashions his experience of the Amerindian other through the productive alterity of his textual means. He uses the experience of the cartographer to fashion a distanced view that will become that of himself as ethnographer, as political scientist, and as ecologist.

As we noted in respect to the relations of the *isolario* and early anthropology, the essays refuse to arrogate the figure or the rights of the other as part of their discourse. Montaigne's critique of papal Rome and Spanish foreign policy orients the diagrammatic mode of the writing toward the sciences of man. The visual and verbal form does not present either the signature or the portrait of a detached observer of man, nor of a figure who acquires his political views after coming to terms with himself. The political effectiveness of Montaigne's relation to New Spain is immediate and clear. Developed through its complex relations to its sources, it owes much to the cartographic register that establishes a focal distance with respect both to the Western Hemisphere and to its own discourse. If we read the text in the terms of the "ocean-river" or *ecoumène* of the globe of our time, the chapters comment with uncanny force on the program of geocide that we have slated for our planet (Harvey 1989). That very program shares many of its beginnings in the conception of the self as a conquering agent that is armed with schematic reason. In order to see two of its manifestations at the end of the sixteenth century and at the threshold of the classical age, we can now conclude this study by way of Lancelot du Voisin and Descartes.

8

La Popelinière and Descartes: Signatures in Perspective

In chapter 7 we discovered that the *Essais* combine the principles of the allegorical landscape with the writing of a historical map. They inherit a cosmographic schema that reproduces in miniature the variety of the world's creations, but at the same time they place the figure of a nascent writing self in dialogue with a contemporary time that cannot be allegorized. The caustic critique of Spanish conquests bears the mark of a writer committed to a strong national cause. Montaigne's writing hovers between a memorial view of the individual subject, an allegorical geography, an art of prediction, and a work of historiography. It moves between the image of the self-possessed individual and the writer who dissolves into the world that his book both invents and embodies. In a real sense, the *Essais* are sketched out as a portrait and a map that appear self-made, obtained through the military arts, citational strategies, modes of plotting, and pictorial perspective.

To give greater definition to the relation between the self and the space of the world toward the end of the early modern era, we can compare the effects of the heterogeneous shapes of the *Essais* to two other pieces of cartographic writing, Lancelot du Voisin's history of the new world, *Les trois mondes* (1582), and René Descartes's *Discours de la méthode* (1637). Both works are carefully plotted in the ways that they display an emergent self through graphic and diagrammatic means. They also inflect politics and history through the relations they establish between geography and chronicle. From these works, two different paths of development are opened for cartographic writing. In the works of the Protestant historian of France, we see a careful rendering of the world as it is, in the force that history and geography exercise on political matters as seen by a Protestant. In those of the philosopher of the *cogito,* the map becomes the internalized or, as it were, introjected form that must be hidden in order for the self-made subject to gain prominence and be endowed with godlike attributes of power in the national space he is constructing. A perspectival object, the signature of René Descartes, is located along an infinitely receding axis that puts the philosopher's name at the vanishing point that disappears into a realm of total and invisible self-control. Exactly how maps figure in these authors' works tells much about the fortunes of cartographic writing at the threshold of the classical age.

The Map of *Les trois mondes*

Lancelot du Voisin, also known as the Seigneur de La Popelinière, is situated at one end of a spectrum that had been opened for historiographers of the sixteenth century. Throughout the century, it was believed that history writing had to adhere to the conventions of literature, to "the literary style established by the *monde des lettrés*" (Ranum 1980: 95), a world in which Montaigne, too, circulates. But the historian, a necessary agent in the course of history, also had to demonstrate political responsibility in his representation of the past. This was the point of view that La Popelinière shared, even though his attitude led to loss of favors that might have come had he taken a more yielding position with respect to royalty. He saw himself as "a historical conscience, or guarantor of historical knowledge" (94). The attitude that welcomed an "active participation in the civic life of the state" (96)—which we have discerned in the areas between the diagrammatic and discursive registers of the *Essais*—has a particular expression in La Popelinière's history of the new world.

Les trois mondes was published in Paris in 1582, a decade after the Saint Bartholomew's Massacre. The book documents the fruits of Magellan's voyages, Protestant attempts at colonization in midcentury, and the overall impact of Spanish conquest upon the Western Hemisphere. It renews faith in colonization in the hope that the French will eventually set foot on a new promised land, the "Terre Australe," that was discovered in 1524 during the first circumnavigation of the globe.[1] Following a design that divides the world according to a cartographic allegory, La Popelinière arranges *Les trois mondes* into three sections that comprise Europe, the Americas, and the unnamed land just beyond:

Je ne m'employeray donc qu'à diviser ce que les hommes jugent habitable, un monde vieil, neuf, & incogneu. Le vieil comprend l'Europe, l'Afrique, & l'Asie. Le neuf, toute l'Amerique avec les terres dites neuves. . . . Puis les autres continents depuis le destroit de Magellan, jusques au Nort, Royaume de Quivira, Anam, & autres contiques comprinses la neuve Espagne. L'inconnu nous est la terre Australe, appellez par les Espagnols & Portug. Terra del fuego, que Fernand Magellan . . . passa soubz le bon-heur, au despens de l'Espagnol, l'an 1521, pour descouvrir la mer du Su[d], par[où]ils cherchoit les Molucques.

[I shall only go about dividing what men believe is inhabitable: an old, new, and unknown world. The old includes Europe, Africa, and Asia. The new, all of America with the so-called new lands. . . . Then the other continents from the Strait of Magellan to the north, the Kingdom of Quivira, Anam, and other land-islands under new Spain. The unknown is the Austral land, called by the Spanish and Portuguese *Terra del fuego,* which Ferdinand Magellan . . . crossed with good fortune, at the expense of the Spanish, in 1521, to discover the South Sea, by which they sought the Moluccas.] (fols. 34–35 r)

The author appears to be taking his cue not only from Pigafetta's account of Magellan's voyage (published in French as *Le voyage et navigation faict par les Espaignolz es Isles de Mollucques* . . . [Paris: Simon de Colines, circa 1528], but also taken up in Thevet's *La cosmographie universelle),* which had drawn extensively on the traveler's account of the voyage that led the Portuguese between the Philippines and Australia en route to the Moluccas and back to Europe.[2] Thevet had included a "map-narrative" that displays Magellan's last battle within the surround of the island of Mactan, embellishing the history of the western Pacific, which had been only approximated in a corner of Ortelius's world map at the beginning of the *Theatrum orbis terrarum.*

Les trois mondes is an apology for travel, to be sure, but it is also a discourse on the new power of maps and mapping in historical writing. In the same area where La Popelinière charts the divisions of the book according to the definition of habitable—or colonizable—lands, he argues that history and geography must be understood as belonging to one another just as light should be understood as pertaining to darkness. "Car comme la Geographie est l'oeil naturel, & la vraye lumiere de l'histoire: tout narré sera tousjours obscur, & ne sçauroit on bien comprendre aucun des cours pour vray qu'il fust, si l'on ne cognoist premierement les lieux, l'humeur du peuple, & la qualité du pays duquel on entend parler" [For as geography is the natural eye and true light of history: all accounts would forever remain obscure if we did not first become familiar with the places, the attitudes of the people, and the quality of the country of which we believe we are speaking] (fol. 35 r). The hard fact of geography will enlighten history. The discourse plays on a chiaroscuro of a world map of many places illuminated and of others left in darkness. Those that seem to be emerging into light, he adds, are the Asian islands in the Indian Ocean, such as Sumatra and Taprobana, "Zeilan," the five Moluccas, "Iappan," and an infinity of other smaller islands "that we can discover on universal maps: especially on those of the learned Mercator and of André Thevet, the cosmographers of our time" (fol. 35 v).

La Popelinière constructs a play of figuration that brings to light certain names and places and that lets others recede into the shade of oblivion. There reigns a rhetoric that mediates between the *graphic truth* of geography and the abstraction of a universal plan of history. The latter is attached to the Protestant mission of seeking new worlds in the time of civil war in France, while the former serves as a guide for the mobilization of the religious cause. Crucial to the enterprise is the need both to name and to leave in the margins the origin and the effect of the history as discourse and diagram.

The remarks on the relation of geography to chronicle and of light to the unknown have a graphic correlative at the beginning of the account. Between folios 4 v and 5 r, there is a world map (the Ortelian *typus orbis terrarum*) that has been inserted according to instructions printed on the verso of folio 4: "La carte des trois mondes doit suivre ceste page" [The map of the three worlds must follow this page]. The reader sees, however, not an allegorical view that divides the globe into three parts but only a reduced copy (16 × 22 cm) of Ortelius's famous world map (33.5 × 49.4 cm) (Figure 8.1). Ostensibly copied from the original or a full-size woodcut in Belleforest's recent *La cosmographie universelle* (Shirley 1987: 171, plate 148), the new title inserted in the upper cartouche invites the spectator to interpret the *mappa mundi* as a representation of the three continents La Popelinière is describing. The inscription enlists a schematic reading at the same time that the text below, translating the quotation from Cicero that had appeared in the 1570 atlas ("Quelle des choses humaines pourroit sembler grande à celuy, auquel avec l'éternité est connuë la grandeur de tout le monde?" [What of human things might appear grand to the one who, with eternity, knows the grandeur of the whole world?]) argues for wonder and chiaroscuro of belief in an eternal creator.

Opposite the map we read the following discourse:

Premier Livre des Trois Mondes

Ce tout puissant, qui tant en general que particulier, nous fait veoir les merveilles de sa grandeur sur toutes choses humaines, elementaires, & celestes: a premierement crée le monde, puis l'a peuplé d'hommes pour les y faire contempler l'excellence de ses oeuvres en la iouyssance de ce qu'il y a voulu produire pour les accommoder. Mais soit que d'accident ou de naturel, soit de contrainte ou volonté,

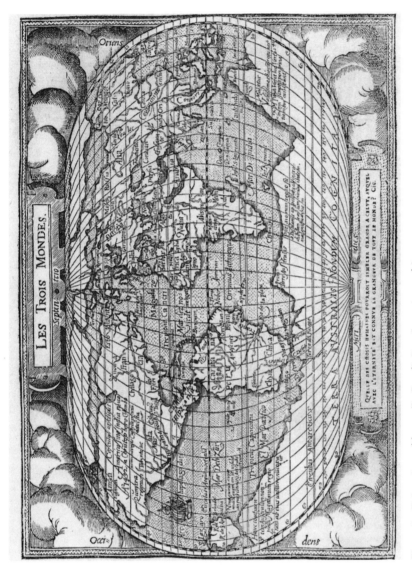

Figure 8.1. Epitomic world map (La Popelinière, *Les trois mondes*)

soit que par hazard ou soigneuse discretion ils ayent cogneu, puis cultivé peu à peu la diversité de tant de terres: le different est vieil & mal resolu, sçavoir si les païs descouvers par ceux de ce temps ont esté incogneus aux premiers peres, ou à aucuns de leurs descendans. Presque tous tiennent pour asseuré, que Dieu poulsant les hommes pour entreprendre choses hautes & extraordinaires, quand & comme il luy plaist: denia aux anciens la descouverte des terres neuves, qu'il a fait rechercher aux Italiens, Portugais, Espagnols, & autres: avec un tel succez toutesfois [map here] en ce qu'ils se sont si diversement portez en la descouverte, conqueste, & maintenue de ce païs : y admirent un merveilleux iugement divin: non moins en l'estrange cruauté des Espagnols (comme ils confessent aux mesmes par leurs escrits) punis par seditions propres, ne pouvans iouïr paisibles d'un si grand bien: qu'au merveilleux naturel des Indiens, richesses incroyables et autres choses prodigieusement estranges que la Nature a produit en ces regions.

[First Book of the Three Worlds
This all-powerful who makes us see the marvels, both in general and in particular, of his [its] grandeur above all human things, elementary and celestial; first created the world, then populated it with men in order to have them contemplate the excellence of his [its] works in the bliss of what he [it] wanted to produce in order to accommodate them. But either by accident or natural causes, by constraint of will or by chance, or careful discretion they might have known, then slowly cultivated the diversity of so many lands: The dispute is old and ill-resolved, that is, of knowing whether the lands discovered in our time were unknown to our first fathers or to some of their descendants. Almost everyone takes for granted that God pushed men to undertake elevated and extraordinary tasks when and wherever he pleased. He denied to the ancients the discovery of new lands and allowed them to be sought by Italians, Portuguese, Spanish, and others, with such success nonetheless [map here] that beyond the notable contrary attitude of these two last nations in which they have so diversely played roles in the discovery, conquest, and colonization of this country, therein they admire a marvelous divine judgment, no less in the strange cruelty of the Spaniards (as they themselves confess in their own writings) punished by their own seditions, unable to rejoice peaceably in such a great gift: than to the natural marvel of the Indians, incredible riches and other prodigiously strange things that Nature has produced in these regions.] (fols. 4 v –5 r)

The discourse is akin to Montaigne's view of the Spanish in the New World, and it begins to take sides in favor of the Portuguese against the colonial system of the *encomienda* in order, later, to have the "others" noted above, that is, the French, succeed them in their example.

Crucial for the enterprise of the argument is the placement of the map in the midst of the text. God is initially named only as "This all-powerful who makes us see the marvels" of the world. But it must be stressed that in the graphic rhetoric *the map is set in the area reserved for God's name.* God is made incarnate in the shape of a world map. The rest of the discourse can be read as a praise of the gifts of the world that are brought to light not with God's help but, rather, because cartographic reason is deified in order to inspire colonization to the west beyond the New World. The invocation of the Christian deity is only a smokescreen for a much more rational and diagrammatic evidence of a world that can be gridded, plotted, and colonized.

No longer does the discourse commingle or become one with the map in a dialogic shape that demonstrates the seamlessness of divine creation of world and language; now the clearly marked division between the map and the text makes God disappear. The disappearance of the origin of creation becomes the justification for the development of the world by entirely pragmatic means. Supreme power and light are invested in the miniature worldview that concretizes the origin and end of God's world with human evidence that is much more immediate than the presence of the deity. God is pushed into remote regions of abstraction, which lay behind the more compelling physical evidence of the map. In short, "Dieu est loin, vive la carte."

The Cartesian Map

It could be argued, to the contrary, that for La Popelinière the inclusion of the epitomic version of Ortelius's map posits the supremacy of God's creation and stands as a sign of His (Her, or Its) presence. In either event, the map emerges from the discourse as something different from writing or the speech that is conveyed through printed characters. But in contrast to Montaigne, a mapping strategy is not embedded in the arguments themselves. In "De la vanité" and other chapters of the later *Essais,* we saw how the work had drawn rhumb lines in and through its discourse, and how the self was plotted according to "supernumerary emblems," or topical wind roses configuring a carefully plotted creation of language and verbal portraiture. Unlike La Popelinière, who takes an extremely graphic, exploitative view of the world and its lands, Montaigne appears to embody what is left of a mystical relation with the universe, in which the self is liable to be anywhere and everywhere at once.

For La Popelinière, the unknown is to be marveled at because it is a site for "diligence & industrie, veu la bonté de la terre" [diligence and industry, given the goodness of the earth] (fol. 2 r), but solely on the grounds that the colonial expansion be reserved for a generation to come. The "second coming" avers not to be apocalypse but a future expedition, emigration, or project of colonization. Montaigne, in contrast to the Calvinist historian's plan for future development, stays at home in order to cultivate a life of imaginary nomadism. A vagabond on his own territory, he travels over the world without expressing a desire to expand a horizon that is seen from his tower in all of its infinity.

Montaigne's manner of travel is studied, mimicked, incorporated, and distorted in the writings of René Descartes. A topos of literary history—but less so in the history of philosophy—requires readers of Montaigne to contrast the articulation of voyage in the *Essais* to the travels and meditations of Descartes's *Discours de la méthode* and Blaise Pascal's *Pensées*. Georges Van Den Abbeele (1991: 1–61) has recently shown that travel in Montaigne's writing is organized according to the dynamics of Freud's oedipal theory. The outward movement, away from a patrilocal area, is connoted by ex-cursion of ex-perience, even expulsion of the sign of the father, Pierre, in the form of textual kidney stones (*pierres*) that afflicted the author when they were lodged in his urinary duct (recounted at the beginning of II, xxxvii, 737). The relation is so ubiquitous and pervasive in the *Essais* (35) that later readers are wont to find themselves adrift where the author follows a mystical and personal itinerary of his own. Partially in dialogue with Montaigne's remarks about his cultivation of textual nomadism, Descartes writes a text that brings a more stable perspective to the movement of self-portraiture. The author of the *Discours de la méthode* maps "certain spatial relations (Holland, the *poêle* [a heated room]) that delimit a warm and privileged interior from which the exterior can be progressively, methodically, appropriated as one's own" (Van Den Abbeele 1991: 61). Montaigne figures, rightly, as a negative model for Descartes insofar as the latter does not imitate the former, who betrays an obsessive penchant for the disappropriative play of creative doubt. Van Den Abbeele's telling comparisons pull both the *Essais* and the *Discours* into a broader arena that includes both psychogenesis and the early modern imagination of space.

Both Montaigne and Descartes assign a cartographic valence to their writing. Spatial rhetoric informs the placement of signs and the distribution of markers in texts that are as much plotted as they are written. It now remains for us to see what happens between the last decade of the sixteenth century and the publication in 1637 of the *Discours,* a work to which Descartes did not initially sign his name. The shifts in the presentation of the self indicate what may also be at work in the domain of cartography. In respect to Cartesian space, Erwin Panofsky (1972) has shown that Hellenistic and Roman concepts and practices of extension lacked measurable continuity and infinity; unlike the equipollent perspective that Descartes inherits, they were not seen "as a homogenous system in which every point would be equally determined by other co-ordinates" and extends "*in infinitum* from a given 'point of origin'" (122–23). Following Nicolas de Cusa, Descartes sets in place the philosophical and mathematical means to determine continuity, infinity, and a perspectival starting point. He also brings back to earth Marsilio Ficino's cosmographic speculations, which had painted the narrative picture of man forging a spiritual path through an infinite universe from microcosm to macrocosm (Ingegno 1988: 236–39). Ficino's philosophy complicated the notion of what it is to know and to discern the knowable, while at the same time he showed that the observable world could not be subjected to mathematical analysis (Ingegno 1988: 262). By contrast, Descartes changes the face of philosophy when he turns the *cogito* into what Panofsky calls a "point of origin" that can extend infinitely into the world.

The innovation of Cartesian reason and its complex relations to earlier theories of space have become commonplaces on well-beaten paths in the histories of science and philosophy. Yet what Descartes accomplishes seems to devolve from the presence of cartographic modes that pattern the writing of the *Discours de la méthode*. Descartes breaks away from Montaigne's nomadic, haphazard, or atomized mode of self-presentation; universalizes into the concept of the *cogito* the specific relation between history, politics, and geography that had marked the later *Essais*; corrects the anamorphic manner of self-portraiture into a deceptively stable and faithfully depicted self-portrait; but he also internalizes the contradictions that characterize Montaigne, earlier cartographers, and even Bouguereau's signatory project in *Le théâtre françoys*. In that atlas, we recall, there emerges between the maps and the textual material a sense of a common project of national representation. A unified country is sought in the dialogue established between the aims of *Le théâtre* and the historical moment of its composition. A national, collective subject—the French citizen—seems to spring from the waters of France's rivers, which flow like the circulatory system of the king's body and assure the pulse and circulation of a great country. In Bouguereau we saw how the design that praises the monarch also depends on that of the common subject or ordinary, unified signature that is obvious in the tracing of all of the nation's toponyms.

Readers of Descartes quickly discover that a similar paradox is couched in the rhetorical and spatial plan of the *Discours de la méthode*. It develops, however, with an uncanny specificity. Published anonymously in 1637, as a preface to the elegantly illustrated treatises *La dioptrique* and *Les météores*, the work follows the plan of a rehearsal of self-discovery. In the spring of 1636, Descartes moved to Leiden (from Utrecht) to oversee the printing of the *Discours* and there appended his technical essays. A well-known mathematician and painter was hired to draw the illustrations for *La dioptrique* and *Les météores*. A publisher's contract was issued on 2 December 1636, to Descartes and Jan Maire, a *privilège* for a French edition being obtained on 4 May 1637, on which date Descartes apparently had his name removed. Sharing affinity with the sixteenth-century *itineraria,* the work melds the figure of travel with that of a discourse (Blanchot 1969: 12–14) that seeks to produce "a credible concept of the self . . . when the self is doubtful or at best a kind of theoretical construction" (Lyons 1989: 155). Independently of but parallel to the history of its printing, one of the tasks of the *Discours* is that of producing a narrator who can slip into the work and, eventually, succeed in legislating what he has both mapped out and has discovered through the vagaries of trial and error. Because it must begin outside itself and then build a framework that will contain the self that could not have inhered in the writing at its origin, the discourse has initiated a tension between a "constative" or fact-producing prose and a "performative" mode that will exemplify—but also contain—the truth that it aims to discover (Derrida 1990: 284).

The writing engages a problem of "translation" or "mediation" between one mode or idiom and another. If this also entails the tension between a diagrammatic and discursive expression, then David Woodward's terminology, with which we began our study of *Les cent nouvelles nouvelles,* can be recalled. Descartes faces the daunting labor of producing a narrative that covers over—camouflages—the difference between two cartographic styles. As the work is concerned with the construction of the self, it must somehow appeal to a center-enhancing mode of plotting, but at the same time, its form, as a discourse and an itinerary set along a path that leads to the *cogito,* must follow the route-enhancing model by which the traveler draws his or her bearings along the way.

With the advent of the creation of a mixed spatial genre, the reader no longer enters into the touristic realm of the kind characterized by the easy ambulations of Estienne's *Guide,* Rabelais's itineraries, or Montaigne's souvenirs of his Italian voyages. By the beginning of the seventeenth century, the "route map" had become a technological object, a specific genre developed for "limited, practical ends" that include constructing or improving roads, establishing defensive networks, and building causeways through marshlands or bridges over rivers. In these maps, cardinal orientation is not important. A linear presentation prevails because the genre appeals to "the services of trained engineers rather than dilettante cartographers or commercial map publishers" (Akerman et al. 1993: 29). Descartes confers this kind of specificity upon his work when he notes almost from the beginning that he envies those engineers "who reap the pleasure of designing new cities over flat spaces that seem to be bereft of relief or even history." Developing what has since become a famous figure emblematizing his philosophy, Descartes remarks,

Ainsi voit-on que les bastimens qu'un seul architecte a entrepris & achevez, ont coustume d'estre plus beaux & mieux ordonnez, que ceux que plusieurs ont tasché de racommoder, en faisant servir de vieilles murailles qui avaient esté bâties à d'autres fins. Ainsi ces anciennes citez, qui, n'ayant esté au commencement que des bourgades, sont devenües, par succession de tems, de grandes villes, sont ordinairement si mal compassées, au prix de ces places regulieres qu'un Ingénieur trace à sa fantaisie dans une plaine, qu'encore que, considerant leurs édifices chascun à part, on y trouve souvent autant ou plus d'art qu'en ceux des autres; toutefois, a voir comme ils sont arrangez, icy un grand, là un petit, & comme ils rendent les rues courbées et inesgales, on diroit que c'est plutost la fortune, que la volonté de quelques hommes usant de raison, qui les a ainsi disposez.

[Thus we see that the buildings a single architect has undertaken and finished are usually better ordered and more handsome than those that several have tried to repair by using old walls that had been erected for other purposes. Thus these old cities that, having only been hamlets at their beginnings, over the passage of time have turned into great cities and are ordinarily so badly plotted (*compassées*) next to these regular places that in his fancy an engineer will trace over a plane, that even still, considering each of their buildings apart, we often find as much or more ingenuity than in those of others; nonetheless, in seeing how they are arranged—a large building here, a small one there—and how they cause streets to bend and be uneven, we might say that fortune, and not the will of a few men using reason, has disposed them thus.] (1902: vol. 6, 11–12)

The text seems to argue for an orthogonal or gridded city plan, but the names that it gives to its designers indicate that the mapping shows signs of inward stress or aberration. First, the hypothetical *ingénieur* is invoked to conjure up the image of a utopian space that a city planner is free to contemplate. The engineer is identified as being among "a few good men" who are armed with reason, that is, an abstraction that replaces an allegory of a designer bearing the attributes of the architect's or cartographer's compass. In the next sentence, the author refers to those "few officers" whose public duties include the difficult task of maintaining private buildings that will serve for "l'ornement du public" [public display]. Then, in staging a scenario of originary times, seemingly inflected by reports of savages from the New World—in what would be a discursive jewel for any psychoanalyst listening to fantasms of bestiality—Descartes shudders at how primitive peoples would have been wise to produce codes of law not equitably but through respect for "les constitutions de quelque prudent législateur" [the constitutions of some prudent legislator] (1902: vol. 6, 12).

The legislator in turn is compared to God, who rules better than any political official. But in the human world, it was the leader of Sparta (implied to have been Lycurgus) who served in this capacity. And in the "sciences of

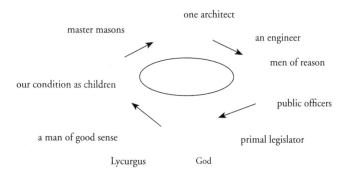

books" (1902: vol. 6, 13) where reason is only probable, or where different authors have added different opinions—in what would resemble Montaigne's ill-joined marquetries of citation—the good work of "un homme de bon sens touchant les choses qui se présentent" [a man of good sense touching on things that are before him] is notably absent (1902: vol. 6, 12). The histories of our own psychogenesis, he suggests, tell as much: As we were infants "governed by our appetites and our preceptors" in our earliest moments of formation, we cannot arrive at the kind of pure and solid judgment that would have been the condition had we been equipped with reason "dès le point de notre naissance, et que nous n'eussions jamais été conduits que par elle" [as of the point of our birth, and as if we might have been led by nothing other than reason] (1902: vol. 6, 13). Descartes goes full circle, returning to the figure of the architect who will "adjust" his life as he might if he were building on old architectural foundations. This life becomes the subject of an engineer's work. In the slyly drawn meander, the text seems to follow an anamorphic circle, or ellipse, as shown, in which the figure of the engineer follows on the heels of that of the architect, who ostensibly is chosen to be an author or a signer of creation replacing the collective architectural labors of medieval master masons. When Descartes returns to the figure of the architect at the end of this movement of chapter 2, he has mediated a center-enhancing plan, which puts the legislator or God at the center of the social compact, with a collective body of humans—in an equipollent plan—who must grow into reason and recognize that they have to work with the institutions that have formed them.

The specter of the Gothic architect or the master mason who uses proportional—not discrete—logic returns to the discourse as a democratic subject. Thanks to the plotting of the enumeration of exemplary figures, the subject has learned much from the lessons of the engineer. In the *Discours,* the "ingénieur" has a specific range of meanings tied to national defense and to mapping. Early in his reign, Henry IV heeded the advice of his economic minister, the duc de Sully, who created the title of *ingénieur du roi* [royal engineer] for military geographers who would be employed to redesign the defensive network of France (Buisseret 1964). Precursers included Nicolas de Nicolaï and, possibly, some of the surveyors who had contributed to *Le théâtre françoys*. A younger generation of cartographers—Jean Errard, Claude de Châtillon, Jean de Beins—produced more detailed maps than those of their predecessors (37), no doubt because their task of reorganizing defensive structures along the borders of France had been primarily devoted to rebuilding ramparts and embattlements. With new forms of artillery came different ways of fortifying walls and conceiving systems of national defense (Ballon 1991: 216). Until the time of Francis I, individual cities were responsible for the maintenance of their protective ramparts. Chaos reigned under different types of management. "In 1598 everything had to be reorganized" (Buisseret 1964: 18). In response to the dilemma, Sully, having become the "surintendant de fortifications," ordered the establishment of credits through *états de fortifications* that were defended by the *ingénieur du roi*, and a *maréchal de logis* [lodging master]. Two engineers were appointed in 1585, then three in 1595, four in 1597, and six in 1611. Most were experienced cartographers who were responsible for the fortification of frontier provinces. Under them were *conducteurs de desseins* who often drew plans for the masters and royal engineers (Buisseret 1992a: 107–8).

A good deal of the refortification occurred in the north and east of the kingdom, between Flanders and the lands to the northeast. When the history of these defensive and cartographic projects is compared to what Descartes makes of the construction of the *cogito,* the metaphor of the "walls" of the old city that will be redrawn by an "engineer" acquires a new and startling specificity. Descartes's philosophical project entails the rebuilding of battlements—*courtines* and *oreillons*—to fend off attack from rhetorical and literal artillery. In doing so, like an *ingénieur du roi*, he draws a provisional code of ethics that follows a simultaneously architectural and cartographic plan. He seems to begin from memory of haphazard enterprises of defensive campaigns prior to the advent of Henry's reign, invokes the image of the "single architect" and engineer who will redesign a city, moves through other city officials, and comes full circle to children and men of "good sense." In the itinerary of names and professions, the discourse moves to and about monarchic and collective bodies. Primitives, children, and groups of people, all of whom are armed with reason, serve as a foil to the sovereign individual who can conceive of and lead a social order on his own.

The cartographic subtext implies that the space that the author is describing is available to anyone and everyone, like a regional projection, but that a regional projection is also conceived according to the laws of monocular perspective. An all-powerful author needs to be placed at the vanishing point of a city-view redesigned by mechanical or artificial means. When "he can formulate the *cogito*, Descartes has to legitimize the incomparable power of the individual. He needs a mono-centered truth, the proper perspective on the world that comes from a unique point of view" in order for the *cogito* to claim for itself a founding role (Goux 1985: 13). It follows that Descartes's association of perspective and reason entails another linkage between monarchic and democratic orders. A universal and universalizing place is occupied by the monarch with the aid of the engineer's drawing, but the rational process being elaborated is made available to any human subject.[3] Descartes draws to its logical conclusion the relation between the king and the national or collective space that had been evident in the gaps between the preface, the maps, and the textual material of *Le théâtre françoys*. Yet Descartes takes the problem a step further in the center-enhancing design of the text, a design that seems to be drawn exactly according to the methods of the *ingénieurs* and the *maréchaux de logis*. The text itself is a map.

The Perspectival Signature: Between Center and Margin

Although the *Discours* appears to be obsessed with its own nomadism, it is no less marked by its need to discern a common site for both the philosopher and the common person of reason.

> Et enfin, comme ce n'est pas assez [he begins the third part], avant de commencer à rebastir le logis où on demeure, que de l'abattre, & de faire provision de materieux & d'architectes, ou s'exercer soymesme à l'architecture, & outre cela d'en avoir soigneusement tracé le dessein; mais qu'il faut aussy s'estre pourvu de quelque autre, où on puisse estre logé commodément pendant le tems qu'on y travaillera; ainsi, affin que je ne demeurasse point irresolu en mes actions, pendant que la raison m'obligeroit de l'estre en mes jugemens, & que je ne laissasse pas de vivre dés lors le plus heureusement que je pourrois, je me formay une morale par provision.

> [And finally, as it is not enough to tear down the house in which one lives before beginning to rebuild it, one needs to acquire training in architecture and, moreover, to carefully draw its blueprint; but it is also necessary to be provided with some place where one can be comfortably lodged while the work is undertaken; thus, so that I would not remain irresolute in my actions while reason would oblige me to be so in my judgments, and so that I would not fail to live as happily as possible, I formed a provisional moral code.] (1902: vol. 6, 22)

The self needs a deontological lodging, a *logis*, where it can house its own spiritual *maréchal*. The fashioning of the provisional ethic takes the form of training in architecture and drafting. The author suggests that what will assure the formulation of the "three or four" maxims is professional training in technical matters. Here and elsewhere, the allusions to the domicile resound with carto-graphic innuendo. In the context of the earlier chapters, it seems as if the au-thor were defining a space from which, once he gets it properly compassed, he might be able to plot out the world at large.[4]

At this moment the chapter launches a rich and almost synthetic cartog-raphy. In an incisive study of "Descartes's Urban Pastoral" (1991) Kevin Dunn argues that the nameless persona of the *Discours* crafts his philosophical project from paradoxes built over the dichotomies of "city and country, civic engage-ment and retirement, labor and *otium*" (93). He performs on the landscape an "ideological operation" that assigns "social functions to spatial configurations" (94). Dunn attributes to a social ambivalence the effect of an "internal com-muting between the values of the urbanized georgic, with its stress on labor for the public good, and the rural values of aristocratic leisure" (98). For him, the city plan of Amsterdam becomes a compromise between, on the one hand, the older, multilateral view of medieval urban space and an area of retreat, soli-tude, participation in social commerce and, on the other, an authoritarian plan and a common political space that gives voice to individual expression. The philosopher finds a "suburban" ethic that will promote "social and ideo-logical commuting" (106–7) in the station wagon of the *cogito*. Hence, the ad-jective *provisional* attenuates everything it modifies, but in doing so it also mobilizes the space of the self being projected out of the topos of the city-as-desert that was first drawn in Strabo's *Geographia*. Given the specific logistical tasks incumbent upon the *ingénieur* of Descartes's time, here the philosophical ideal of self-discovery, the charting of an adequate itinerary between the values of the city and the country, and the task of self-promotion in the vernacular idiom betray, in a thematic register, the mix of mapping and subjectivity.

The cartographic texture of the discourse is felt first, and most immediately, in the curious presence of the *poësle* (*poêle*) where Descartes establishes resi-dence and then, second, in the literal sense of perspective that maps out the overall plan of the *Discours*. In the warmth of the *poësle,* Descartes happened upon the comparison between the project of creating the subject and city planning and national defense. He "was then in Germany, where the occasion of wars, that are not yet over" (1902: vol. 6, p. 11) had called him. Where the depiction of the time that Descartes spent in the *poësle* can be dated to the winter of 1619, the oblivion of his period of contemplation stands, inversely, as his effort to get out of history. Without need or passion, "je demeurois tout le jour enfermé seul dans un poësle, où j'avois tout loysir de m'entretenir de mes pensées" [I spent an entire day enclosed in a heated room, where I had leisure enough to entertain myself with my thoughts] (11). Therein emerges the figure of the old city that would be replaced by the engineer's fantasy of a new network built upon a tabula rasa.

The singularity of the moment, in which the one, the *je,* spends one whole day in one room, is echoed in the labors of the one architect who maps out a grid upon one single and smooth surface. The *poësle,* a sort of toponym, marks a geographic valence by being synonymous with the northern region in which the word, along with its attendant thermal properties and the space it designates, is customarily located. The substantive verifies the speaker's account by designating the area where war has required considerable defensive investment. But as the heated room accrues evidence of the author's sojourn in the north, it also tends to disappear into the drift of thoughts that lead to the formulation of the provisional moral code. When the *poësle* recurs in the context of chapter 3—when the author wanted to get to the end of his mental itinerary as much "en conversant avec les hommes, qu'en demeurant plus long tems renfermé dans le poisle ou j'avois eu toutes ces pensées" [by conversing with others as remaining enclosed for a longer time in the heated room where I had had all these thoughts]" (55)—the proximity of *poësle* to the author's *pensées* leads to a quasi confusion of the space and the abstract forms that are generated within.

Is the text crafting a coordinate point, a perspectival object, in which the author's relation to the unknown—himself—begins to make the process of thinking synonymous with the space and qualities of the closed room? "Poelle," what Cotgrave calls "a stove, or hot-house," is also related to a "pail" or plumb that is suspended from a rack or tripod, signaling the force of attraction ("*poisle*"). An abstract force, gravity, is concretized in the reference to a stove (and its pots and pails) and the heated environs. At the same time the figure of *pesée,* weight, inflects the product that emanates from the area, *pensée.* Mixed into the reference is the art of surveying space by means of a theolodite, an instrument that had figured in recent books on surveying (Figure 8.2). Related to earlier works of geometry and cosmography, like those of Apian or Finé's Bovelles, the theodolite offers a solid base on which to mount a table and, no less, to take readings on both horizontal and vertical planes.[5] It also conveys the presence of a more general and current figure, the mariner's plumb line, that had lately appeared in practical atlases such as *The Mariner's Mirror* (London, 1585).

In addition to an allusion to the technology of mapping, an ineffable factor, heat, seems to meld *poësle, poisle, pesée,* and *pensée.* The subject who comes to

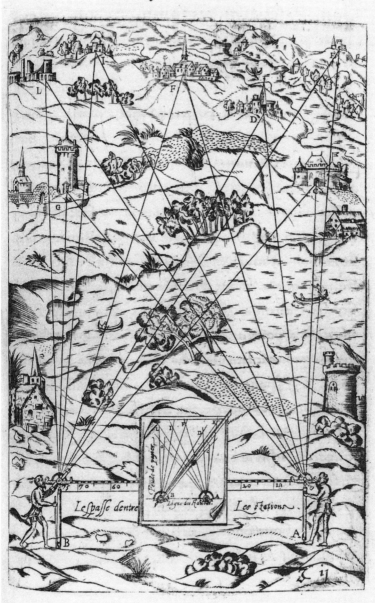

Figure 8.2. Philippe Danfrie, *Declaration de l'usage du graphomètre*

an idea of his sovereignty in the warmth of the room is also the figure, in the *Méditations*, who discovers the common truth of variability in the changing properties that beeswax displays according to its proximity to the stove. It is implied that a theory of climes or degrees of latitude is established through the thermometric figure. But at the same time, since apiculture was a traditional icon for a common nation and society of subjects, the "self" who discovers the need to argue for the existence of God locates his thinking being squarely between a position of sovereignty and commonality. A universal condition can be imagined by allusion to climatic differences, but that same condition is fathomed through the labor of mental cartography.

The end of the third part of the *Discours* dots the *i* of its point. Once he is armed with his provisional ethic, after nine years, the author discovers that he can be anywhere he wishes to be. He thus comes to the end of a stage in his travels and arrives at the midpoint, the chosen milieu, of his discourse. He realizes his desire to be and show what and who he is:

> Mais ayant le coeur assez bon pour ne vouloir point qu'on me prist pour autre que je n'estois, je pensay qu'il faloit que je taschasse, par tous moyens, à me rendre digne de la reputation qu'on me donnoit; et il y a justement huit ans, que ce desir me fit resoudre à m'esloigner de tous les lieux ou je pouvais avoir des connoissances, & à me retirer icy, en un païs où la longue durée de la guerre a fait establir de tels ordres, que les armées qu'on y entretient ne semblent servir qu'a faire qu'on y jouisse des fruits de la paix avec dautant plus de seureté, & où parmi la foule d'un grand peuple fort actif, & plus soigneux de ses propres affaires, que curieux de celles d'autruy, sans manquer d'aucune des commoditez qui sont dans les villes les plus fréquentées, j'ai pû vivre aussy solitaire & retiré que dans les desers les plus escartez.

> [But having courage strong enough not to wish that I would be taken to be someone other than who I was, I thought that I would have to try, by every means possible, to make myself worthy of the reputation being conferred upon me. And now only eight years later, this desire gave me the resolve to get away from all places where I might be known and to withdraw here, into a country where the long duration of the war has caused such orders to be established, that the armies that are being sustained appear to aid only in everyone's joy in partaking of peace with no less assurance, and where among the crowd of an active and great people, taking more care in its own affairs than being curious about those of others, without lacking any of the comforts that are in the most bustling cities, I have been able to live as solitary and withdrawn as in the most remote deserts.] (vol. 6, 30–31)

At the end of the carefully drawn itinerary of this sentence, we would not be wrong to see in the author's meditations a staging of a self-made map. Descartes portrays himself in the very course, the route, of the sentence that comes to an invisible end. The point between the third and fourth chapter of the meditation remains, like the "plus bel endroit et milieu de chaque paroy" that Montaigne's hypothetical painter chooses for his vanishing design, the point of disappearance and transcendence visible within the graphic plan of the *Discours*. The work that Descartes had likened to a "story," a "fable" (vol. 6, 5) containing some noteworthy examples, is also invested with a pictorial and cartographic design. He has been able to live as hermetically solitary and withdrawn as in "les *des*ers les plus *escartez*," that is, as in the perspectival object, his own proper name, which is folded into the very figure of an abstract countryside. Far from being the denial of the "desert" that Descartes contrasted with Paris in a famous letter to Ferrier (18 June 1619, in 1899: vol. 1, 119–20), Descartes's name is now conjoined to the extension of the north. In the letter he invited his correspondent *not* to visit him to collaborate on a project of grinding lenses, but a seductive invitation is nonetheless put forward. From Amsterdam, Descartes said,

> Je n'ose pourtant vous prier de venir icy; mais je vous diray bien que si j'eusse pensé à cela, lorsque j'estois à Paris, j'aurois tasché de vous amener; et si vous estiez assez brave homme pour faire le voyage, & venir passer quelque tems avec moy dans le desert, vous auriez tout loisir de vous exercer, personne ne vous divertiroit, vous seriez éloigné des objets qui peuvent vous donner de l'inquiétude; bref vous ne *feriez* en rien plus mal que moy, et nous vivrions comme *frères*.

> [All the same I cannot beg you to come here; but I will tell you that although I had given thought to it when I was in Paris, I would have tried to bring you here; and were you strong enough to make the journey and come to spend some time with me in the desert you would be entirely free to do what you wish, no one would distract you, you would be far from objects that might cause disquiet; in short, you would be no worse off than I, and here we would live like two brothers]. (vol. 10, 14, emphasis added)

A fantasied conjunction will take place on a lexical map where words, such as anagrams and adventitiously drawn connections, will allow the imagination to do what is less conceivable in the realm of experience. Here Descartes drafts the beginning of a process of appearance and disappearance that is fixed in place at the end of the third part of the *Discours*. Descartes's signature at the vanishing point of the text becomes the figure that gives reason to—is the *raison d'être* of—the landscape of an infinite world.[6] The consequence of this tactic of self-inscription is that the diagrammatic or cartographic aspect of the *Discours* relieves the author of any obligation to make any proof of the existence of God.[7] At the point reserved for God, Descartes inscribes the anagram, what elsewhere Descartes calls this "artifice de peu de poids" [an almost weightless artifice] (Hallyn 1992: 19–37).

The anagram floats in the text just as the art of surveying and engineering falls into it with such affected gravity. The anagram is connected to the schemes of mapping, furthermore, in the combination of diagrammatic and discursive elements of Descartes's *Rules for the Direction of the Mind*. In that unfinished work of twenty-one axioms defining the bases of Euclidean geometry in the context of logic, Descartes moves from discourse to space (as the gridded character of multiplication and squaring indicates in Rule 18) (vol. 10, 466). At every point in the work, he asks his reader to remember the step-by-step process of his rules, but only to the degree that the reader can also grasp all of their steps at once. In other words, discourse and map are seen as being complementary and identical in the Euclidean memory theater. They become so by dint of the anagram: "Permulta quoque sunt ex levioribus hominum artificiis, ad quae invenienda tota methodus in hoc ordine disponendo consistit" [There exists, too, many of the lighter things of man's artifice, in the invention of which the whole method consists in the disposal of this order], and furthermore, "if you wish to construct the best anagram possible by transposing the letters of a name, there is no need to pass from one stage to the next, nor to distinguish the absolute from the relative." The task, he says, is "ita non longus erit, sed tanùm puerilis labor" [not tedious but merely a child's labor] (vol. 10, 391). The anagram participates in the haptic activity that will wander about, traverse, or scan [*perlustrare*] all the possible ways that lead to any problem that the mind can solve (388).

Thus the anagram, nascent in the letter to Ferrier, is theorized in the *Rules* and mobilized in the *Discours,* where it figures as a perspectival signature. In the autobiographical context, its art becomes rarefied, refined, and politicized. The name becomes a common object, a common name, but a name hidden in a text-map, synonymous with *des cartes*, a partial sum of maps born of his carefully charted meditation. The inscription bears an almost uncanny resemblance to the invisible centering of the self that Oronce Finé had theorized in the *Protomathesis* and drawn up in his topographical map of 1543. At the same time, the spatial signature, the discrete point that Descartes marks with his name, belongs to a grid that assigns equal and total, authorial and lectorial, value to every discursive element held within the weave of the *Discourse.*

A Saturation of Names

In La Popelinière's account of the "third world" that would soon be populated with new generations of reformed Christian soldiers, we saw that the map stood in place of God, or in fact became God, "ce tout puissant." Now, in the Cartesian argument for the autonomy of the self, the signature of the author stands at the point where the work, conceived as a "discursive picture," indicated a site reserved for God. La Popelinière associates the world map with a supreme cause, but, unwittingly it seems, he also infers that, since God is a map and since maps are readily available to whoever wishes to use them, the self can be spatially fashioned by readily accessible means. Descartes lodges his name in the center of the kingdom of the *Discours*. He can be seen there reigning as a hidden god, or as a signature both present and absent that would be the perspectival object of the autobiographical itinerary. If we pursue further the comparison, other issues become clear. First, if Descartes's name is "concealed" in the text, it figures as a lexical point that is no different from any other in the work. It does not gain prominence unless we detect the hidden agenda that uses map and text as coextensive surfaces.

In contemporary and military and logistic maps that the *ingénieurs* and *maréchaux de logis* were making for limited, strategic purposes, place-names begin to proliferate so much that all cities and towns appear to acquire equal importance. In Jacques Fougeu's drawing of the mouth of the Somme River (1600, illustrated in Buisseret 1992a: 111, figure 4.7), 140 place-names are visible; by comparison, there are only 12 in the same area of Jean Surhom's rendering of the same locale in Bouguereau's *Théâtre* of only six years earlier. And Damien de Templeux's maps in the 1619 edition of Jean Leclerc's atlas (Ile-de-France [Figure 8.3], the Valois region, the Beauvais, Beauce, and Champagne, with Normandy added in the 1621 edition) are studded with toponyms bearing equal value. Fougeu precisely located many more names, no doubt to tell where soldiers could be lodged and fed in the course of battles and campaigns. The representation of real space is far more exact than on any maps that had appeared in major atlases.[8]

The expanding number of toponyms in the maps drawn and printed between the time of Bouguereau and the end of Henry's reign show that a consciousness of a collective population of subjects was materializing in graphic and strategic ways. Fougeu's maps and those of other engineers would have been "used to approximate the populations of a given region, or to calculate, for example, the general sum of taxation in a given place," notes David Buisseret, but only with the advent of the reign of Louis XIV and the impact of Nicolas Sanson would "this kind of administrative cartography be put to use" (1992b: 115). Now, if we look again at the *Discours* in light of the new and precocious turn in local mapping, it would seem that Descartes's signature, like a common place-name, dissolves into the general pattern of an anony-

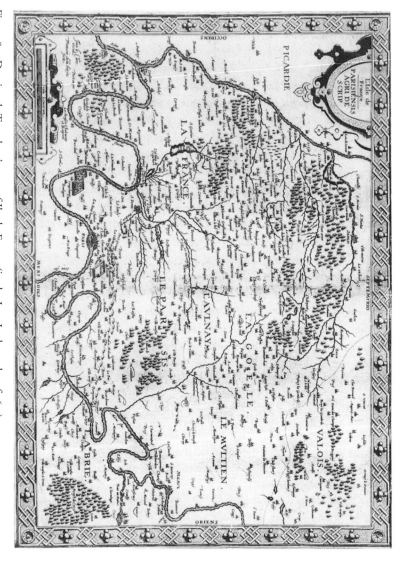

Figure 8.3. Damien de Templeux's map of Île-de-France (in the Jean Leclerc atlas of 1619)

mous and collective discourse in order to become a subject within the language and the space of the French kingdom. His text-map would be another of those equipollent guides that assign equal importance to all areas just as, in a utopian political world, every subject would be created and appraised as equal to all others.

Second, Descartes's signature also emerges into visibility insofar as its own cartographic sign guarantees its privilege: Descartes would reign, solitary and withdrawn, over "les desers les plus escartez." The philosopher becomes the sovereign of his fabulous kingdom, which is everywhere and nowhere. He surges out of a common space, like a prominent place-name in an engineer's atlas, that attributes strategic importance to cities, bridges, ferry points, and the like.[9] Descartes's inscription of himself as a divine place-name also belongs to the strategic tradition that we have followed, beginning with the convergence of northern and southern modes of seeing and ciphering the world, leading to the signature effects that Oronce Finé and literary writers, such as Montaigne, set into the perspectival order of their cartographic or descriptive projects. In this way, Descartes becomes the subject and object of his own cartography: a self-made map. He ratifies the centering projects that hold to early modern literature, mapping, and the visual arts.

But third, if we heed the tension of the name's simultaneous dissolution into and emergence out of the field of the discourse, then Descartes becomes, in one blow, an engineer, a surveyor, a philosophical writer, and an empirical topographer. How? Descartes studies himself and his worlds exactly as might have a Templeux or a Fougeu. The latter, working with his team of assistants, could have initiated a regional survey by taking the projection of a province, such as one of Bouguereau's printed maps, and then working in the area itself with surveying instruments, such as a *graphomètre*, slowly adding details, filling lacunae, and correcting imprecisions. But he would nonetheless have used the grid model to move between an initial meridian and an environing space crosshatched with longitudes and latitudes. With respect to the *Discours*, the self would stand as a beginning that is disguised or else modified by surrounding names and places. It would, in the words of Erwin Panofsky, be a paradoxical point where is concretized both "a triumph of the distancing and objectifying sense of the real" and "a triumph of the distance-denying human struggle for control," seen "as much as a consolidation and systematization of the external world, as an extension of the domain of the self" (1991: 67-68). One can move into space by surveying and arrogating it, and one can make it virtual, seemingly self-made, when a cartographic process is adjusted to the imagination of one's origins, growth, works, memory, and living itineraries.

9

Conclusion

At the outset of this study, four principles were drawn from a psychoanalytical lexicon to mark an itinerary that began with Jean Fouquet and ended with Descartes. It seemed fitting to begin with a riddle that straddles both the early modern era and our own times and lives. As inhabitants of the world, we surmise over and over again, every day of our existence, that no sufficient reason exists to explain why or whether we ought to be alive. Nothing in a great book of nature or a sacred Bible can argue away the utter gratuitousness or absurdity of human life on our planet. It is that question, surmised Piera Aulagnier, that can lead either to a dangerously psychotic condition or to a reasonably healthy degree of subjectivity. The ethnographer Claude Lévi-Strauss, whose work is strongly grounded in exploration of the Renaissance and who has forever enjoyed looking at the world with a "gaze from afar," concluded, in a postscript to a reading of the "Apologie de Raimond Sebond" (in 1991: 218), that in all intellectual sincerity, we can only offer cosmetic reasons for granting humans the right of temporary residence in the nature of things. The gratuitousness of human presence in the world could not have failed to vex cartographic writers of the early modern age as well.

Similar expressions of universal doubt inaugurate an existential relation between subjectivity, writing, and cartography.[1] Those same manifestations of suspicion are heard when we listen to analysts—Aulagnier, Rosolato, McDougall, Mijolla-Mellor, and others—who attest that subjects who initiate and work through the labors of self-study begin by appraising the crushing realization of spacelessness, atopia, and atemporality that mark the core of human life. These interpreters show that healthy subjects do not deny or repress the traumatic consequences of these everyday thoughts, but that they accept, live, and continually cope with them. All suggest that one way of dealing with the effects of spatial deracination is the slow and deliberate invention of *topical fictions* that serve as practical illusions for living in the world. They engage the creation of sites and events that attach affect and drive to discourse and to locale. One analyst (Félix Guattari) baptized them in the name of the "invention of existential territories." But they can also mean that a subject fashions, from shards of the geographic side of bodily impressions and memories, a "world-theater" that grants a privilege to one's activity of playing within its arena. If we pause to reflect briefly on the onslaught of doubt and skepticism that marked early modern France (among other studies, Febvre 1968; Gauna 1992; Busson 1993), it becomes tempting to follow a parallel that emerges between the grounding condition of the psychoanalytic subject that analysts describe and the historical subject that emerges in the early modern cartographic era.

The cartographic impulse that we have witnessed both in language and in mapping can be interpreted as a means of working with doubt or coping, before it is stated as such, with the Pascalian wager that human beings, having no reason to be, would do well not to inhabit a world lost in infinite space. The cartographic drive amounts in part to that which denies a denial, doing so by means that analysts have conceived in vocabularies strikingly derivative of what cartographers mobilized throughout the Renaissance. A drive to locate and implant oneself in a named space; a drive to imagine necessary connections between the "I," the locale of its utterance, and the origins of its birth; a sense, imposed from without and from within, that one's idiom belongs to an integral nation imagined as an erotic and as a maternal object; a perceived need to burrow into and circulate about a body, a world, and a nation, of which all three components give credence and an illusion of heritage to the ego—such are the elements of the cartographic subjectivity that emerge from the bodies of writing and mapping analyzed above.

A quadrant of principles (the relation to the unknown, the perspectival object, the pictogram, the signature) was used to map out an itinerary of cartographic writing. Biological and gendered features pertaining to the function of identity were projected onto an ostensibly neutral (hence "veracious") surface of early modern maps and their discourses. In discovering that the latter were far from being either neutral or endowed with a God-given truth, we discovered how the programs of subjectivity, selfhood, nationhood, and identity exploited a growing body of cartographic writing. But wonder of wonders, when analysis was made of painting, narrative, poetry, and typographic manifestos, the somatic register of experience, vital to the theories that launched the study, may have disappeared under the dull gloss of analysis or hopelessness of erudition.

Processes used to inform the readings may have been marginalized, if for no other reason, merely because the cartographic writer had been held to be masculine. His firm sense of identity depended on the aggressive determination of his labors in a male world: Geoffroy Tory fetishizes puncheons and presses in a studio inhabited by male masters and apprentices; Oronce Finé encloses his male name in the matrix of a historiated letter designed in the same space; the mature Rabelais heralds himself as a doctor who has grown from a proto-scientific milieu inhabited by a few good Pantagruelic men; Thevet and Belleforest project hyper-masculine images of the logophile, anticipating with their competing images the Cornelian adventurer-poet-historian (one thinks of the "Matamore" of *L'illusion comique,* with its swashbuckling braggadocio).

But these self-wrought images are also contravened by history if we consider Maurice Bouguereau as a harried editor in a printer's sweatshop on the rue de Scellerie in Tours, a figure subject to division of labor, fighting against impending deadlines, worrying about the future of the Protestant cause; La Popelinière as a windy ideologue at odds with his Catholic enemies, seeking the idea of Protestant utopias in Australian *terrae incognitae* at the cost of being rejected by the Parisian court; Descartes, a clever "*ingénieur*" who implies that the *malin génie* who inhabits him is the espionage agent-cartographer or the fretting scientist, a lens grinder, busily covering his traces as he commutes to and from Holland and Paris.

By folding the figures that exude anxiety in the later years of the sixteenth century back over the founding works, we discover that issues of gender, origin, eros, and identity may not have been so firm as the writers so projectively identified them. Tory invites an ambivalent view of the letter that pluralizes many tonal differences of gender within its own form. Finé's writing adheres to Tory's vision, and it evinces an extremely delicate mixture of traits that confuse the phallus and the matrix, the stylus and the heart, and political and personal agendas as well. Rabelais's admiration of oversexed and sterile tricksters, along with his contempt for Picrocholine phallocrats, puts a chink in the armored image of a wise Pantagruel who seems too paternalistic for his own good. André Thevet leaves the reader of the fragmentary *cosmographie universelle* with the fantasy of the author trying to crawl up into the womb of the word "ocean," the key to the vault of a compendium of masculine writing built upon a *cul-de-lampe.*

A bodily register tends to inhabit the truth that the cartographic writer wishes to display. It is clear that the project of mapping the self and the world is built on energetic foundations and that, try as it may to neutralize itself to gain an aura of truth and of a world living under the sign of progress, the budding science that emerges in the persona of a self-contained philosopher-engineer arches back to an imagination tied to fantasies of different kinds. These can include fears of miscegenation and perversion, as Gillies has so elegantly shown about the Shakespearean heritage (1994: 13–19), or the association of alterity and broadsheet images of Ubangis, cannibals, and vamps of the kind that Holbein drew for Sebastian Münster. Or they can include the expression of terror that borders on science and comedy in the bestiaries of Conrad Gesner or in the world theaters of monstrosities that writers such as Pierre Boaistuau and the cosmographers delight in putting on view.[2] Cartographic writing, indeed, appears to be produced *as if* to discover and slowly expunge this material by reengaging primal scenes, by recalling good and bad maternal objects, by invoking fantasy substitutes such as Amazons and alligators to designate dubious relations between the self and its kin, or by taking refuge in armor and mail that associates the logistics of conquest with the cartographer's spiritual and spatial enterprise.

In order not to let a history of progress or erudition eat away at either the energetic foundations or the gendering conditions of these writings, or to even downplay the necessary reinvention that goes with the rereading of early modern cartographic writing, I would like to end at the point where Michel de Certeau began his *L'écriture de l'histoire* (1982a). As an emblem and a frontispiece to the work, which argued for Freudian means to call into question the authenticating effects of historiography (and some of the technocratic bases of its practice in European and U.S. academies), de Certeau chose Jan van der Straet's famous copperplate engraving illustrating *Vespucci Discovering America* (1624). In the fantastic dream-image of encounter, conquest, and discovery, an armor-clad Vespucci (Figure 9.1) has descended from an ocean vessel to plant his staff and ensign on the earth and now gazes at the nude and nubile body of the continent allegorized before his eyes. Vespucci casts his gaze toward America. For de Certeau, the engraving sums up much of the labor of historiography, a fairly gendered occupation of Western modes of production, that fixes into a secure place the colonized, the other, the indigenous subject, and, no less, the female (see also Rose 1992). The implicit violence suggested in the figure of a clothed male beholding a naked female underscores the prurience that goes with the discovery that is the bait and inspiration of conquest. And the allegorical landscape (Panofsky 1971), in which a world of metallic appara-

Figure 9.1. Jan van der Straet, *Vespucci Discovering America*

tus on the left side contrasts with the neolithic technology of hammocks, wooden roasting grills, and massive clubs on the right, places the Italian traveler at the threshold of a takeover, translated in the graven lines of the copperplate as an impending rape by Europe of America.

The depiction further underscores de Certeau's themes of the violence entailed in the operation of naming (1982: ch. 7). Amerigo imposes himself upon the New World in the armor of a name and a gonfalon. His gaze literally enacts the performative, "I declare that I own you in my own name." The hitherto unknown areas of the world and its unnamed or unnamable practices (seen in the background) over an expanding horizon of *terrae incognitae* fall under the purview of the male voyager. At the same time, suggests de Certeau, the image avows its own failure to represent the event of a primal scene of discovery because it does not speak. The performative is silent; a subject position cannot be located (Benveniste 1966; Metz 1991). A mute caption below reports in writing what is said to be "taking place." The weakened deixis of the image cannot quite establish the power relations that the allegorist wishes, it is implied, to put forward through the choice and staging of the iconography. The image that belongs to a set of illustrations celebrating new technologies covertly avows its own incapacity to control the American who is disarming in her generosity.

In view of what we have seen in the passage through Franco-Burgundian materials of the later fifteenth century; in the works of the humanists Tory, Finé, and Rabelais; in those of Thevet, in the *isolarii,* and in cosmography; in Montaigne's *Essais;* in the collaborative and unfinished stamp of Bouguereau's *Le théâtre françoys;* in the Protestant vision of the colonization of Australia under the aegis of a map-god, an epitome of Ortelius's *mappa mundi* in the name of this "tout puissant"; and finally, in the course of Cartesian ambulations and burrowings into vanishment, we can discern an extensive spatial and cartographic measure suffusing van der Straet's image and determining much of what it says.

Three details—hammock, astrolabe, and the gaze—can serve to sum up the principles of cartographic writing developed above. First, America is portrayed not thrust down by the other but as a subject who rises to greet the other's coming. As if putting into bodily pose the structures of Amerindian myth that *welcomes* the disembarkment of the stranger (in contrast to the European who sees himself mirrored in her [Lévi-Strauss 1991]), the native greets the observer as she rises from the hammock, the nocturnal site of dreams, in the light of day. Iconography current since portolano charts, maps of the Dieppe School, and early printed reports had shown the hammock to be an attribute of the new and dubious Eden. Here, however, its tessellated weave extends across the span of the image, like an anamorphically drawn cartographic grid of the kind that cartesian engineers would conceive for city planning and centuriation (Edgerton 1987: 21–22).

The object that is discovered in the neolithic world before Vespucci's gaze *already* contains the very technology that will be used to appropriate the populations of the newly discovered Adamic world. As if extending in a taut fashion what had been a loosely crumpled festoon in the American alcove at the bottom of Ortelius's allegorical title page to the *Theatrum orbis terrarum,* the hammock (Figure 9.2) belongs to two orders at once. One, an ethnographic cliché, rises from the illustrated atlases and sheet maps of the sixteenth century, registering one object among a panoply of flora and fauna recently registered in atlases and compendia. The other, of more difficult form, mixes archaic and modern technologies. It is a hammock, but it is also a system of graticules, an equipollent design used to accord equal valence to anything in its webbing. On its "male" technological attributes reposes the ultimate object of Vespucci's gaze, the flaming buttocks and midsection of the female. A relation to the unknown is already configured in well-known cartographic terms.

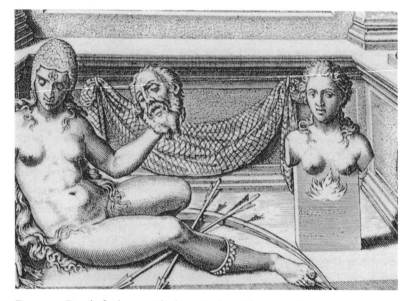

Figure 9.2. Detail of title page, Abraham Ortelius, *Theatrum orbis terrarum*

The hammock provides the very perspective for the framing and the object of the male's desire. Desire for the other is seen in the grid-fetish that happens to be confused with the female.

But curiously, second, the astrolabe that Vespucci carries in his left hand is set so directly over the hammock that the object of one technology seems to be glued to the other (Figure 9.3). At the point of contact between the hammock and the astrolabe is spotted, like a vanishing point, the meeting of two ways of seeing, plotting, and living in the world. The astrolabe carries a long iconographic history that reaches back to the earliest images of Ptolemy. In Oronce Finé's first self-portrait (Figure 3.7), Ptolemy was patterned after a woodcut in a Parisian edition of Johannes de Sacro Bosco's *De mundi sphaera* (Figure 3.8). Finé shows us that Ptolemy had often been imagined holding the tool of his trade up to the sky, so that it rests between the geographer's gaze and the firmament beyond. Vespucci inherits the same pose, but now the astrolabe is set on a horizontal axis, on a line that will allow the traveler to mark off sites, people, and things that remain not above, not in the celestial realm, but in the material world before one's eyes. Vespucci now conquers in travesty of Ptolemy, his arm lowered and extended in order to look westward. Nonetheless, a cosmographer still inhabits the conqueror; the founding father of humanist mapping remains present, albeit in a distant way that indicates where

Figure 9.3. Detail of Figure 9.1: astrolabe and hammock

new inventions found some of their origins. The gaze set upon nubile America was that which had belonged to the idealized image of the studious geographer of Alexandria whose desire was trained on the heavens.

Here, third, we see how the fortunes of the conquest are summed up in Vespucci's gaze. The drive for maternal and erotic objects that had gone unnamed in the method and style of much cartographic writing is now clearly betrayed. Eros, gender, and alterity, in sum, everything that had seemed marginal to the enterprise of mapping the world, are now admittedly essential to it. In this sense, the self who is Vespucci cannot be named Amerigo without gazing at a relation to the unknown or without avowing an umbilical tie to *terrae incognitae.* Fathoming the illusion he takes to be America, he focuses on the inner side of his pupils, aiming his gaze at the mirage of his own imagination. Where he finds his origin in the virtual feminization of himself, in the female he believes arising from his own cartographic hammock, his map is surely self-made.

Notes

Introduction

1. These remarks draw on Emile Benveniste's classic study of discourse in relation to history (1966). See also, with respect to the problematic condition of deixis, Kinser 1990: ch. 1; Saenger 1982: 367–414; Metz 1991: introduction; Zumthor 1987: 107–28 and *passim*; Le Goff 1991: esp. 126, 234–41.

2. Richard Helgerson has argued that in English cartography in the Elizabethan age, the cartographer Christopher Saxon, a dutiful subject of the king, is metamorphosed into a protodemocratic subject who, however paradoxical his status may be, also gains agency through increasing self-consciousness and mastery of the represented world that owes its existence to his many talents. The cartographers create a "cultural entity" that, it is claimed, is only represented in the maps. By fashioning that entity, "they also brought into being . . . the authority that underwrote their own discourse. They thus made themselves" (1986: 81; 1992: 147). As Helgerson later remarks, the nation, formerly opposed to the state, begins to make "claims of its own" (1992: 296) by way of its cartographers.

3. See Harley 1989. Noteworthy in this pathfinding essay is that Harley, stressing deconstruction as it is filtered through its best readers (e.g., Edward Said and Christopher Norris), does not engage the areas in which Freudian psychoanalysis is crucial to the elaboration of the philosophy associated with Jacques Derrida. No less pertinent is Harley's tendency *not* to include sixteenth-century maps and mapping under the purview of what can be deconstructed, thus implying that Renaissance maps are liable to be self-deconstructing in their aggressive representations of nation and self-identity. He does advocate a *literary* reading of the rhetoric of cartography (11) that I will follow and also reverse in this book, at least insofar as I will attempt a *cartographic* analysis of literary texts.

4. One feels, concludes Stephen Greenblatt, "an overwhelming need to sustain the illusion that we are the principal makers of our identities" (1980: 257). He develops the same point in spatial terms in *Marvelous Possessions* when showing that colonization is based on a culture's perceived need to acquire a protective zone between itself and the world in order to gain authority. The need turns against the self, he adds, when the solidity of experience is weakened by the attraction of alterity, when "it becomes increasingly difficult to find a stable signified to which the whole thesaurus of exotic signifiers may be referred" (1991: 47). He captures the difference between the "possessed" and "dispossessed" individual that C. B. Macpherson has studied in *The Political Theory of Possessive Individualism* (1962: 17–46).

5. In *Topophilia,* Yi–Fu Tuan contends that the sixteenth century witnessed a great shift from a cosmic to a two-dimensional representation of reality (1990: ch. 6). His conclusions are mobilized for strong political ends by David Harvey in *The Condition of Postmodernity* (1989). Harvey notes that increasing compressions of space and time result from the relation of the growth of capitalism to shrinkages of relay, feedback, and extension. The initial sign of that development is the transition from cosmography to topography. Gilles Deleuze studies the relation between the "self" and the "other" through the dialogue of "discursive" and "visible" formations in his *Foucault* (1986: esp. 50–51, 66–75).

6. Michel de Certeau shows that "the masked law" of the historian follows a sinous line of orientation that begins in the present, moves into the past, and curls back to the present. The historian seeks to find and generalize in the documents of the past what he or she is unable or unwilling to state about the present. Thus, a work of history is a document of an unstated discourse in the present (1982a: ch. 2). Those areas in which the subject "gets lost" are usually between what is visual and what is lexical. These are also areas where the authority of "truth" is suspended, as in early modern maps that are decidedly false. That they are of greater interest to us than accurate maps is in fact the truth of their being. Carl Wheat has located the disruptive effect that we seek in the study of maps in the charge he invests in what he calls the "visual" quality of the discipline: "The relevance and import of any given map, however well described it may be, can fairly be gleaned only by inspecting the map itself, for the understanding of a map is essentially a visual experience" (1957: 7–8); that is why he underscores the importance of error in early mapping: "But, with all their faults—sometimes even because of them—(maps), better than any other documents, illustrate the story of *developing thought* and understanding to vividly reflect the advance and the unfoldment of knowledge" (8, emphasis added). Wheat is stating what the late psychoanalyst Piera Aulagnier stated about the nature of truth: "La vérité, c'est une erreur non encore reconnue" [truth is an error that has not yet been recognized] (1982: 7–8). Recently Matthew Edney (1993) has shown that even *scientific* mapping after 1800 is fraught with distortion. His point bears out what J. B. Harley, in post-1988 writings, states about the relation of cartographic truth to the "silent agendas" of power structures. Whether a map is produced under the banner of cartographic science—as most official maps have been— or whether it is an overt propaganda exercise, "it cannot escape involvement in the processes by which power is deployed" (Edney 1993: 279).

7. The concept is studied in various places in Rosolato's *La relation d'inconnu*

(1978) but is summarized on 7–18 and 254–79. Here and elsewhere: All translations from the French are mine.

8. See Dainville 1964b. Père François de Dainville's dictionary is still one of the finest studies of geography and its history.

9. It is tempting to cite Gilles Deleuze's and Félix Guattari's *Rhizome* (1976) to figure the ramifying lines and connections that produce an image of moving surfaces of lines that web the earth. Their title is inspired as much by mycology (e.g., Miller 1971) as by Claude Lévi-Strauss's depiction of his associative imagination that spreads over the surface of things, that scans and lets the eye rove about, willy-nilly, without the control of rectilinear reason (Lévi-Strauss 1955), in imitation of the unknown workings of the savage mind.

10. In a fairly common obsession, amateurs of maps often seek to find the names of the places where they were born or raised. We generally look for an originary site for our own past and then move out to other places that are more tenuously connected to the point of beginning. As we shall observe in the topographical map of Oronce Finé, even cartographers indulge in the same practice in the art of composition (which Père François de Dainville, 1970, mentions in passing).

11. With respect to Montaigne's child, see Lawrence Kritzman's "My Body, My Text," in Kritzman 1991.

12. See chapter 3, on Oronce Finé. Serial and recombinant structures of space and volume are taken up in Claude-Gilbert Dubois's "Taxonomie et poétique: Compositions sérielles et construction d'ensembles dans la création esthétique en France au XVIe siècle," reprinted in Dubois 1992: 171–85. J. B. Harley studies how engravers exploited the unknown through the creation of images of cannibalism in the margins of maps: "With such images an identity was built up about the American Indian," where new knowledge is interpreted to "revert to earlier myths and misconceptions" (apropos Holbein's illustration of the Huttich and Grynaeus world map of 1537) (Harley 1990a: 86).

13. In *The Mystic Fable 1: The Sixteenth and Seventeenth Centuries*, translated by Michael B. Smith (Chicago: University of Chicago Press, 1992), 80 and passim.

14. The relation of the perspectival object to visibility is studied in Rosolato 1993: ch. 3; 1985; 1978: 199–210 (along with that of the screen memory).

15. "Theater" is used in a cartographic sense appropriate to the tradition of the *Theatrum orbis terrarum* but also with reference to the dynamic space where the "I" or the "self" sees itself engaged in a public space (of kin, of others, of economic and political forces), such as what Joyce McDougall describes in *Theaters of the Mind* (1991: introduction and ch. 1).

16. Two instances illustrate this exactly. First, McDougall (1991: ch. 6) recounts how her successful analyses are cued on the ways that certain words will instantiate a patient's ever abnormal theatrics. She notes, in fact, that the most irksome and frustrating analysands are those who convey a falsely normal discourse that refuses to let itself be summoned by its own doubt or to allow attention to be drawn to whatever makes it peculiar. She calls these patients "normopaths." They are often victims of formations that lead to sadism and to what she calls "neo-sexualities" (also in her *Plea for a Measure of Abnormality*, 1992). Her points are confirmed for Proust's literary sphere by Hendrika Halberstadt-Freud in *Freud, Proust, Perversion, and Love* (1991: 62–64), where the per-

spectival object is used neither to regress nor to advance the course of analysis. Second, in *Cartographies schizoanalytiques* (1989, ch. 1), Félix Guattari shows how the state of depression of a vocalist who had recently lost her mother is lifted when she correlates the two octaves she lost in the process of grieving to find an explanation for a musical tone that had been unavailable to her imagination (37–39). The contraction of the vocal chords is "singularized" in a somatic area to show how the singer is coping with the loss. Guattari argues, thus, for a remobilization of subjective mapping to "recuse fixed cartographies and invariants of law in the domain of subjectivity" (36). The shape of the referent, its sound, and a new meaning (produced by amphibology) constituted a perspectival object that set constructive thinking into motion.

17. The formal and historical aspects of perspective and expansion are recounted in Edgerton (1975 and 1991), but they are grounded in Panofsky's classic *Perspective as Symbolic Form* (1991). Rosolato (1985: 123–32; 1993: 29–52) treats perspective in terms of the origins of sensuous affect, in the at once projective activity (the infant looks into or toward the world of light, color, and tone before its eyes) and its projective counterpart (the infant closes its eyes to fend off menace, hence negotiating with the real in a space and time prior to the mirror stage). He adds that Claude Lorrain's landscape paintings can be studied psychoanalytically insofar as their vanishing points meld the seascapes with a strongly motivated appeal of the unknown (what is beyond the shoreline) or with geographies that are at once plotted and held up as ideal spaces (1985: 305–16). We shall note that cartography can be viewed in the same way.

18. The spectator's or reader's *free attention* is not, as Louis Marin shows (1981: 336), to be confused with free association; it is, rather, an "intermediary space" of movement and determination (1993: 232). In the work of analysis of art or literature that is not unrelated to the analytic scene, attention is directed toward a text or figure, but the play of signs and spacings between the object and the viewer controls to a degree the act that is producing meaning. A coordination has to occur. The perspectival object would be those median points that emerge between the spectator or reader and the object. In an analytic situation, where deixis is much stronger, the *objet de perspective* would become evident to the speaker and his or her realm in view of the listening interlocutor. Studies of the vital and creative agency of dedifferentiation include Anton Ehrensweig's *The Hidden Order of Art* (1973), which Rosolato (1978: 173) uses to depict oscillation between self and other. Also, Jean-François Lyotard (1973) and, more recently, Claude Gandelman (1991) have appealed to Alois Riegl's concept of haptic readings to counter the forces of a centering or of a narrowing attention, what in psychoanalysis might be likened to projective identification (McDougall 1989: ch. 4). The haptic process, in which attention gives preference to an optical activity in the lexical world, is also at the basis of Walter Benjamin's poetics of translation and viewing in *Illuminations* (1971).

19. "Hidden agenda" is a metaphor in Harley's work and is itself almost a perspectival object. It figures in the title of one crucial article about cartographic dissimulation of power, "Silences and Secrecy: The Hidden Agenda of Cartography in Early Modern Europe" (1988b), it recurs in "Deconstructing the Map" (1989: 3), and it works as a concept explaining conquest and the illusion of truth in "Texts and Contexts in the Interpretation of Early Maps" (1990: 3–15, esp. 12–13).

20. As shown by Josef Konvitz (1987) and James E. King (1949).

21. In *L'apprenti-sorcier et le maître-historien* (1982), Piera Aulagnier argues that history

is like the unconscious in that it always prefers to say no to what the subject believes to be his or her own possession. The trials of becoming a subject include battles between the emerging, self-centered individual and the force of history, which divides and shatters that individual at all times (8–14). Her analysis charts in clinical terms what Richard Helgerson noted (see n. 2 above) about the fortunes of Christopher Saxon's mapping of the British Isles: The map maker, once a dependent displaying obeisance to royal authority, begins to acquire a signature as a national, both individual and democratic, subject when his project rivals and overtakes the authority for whom it had been destined.

22. Michel de Certeau (1990) contends that reading can be an actively vagrant, nomadic examination of ideological materials. This point of view is sustained in his reading of images and their textual counterparts in a study of Hieronymous Bosch's *Garden of Earthly Delights* in *The Mystic Fable* (1992: 49–78), in which the meaning of a "bird's-eye view" that is, a three-quarter, tilted perspective on the landscape, is made literal. The painting is a map constructed according to that design, but it is identical to the many "bird's-eye views" we obtain in noticing birds that gaze upon us from the painting. The rebus at the basis of de Certeau's analysis is essential to the trajectory of reading that crosses images and languages in a both pictorial and cartographic space.

23. Elsewhere in the same issue, in "Pictogramme et critique littéraire," I have attempted to delineate how wit maps out other spaces within the geography of literary creations (Conley 1991b: 269–79).

24. See the personal communication in the epigraph to Terdiman 1992: 2; and de Certeau 1982b.

25. François Rigolot, (1976, 1977) charts the history of the movement between motivation and demotivation of proper names and their implied referents. What seems at first to be a strong link between language and place becomes, as in the history of cartography, increasingly arbitrary as the sixteenth century unfolds.

26. Gilles Deleuze remarks of Michel Foucault's work on diagrammatic thinking: "A diagram is a map, or rather a collage of maps. From one diagram to another, more maps are drawn. Therefore, no diagram can exist that, next to the points it connects, would be relatively free of unlinked [*déliés*] points, points of creativity, mutation, resistance. . . . By means of the 'battles' that define every epoch, and the style of those battles, we can understand the succession of diagrams, or their new linkages over different discontinuities" (in "Un nouveau cartographe," in Deleuze 1986, 51).

27. Travel accounts quickly became viable commodities in the book and map trade. Editors no doubt realized that most readers did not need to voyage in reality and that the sales of translations of materials treating of the old and new worlds would satisfy most appetite for travel (see Atkinson 1935; Eisenstein 1980).

28. Elizabeth Eisenstein underscores the debt that the revolution and expansion of print culture owe to its affiliation with cartography in "The Book of Nature Transformed" (1993: ch. 7).

1. Franco-Burgundian Backgrounds

1. Henri Focillon calls Fouquet's art "modern in the profound science of living forms, through the exquisite poetry of the landscape, and in the manner of the grandeur

of his illustrations of history. But he belongs above all to the French Middle Ages, not only in his mysticism, in the iconography of Paradise that is comprised, like a church portal, with archivolts of the elected and with seraphims, not only by the order shared with theater and by the lively image of the mystery of Saint Apollinaire, but also with the ties that link him directly to monumental sculpture in his large portraits. . . . He interprets the figure as a solid in space, as a block of stone colored with a slightly fleshy tone. . . . Where van Eyck labors with patience in the detail of analysis, and pursues his quest for the particularity of the line and the play of values into the infinitely tiny areas of living substance by presenting his model so as to underscore the entire intensity of his studies of the figures, Jean Fouquet constructs his portraits in large masses, in simple, delicately rendered stagings. These strong foundations, this supple modeling are those of French sculpture found in the royal workshops at the end of the fourteenth century. Fouquet made use of its heritage" (1938: 358; see also Focillon 1936).

2. Erwin Panofsky remarked that, by the first third of the fifteenth century, the proliferation of heraldic signs was symptomatic of "an aristocracy made self-conscious by a permanent threat of intrusion" by a different social order. Upper classes "developed a kind of defense mechanism which lead to an overstylization . . . foreign to the unchallenged feudalism of the past and to the secure bourgeoisie of the future" (1971: 68). The nouveau riche outdid the old nobility by overstylizing and overloading with connotations the forms it saw attached to long-standing classes above its station.

3. The mix of language and perspective in the *nouvelle* might be likened to Henri Focillon's description of what he calls an "experimental stage" in the life of forms of art, a stage in which artists confront massive problems by adopting a variety of different approaches. Not finding any adequate solution, the creator works in an unfinished dialogue that mediates the problems encountered. Focillon describes the creative process in the experimental stages of Romanesque and Gothic art in *Vie des formes* (1939).

4. White adds that "the genius of Fouquet" (1987: 230) can be attributed to the synthetic system of perspective mixed with the "frank empiricism" of observation. Pächt shows how the Master of Mary of Burgundy "wanted the frame to allow a view at close-range . . . , of an interior or even of a distant landscape" (1986: 200). The remark can be applied to various texts of the same period in which the frame encloses a diagrammatic configuration of words and graphs.

5. David Woodward (1990) summarizes the differences between space represented in equipollent, route-enhancing, and center-enhancing modes of projection. Equipollent grids, which he traces to Roger Bacon's *Almagest*, acquire extraordinary power in the Renaissance. "It was the deceptively simple concept of plane coordinates, with its ability to assign the same importance to every point on the map and so control the accuracy of positions over its entire face, that was to become adopted for world cartography" (120). The same system can hold for textual surfaces, except that the vagaries of composition and perception allow narrative to be mapped according to all three systems at once. The analysis that follows will argue that a center-enhancing narrative mode also betrays an "equipollent" sensibility in language (its wit exploding everywhere at once); at the same time, like a narrative, the tale has to follow a route from an initial imbalance to a conclusion. The approach used here contrasts with the more strictly rhetorical reading of short prose in the essays included in Jean Lafond's *Les formes brèves de la prose et le discours discontinu (XVIe-XVI siècles)* (1984). The proto-

cartographic reading may in fact be closer to what, more recently, Michel Jeanneret labels a "modular" style of narrative, that is, a writing that can be apportioned and segmented *comme on voudra*, for the purpose of "expressing a composite and segmented view of the world," and that has a "do-it-yourself" (1993: 101) format that depends, like the study of a map, on the roving eye and ear of the spectator, reader, or auditor.

6. *Les cent nouvelles nouvelles*, in Jourda 1965: 206–7. Judith Bruskin Diner has rendered an excellent modern English version in *The One Hundred New Tales* (1990: 199–200, with an updated and complete bibliography, xi–xl). We should recall that any transcription of the tales into modern typography, as in this or other modern editions, is tantamount to an interpretation and a translation. The shape and disposition of the Gothic letters in the Glasgow manuscript or in incunabular editions engender meanings that are muted or displaced when the story is set in Roman characters (cf. Saenger 1989), for which spacing of letters is important for recombinations of meaning. If reading is silent, deictic control of meaning is weakened: Thus connections among letters and vocables become multidirectional.

7. "The preparation leading to the punchline is well drawn: we learn incidentally that the grandmother is the father's mother, the element without which the story has no meaning. On a purely technical level, all matters of good taste set aside, this tale is quite acceptable; its brevity (58 lines) is interesting in that it legitimates *a clearer view of its technique*" (Dubuis 1973: 116, emphasis added) despite, he adds, its regrettable failure to include a "conclusion" ("the heavy-handedness is not enough, however, to condemn the collection"). As Gillies (1994: 18) has shown about cartography, violence, and Shakespearean drama, a scenario of miscegenation undergirds the articulation of linguistic space.

8. Lorian (1973) and Rasmussen (1958) take up the doubling of substantives, markers of orality ("le dict curé," etc.) as evidence of *amplificatio, chicane,* or a "curial" style that is constantly subject to parody.

9. The pun on *peine* as *travail* and *plume* is ubiquitous in rebus literature, which is born at almost the same time in northern France and Flanders (Céard and Margolin 1986: ch. 1). The rebus, like the ciphered prose of *Les cent nouvelles*, moves amphibiously between image and text; it asks the reader not to respect grammar but to multiply forms by dividing and rearranging their composite elements. Estienne Tabourot printed illustrated conundrums using "vos tours me donnent peines" and "peines en travail" (1583: ch. 1).

10. In their tendency to yield sums and products greater than their individual units, the tales are an early reflection of what Michel Jeanneret (1991) calls "*débordement*," a will to establish barriers that are exceeded from within; a model of writing is discovered and exploited by making more of itself without transgressing the laws of its form.

11. Kenneth J. Knoespel (1987) studies indeterminate relations between language and mathematical figures in early-modern writing. He argues that with John Dee, as late as the 1570s, numbers and equations are attached to language, and that only later will scientific authority be conferred upon them. When they become detached from their verbal ground, they are no longer called into question by their "other." A premodern fluidity of figure and word holds in this story. Though heterogeneous, the two elements are part of each other. Their dialogic condition confirms what Jacqueline

Cerquiglini (1989) notes about vocables and images in respect to Guillaume de Machaut and Christine de Pisan.

12. Michel de Certeau notes that in early landscape painting the spectator discovers that he or she can move and change positions. Following E. H. Gombrich, he shows that landscape means, in a broad sense, "a reciprocity between places" and not just the "autonomy of a background to the figures of a painting" (1987: 18). Displacements of the eye "ceaselessly change the painting" just as they also reconfigure, as we see in the flickerings of meaning and graphic points in this *nouvelle,* the drive of a narrative. This point will be taken up in the discussion of Bouguereau, in chapter 6.

13. Noise indicates interference along the edges between seasons in medieval literature. Dialogue of universal forms, in which myth and ritual (like that of tale-telling) mediate seasonal and generational changes, is studied in Lévi-Strauss 1962: 335–45. The violence of abrupt shifts of seasons is likened, Lévi-Strauss adds, to too wide differences in ages between men and women who are to be married. A woman whom a social group considers too old for marriage to an eligible bachelor is designated a *femme pourrie.* With its cosmic violence and implicit parallel between the grandmother and a "rotten" sexual partner, the fiftieth tale taps into the same expressive vein. (See also note 8.)

14. Molinet 1933: vol. 2, 749). This and other quotations are drawn from this critical edition.

15. Paul Saenger and Michael Heinlen remind us that print culture exerted enormous control on the play of medieval writing. The visible aspect of print, with its insertion of new punctuation marks, capital letters, foliation, and paragraphs and its blackening of the page, conferred upon its technology a new authority: "Under the influence of printing, reading became increasingly an activity of passive reception (Saenger and Heinlen 1991: 225–58, esp. 254–55).

16. "Visible" and "utterable" are understood in their broadest virtual sense. They are neither what is before the eyes nor what is heard, understood, or spoken. Each can be—or risks being—seen and heard insofar as they embody the concepts and practice of the visible and the utterable. Gilles Deleuze notes that for Michel Foucault these terms designate *conditions of their own possibility,* and that when they are treated together—as they are in most writing of the later fifteenth and early sixteenth centuries—each "reaches its own limit that separates it from the other, a visible that can only be seen, an utterable statement that can only be spoken. And yet, the very limit that separates each from the other is also the common limit that ties the one to the other," a point of view that is taken to be "singularly close to contemporary cinema" (1986: 66, 72). Foucault (1973) argues that coincidences and differences between visible and lexical material jostles orders of reason that have since been lacquered over the medieval imagination. The point is not lost on Jacqueline Cerquiglini, as can be seen in her studies of the graphic and lexical crisscrossing of late-medieval poetry (for example, 1989: 110–26, esp. 113–14).

17. Quoted in Molinet 1933: vol. 3, 875.

18. In manuscripts, the compass is used to outline the legs of the body or to open angles. Anne-Marie Lecoq (1987: 96) notes how Jean Dumoulins equivocates on the geometer's instrument and the staging of the body in a manuscript prepared for Louise de Savoie. Prudence is armed with a giant compass that inverts the letter of V(irtue).

19. Samuel Y. Edgerton, Jr., reviews the cartographer Roger Bacon's optical theory,

which pertains here. Quoting (and translating) the *Perspectiva*, Edgerton states: "'Vision must perform the act of seeing by its own force. But the act of seeing is the perception of a visible object at a distance, and therefore vision perceives what is visible by its own force multiplied to the object'" (1991: 100–103, quote on 100). In this sense, a species emits rays in the way that its members speak; these rays move toward each other. No wonder, then, that facetious writings rehearse these scenes of desire that move concomitantly from the perceivers who "see" to their objects through the visible filter of printed speech. We recall the farmer, perched on the top of a tree, who mistakes his missing goat's tail for that of a woman's sex as it is gazed upon by her lover in *Les cent nouvelles nouvelles* (xii): The lover, "ce vaillant homme va passer temps à son devant (that of the lady) regarder, et, si sans honneur on le peust dire, il ne fust pas content si ses mains ne descouvrirent à ses yeulx les secretz dont il se devait passer d'enquerre. Et comme il estoit en ceste parfonde estude, il disoit maintenant: 'Je voy cecy! Je voy cela! encores cecy! encores cela!' et qui l'oyoit, il veoit tout le monde et beaucoup plus" [This valiant man is going to spend his time looking squarely at her frontside and, if it can be said without honor, he wasn't happy *if his hands did not show his eyes* the secrets that he was not supposed to think about. And as he was in that profound meditation, he now uttered, 'I see it here! I see it here! And over there!' And he who heard it saw the whole world and a whole lot more] (Jacob 1858: 96–97). A narrative counterpoint is established, in which, again, point of view shows how the viewer goes into space: The lover, from a close angle (gazing at the origin of the angle before him) sees the entire world "and a whole lot more," whereas, from afar and on top of the bushy (*houchie*) tree from which he looks, the farmer only discerns a goat's tail.

20. Cynthia J. Brown notes that for André de la Vigne the deferment between invocation of the patron's name and that of authorial inscription stresses the "creative process" within the development of the poem. The signature embodies and summarizes the design of force (1991: 114–15). Her work on Molinet (1988) orients the relation of space and signature toward autonomy derived from techniques in incunabular culture and poetic craft. The conclusions about the "ego-centering" effect of the signature are remarkably synthesized in *Poets, Patrons, and Painters* (1995: 153–58).

21. Martin Jay (1988: 2–23) and Norman Bryson (1988: 107) have insisted that the early modern period is defined by the emphasis it places on visibility as a sign of truth and a grounding of politics. In poetry and in travel accounts, it is often difficult to distinguish between a symptom of cultural change, such as the shift from an aural to a visual culture, and a cliché. Poets appeal to the eye so profusely that the reader wonders if they are also calling attention to themselves and to the graphic dimensions of their writing.

22. In Tony Campbell's discussion of the Lübeck map (1987a: 121).

2. The Letter and the Grid

1. References in the text to the *Champ fleury* are to J. W. Jollife, ed., facsimile of the British Musuem Copy 60. e 14 (Paris: Geofroy Tory et Gilles Gourmont, 1529). The Hague: Mouton, 1970.

2. Gisèle Mathieu-Castellani notes how Agrippa D'Aubigné, in the *Hécatombe à*

Diane, the late-sixteenth-century apologist for Protestantism and the author of poetry that politicizes the diction of Pierre de Ronsard, appeals to Tory's graphic and even cabalistic views of writing (1991: 80–82). Estienne Tabourot inverts Tory's Platonic allegories of writing in the opening chapters of his chapbook, *Les Bigarrures* (1583). As we shall see, Montaigne also shares the same view of printed characters. The cabalistic traits of Tory's work are developed in Claude-Gilbert Dubois, "La parole est pennigere" (1992: 27–51).

3. William Mitchell (1992) argues that computer-generated images revolutionize our sense of the history of writing, photography, and image making. The basis of new technology, the pixel, is the digitized unit that can be electronically stored and is always available for recombination. The possibility of new configurations and their range of recombination mirror Tory's diagrammatic imagination. The minuscule square that founds the *lettre quarré* is comparable to the pixel.

4. The curious orthography of *caiet* for *cahier* spells out the art of perspective contained in the book. It draws our attention to the automatic association that the sixteenth century habitually made between a "notebook" and a quire (from *quaternio*), a square folded into four parts, or a grid of pixel-like pages atop one another. The materiality of the meaning is not lost on the navigator-poet John Donne, who plays on the relation of paper sheets to the orientation of the church in his "Hymne to God my God, in my sicknesse."

5. "Je dis invention, pource que ie nay point veu dautheur Grec, Latin, ne François qui aye escript ne figure ces choses comme iay de present" [I say invention, because I have never seen a Greek, Latin, or French author who has either written or figured these things as I presently have] (fol. xvi v).

6. "Cas: m. *A case, cause, matter, thing; also, a crime, offence; fact; also, esteeme, account, reckoning of; also, the priuities (of man, or woman)*" (Cotgrave 1611). Tory elaborates on this in his explanation of the letter *G* (fol. xlii), a crucial moment in the book, where the rebus and device are theorized and exemplified.

7. By the fifteenth century, national signatures were developed along the lines of architectural signatures. In a great study of the building of the Milan cathedral, James Ackerman (1991: 211–68) has shown how Lombard master masons at Milan rejected flying buttresses because they did not "fit" their vision of the cathedral that was underway.

8. Roland Sanfaçon (1971) has demonstrated that the flamboyant is above all a national style that is dotted over French territory and yet has variation (we can add, like the Romanesque and Gothic). The mixed effect produces a "Frenchness" of architectural idiom by the beginning of the sixteenth century. He develops a point that Henri Focillon tenders (1934 and 1938: vol. 2) in his brilliantly suggestive description of a national style that burns with different degrees of intensity, seen in baroque effects of irreality and of mystical gleam. The illustrations in Cali (1968) prove the validity of these remarks.

9. A classical instance of what in psychoanalysis is called the "anticipation" of the signifier, where, as Jacques Lacan noted, "le signifiant de sa nature anticipe toujours sur le sens en déployant en quelque sorte au devant de lui sa dimension" [by its own nature, the signifier always anticipates the meaning that is somehow deployed before in its own dimension] (1966: 502). Lacan returns to the early history of movable type—

the context of Tory—to affirm that the letter is in actuality "the essentially localized structure of the signifier" (501), a point that almost every early modern writer and engraver probably took to be an axiom of language.

10. Tory underscores that Roman models are *already* on French soil, "in an old section of the city near Avignon on the Rhône, said and named Aurenges [Orange]" (fol. xx v).

11. Alan Tormey and Judith Farr Tormey report that the art of intarsia developed in Florence, where eighty-four workshops were active in 1484. "From the outset the practice of intarsia had required a sophisticated understanding of applied geometry and precise means of measurement for the cutting and fitting of the pieces of wood that made up the final composition and gave it its characteristic shading and texture" (1982: 137). They add that a "systematic self-reference" is part of the design of intarsia, and that these designs coordinate (as we see in Tory's allegories) the metaphysical elements of the earth with given solid forms. The cube equaled the earth, the octohedron air, the tetrahedron fire, the icosahedron water, and the dodecahedron the universe. By the 1550s, the intarsia lost eminence. Michelangelo, they add, felt that "all the reasonings of geometry and arithmetic and all the proofs of perspective" were of no use to a man who could not see (142–43). But in 1588, Montaigne, a writer who resists all chronology, ostensibly arches back to the artist Tory in his famous comparison of his *Essais* to an "ill-joined marquetry" (1962: 941).

12. Tory begins with the vertical, as if to confirm that the initial axis requires inspiration that will be matched by the labor on the horizontal axis. Tory's analogy influences much later theories of mimesis and diegesis, of the paradigmatic and syntagmatic axes of writing (e.g., Genette 1966; Barthes 1973).

3. Oronce Finé

1. Karrow (1993: 168) revives the debates surrounding "the proper vernacular spelling and pronunciation of the name" and opts for *Fine* instead of Finé (from Finaeus). It appears that the cartographer played on the ambiguity in his poetry throughout his career. The Latin shape inevitably gives way to a French inflection, but at the same time the cartographer exploits the manifold meanings of completion and refinement. The signature is totemic, associated with the dolphin of Dauphiné, but it is also evidence of *anthonomasia*, the blending of proper and common names.

2. Accounts of Finé's life and works include Thevet 1584, Gallois 1890a, Ross 1971, Hillard and Poulle 1971, Hamon 1975, Poulle 1978, Broc 1987, Pastoureau 1992, and Karrow 1993. Karrow's account is rich, accessible, judicious, and comprehensive. After Ross, it is the most complete biographical and bibliographical guide.

3. Finé's work is reflected, for example, in David C. Lindberg's account of the medieval cosmos and of astrology in his *Beginnings of Western Science* (1992: 245–80).

4. Mary Douglas argues that the trickster belongs to primitive myths that are "phrased to satisfy a dominant social group [and that address] the problem of how to organize together in a society" (1984: 91). The trickster defines the borders by surveying the areas that are within and beyond the group that he or she internalizes and distorts by tomfoolery.

5. Kenneth Nebenzahl (1986) adds that Reuwich's map is affiliated with a tradition of biblical maps that begins with Eusebius but that pays special heed to what he records from observation.

6. Reviewed in Davies 1911.

7. Ocean-going ships used overlapped planks and were more solidly constructed than were the Mediterranean caravels. Breidenbach's woodcut depicts only a sea-going ship.

8. Jean Céard and Jean-Claude Margolin note that the heterogeneity of the rebus—its uneasy relation that plays with the ostensive truth of knowledge at the time of the Renaissance—resisted study (1986: vol. 1, 15). The same would seem to hold for the combination of wisdom and humor that Finé embodies in his signature effects.

9. The images are also reproduced and commented upon in Lecoq 1987: 261–63. Not an immortal ballad, the poem roughly translates thus: "O Christians, both young and old, / Royalty, barons, princes, merchants seeking gold, / Open your hearts and peel your eyes, / No, be not tardy but do then defy, / Those Turks and pagans who'll know your acts, / Irremissive they'll be in deeds and facts, / Until you, in sending their filth to demise / See and follow the cross to Paradise. // Frenchmen, valiant, mounted on steed, / Inseparable from the Catholic creed, / Noble princes, and virtuous indeed, / Ever true, display your proudest face, / Think, in sum, of this iniquitous race, / Horrible, infected—that we must abolish. / Saved be those who wish, yes, to / See and follow the cross to Paradise. // Jesus has, with his precious blood, / Redeemed you & been given to his father / Now why not take the vicious Turk, the other / And kill him and so Him avenge, rather: / Your strong heart will not be so austere / If you fail to kill what you ever fear, / If you want, in this world of misery, to / See and follow the cross to Paradise. // Prince, you would gain solace, too / By killing these evil souls in blazing cries, / For thus you could never do better than to / See and follow the cross toward Paradise. // Finis."

10. Ruth Mortimer traces the history of the woodcut in the *Harvard Catalogue of Books and Manuscripts,* in entry 432 (539–40). She notes that "this is the earliest known woodcut by Finé." Joannes Hamman's 1496 edition of Regiomontanus's *Epytoma in almagestum ptolomei* originated in Venice. Finé copied the design but added the figure of Astrologia, "probably suggested by a Venetian illustration for editions of Sacro Bosco to which Peurbach's text was appended" (540). Yet, she notes, other editions of Sacro Bosco were probably available, including versions published in Venice and Paris. The same block is used in Simon de Colines's edition of Sacro Bosco in 1521 (the edition used for the illustration above), 1527, and 1531. Mortimer suggests that on grounds of "fine workmanship," Finé's title page woodcut in the *Protomathesis* merits comparison with this early illustration. There clearly seems to be a greater shift toward an integral representation of the self than is suggested by craft alone.

11. Edgerton (1991: 201–3) notes that the woodcut might have been a source for Raphael's sketch for Astronomy (ca. 1509) and that the form offers resistance to engravers, as might the Florentine tradition of the *mazzocchio,* a geometric representation that in fact became a stylish coiffure in the 1480s (Schefer 1976).

12. Richard Ross (1971) speculates that the cartographer may, in fact, have been imprisoned in 1524 for having predicted events that would mediate the career of Francis I. Robert Karrow also notes that Finé's interest in astrology may have led him to prison (1993: 175).

13. André Thevet (1557) will show how the Tupinamba bury their kin by digging a capacious grave that will hold the body of the beloved as well as all the items that were dearest to the person. The encrypting process in Finé's initial is not without a certain parallel.

14. In, as we shall note, Bovelles (1542: fols. 32–44).

15. Robert Brun argues that Oronce Finé and Geoffroy Tory embody two of the most decisive advances in the illustrated book from 1530 to 1550 (1930: 57 and 65). Finé becomes a school and signature of his own and can thus be identified through the presence of various motifs, including cartographic implements (square, compass, and astrolabe) but also the initials of a signature. Brun argues that a *style* is born, but he does not study the history of the signature in the terms of a psychogenesis of an emerging subject being projected here.

16. See Jeanneret 1987: 249–51. Jean Céard and Jean-Claude Margolin (1986) study the bifurcating path that the model follows: In moving upward, to the celestial spheres, image writing is likened to hieroglyphics; going downward, toward the body and earthly matters, the rebus conflates the form of writing with objects and corporal matter.

17. An arresting and colorful reproduction of the Sylvanus *mappa mundi* and projection of *Gallia* can be found in Allen 1992: 24–27.

18. In Martineau et al. 1975 and 1979. Heller (1971) outlines the mystical and theological themes of the dialogue, while Cottrell (1993) relates them to a dialectics of desire that pertains to the birth of subjectivity.

19. The appeal to anthonomasia, the trope confusing proper and common names, is clearly intended: Lecoq (1987) uses the device to illustrate the back cover of her book, as an enigma of her name and that of her research on imperial iconography in the time of Francis I.

20. One of the striking features of the Cimerlino copperplate copy of the map (1566) is the curvilinear aspect of the letters. They are seen anamorphically, at one with the bend of the world. The new torsion that the engraving process confers upon the letters is strikingly visible in the upper-case letters that describe the continents in the southern hemisphere.

21. In the later years of the sixteenth century, Finé's map may have been known for the traits that Cimerlino disengages in his 1566 copy. In *Le moyen de parvenir* (ca. 1610 but crammed with material dating to the Wars of Religion), a banquet-genre that stages the universality of time and space, Finé figures as a dinner guest. He listens to the story of a woman who falls buttocks-down into a tub of butter. The imprint that she leaves resembles the shape of the cordiform map. See Conley 1992b.

22. Robert Karrow promises an introduction and a new edition of this map (1993: 179, 698). Its influence on Mercator's similar projection (in Shirley 1987: entry 66; Nordenskiöld 1973) is clear; its depiction of the imagination of the New World in 1531 is no less striking, as demonstrated by Charles V. Langlois (1923).

23. In her forthcoming study of French cartography in the sixteenth century (to appear in *The History of Cartography 3: Early Modern Europe*), Mireille Pastoureau emphasizes the importance of Finé's role in regional mapping. I am grateful to David Woodward, who generously allowed me to read the manuscript draft.

24. Fol. 2 v. The poem can be translated thus: "Oronce's Circular Rhyme / Above all

Figure N.1. U.S. postage stamp: love as a cordiform projection

the arts said to be liberal / Seeing everyone, both learned and rural, / The first, after what is arithmetic / Is namely the one called geometric. / In order to accede to the empyreal // All artisans and people mercurial / Who seek secrets that are inaugural / Must calculate with the practical / Above all the arts. // God created the body, and each animal / From the heavens down to every mineral / Through number, weight, & harmonic measure. / Happy are those, with knowledge, to be sure / Who know every secret, each so general / Above all the arts."

25. The fate of Finé's work parallels, to a certain degree, what Michel de Certeau notes about mystical thinking. When the latter can be called "mysticism" (in the seventeenth century), whatever was mystical has become history, for when the dynamics can be put into a substantive, the mystical relation turns into an intelligible object and is no longer a driving, unnamable force (1992). The work also becomes a victim of its own innovation: The world of figuration, overtaking that of mystical language, becomes synonymous with science. Through the latter, if we follow Knoespel's hypothesis (1987), the work is silenced. But Finé has not vanished: In our day we see the U. S. Postal Service produce a 29-cent stamp that displays a cordiform map over a stippled background, under the sign of "Love," which harks back to the context in which the 1534 map was issued (Figure N.1). The meridian is placed adjacent to the Canary Islands, exactly where Finé placed it in his version. The heart floats in the stippled cosmos, just as the cordiform heart was set in the heavens that Finé drew in his many depictions of the firmament. The motif abounds in Valentine literature and is evident even in the 1993 movie *Sleepless in Seattle,* in which we glimpse a globe whose ecliptic

band is defined by a series of cut-out hearts. The relation of love that the sentimental film espouses is defined by the stippled dots in the shots of the map of the United States, on which are traced the paths between Seattle and the eastern seaboard.

4. Words à la Carte

1. Rabelais 1955: 190–91. All quotations of Rabelais will be drawn from this edition.

2. Terence Cave (1991: 171–82) coins the term "language map" to describe the author's expansion of graphic and textual space from limited sources in the comic theater of the fifteenth century. Points of comparison include the trickster's polyglot ruses in the fifteenth-century *Farce de Pierre Pathelin*, early printed grammar books, and the diagrammatic comparison of languages that Charles de Bovelles—the humanist cited in Tory and whose work was later reedited and illustrated by Oronce Finé—sets forth in *De differentia vulgarium linguarum et gallici sermonis varietate* (1533). The term is a viable one that can also describe Rabelais's textual expansion of cartographic models. Cave rightly notes that "the Pathelin map [persists] beneath or behind the Rabelaisian one, if only because, despite the centralization of France and the normalization of French in the seventeenth century, regional languages continued to flourish with great vigor until nineteenth-century educational reforms begin to marginalize them" (180). In effect, the centralizing influence of the map and educational reform is an effect of what is begun here and extended, as we shall see, into Maurice Bouguereau's *Théâtre françoys* (1594). On the relation of Tory to Rabelais, see also La Charité 1979.

3. Comparative studies of Rabelais and Joyce are legion, and for good reason: *Ulysses* cribs passages from *Gargantua* (for example, the dog sniffing the bone in the prologue of 1534) in order to show that, like Rabelais's language, Joyce's exceeds Homer's by being at every point a part of a whole, and to show that very whole in the shape of a detail. Seen in this light, the Rabelaisian side of Joyce undoes the will to produce the total and redemptive work of immortality that critics are now calling into question (e.g., Bersani 1990).

4. A critic like Jacques Derrida might have called this an effect of double invagination, or of an outward, extensive movement of self-dissemination, as he shows in the relation among language, numerical figures, and the art of folding in *La dissémination* (1972a: ch. 4).

5. Two magnificent studies of Rabelais, by Cave (1979) and Jeanneret (1987), appeal to this originary moment in the psychogenesis of Rabelais's heroes. For Cave, the cornucopian text is endlessly productive on the basis of its fear of a void at its origin. For Jeanneret, the festive text of *Gargantua* shows how an infant passes from not distinguishing mouth and sphincter, or words and food, to a condition of intermittance—a blinking recognition of the symbolic realm—when it discovers that it cannot talk and eat at the same time. Flux gets differentiated; an art of spacing and difference is born with the advent of civility.

6. Schwab (1984) extended Mikhail Bakhtin's concept of the dialogic to include Jacques Lacan's mirror stage and the transitional object (Winnicott 1971). She notes

that the subject grows into language from the differences it perceives in a massive presence of languages that are aural, textual, imagistic, olfactive, and tactile.

7. References to book and chapter—rather than page number—are set thus: between parentheses are indicated, first, in upper-case roman numerals, the volume (I = *Gargantau*; II = *Pantagruel*; III = *Le tiers livre*; IV = *Le quart livre*), and second, in lower-case roman numerals, the chapter number.

8. Jean-François Lyotard, in *Le post-moderne expliqué aux enfants* (1985), which is aligned with the spirit of the childhood of Rabelaisian giants, reiterates that most modern literature derives from parataxis. The paratactic style grounds "the postmodern condition" insofar as causal and logical ties, suppressed from propositions and narrative orders, give way to a free play of sensation that can move across otherwise demarcated barriers. The author, in fact, takes the role of what resembles the benevolent "grandfather" (a variant of Grandgousier) to his readers (little Pantagruels), thus sustaining what Walter Friedlander called the "grandfather law" that assures artistic renewal (1957).

9. In the introduction to *The Graphic Unconscious in Early Modern French Writing* (1992a) I delineated how traits of the letter acquire paratactic virtue. The printed form can be a memory of an impression, or the contact of a paradigm-puncheon with the paper that receives it; a unit of meaning independent of the context (such as Tory's allegorical letters); an enigma or a vanishing point that resists being deciphered. When the letter functions as a relay of meaning, it does not require the reader to "invent" the world anew or to map a course of deciphering (7–14).

10. Dean MacCannell (1976) shows that tourism organizes attitudes toward social life and is not a "repository" or a reflection of facts or things past. We can add that what may appear to be nostalgia when presenting images of a nation as it might have been "traditionally" can be a nostalgia that organizes other policies and agendas.

11. "Aller à Angiers" meant "to fall into the shit" of life, at least as the idiolect of Rabelais's master, François Villon, implied in the *Lais* of 1456 (as glossed by Kuhn 1967: 109); Kuhn adds that in popular language "aller à Bourges" also signified *se faire pédéraste* (a meaning that is fitting in the context of education and pedagogy).

12. Lestringant's analysis of the "transgressive" latency of the *Guide* is aligned with de Certeau's view (1982a: ch. 6; 1990: chs. 7–8) of popular hagiography and of walking and reading serving as tactical operations in the practice of everyday life, where the constitution of the land "in current and ever-available memory of a past gone by" or invented through myth is such that the work can open onto "other trajectories than those that the flat and enclosed extension of a map offer to the reader" (439). What is implied by de Certeau's remark is that the text of Signot, Rabelais, or Estienne jostles the fixing traits of diagrammatic logic. Lestringant adduces the point by showing that from 1553 to 1600 fourteen printings of Estienne's *Guide* allowed new uses to develop, one of which was a hidden itinerary that Protestants followed to find refuge in Switzerland.

13. The author of *A la recherche du temps perdu* habitually signals events determining the structure of the novel by a number, which contrasts with the descriptions of recurring actions. *Une fois, un jour*, or other flags signal the coming of a singular event that rises out of the continuum of *toujours, le samedi, souvent*, and so on. As in Rabelais, these flags mark the conflation of the space of memory with the time that we see congealed in the printed characters.

14. The two meetings share much with Marcel Mauss's study of archaic exchange in "Essai sur le don: Forme et raison de l'échange dans les sociétés archaïques" (in Mauss 1973) and in fact parallels Lévi-Strauss's parable of his meeting with the Nambikwara (1955: 337–49), where he witnesses a first moment of conflict that gives way to—but is never obliterated by—exchange. The structure, broadly studied by Sahlins (1972: 149–83), inflects other moments of the Rabelaisian voyage (the beginnings of the Picrocholine wars, *Gargantua*, xxvii) and a good deal of travel literature of the Renaissance (Thevet, Léry), as de Certeau (1982a: ch. 5) has shown in his study of heterology in an analysis of Léry's *Histoire d'un voyage faict en la terre du Brésil* (1578). More recently, Lévi-Strauss (1991: 277–97; see also ch. 5) has shown that the drama of the European conquest of (ideologized as "encounter with") the New World hinged on the native Americans' propensity in their myth and ritual to leave open a space for the other, while the Europeans could only see the other as mirrors of themselves. The two meetings can be read in this fashion.

15. We have seen that the *spacing* of Tory's letters seems to contravene his allegories. Here, too, the freewheeling practice of anagram turns the last words of the moralized parable into the filth that stains the Limousin's pants. *Rochiers de la mer* implies *or chier la merde*, an action (*chier*) embroiled in its effect. The lesson of the tale is not well taken in the shape of its printed form.

16. In a recent study of Panurge and the Turks, Timothy Hampton takes the trickster's origins a step further. Because Panurge has escaped from both dogs and an empire opposed to the Christian imperium, we face a radically different type of encounter that "becomes the site for both an exploration of the limitations of humanist allegorical interpretation and a tension between history and fiction" (1993: 74). The episodes involving Panurge indicate "the rhetorical contradictions in Christian humanism's attempt to allegorize the contemporary non-Christian other" (74). Hampton's study confirms that space is at stake in a historical battle between different modes of belief.

17. The collapsed logic is identical to Freud's "cauldron argument" that he used in psychoanalysis to illustrate the process of logical absurdity.

18. Michel de Certeau (1987: 15–17) has shown how visual speech marks the mystical discourse of Nicolas de Cusa's *De Icone*. Speakers "see" each other through languages and points of view in such a way that they can utter to one another, in response to a phatic question that has not been posed, "You too?" The parallels between the mystical geographer's structure of spatial communication and that of Panurge and Pantagruel are arresting.

19. Hampton (1993) shows that Panurge defines the edges of the Christian world because of his return from the lands of the Turks. Panurge invokes a European theater of operations where the Catholic kings attempt to erect their national identities through opposition to the infidels who have taken the Holy Land. Hampton's argument hinges on the way the narrator likens Panurge to dogs, emblems of the nonhuman. We can add that Tory calls the letter *R* the "canine" letter, expressive of rage. "Quant ung homme est en ire, ou rechigne, ou courouce, on dit quil est de quelque chose irrité. C'est a dire, exasperé. Et ce, pource qu'il ne scauroit dire une doulce parolle, mais toute aspre, grieve, & plain des lettres faisant strideur lesquelles lettres sont RR. repetée, & asprement pronuncees." [When a man is ired, or grim (Cotgrave translates *rechigne* as "dogged"), or angered, it is said that something irritates him. That is, exasperated.

Hence, because he couldn't utter a gentle word, but only what is bitter, grievous, and full of strident letters that are RR repeated and bitterly pronounced.] (f. lv. r). Panurge's words act out this very condition. His imbalance is owed in part to his canine character, which moves between humans and animals. As Deleuze (1980) would say, he "becomes-animal."

20. We should recall that in the medieval world, the eye tends to move into space, to emit natural spirits, and thus to go toward an apprehension of things; this is the opposite of our modern experience of being blitzed or zapped by images and forms that assail us from all directions. The way that a list serves to uncover the reader's habits is crucial to the way we imagine how early modern maps were read. See de Certeau 1987: 19; de Bruyne 1946: vol. 2, 112–13, 155–79; and Lindberg 1976, 1992: 307–15.

21. François Bon (1990) suggests that the whole creation moves from these four episodes in a style of *ampliation*, or enlargement. A central, divided point, generates the comic novel.

22. The diagram is used here to show the relations of tension that Deleuze (1985: 51) studies through enunciation and visibility, where a unit of difference never stabilizes but continues to produce further tension from the irreconcilable mix of space and of discourse.

23. In Panurge's lusty tale explaining why French leagues are shorter than their German counterparts (xxiii), the fable of the surveyors' markers along the road does in fact have evidence in the *scala leucorum* of contemporary maps. Ribald myth and cartographic fact are conjoined.

24. In Lucien of Samosata 1961: 142–55.

25. Nordenskiöld 1973: 142–95 includes a complete version of the 1490 Rome edition from which later copies were made.

26. David Woodward shows that printers faced difficulty in aligning spaces cut into wood blocks with names printed on lead forms inserted within (1987: 194–95). See also R. A. Skelton's discussion of typeset names in his introduction to Münster's edition of *Claudius Ptolemaeus Geographia* (Skelton 1966b: xii–xiii).

27. François Rigolot (1982) argues that a visual rhetoric informs *Pantagruel*. Following Charles Singleton's studies of center and circumference in Dante, Rigolot notes that a center is left for an enigma that generates textual production or *événement poétique majeur* (145–46). The same holds here, except that now the identities at the periphery leave open a mobile textual center that is scattered everywhere through the toponyms. Hence, the strange orthography of *cyre* for *sire* marks the moment when discourse anticipates its concurrently spatial and verbal movement. M. A. Screech notes rightly that the unusual spelling "increases the comedy, suggesting that Picrochole is a new Cyrus the Great, as well as indicating the current (false) etymology of Sire from *Kurios*, 'lord'" (1979: note 31, 166–67). He shows that Picrochole's last words in the chapter, "Qui s'aymera, si me suyvra," parody those of Cyrus. In doing so, the parting shot counterpoints the beginning. In between, the words vary on the incipit before returning to the five characters of the surname hidden in Picrochole's last remark.

28. Frank Lestringant shows how conquest and naming—as well as dissimulation and defeat—go hand in hand with the ruses of historians and travelers (1981: 220). He begins from Louis Marin's remarks about discernment (seeing and naming) and power (1973) and recoups what J. B. Harley stated in respect to the hidden agendas that are at

work in mapped representations (1990a: 12–15). The historical background in which human subjects are "fixed" in space is noted in Rigolot 1977: 24ff. Samuel Kinser shows that *Le quart livre* verbalizes scenes adorning Olaus Magnus's 1539 (Venice) *Carta marina* (1990: 64–66, 99–103). His observations confirm that the writer uses maps to generate textual distortions of space and language. The relation between image and text also tells us why, despite the expanse of knowledge that Abel Lefranc (1905) offers, he does not problematize the distortions engaged in mimetic transfer when materials of one medium are mapped onto others. Gargantua does not claim cartographic interest: "En résumé, il apparaît clairement que, dans ce premier livre, tous les éléments d'ordre géographique ou topographique sont *strictement empruntés à la réalité* et que l'imagination du conteur n'est intervenue en rien pour les transformer ou les combiner arbitrairement" [In sum, it clearly appears that in this first book, all the geographic or topographical elements are strictly borrowed from reality and that the storyteller's imagination in no way intercedes to transform or combine them arbitrarily] (5–6, emphasis added).

29. Skelton notes that Sebastian Münster used the Psalms (e.g., 104), which "praise God's work on the face of the earth to justify geography" (Skelton 1966b: ix).

30. See the inner cover of Rodney Shirley's *The Mapping of the World* (1983). In his discussion of the map, he calls special attention to the depiction of the north. "Four islands make up the north polar regions. The separate island of Greenland is named, and a large promontory marked *baccalar* (supposedly Labrador) extends from the North American land mass into the Atlantic" (75). Rabelais's text takes these discoveries into account.

31. In Grynaeus 1532, which relates accounts of travel up to Vespucci and Columbus. If a biographical approach were to be taken, the book could be said to figure in the world of Rabelais's knowledge.

5. An Insular Moment

1. M. A. Screech (1958) grounds a political and historical reading of the third book that is amplified in his critical edition of the *Tiers livre* and in the monumental *Rabelais* (1979). Despite a schematic and abbreviated form, its paradoxes notwithstanding, Saulnier 1957 remains a work that cannot be refuted, if only for the beauty of its design. For Saulnier, the new, older Panurge of post-1546 writings is a wanderer, an everyman, who seeks answers to the deeper enigmas of creation as he lives in an age where direct statement about topical issues gets risky. Panurge becomes a nomad who travels from one area to another, in quest of meaning in a world that refuses to yield any explanation of its design. Saulnier's work engages a geography of quest that indirectly serves as a background to Samuel Kinser's recent *Rabelais's Carnival* (1990), a book that offers a compelling view of the unsettling, deracinating effects of travel and irony. Showing how the text is an ekphrastic description of Olaus Magnus's 1549 map of the North Atlantic, Kinser draws to a strong conclusion what Saulnier may have been reticent to remark about the violence and cynicism that color the last pages of Rabelais's oeuvre.

2. See chapter 4, which cites the promise the author will clearly fail to respect.

3. Ekphrasis is understood here as "a particular case of description or narrative" in

which "the ekphrastic text represents in words a plastic representation" (Riffaterre 1994: 211), but also a double effect of being at once a picture and a verbal image.

4. Henri Estienne translates the Greek as *monachus, quasi bellus senex*. The most compelling analysis of Rabelais and the *isolario*, with emphasis on Hiere Islands in the *Quart livre*, is Lestringant 1988a. The connections that Lestringant establishes with Bordone, Thevet, and chapter 57 show how a pattern of isolation reigns in the fourth book. The cosmographic features of the island are taken up in Allen 1977.

5. See Dilke 1987: 244–45 and the illustration from *In somnium Scipionis expositio* (Macrobius 1483: 300).

6. See Lestringant 1991a. Karrow 1993: 529–46 offers a concise review of the cartographic production.

7. "The island," notes Frank Lestringant, "appears to some degree contaminated by the marine world in which it is located, and thus displays a founding ambiguity: formed by land, the island is nonetheless defined by the surrounding sea or lake. Its nature is, therefore, essentially hybrid" (1980b: 470).

8. James Akerman (1991b) shows that the atlas structure evolves from the *isolario*, along with navigational books and cityscapes, by according privilege to the illustrated material. Using Mireille Pastoureau's definition of an atlas as a book in which maps prevail over textual material, he implies that in its evolution toward an atlas, the island book loses its verbal surround as it develops increasingly accurate visual treatments of islands.

9. Readers of Thomas More's *Utopia*, Louis Marin reminds us, are aware of the ways that the *isolario* can be used to put forward and dissimulate political issues, or how the form exploits the concepts of allegory by using an "image" to utter what a text cannot state, or vice versa. Marin notes that, with a spatial play of different and multiple forms, we discover "the site of production of a representative figure, of a picture in the text that had been put there, to dissimulate by way of its metaphor historical contradiction—a historical tale—by projecting it upon its screen" (1973: 87).

10. See Shirley 1987: 75–76, plate 61. He notes that Bordone's later editions follow the 1532 material in a reprint of Bartolommeo dalli Sonetti's *Isolario* (originally 1485). The idea for the rhumb lines that update the original may have been inspired by Rosselli's marine chart of the world (Florence, 1508), which uses the *marteloio* system to define the axis (near the Fortunate Islands), the polygonal circle of lines embracing the New and Old Worlds (in Nebenzahl: 1990, plate 17A). The *marteloio* system is studied in Mollat du Jourdain and Roncière 1984.

11. See Shirley 1987: 150–51, plates 108, 109. New plates were added in 1586. Maps from Porcacchi's plates "were inserted into occasional books of travel and topography emanating from Venice over the next hundred years" (175).

12. Thevet's life and works have been studied meticulously in Lestringant 1991a, 1991b.

13. At the same time that Lévi-Strauss praises Thevet and Jean de Léry as our keenest witnesses of discovery, he adds that the conscience of the period lacked a sense of the "style of the universe" and that these voyagers could not possess the traits needed for "scientific reflection."

14. There is an error in pagination in the Newberry Library copy (Case G 117.88).

15. "Zero-degree" focalization is tantamount to omniscience. It could be said that

Bordone's prose exemplifies Genette's concept of this strategy of truth, developed in *Figures III* (1972).

16. The term "intravagate" is not a neologism. Early ethnography is built upon the same modes. Claude-Gilbert Dubois writes of Montaigne's use of *enstasis*, a tendency to be both in the material of his writing, as a self marked everywhere on the printed page, and also a figure apt to assume the point of view of the other. He (and Thevet) do so without, however, seeing the other as a mirror of the self. Montaigne's extravagations are, in fact, intravagations (Dubois 1985: 227).

17. These were heralded in the secret writings of hieroglyphs illustrated in Thevet's *La cosmographie de Levant,* and they are subject to more consistent editorial control in *La cosmographie universelle.* It might be added that the work mixes two different "speeds" of decipherment. One, in the image, intends to offer an immediate view of singularity, while the other, the discourse, labors slowly to produce "intrasubjective worlds of facts and arguments" (Gombrich 1978: vol. 2, 190) that will correct what comes too simply or erroneously through the Platonic quality of the image.

18. In his study of the same myth that draws on the same pages of Thevet, Alfred Métraux argues that the Tupinamba endow transformational virtue upon most of their deities. The gods are "less creators than transformers" (1928: 7).

19. A reader is tempted to see the German trace of *Ebene,* or planar surface, in the text. The word evokes the haptic quality of reading and seeing the world together. *Ebene* would also refer to the work and its mode of illustration, and signal cosmographic sources that reach back to Münster and Pieter Apian by way, perhaps, of Oronce Finé, one of Thevet's declared mentors. French relations with German cartography are taken up in Gallois 1890b. Claude Gandelman studies the haptic/optic distinction in his *Reading Pictures, Viewing Texts* (1991: 4–5).

20. See Marcel Mauss, "Don, contrat, échange," in Mauss 1969: vol. 3, 46–51. Lestringant notes that the Pierre Thevet who received the gift purchased on the shores of the Red Sea died in 1575 (1991a: 24). He does not connect the effect of the *gift* to the brother's death as it is represented within the text.

21. Frank Lestringant summarizes the major tenets of his *L'atelier du cosmographe* thus: The "theoretical" or erudite geography that the humanists celebrated in their editions of Ptolemy in the early years of the sixteenth century had entailed a wholesale rejection of the accurate representations that artists and navigators made in the portolano tradition. These came back—like the repressed—to haunt cosmographers, since they were part of the world of experience and observation that heralded a pragmatic and measured picture of the earth's surface. The maps of cosmographers like Thevet and Guillaume le Testu are anachronistic insofar as they "do not show a definitive state of the world," but they are also modern, conceived as a mosaic, assembled within a floating space of fragmentary accounts. Both engage a "play between the geometrical whole of the sphere and empirical fragments of hydrography, and between the parts of the world themselves," in which "a moving space" is born, in which the imagination and instrumental reason are confused (1991c: 165, 167). Tony Campbell reaches similar conclusions (1987b: esp. 372, 444).

22. Wilda Anderson (1990) argues that Diderot envisions the world as a flowing mass of shapes that are in perpetual movement between subject and object. Her view of

a dynamic rapport among subject, world, and affect seems akin to what readers evince in Thevet.

23. The work is described at length in Frank Lestringant's appendix to Pastoureau 1984: 481–95. See Hair, 1982; Lestringant 1991a: 319–22, passim; 1991b: 156–74.

24. Lévi-Strauss cites the first and last sentences of the passage (1991: 282–83).

25. Van Den Abbeele notes how Thevet's cosmography resists essentializing gestures through its myriad combinations of duplicity and singularity (1992b: 34). We can take singularity in its most concrete sense, in its relation to the island book that allows the imagination to move about almost unconsciously. Thevet's style of thinking and writing effectively renews cosmography at the very points where its own form can account for the changes taking place in the idea of the world's mass and surface. The text allows for change and revision where other cosmographies do not. In, for example, Alonso de Santa Cruz's *Islario general de todas las islas del mundo* (Madrid, 1540–1542), the desire to produce a cohering whole is betrayed by the same author's project of writing a history of the Catholic monarch *elsewhere*. One genre is separated from the other so that history—especially that of the Iberian experience in the Americas—does not color the cosmography, so that new views of isolated space and human practices do not break into the chronicle of the writer's patrons. Avoiding the problems that Thevet takes up, "in the *Islario* (Santa Cruz) limits himself, in order not to deflower his great future work (the *Crónica del Emperador Carlos V*), to a geographical reconnaissance of coastlines and islands of which cartographic illustration is an essential element" (Naudé 1992: 114).

6. An Atlas Evolves

1. See Simonin 1992: 171–72, passim: "It is true that [Münster's] methods, like Belleforest's, appealed to everyone's collaboration and to readings and were led to make legends timeless" (181). Simonin also notes that "the beginning of the 1570s is marked by aggressive and ambitious commercial enterprises" (1987: 434–35), like those of Georges Braün's *Theatrum urbium praecipuarum mundi* (1572, French translation, *Théâtre des différentes villes du monde*) and Ortelius's atlas. Belleforest's publishers, Chesneau and Sonnius, had the ambition of "being at the origin of financing a national product or, at the very least, of arrogating for themselves the possibility of retailing a 'description of France' that might well have been inserted in the revised and enlarged edition of Münster" (Simonin 1987: 435). The model for the "French" Münster would have included Antoine du Pinet's *Plantz, pourtraitz et description de plusieurs villes et forteresses* (Lyon: Jean d'Ogerolles, 1564) (illustrated in Pastoureau 1984).

2. Belleforest had worked with and even pilfered material from Thevet in the preparation of *La cosmographie*. Simonin (1992: 39–40, 179–82, 219) follows their collaboration as of 1553. Belleforest's admiration for Thevet is marked in liminary pieces in the prefaces to *La cosmographie de Levant* and *Les singularitez*. Their ensuing enmity has become legendary.

3. The importance of this shift in the physical conception of the book cannot be overstated if it were hypothesized, following Michel Foucault (1966), that an epistemology of representation comes into existence when the atlas replaces the universal

cosmography. The labor of analogy that allowed discourse to flow endlessly into and through the illustrations that defined the cosmography is now obsolete; a rational mode of formatting replaces the organic and animistic shape of the former encyclopedia. When Ortelius's work is seen juxtaposed to Belleforest's, we see that the "science of the sixteenth century leaves the deformed memory of a mixed and unruly knowledge in which all of the world's objects could formerly be likened to the chance of experiments, of traditions, and of beliefs. From now on the handsomely rigorous and constricting figures of analogy will be forgotten. They will be held forth as signs of the reveries and the charms of a knowledge that had not yet become rational" (Foucault 1966: 65).

4. In Deleuze's terms, modulation and relation to a mean replace a permanent law of creation or authority (1988: 26). The reader of Ortelius compares maps not on a basis of the truth of their representation but on that of variation of shape with respect to the unifying style of engraving. An entirely new—or "baroque"—mode of reading and seeing is established.

5. Once again we are reminded of Focillon's principle of the "life of forms" in a culture, in which, in an "experimental" phase, one sees mixed together "a mobility and diversity" of attempts to define and to solve a variety of problems (1938: 1, 127).

6. Dainville's study, "Le premier atlas de France, *Le Théâtre françoys* de M. Bouguereau, 1594," first appeared in the *Comité des travaux historiques et scientifiques, Actes du 85e congrès national des sociétés savantes, Chambéry-Annecy, 1960, Section de géographie* (Paris: Bibliothèque nationale, 1961) and is reprinted in *La cartographie reflet de l'histoire* (Geneva: Slatkine Reprints, 1986), 295–342. The contents are summarized in the "Bibliographical Note," introduction to the facsimile edition of Maurice Bouguereau, *Le Théâtre françoys* (1966: vi–xvi). The evolution of Bouguereau's composite creation into the Leclerc atlases (1619–1632) is documented in Père Dainville's companion article, "L'évolution de l'atlas de France sous Louis XIII: *Théâtre géographique du royaume de France* des Le Clerc. 1619–32 (1963) (and reprinted in *La cartographie reflet de l'histoire*, 346–97). All reference to Bouguereau's work will be taken from the Theatrum Orbis Terrarum facsimile edition.

7. The history of the choice and arrangement of allegorical figures on title pages of tributary books of fortification and edification affords comparison. Mars, for example, gives way to Bellona. Minerva is chosen to represent acuity and ingenuity (*ingegno*). Bouguereau's title page anticipates what seventeenth century manuals will choose for the promotion of military action and fits in the line of development that John R. Hale traces (1964).

8. The design is textualized at the end of the synoptic table listing the sixty-three kings of France, the length of their reigns, the dates of their death, and their places of burial. The work looks to the future in the sentence that breaks the columnar order of the ensemble: "Mais sa trop grande bonté nous presage que sa Misericorde & Pardon sur iceux [his enemies] les amenera avec ses bons sujets à reconciliation & obeissance deuë a sa Majesté, affin que le recognoissans de coeur, de voix & de courage, la Paix nous soit envoyée du Ciel sous sa domination, pour tous ensemble n'avoir qu'un Dieu, un Roy, une Foy, & une Loy" [But his extraordinary beauty makes us foresee that kindness and pardon upon his enemies will lead them, with his good subject, toward reconciliation and obeisance due to his Majesty, in order that, recognizing bravery, voice,

and courage, peace will be sent to us from the Heavens under his dominion, so that together everyone will have only one God, one King, one Law, and one Faith].

9. Jacques Lacan cites the anamorphic death's head in Holbein's *Ambassadors* to map out the laws of desire. "All that shows us that in the very heart of the epoch (the early modern age) in which the subject is outlined and where geometrical optics are sought, Holbein makes visible for us something that is nothing other than the subject as if turned into nothing (*néantisé*). . . . But we have to look further into the function of vision. We shall thus see being outlined from its basis, not the phallic symbol, the anamorphic phantom, but the gaze as such, in its driving function, exploded and stretched out, as it is in this painting. This painting is nothing other than what any painting is, a trap for the gaze" (1973: 83). The drive to conquer that is glimpsed between the portrait and the map is evinced in the analyst's appreciation of a first major pictorial expression of anamorphosis.

10. The page renews a fifteenth-century model of a "speaking gaze," what Michel de Certeau (1987: 14) calls a "simultaneity of stupefactions" in the spatial organization of discourse and painting in Nicolas de Cusa's *De Icone*.

11. In his introduction to an English edition of the *Theatrum* (1606), Ortelius states that the reader will be able to treat the book the way that princes used to look at maps. In the ideological stratum of his introduction, he implies that the buyer will be able to become a nobleman in miniature. "For there are many that are much delighted with *Geography* or *Chorography,* and especially with Mappes or Tables contayning the plotts and descriptions of Countryes, such as there are many nowadays extant and every where to be sold: . . . who when they have that which will buy them, would very willingly lay out the money, were it not that by reason of the narrownesse of the roomes and places, broad and large Mappes cannot so be opened or spread, that every thing in them may easily and well be seene and discern'd. For . . . those great and large *Geographicall* Maps or Chartes, which are folded or rowl'd up, are not so commodious: nor, when any thing is peradventure read in them, so easie to be look'd upon. And he that will in order hang them all along upon a wall had need have not only a very large & wide house, but even a Princes gallery or spacious Theater. This I having often made triall of, I began to bethinke my selfe, what meanes might be found to redresse these discommodities. . . . And at length me thought it might be done by that meanes which we have observed and set downne in this our booke, to which I earnestly wish that every student would affoord a place in his Library, amongst the rest of his bookes" (cited in Akerman: 100).

12. In his quatrains "Sur le Tres-Chrestien Roy de France, & de Navarre, Henry quatriesme de ce nom" (fol. 8 r), which are written to explicate the picture, Bouguereau draws attention to the allegory of the elliptical scheme: "Quiconque ayme le fard, sejour icy ne fasse, / Ce Roy n'a iamais eu le visage trompeur, / Que si voir on pouvoit son coeur comme sa face, / Nostre oeil confesseroit n'avoir rien veu si pur." [Whoever loves mascara, repose here do not take: / This king has never shown a face to be fake, / And if we could see his heart as we do his visage / Our eyes would avow they see the purest image.]

13. The play among letters, the checkerboard, and fate is the subject of Rabelais's *Tiers livre*, chapter 25 (421). Jean Céard notes that "the anagram was never without relation to divination" (1982: 420).

14. The allure of perfection that is intended seems to anticipate strategies that Louis Marin analyzes in "The King and his Geometer" in Marin 1988: 169–79.

15. See Dainville 1964b: 133–64 on the importance of potamography and other "terms, signs, and colors" of early modern maps.

16. Mercator wrote to Ortelius, marveling at how regional descriptions can be "collected into one manual, which can be bought at small cost, kept in a space wherever we please" (translated and cited by Koeman, in Karrow 1993: 9). The ideology of *brevitas,* of compactness and worldliness, might extend further into the relation of cartographic development and the spread of Protestant belief. Catherine Delano Smith (1992) has shown how Protestant Bibles append maps to coordinate graphic logic with Scripture.

17. [Premier of the French, whose ship always afloat, / Already off to Spain, in order to herald your name: / Remark your Henry, whose everlasting fame / Iridescent in the sky, will make you gloat: / Saved, now let BOURBON be what you note.]

18. Dainville (1985: 326–27) studies the provenance of de Jode's map, arguing that Bouguereau did not copy a Flemish map of the region but that it is a direct copy of a French map that de Jode took from Bouguereau himself. He attributes a map of the region to Macé Ogier (executed in 1539), which was edited in 1565: "Though Bouguereau's copy . . . was clearly closer to the original than the Flemish maps, we can ascertain that (Macé's) map had been the oldest of all those of the French provinces." (327).

19. We have seen that the engraver plays a strong role in the work that bears the name of the cartographer. The work of Nicolaï is no exception. His illustrator, Lyon Davent, as Catherine Grodecki shows, was "the faithful interpretor of the work of others, whence the excellence of the plates taken from greater masters" (1974: 348). That Davent was associated with the Fontainebleau school shows where the Mannerist style and cartographic imagination converge in the 1550s.

20. Dainville notes that woodcut maps had followed manuscript practices by dotting areas that had been marked with sepia-ochre colors to designate elevations or, more correctly, by putting wide hatching to represent "sawtooth," "rooster–comb," or "sugarloaf" alignments with white or light summits above dark bases. By the middle of the sixteenth century, with the advent of copperplate engraving, mountains are conventionally treated by alignments of molehills or ranges of sugarloaves "that give no idea of surface, altitude, or slope. . . . They are always of the same height, always smoothly rounded, shaded by concave and soft lines, from East to Southeast, because the engravers work with the source of light coming from the left" (1964b: 167–68).

21. Belleforest's text is taken from the Newberry Library copy of *La cosmographie universelle de tout le monde* . . . (Paris: Michel Sonnius, 1575). (All citations from Belleforest are from this source.)

22. *Le sententiose imprese, et dialogo del Symeone. Con la verificatione del sito di Gergobia, la Geografia d'Ouernia, la figura & tempio d'Apolline in Velay: & il suo hieroglifico monumento, natività, vita & epistaffio* . . . (Lyon, 1560) (Karrow 1993: 527).

23. In a related piece, the same author notes, "Is not the dream of the Renaissance that of transforming the visible into an entirely legible world, but without calling into question its 'translatability' of the entirely legible into something entirely intelligible, all the while the conditions of transposition are never considered? At the heart of this problem, however, surges forth, unexpectedly, the relation with the unknown" (Mathieu-Castellani 1990: 9).

24. For example: "La chose qui plus anoblit une Province, sont les fleuves: que si Italie par plusieurs nobles Fleuves, comme le Pau, dit en Latin Frianus, le Tybre à
Romme & autres, ha esté recommandé des Historiographes. Et la Germanie pour le
Danube, & le Rhin qui despart & separe Gaule à Germania. Je veux bien en ce petit
livre demontrer, que la Gaule ha des fleuves aussi nobles & en aussi grand nombre que
Provinces ou nation qui soit en Europe: & prendray mon commencement au Rhosne,
qui est le chef, & comme Roy entre les fleuves des dites Gaules" [What most ennobles
a province are its rivers: Just as was Italy by several notable rivers, such as the Po, in
Latin the Frianus, the Tiber at Rome, and others, as historiographers emphasize. And
in Germany there is the Danube, and the Rhine, that splits and separates Gaule from
Germania. In this little book I want to show that Gaul owns rivers as noble and numerous as those of any province or nation in Europe: and I'll begin at the Rhône that is the
leader, or king, among the rivers of Gaul] (Estienne 1558: 113). Rivers provide a useful
image that can be purveyed: Bouguereau exploits the ideology at work in Estienne to
produce a tourism and a geographic image of the nation that still pervades the *Guide
Michelin*.

25. Thus: "La plus fertile, douce, saine, & nourissante rivere qui soit en l'Europe,
c'est de la Seine que je parle, laquelle ayant sa source en terroir des anciens Langrois . . .
prend doulcement course sans porter bateau de compte . . . se ioint à l'Aulbe, qui se
vient engoulphrer en la Seine pres de Mery, & deslors Seine enflant ses flots, se fait
aussi eslargir ses limites, arrousant le pays Champenois, iusques à ce qu'elle s'aggrandit
& devient plus puissante par la reception qu'elle fait de l'eau de Yonne . . . apres elle
reçoit en ses bras, la riviere de Loin. . . . Apres que Seine est enflée des flots de
Marne . . . avant de se lancer ses bras de l'Océan, reçoit encor plusieurs petites ri-
vières . . . & autres que je ne puis vous deschiffrer. Tant y a que entre tous les fleuves de
France, on peut dire que la Seine a des privileges qui luy sont tous propres, elle estant
doulce, paisible, non ravissante, ny rongeant, & gastant les terres qui lavoysinent, peu
souvent sortant de ses limites, & des plus navigables de l'Europe, non guere frequente
en abisme, & fosses tourbillonneuses, non dangereuse aux nageurs, ny fascheuse à ceux
qui y naviguent, & en somme n'y a fleuve en Europe, qui au pris de cestuy cy, n'aye de
bien de grandes incommoditez . . . : en somme la Seine est toute navigable, fertille,
abondante, gracieuse, saine, portueuse, sans rochs, ny escueils, & la plus asseurée
d'entre les rivieres de France: qui est cause que la grande cité de Paris abonde, en tout
temps de tout ce qui est requis pour la vie des hommes, ceste riviere luy servant comme
une corne d'abondance" [The most fertile, the sweetest, healthiest, and most nourishing
river that flows in all of Europe is the Seine of which I speak, having its origin in the
homeland of the former Langrois, whence she flows softly without bearing any boat of
size; she joins the Aulbe, that becomes engulfed in the Seine near Mery, and from there
the flow of the Seine swells; she broadens her shores, fertilizing the Champenois region
until she grows and strengthens when she receives the waters of the Yonne, and after,
she receives in her arms the River Loin. . . . Soon the Seine is swollen with the currents
of the Marne, but before throwing her arms into the ocean, she still receives a few little
rivers and others that I cannot enumerate for you. Among all the great rivers of France
it can be said the Seine has privileges of her own, for she is soft, peaceful, not ravishing,
not threatening, never spoiling the land by which she flows, rarely swelling over her
shores, and she remains one of the most navigable in Europe, rarely pocked by eddies,

Figure N.2. Totem and edge of map: detail of Wolfgang Lazius's 1561 map of Austria

or whirlpools, never dangerous for swimmers, nor contrary to those who sail upon her, and in a word there is no river in Europe that, in comparison to the Seine, has so few disadvantages. . . . In sum, the Seine is entirely navigable, fertile, abundant, gracious, healthy, buoyant, without rocks or shallows, and she is the surest of all rivers of France, which explains why the great city of Paris thrives on her shores, getting from the river everything necessary for human life, the river serving the city as if she were a horn of plenty] (vol. 2, 228–29). The description ends on its own figure of a horn of plenty, the emblem of *copia* turning into *fluvia,* which turns on the homonym of a *rivière Seine/saine.* Proven are the "healthy" ideals of the nation by the authority of a homonyn.

26. The meeting of anatomy and cartography is probably most precociously illustrated in the work of Wolfgang Lazius. Behind his depictions of Austria he places the national totem, an eagle, whose head is seen at the top and whose talons are seen below. The oval maps resemble splayed charts of a dissected eagle, the rivers made analogous, by juxtaposition, to the bird's intestinal network. See Bernleithner 1972 (Figure N.2).

27. The river as a memory-image of a genealogical tree persists in later literature. In 1738 the Abbot Jean Delagrive, reports Josef Konvitz, mapped the Seine with all its tributaries in the order in which they merged (1987: 109–10). The description was "far from useful" and ran contrary to the cartographer's scientific mission. In 1766, after compiling maps of the Seine from Paris to the Atlantic (in ten sheets), Philippe Buache drew a schematic chart "in which the river and all its tributaries were depicted as straight lines in exact proportion to their actual length, arranged as a genealogical chart might be but with a rigor and a purpose totally absent from Delagrive's schematic outline" (110).

28. From this perspective, the project of *Le théâtre* parallels that of Christopher Saxon, for whom a new ideology of place and of identity emerges in opposition to a monarchic model of leadership, as shown by Richard Helgerson (1986: 50–85). Yet the complexity of Bouguereau's atlas betrays Helgerson's conclusion that, in the France of Henry IV, "maps seem to have functioned in untroubled support of a strongly central-ized monarchic regime" (81).

7. Montaigne

1. All references to the *Essais* are from the *Oeuvres complètes,* edited by Thibaudet and Rat (Montaigne 1962).

2. Montaigne does not follow—as Nina Catach would argue (1968)—the rules of a substitutive code of printed writing. Other registers of meaning and of expression are embedded in the graphic shape of signifiers. The latter, as Citton and Wyss (1989: 10–18) note, pertain to a level of expression that phonetic meaning does not control. For this reason, in the reading of Montaigne and of cartographic writing in general, a Saussurean model of the sign is far less effective than that of Hjelmslev (1969), for whom, as Deleuze and Guattari argue (1980: 58–59), a tonal range of meanings fans out between the signifier and the signified, despite its return to a metaphysical plan of lan-guage (Meschonnic 1975: 227).

3. Longeon (1989: 79–80) reproduces the significant articles. He adds that they "do not introduce a revolution in practice, but they consecrate the fact that Latin is already so far removed from popular use that it is the cause of too much 'ambiguity' and 'incer-titude' in a domain that cannot support either the one or the other" (79). De Certeau, Julia, and Revel project the issue from the sixteenth century (Charles de Bovelles) to the Revolution of 1789, where they see "a constitutive will" that is experienced in con-formity with a rational scheme—offered by the "search for an origin"—that both is French and is located upon the land on which French is spoken (1975: 83–85). As we observed in chapter 6, this is the space Bouguereau surveys through cartographic means.

4. The point has been studied in Butor 1968, and Rigolot 1982, and has since been used for political and historical reevaluations of the *Essais* (Henry 1987; Conley 1992c).

5. The historiated initials of Apian's workshop, drawn in the context of globes, are illustrated in Butsch 1969: plate 189. The upper-case A or V, allegorized as a geometer's instrument, had long marked illustrated manuscripts. We recall that for Tory and his age the compass was a sign of Prudence. It also figured in the idiolect of Jean Thenaud's pictogrammatic counsel to Louise de Savoie, as well as in the idiolect of François Demoulins (Lecoq 1987: 75, 96). By midcentury, its symbolic content had become common usage (Terverant 1958: *compas*). For this reason, we are obliged to depart from Rigolot's observation that "the author of the *Essais* does not take an interest in the spatial possibilities of language or, as current expression would say, the 'analogical motivation of the signifier'" (1988: 205–6).

6. Montaigne's servitude to both travel and household affairs, notes Alfred Glauser, is "translated in a spiked prose that suggests a world of locks, hinges, or ironwork. Its very texture promotes the idea of a prison" (1972: 105).

7. "C'est l'indiligent lecteur qui pert mon subject, non pas moy; il s'en trouvera tousjours en un coing quelque mot qui ne laisse pas d'estre bastant, quoy qu'il soit serré" [It is the indiligent reader who loses my subject, and not I; somewhere he or she will always find in it a corner of a word that is not sufficient, although it is tightly embedded] (973).

8. The implication of order and play are developed in Conley 1988.

9. Claude-Gilbert Dubois (1977: 159–62) explains the temporal and spatial coordinates of this type of history.

10. López de Gómara 1943: chs. 47, 48, pp. 164–69. (In English: *Cortez: The Life of the Conqueror*, trans. and ed. Lesley Byrd Simpson [Berkeley: University of California Press, 1964], chs. 47, 48, pp. 105–7). Montaigne's source is an Italian translation (Venice, 1576) by Cravalix.

11. Claude Lévi-Strauss (1958: 147–80) touches on the dual structures among some of the cannibals (the Bororo) that Montaigne takes up by way of André Thevet and that he will embody in his writing of friendship.

12. In the opening lines of his study of "Des cannibales," Michel de Certeau notes that the topography of the essay "places into question both the text's power of composing and distributing places, its ability to be a narrative of space, and the necessity for it to define its relation to what it treats, in other words, to construct a place of its own" (1986: 67). One area will be the space that Montaigne "opens for the other," while another will be the alterity it ascribes to the surface of the printed page and emblematic design of the *Essais*. The point inflects what we have noted at the end of chapter 5.

13. See the surrounding context in Thevet 1557: fols. 69–74.

14. See Zerner 1969. Connections between the Fontainebleau style and Thevet's illustrations are suggested in Marchand and Parent 1984: 67–82, 257 and passim.

15. Here emerges an encounter with a prevailing theme of Spanish historiography: Gómara and Thevet establish hyperboles of objectivity that tend to give credence to the ocularity or the truth of their "science." "Francisco López de Gómara se adhiere, en su 'Historia General de las Indias' (1552)," remarks Victor Frankl (1963: 87–88) "enfáticamente a la tesis de que la experiencia constituye la única fuente de la verdad en historia, a pesar de que el mismo escribió su Historia sin haber estado en Hispano América" [Francisco López de Gómara adheres . . . emphatically to the thesis that experience constitutes the unique source of truth in history, all the while he wrote his history without having spent any time in Hispanic America]. He and Thevet are secondary eyewitnesses who ground their truth in the contradiction of the immediacy of their written sources. In other words, the printed page and its illustrations of text and image produce the effect of untrammeled marvels. By contrast, in his avowedly tertiary contact, Montaigne comes closer to his origin as he takes an increased distance from it.

16. Michel de Certeau remarks that Montaigne's voice "circulates in the space of cannibalistic orality" (1986: 77) and constantly must return from one world and go back and forth to the other.

17. The remark is similar to what Claude-Gilbert Dubois calls *enstasis* (1985: 223–25), where Montaigne is at a double center, a blind point, around which the autobiography turns. See also chapter 6, note 8.

18. A similar paradox results from Gisèle Mathieu-Castellani's reading of "D'un

enfan monstrueux" (II, xxx), an essay in the second book that corresponds to "moderation" and "cannibales" both numerologically and thematically (1988b: 222–24).

19. The last sentences of "Des cannibales" thus ground the structure of a tradition of social criticism and fable that Montesquieu will use for his *Lettres persanes*, and that has since been used frequently in political fables. No doubt Jonathan Swift's *Gulliver's Travels* also shares much with the tactic used here.

20. Simultaneity of the two points of view that are Montaigne's and the Amerindians' tends to negate the sense of delay inscribed in Jean Starobinski's reading of this passage, in which he shows how political action is only gained by a movement that goes from the self to the other: "Adhérer étroitement à la vie sensible, puis, par sympathie, étendre cette adhésion au-delà des limites de la vie personnelle, c'est vivre dans la non-violence, où, du moins dans la moindre violence" [To stick closely to sensible life, then, through friendliness, to stretch this adhesion beyond the limits of personal life, is to live in non-violence or, at best, in the least violence] (1982: 301). Delay allows his reading to bind social criticism with what appears to be the *Essais*'s thematically conservative view of political institutions. The optical facets of the text, the simultaneity of its events, and the self-contained structure of the chapter do not allow such thematic "movement" to emerge from the writing.

21. Some of the network has been elaborated in Sayce 1972 and in Conley 1978. John O'Neill (1988: 188–209) has reviewed the principal literature on "Des coches."

22. See also engraving 37, "Cérémonies pour la venue de la future reine," illustrated in *La Renaissance et le nouveau monde* (Lestringant 1984: 96). In his contribution to this volume, "Theaters of Cruelty," Frank Lestringant specifies how de Bry uses las Casas's *Brevísima relación de la destrucción de las Indias* to illustrate the horrors of anthropophagia for a European public (207).

23. The Mexican religion is also taken up in chapter 72 of Thevet's *Singularitez*. Roger Schlesinger and Arthur P. Stabler furnish a bibliography (e.g., C. A. Burland, *The Bases of Religion in Aztec Mexico*; B. C. Brundage, *The Fifth Sun;* and David Carrasco, *Quetzalcoatl and the Irony of Empire*) in their *André Thevet's North America: A Sixteenth-Century View* (1986: 170–71).

24. See Lestringant 1980a: 9–26; 1988b: 51–85 and Pagden 1982.

25. That is, a variegated and layered sum of verbal affinities that circulate within or through words, and by which their forms and shapes acquire the archaic function of motivating various analogies. The style is as old as what Cratylus puts forward in Plato's dialogue of his name, and it is invoked with no less conviction by Claude Lévi-Strauss when he notes, referring to the *Essais*, that "la pensée populaire prétend se fonder sur l'expérience mais met aussi en oeuvre toutes sortes d'équivalences symboliques sur le plan de la métaphore" [popular thought claims to be founded on experience but also puts to work all kinds of symbolic identities based on the plan of metaphor] (1985: 11).

26. Bataillon reviews them: from the Inter Caetera of 1493, papal bulls, he recalls, were political instruments that the Spanish monarchy invoked to justify its conquest of the New World (1971: 58). See also Vincent 1975: 111–99.

27. See Michel de Certeau 1982a: 224.

28. Patrick Henry has taken up Montaigne's defensive stance in view of papal censure (1987: 3–23).

29. Olive Dickason notes that Europeans used torture (notably absent from the firsthand accounts but mentioned in Montaigne's) to punish offenders in the growing centralized monarchy (1984: 56–57). By contrast, Amerindians were seen using torture against enemies in order to consolidate a tribe's position with respect to the outside world. The most telling accounts in English of Aristotle's use and abuse are Hanke 1959, 1974.

30. Geoffroy Atkinson (1935) lists two French translations: las Casas's *Tyrannies et cruautés des espagnoles* (Anvers, 1579; Paris, 1582) and his *Histoires des insolences et cruautés. . . .* (Paris, n.d.). De Bry's illustrations (1598) confirm what had been obvious since the early years of the century. They are inspired by the first Latin edition (Frankfurt, 1594) of Las Casas's *Brevísima relación de la destrucción de las Indias* and accompany *Benzoni's Historia del nuovo mundo* (1550). Citing Pierre Chaunu, Marianne Mahn-Lot remarks that Dutch editions of the *Brevísima relación* became the weapons of psychological warfare aimed against Spain (1982: 252–53).

31. The affinities between Freud and Montaigne are well known. "Freud has more in common with Proust and Montaigne," notes Harold Bloom, "than with biological scientists, because his interpretations of life and death are mediated always by texts, first by the literary texts of others, and then by his own earlier texts, until at last the Sublime mediation of otherness begins to be performed by his text-in-process," from "Freud and the Sublime," quoted in Malcom Bowie 1987: 8. Bloom notes that certain writers read and assimilate each other without needing to have any empirical relation to each other; nor does an antecedent text necessarily form a pregiven source for a later one: Often a later work will reread and effectively complicate matters that had gone unquestioned in earlier ones. The argument shows where a "map of misreading" (Bloom 1975) can change the picture of both literary history and historiography in general. The hypotheses repeat what Michel de Certeau determines through a psychoanalytic reading of Freud and history (1982a: 312–58).

8. La Popelinière and Descartes

1. See Lestringant's account of La Popelinière and Richard Hakluyt, Portuguese exploration, and Francis Drake in *Le Huguenot et le sauvage* (1990: 234–36, 259–61). The Portuguese are the inverse of the Spaniards insofar as they are represented using negotiation, rather than gunpowder, to develop new lands. "The so-called 'Portuguese model' definitely allows the Huguenot minority to unite good conscience with colonial ambition" (261). Hence the interest in a continent that the conquistadores had not yet reached. The quotations that follow from *Les trois mondes* (Lancelot du Voisin, Seigneur de La Popelinière, 1582) are taken from the Newberry Library copy. That Australia was the site of utopian thinking is the topic of David Fausett's introduction to *Writing the New World: Imaginary Voyages and Utopias of the Great Southern Land* (1993: 1–26).

2. Skelton (1969) edits and translates Pigafetta's account, while Nebenzahl (1990: 80–83) reproduces illustrations of the islands from the only extant manuscript.

3. Goux notes that "no longer can God only know objectively what is. A singular, ego-centered subject can also be, as such, the subject of science, the objective spectator

of the world. Such is what perspective postulates, like the *cogito*: Absolute subjectivity does not contradict but makes possible perfect objectivity" (1985: 20).

4. Two topics that inspire a comparison of Montaigne and Descartes are travel and domestic space. Throughout the *Discours,* Descartes rearticulates the theme of travel that runs through "De la vanité," but he also appears to rework the description of Montaigne's writing space—developed in "De trois commerces" (III, iii)—through the evocation of the *poêle* or heated room (shown well in Van Den Abbeele 1992: 18, 60). The self that Descartes seeks to produce is laced with oedipal innuendo referring to the *Essais.*

5. The later history of the theodolite in triangulation is studied in Brown 1977: 259–64 and Greenhood 1964: 16.

6. The style of the author's inscription of his name has anamorphic properties. Like the zigzagged portrayal of the death's head in Holbein's *Ambassadors,* or the woven presence of the skull in the breast of a lover in the Amboise tapestry (1502, in the Cleveland Museum of Art), here the signature becomes a visual object that mobilizes a continuous process of regress and egress. One commentator has noted that for Jacques Lacan the era of the "subject" begins when one asks, "what in this graphic space, does not show, does not stop not writing itself? The point at which something appears to be invisible, the point at which something appears to be missing from representation, some meaning left unrevealed," becomes the point of origin of the "Lacanian gaze. It marks the absence of a signified; it is an unoccupiable point, the point at which the subject disappears" (Copjec 1987: 69). The point is both affirmed and denied in that there is no absence of a signified, but a collage of two terms, God and Descartes, that reveal a sovereign presence of mapping.

7. Van Den Abbeele also notes that the graphic instance of the signature returns to the *Discours,* but he stresses that from the privileged interior an exterior "can be progressively, methodically, appropriated as one's own" (1992: 16). A mastery and possession of nature will ensue in chapter 6. The outward movement follows Edgerton's remarks (1987: 10–14) about the quincunx plan that allows the west to conquer and colonize surrounding world.

8. "Fougeu's manuscript maps are more detailed than any printed map of the period, including those of the atlases of Bouguereau, Ortelius, Mercator, etc. The latter contain between 10% and 20% of the place-names indicated on Fougeu's maps. They are far more carefully drawn than Fougeu's maps, but they are less complete, and often much less precise" (Buisseret 1992b: 114).

9. See the example of Jean de Beins's remarkable views of Grenoble and the Dauphiné, in Dainville 1968, one of which is copied in Buisseret 1992a: 110, figure 4.6 and another in 1992b, plate 7.

9. Conclusion

1. The expression of "belief" stated here has echoes in what Michel de Certeau, in *La faiblesse de croire* (1988), calls "the weakness of belief," a force constitutive of a politics that affirms, nonetheless, a subject's right to take discursive positions in the space and time in which he or she is located.

2. Jacob (1992: 334–35) reiterates that many of the intentions behind the inventory of monstrosities are related to a praise that uses encyclopedic means to prove "the glory of the Creator," and to test the reader's credulity, through the accumulation of monsters and marvels, thus measuring his or her degree of faith. These examples, however, produce unattached affective charges that reason and ideology strive to link to a rhetoric of causes.

Works Cited

Ackerman, James S. 1991. *Distance Points: Essays in Theory and Renaissance Art and Architecture.* Boston: MIT Press.

Akerman, James. 1991. "On the Shoulders of Titan: Viewing the World of the Past in Atlas Structure." Ph.D. diss., Pennsylvania State University, Department of Geography.

Akerman, James, and David Buisseret. 1985. *Monarchs, Ministers, and Maps: A Cartographic Exhibit at the Newberry Library.* Chicago: Newberry Library.

Akerman, James, David Buisseret, and Robert Karrow. 1993. *Two by Two: Twenty-Two Pairs of Maps from the Newberry Library Illustrating 500 Years of Western Cartographic History.* Chicago: Newberry Library.

Allen, Phillip. 1992. *The Atlas of Atlases: The Map Maker's Vision of the World.* New York: Abrams.

Allen, W. Sidney. 1977. "*Kalóyeros:* An Atlantis in Microcosm?" *Imago mundi* 29:54–71.

Anderson, Wilda. 1990. *Diderot's Dream.* Baltimore: Johns Hopkins University Press.

Apian, Pieter. 1551. *Cosmographie.* Paris: V. Gualtherot. French translation of 1529 *Cosmographicus Liber Petri Apiani Mathematici studiose collectus.*

Atkinson, Geoffroy. 1935. *Les nouveaux horizons de la Renaissance française.* Paris: Droz.

Auerbach, Erich. 1956. *Mimesis: The Representation of Reality in Western Literature.* Translated by Willard R. Trask. New York: Doubleday.

———. 1984. *Scenes from the Drama of European Literature.* Minneapolis: University of Minnesota Press.

Aulagnier, Piera. 1975. *La violence de l'interprétation: Du pictogramme à l'énoncé.* Série Le fil rouge. Paris: Presses Universitaires de France.

———. 1982. *L'apprenti-sorcier et le maître-historien.* Série Le fil rouge. Paris: Presses Universitaires de France.

———. 1987. *Un interprète en quête de sens.* Paris: Ramsey.

Bagrow, Leo. 1964. *History of Cartography*. Revised and enlarged by R. A. Skelton. London: Watts.

Ballon, Hilary. 1991. *The Paris of Henry IV: Architecture and Urbanism*. Cambridge, MA: MIT Press.

Baltrušaitis, Jurgis. 1931. *La stylistique ornementale dans la sculpture romane*. Paris: Leroux.

———. 1977. *Anamorphic Art*. New York: Abrams.

Barthes, Roland. 1973. *Eléments de sémiologie*. Paris: Gonthier.

Bastide, Roger. 1970. "Le rire ou les courts-circuits de la pensée." In Jean Pouillon and Pierre Maranda, eds., *Echanges et communications: Mélanges offerts à Claude Lévi-Strauss à l'occasion de son 60ᵉ anniversaire*, vol. 2, 954–63. Paris: Mouton.

Bataillon, Marcel. 1959. "Montaigne et les conquérants de l'or." *Studi francesi* 9:353–67.

———. 1965. *Etudes sur Bartolomé de Las Casas*. Paris: Centre de Recherches de l'Institut d'Etudes Hispaniques.

———. 1971. *Las Casas et la défense des indiens*. Paris: Julliard.

Bateson, Gregory. 1972. *Steps to an Ecology of Mind*. New York: Ballantine Books.

Benjamin, Walter. 1971. *Illuminations*. Translated by Harry Zohn. New York: Schocken.

———. 1977. *The Origins of German Tragic Drama*. Translated by John Osborne. London: New Left Books.

Benveniste, Emile. 1966. *Problèmes de linguistique générale*. Vol. 1. Paris: Gallimard.

Bernleithner, Ernst, ed. 1972. *Wolfgang Lazius, "Austria" (Vienna 1561)*. Sixth series, vol. 2. Amsterdam: Theatrum Orbis Terrarum Ltd.

Bersani, Leo. 1990. *The Culture of Redemption*. Cambridge, MA: Harvard University Press.

Blanchot, Maurice. 1969. *L'entretien infini*. Paris: Gallimard.

Bloom, Harold. 1975. *A Map of Misreading*. New York: Oxford University Press.

Bodin, Jean. 1962. *The Six Books of a Commonweale*. Edited by Kenneth Douglas McRae. Facsimile reprint of the English translation of 1606. Cambridge, MA: Harvard University Press.

Bon, François. 1990. *La folie Rabelais: L'invention du "Pantagruel."* Paris: Editions de Minuit.

Bonnerot, Jean, ed. 1936. Charles Estienne, *La guide des chemins de France*. 2 vols. Paris: Champion.

Bony, Jean. 1983. *French Gothic Architecture of the Twelfth and Thirteenth Centuries*. Berkeley and Los Angeles: University of California Press.

Bordone, Benedetto. 1966. *Libro . . . de tutte l'isole del mondo*. With an introduction by R. A. Skelton. Facsimile reprint of 1528 edition, Venice. Amsterdam: Theatrum Orbis Terrarum Ltd.

Bouguereau, Maurice. 1966. *Le théâtre françoys*. Second Series, vol. 5. Facsimile edition, with introduction and notes by Père François de Dainville, of 1594 edition, Tours. Amsterdam: Theatrum Orbis Terrarum Ltd.

Bovelles, Charles de. 1542. *Livre singulier et utile, touchant à l'Art et Pratique de Geometrie*. Paris: Simone de Colines.

Bowen, Barbara C. 1991. "Rabelais and the Library of Saint Victor." In Barbara C. Bowen and Jerry C. Nash, eds., *Lapidary Inscriptions: Essays Offered to Donald A. Stone, Jr.*, 159–70. Lexington, KY: French Forum Monographs.

Bowie, Malcolm. 1987. *Freud, Proust, and Lacan: Theory and Fiction*. Cambridge, Eng.: Cambridge University Press.

Brault, Gerald J. 1966. "*Ung abysme de science*: On the Interrelation of Gargantua's Letter to Pantagruel." *Bibliothèque d'Humanisme et Renaissance* 28:615–32.

Brennan, Teresa. 1993. *History after Lacan*. London: Routledge.

Broc, Numa. 1980a. *La géographie de la Renaissance (1420–1620)*. Paris: Bibliothèque Nationale.

———. 1980b. "Quelle est la plus ancienne carte 'moderne' de France?" *Annales de géographie* 92 (Sept.–Oct. 1983): 513–29.

———. 1987. "Les cartes de France au XVIᵉ siècle." In Frank Lestringant and Jean-Claude Margolin, eds., *Voyager à la Renaissance*, 221–41. Paris: Aux Amateurs de Livres.

Brown, Cynthia J. 1988. "L'éveil d'une nouvelle conscience littéraire en France à la grande époque de transition technique: Jean Molinet et son moulin poétique." *Le moyen français* 22: 15–35.

———. 1991. "Text, Image, and Authorial Self-Consciousness in Late Medieval Paris." In Sandra Hindman, ed., *Printing the Written Word: The Social History of Books, circa 1450–1520*, 103–42. Ithaca, NY: Cornell University Press.

———. 1995. *Poets, Patrons, and Painters: Crisis of Authority in Late Medieval France*. Ithaca, NY: Cornell University Press.

Brown, Lloyd A. 1977. *The Story of Maps*. 1949. Reprint, New York: Dover Books.

Brun, Robert. 1930 and 1969. *Le livre français illustré de la Renaissance*. Paris: Alcan. Reprint, Paris: Picard.

———. 1934. "Un illustrateur méconnu: Oronce Finé." *Arts et métiers graphiques* 41 (May):51–57.

———. 1969. "Maquettes d'éditions d'Oronce Finé." In *Studia bibliographica in honorem Herman de La Fontaine Verwey*, 36–42. Amsterdam: Hertzberger.

Bruyne, Edgar de. 1946. *Etudes d'esthétique médiévale*. 3 vols. Bruges: de Tempel.

Bryson, Norman. 1988. "The Gaze in the Expanded Field." In Hal Foster, ed., *Vision and Visuality*, 87–114. Seattle, WA: Bay Press.

Buisseret, David. 1964. "Les *ingénieurs du roy* au temps de Henri IV." *Bulletin de la Section de Géographie* 77:13–84.

———. 1984. *Henry IV*. London: Allen & Unwin.

———. 1992a. Introduction and "Monarchs, Ministers, and Map in France before the Accession of Louis XIV." In David Buisseret, ed., *Monarchs, Ministers, and Maps: The Emergence of Cartography as a Tool of Government in Early Modern Europe*, 1–4, 99–123. Chicago: University of Chicago Press.

———. 1992b. "L'atelier cartographique de Sully à Bontin: L'oeuvre de Jacques Fougeu." Le XVIIᵉ Siècle 44, no. 1 (Jan.–Mar. 1992): 109–15.

Busson, Henri. 1993. *Le rationalisme dans la littérature française de la Renaissance*. Reprint, Paris: Vrin.

Butler, Pierce. 1940. *The Origin of Printing in Europe*. Chicago: University of Chicago Press.

Butor, Michel. 1968. *Essais sur les "Essais."* Paris: Gallimard.

Butsch, Albert Fidelis. 1969. *Handbook of Renaissance Ornament.* With new introduction and captions by Alfred Werner. New York: Dover Books.

Caesar, Julius. 1917. *The Gallic War.* Translated and edited by H. J. Edward. Loeb Classical Library. Cambridge, MA: Harvard University Press.

Cali, François. 1968. *L'ordre flamboyant.* Paris: Armand Colin.

Camille, Michael. 1992. "Reading the Printed Image: Illuminations and Woodcuts of the *Pèlerinage de la vie humaine* in the Fifteenth Century." In Sandra Hindman, ed., *Printing the Written Word: The Social History of Books, circa 1450–1520,* 259–91. Ithaca, NY: Cornell University Press.

Campbell, Tony. 1987a. *The Earliest Printed Maps.* Berkeley and Los Angeles: University of California Press.

———. 1987b. "Portolan Charts from the Late Thirteenth Century to 1500." In Harley and Woodward, 1987: 371–463.

Cassirer, Ernst. 1979. *The Individual and Cosmos in Renaissance Philosophy.* 1953. Reprint, Philadelphia: University of Pennsylvania Press.

Castelnuevo, E. 1966. Introduction and "Le maître du 'document humain.'" In *Fouquet.* Chefs d'oeuvres de l'art—Grands peintres. Paris and Milan: Fabbri Editori.

Catach, Nina. 1968. *L'orthographe française à l'époque de la Renaissance.* Geneva: Droz.

Cave, Terence. 1979. *The Cornucopian Text: Problems in Writing in the French Renaissance.* Oxford: Clarendon.

———. 1991. "Panurge, Pathelin, and Other Polyglots." In Barbara C. Bowen and Jerry C. Nash, eds., *Lapidary Inscriptions: Essays Offered to Donald A. Stone, Jr.,* 171–82. Lexington, KY: French Forum Monographs.

———. 1995. "Travelers and Others: Cultural Connections in the Works of Rabelais." In Jean-Claude Carron, ed., *François Rabelais: Critical Assessments,* 68–80. Baltimore: Johns Hopkins University Press.

Céard, Jean. 1982. "Jeu et divination à la Renaissance," In Philippe Ariès and Jean-Claude Margolin, eds., *Les jeux à la Renaissance,* 405–20. Actes du XXIIIe colloque international d'études humanistes. Paris: Vrin.

Céard, Jean, and Jean-Claude Margolin. 1986. *Rébus de la Renaissance: Des images qui parlent.* 2 vols. Paris: Maisonneuve & Larose.

Cerquiglini, Jacqueline. 1989. "Histoire, image: Accord et désaccord des sens à la fin du Moyen Age." *Littérature* no. 74 (May): 110–26.

Certeau, Michel de. 1982a. *La fable mystique.* Paris: Gallimard. In English as *The Mystic Fable 1: The Sixteenth and Seventeenth Centuries.* Translated by Michael B. Smith. Chicago: University of Chicago Press, 1992.

———. 1982b. "Lecture Absolue." In L. Dällenbach and Jean Ricardou, eds., *Problèmes actuels de la lecture,* 65–81. Clancier-Grènaud.

———. 1986. *Heterologies: Discourse on the Other.* Translated by Brian Massumi. Minneapolis: University of Minnesota Press.

———. 1987. "The Gaze Nicolas of Cusa." *Diacritics* 17, no. 3 (Fall): 2–38.

———. 1988. *La faiblesse de croire.* Paris: Editions du Seuil.

———. 1990. *L'invention du quotidien 1: Arts de faire.* Paris: Gallimard/Folio.

———. 1992. "Mysticism." Translated by Marsanne Brammer. *Diacritics* 22, no. 2: 11–25.

Certeau, Michel de, Dominique Julia, and Jacques Revel. 1975. *Une politique de la langue: La Révolution française et les patois*. Bibliothèque des histoires. Paris: Gallimard.

Champier, Symphorien. 1539. *Cathalogue des villes et citez assises es troys Gaulles, avec ung traitez des fleuves et fontaines, illustré de nouvelles figures*. Paris: Denys Janot.

Citton, Yves, and André Wyss. 1989. *Les doctrines orthographiques du XVIᵉ siècle en France*. Geneva: Droz.

Colie, Rosalie. 1966. *Paradoxica Epidemica: The Renaissance Tradition of Paradox*. Princeton: Princeton University Press.

Conley, Tom. 1978. "Cataparalysis." *Diacritics* 8, no. 3: 41–59.

———. 1988. "*De capsula totæ:* Lecture de 'Trois commerces.'" *L'esprit créateur* 28, no. 2 (Spring): 5–12.

———. 1991a. "Montaigne en montage: Mapping 'De la vanité' (III, ix)." *Montaigne Studies* 3, edited by Robert Cottrell: 224–48.

———. 1991b. "Pictogramme et critique littéraire." *Topique: Revue freudienne* 46: 269–79.

———. 1992a. *The Graphic Unconscious in Early Modern French Writing*. Cambridge, Eng.: Cambridge University Press.

———. 1992b. "Mapping Beroalde: Between *Le moyen de parvenir* (1610) and *Le palais des curieux* (1612)." In Michael Giordano, ed., "Studies on Beroalde de Verville," *Seventeenth Century Studies* no. 72: 83–107.

———. 1992c. "An 'Allegory of Prudence': Text and Icon of 'De la phisionomie.'" *Montaigne Studies* 4:156–79.

———. 1992d. "Pierre Boaistuau's Cosmographic Stage: Theater, Text, and Map." *Renaissance Drama* 33, no. 2, new series: 59–86.

Copjec, Joan. 1987. "The Orthopsychic Subject." *October* no. 49:53–71.

Cotgrave, Randle. 1950. *A Dictionarie of the French & English Tongues*. Facsimile of 1611 (London) edition with introduction by William S. Woods. Columbia: University of South Carolina Press.

Cottrell, Robert D. 1993. "Inmost Cravings: The Logic of Desire in the *Heptameron*." In Mary McKinley and John D. Lyons, eds., *Critical Tales: New Studies of the "Heptameron" and Early Modern Culture*, 3–24. Philadelphia: University of Pennsylvania Press.

Curtius, Ernst Robert. 1963. *European Literature and the Latin Middle Ages*. Translated by Williard Trask. New York: Harper.

Dainville, François de, S.J. 1940. *La géographie des humanistes*. Paris: Beauchesne.

———. 1961. "Le premier atlas de France: *Le théâtre Françoys* de M. Bouguereau, 1594." *Comité des travaux historiques et scientifiques: Actes du 85ᵉ congrès national des sociétés savantes, Chambéry-Annecy 1960, Section de Géographie*. Paris: Bibliothèque Nationale.

———. 1963. "L'évolution de l'atlas de France sous Louis XIII: *Théâtre géographique du royaume de France* des Le Clerc. 1619–32." In *Comité des travaux historiques et scientifiques: Actes du 87ᵉ congrès national des sociétés savantes, Poitiers, 1962. Section de Géographie*, 1–51. Paris: Bibliothèque Nationale.

———. 1964a. "Jean Jolivet's 'Description des Gaules.'" *Imago mundi* 18:45–52.

———. 1964b. *Le langage des géographes*. Paris: Picard.

———. 1968. *Le Dauphiné et ses confins vus par l'ingénieur d'Henri IV Jean de Beins.* Geneva: Droz.

———. 1970. "How Did Oronce Finé Draw His Large Map of France?" *Imago mundi* 24:49–55.

———. 1986. *La cartographie reflet de l'histoire.* Ed. M. Mollat du Jourdain et al. Geneva: Slatkine Reprints.

Danfrie, Philippe. 1597. *Declaration de l'usage du graphomètre.* Paris.

Davies, Hugh W. 1911. *Bernhard von Breydenbach and His Journey to the Holy Land, 1483–1484: A Bibliography.* London: Leighton.

Davis, Natalie Z. 1960. "Sixteenth Century French Arithmetics on the Business Life." *Journal of the History of Ideas* 21:18–48.

———. 1966. "Publisher Guillaume Rouillé, Businessman and Humanist." In R. J. Schoeck, ed., *Editing Sixteenth Century Texts,* 72–112. Toronto: University of Toronto Press.

Deleuze, Gilles. 1986. *Foucault.* Paris: Editions de Minuit.

———. 1988. *Le pli: Leibniz et le baroque.* Paris: Editions de Minuit.

Deleuze, Gilles, and Félix Guattari. 1976. *Rhizome.* Paris: Editions de Minuit.

———. 1980. *Mille plateaux: Capitalisme et schizophrénie 2.* Paris: Editions de Minuit.

Demerson, Guy. 1981. "Les calembours de Rabelais." In Halina Lewicka, ed., *Le comique verbal en France au XVIe siècle,* 73–93. Warsaw: Les Editions de l'Université.

———. 1986. *Rabelais.* Paris: Balland.

———. 1994. *Humanisme et facétie: Quinze études sur Rabelais.* Orléans-Caen: Editions Paradigme.

Derrida, Jacques. 1972a. *La dissémination.* Paris: Editions du Seuil.

———. 1972b. *Marges de la philosophie.* Paris: Editions de Minuit.

———. 1990. "La philosophie dans sa langue nationale" and "Les romans de Descartes ou l'économie des mots." In *Du droit à la philosophie,* 283–341. Paris: Galilée.

Descartes, René. 1898–1910. *Oeuvres complètes.* Edited by Charles Adam and Paul Tannery. 10 vols. Paris: Léopold Cerf.

Dickason, Olive. 1984. *The Myth of the Savage in the New World.* Alberta, Canada: University of Alberta Press.

Dilke, O. A. W. 1987. "Itineraries and Geographical Maps in the Early and Late Roman Empires." In Harley and Woodward 1987:234–57.

Diner, Judith Bruskin, trans. and ed. 1990. *The One Hundred New Tales (Les cent nouvelles nouvelles).* Garland Library of Medieval Literature 30, series B. New York and London: Garland Publishing.

Douglas, Mary. 1984. *Purity and Danger: An Analysis of the Concepts of Pollution and Taboo.* 1966. Reprint, London: Ark Paperbacks.

Drapeyron, Ludovic. 1889. "L'image de la France sous les dernier Valois (1525–89) et sous les premiers Bourbons (1589–1682)." *Revue de géographie* 29:1–15.

Dubois, Claude-Gilbert. 1977. *La conception de l'histoire en France au XVIe siècle.* Paris: Nizet.

———. 1985. *L'imaginaire de la Renaissance.* Paris: Presses Universitaires de France.

———. 1992. *Mots et règles, jeux et délires: Etudes sur l'imaginaire verbal au XVIe siècle.* Preface by Gilbert Durand. Caen: Editions Paradigme.

Dubuis, Roger. 1973. *Les cent nouvelles nouvelles et la tradition de la nouvelle en France au Moyen Age*. Grenoble: Presses Universitaires de Grenoble.

Dunn, Kevin. 1991. "'A Great City Is a Great Solitude': Descartes's Urban Pastoral." *Yale French Studies*, no. 80:93–107.

Edgerton, Samuel Y., Jr. 1975. *The Renaissance Rediscovery of Linear Perspective*. New York: Basic Books.

———. 1987. "From Mental Matrix to 'Mappamundi' to Christian Empire: The Heritage of Ptolemaic Cartography in the Renaissance." In David Woodward, ed., *Art and Cartography: Six Historical Essays*, 10–50. Chicago: University of Chicago Press.

———. 1991. *The Heritage of Giotto's Geometry: Art and Science on the Eve of the Scientific Revolution*. Ithaca, NY: Cornell University Press.

Edney, Matthew H. 1993. "Cartography without 'Progress': Reinterpreting the Nature and Historical Development of Mapmaking." *Cartographica* 30, no. 2–3 (Summer-Autumn): 54–68.

Ehrensweig, Anton. 1973. *The Hidden Order of Art*. Berkeley and Los Angeles: University of California Press.

Eisenstein, Elizabeth L. 1980. *The Printing Press as an Agent of Change: Communications and Cultural Transformations in Early Modern Europe*. 2 vols. in 1. Cambridge, Eng.: Cambridge University Press.

———. 1993. *The Printing Revolution of Early Modern Europe*. Cambridge, Eng.: Canto Books, Cambridge University Press. [Abbreviated edition of *The Printing Press . . .*]

Estienne, Charles. 1552. *Le guide des chemins pour aller & venir par tout le Royaume de France & autres païs circonvoisins. Reveue & corrigée outre les precedentes impressions*. Lyon: Benoist Rigaud & Ian Saugram.

Fausett, David. 1993. *Writing the New World: Imaginary Voyages and Utopias of the Great Southern Land*. Syracuse, NY: Syracuse University Press.

Febvre, Lucien. 1968. *Le problème de l'incroyance au XVIᵉ siècle*. 1943. Reprint, Paris: Albin Michel.

Finé, Oronce. 1532. *Protomathesis: Opus uarium, ac scitu non minus utile quàm iucundum, nunc primùm in lucem foeliciter emissium . . .* Paris: Gerardi Morrhij & Ioannis Petri.

———. 1551. *Le sphère du monde, proprement ditte cosmographie, composee nouvellement en françois, et divisee en cinq livres, comprenans la premiere partie de l'astronomie, & les principes universels de la geographie et hydrographie. Avec une epistre, touchant la dignité, perfection & utilité des sciences mathematiques*. Paris: Michel de Vascosan, demeurant rue Saint Iaques à la fontaine.

———. 1556. *Regii mathematicarum professori, De rebus mathematicus, hactanus desideratis, Libri IIII . . .* Lutetiae Parisiiorum, Anno Christi Servatoris M. D. LVI (1556). Ex Officina Michaëlis Vascosani, via Jacobæ ad insigne Fontis. Cum Privilegio Regis.

Focillon, Henri. 1936. "Le style monumental dans l'art de Jean Fouquet." *Gazette des Beaux Arts*, 1936.

———. 1938. *L'art d'Occident*. 2 vols. Paris: Armand Colin.

———. 1939. *Vie des formes*. Paris: Presses Universitaires de France. Reprint 1968.

Fontaine, Marie-Madeleine. 1984. "Quaresmeprenant: L'image littéraire et la contestation de l'analogie médicale." In James A. Coleman and Christine Scollen-Jimack, eds., *Rabelais in Glasgow*. Proceedings of Glasgow Colloquium, December 1983, 87–112. Glasgow: Glasgow University Printing Unit.

Foucault, Michel. 1966. *Les mots et les choses: Une archéologie des sciences humaines.* Paris: Gallimard.

———. 1973. *Ceci n'est pas une pipe.* Montpellier: Fata Morgana. In English as *This Is Not a Pipe.* Translated by James Harkness. Berkeley and Los Angeles: University of California Press, 1982.

Francastel, Pierre. 1967. *La figure et le lieu: L'ordre visuel du quattrocento.* Paris: Gallimard.

Frankl, Victor. 1963. *El 'Antijovio' de Gonzalo Jiménez de Quesada y las concepciones de realidad y verdad en la epoca de la contrareforma y del manierismo.* Madrid: Ediciones Cultura Hispanica.

Friedlander, Walter. 1957. *Mannerism and Anti-Mannerism in Italian Art.* 1924. Reprint, New York: Columbia University Press.

Friedrich, Hugo. 1968. *Montaigne.* Translated by Robert Rovini. Paris: Gallimard.

Frye, Northrop. 1969. *Anatomy of Criticism.* New York: Atheneum.

Fumée, Martin/López de Gómara, Francisco. 1587. *Histoire generalle des Indes . . . augmentee en ceste cinquiesme edition de la description de la nouvelle Espagne, & de la grande ville de Mexicque, autrement nommee Tenuctilan: composee en espagnol par François Lopez de Gomara, & traduite en françois par le S. de Genillé Mart. Fumée.* Paris: M. Sonnius.

Gallois, Lucien. 1890a. *De Orontio Finaeo Gallico geographo . . .* Paris: Leroux.

———. 1890b. *Les géographes allemands de la Renaissance.* Paris: Leroux.

———. 1891. "Les origines de la carte de France: La carte d'Oronce Finé." *Bulletin de géographie historique et descriptive* 6:18–34.

———. 1935. "La grande carte de France d'Oronce Finé." *Annales de géographie* 44:337–48.

Gandelman, Claude. 1991. *Reading Pictures, Viewing Texts.* Bloomington: Indiana University Press.

Gauna, Max. 1992. *Upwellings: First Expressions of Unbelief in the Printed Literature of the French Renaissance.* London: Associated University Presses.

Geertz, Clifford. 1990. *Writers and Lives: The Anthropologist as Author.* Princeton: Princeton University Press.

Genette, Gérard. 1966. *Figures I.* Paris: Editions du Seuil.

———. 1972. *Figures III.* Paris: Editions du Seuil.

Gillies, John. 1994. *Shakespeare and the Geography of Difference.* Cambridge, Eng.: Cambridge University Press.

Gingerich, Owen, ed. 1975. *The Nature of Scientific Discovery: A Symposium Commemorating the 500th Aniversary of the Birth of Nicolaus Copernicus.* Washington, DC: Smithsonian Institution.

Glauser, Alfred. 1966. *Rabelais créateur.* Paris: Nizet.

———. 1972. *Montaigne paradoxal.* Paris: Nizet.

Godzich, Wlad, and Jeffrey Kittay. 1987. *The Emergence of Prose: An Essay in Prosaics.* Minneapolis: University of Minnesota Press.

Gombrich, Ernst. 1978. *Symbolic Images and the Art of the Renaissance.* 2 vols. New York: Phaidon.

Goux, Jean-Joseph. 1985. "Descartes et la perspective." *L'esprit créateur* 25, no. 1: 10–20.

Graham, Victor E. 1978. "Gabriel Syméoni et le rêve impérial des rois de France." In Louis Terreaux, ed., *Culture et pouvoir au temps de l'humanisme et de la Renaissance*, 299–309. Paris: Champion.

Gray, Floyd. 1974. *Rabelais et l'écriture*. Paris: Nizet.

———. 1994. *Rabelais et le comique de la discontinuité*. Paris: Champion.

Greenblatt, Stephen. 1980. *Renaissance Self-Fashioning: From More to Shakespeare*. Chicago: University of Chicago Press.

———. 1991. *Marvelous Possessions: The Wonder of the New World*. Chicago: University of Chicago Press.

Greenhood, David. 1964. *Mapping*, rev. ed. Chicago: University of Chicago Press.

Grodecki, Catherine. 1974. "Le graveur Lyon Davent, illustrateur de Nicolas de Nicolaï." *Bibliothèque d'Humanisme et Renaissance* 36, no. 2 (1974): 347–50.

Grynaeus, Simon. 1532. *Novus Orbis Regionum ac Insularum veteribus incognitarum, unò cum tabula cosmographica, & aliquot alis consimilis argumenti libellis, quorum omnium catalogus sequenti patebit pagina . . .* Paris: Jehan Petit.

Guattari, Félix. 1989. *Cartographies schizoanalytiques*. Paris: Galilée.

Guillaume, Jean. 1985. "L'escalier à vis dans l'archecture de la Renaissance." In Jean Guillaume, ed., *L'escalier dans l'architecture de la Renaissance*, 24–47. Paris: Picard.

Hair, P. J. H. 1982. "A Note on Thevet's Unpublished Maps of Overseas Islands." *Terrae Incognitae* 14:105–16.

Halberstadt-Freud, Hendrika C. 1991. *Freud, Proust, Perversion, and Love*. Amsterdam and Lisse: Swets & Zeitlinger.

Hale, John R. 1964. "The Argument of Some Military Title Pages of the Renaissance." *The Newberry Library Bulletin* 6, no. 4 (March): 91–102.

Hallyn, Fernand. 1988. "Le paradoxe de la souveraineté." In Jean Céard and Jean-Claude Margolin, eds., *Etudes Rabelaisiennes 21: Rabelais en son demi-millénaire. Acte du Colloque International de Tours, 1984*, 339–45. Geneva: Droz.

———. 1992. "Un artifice de peu de poids . . . (Poésie expérimentale au XVIIe siècle)." *Théorie Littérature Enseignement* 10 (Fall): 19–38.

Hamon, P. 1975. "Oronce Finé." *Dictionnaire de biographie française* 13:1370–71.

Hampton, Timothy. 1993. "'Turkish Dogs': Rabelais, Erasmus, and the Rhetoric of Alterity." *Representations* no. 41 (Winter): 58–82.

Hanke, Lewis. 1959. *Aristotle and the American Indians: A Study in Race Prejudice in the Modern World*. Bloomington: Indiana University Press.

———. 1974. *All Mankind Is One: A Study of the Disputation between Bartolomé de Las Casas and Juan Ginés de Sepúlveda in 1550 on the Intellectual and Religious Capacity of the American Indians*. DeKalb: Northern Illinois University Press.

Harley, J. Brian. 1988a. "Maps, Knowledge, and Power." In Denis Cosgrove and Stephen J. Daniels, eds., *The Iconography of Landscape*, 277–312. Cambridge, Eng.: Cambridge University Press.

———. 1988b. "Silences and Secrecy: The Hidden Agenda of Cartography in Early Modern Europe." *Imago mundi* 40:57–76.

———. 1989. "Deconstructing the Map." *Cartographica* 26, no. 2 (Summer): 1–20.

———. 1990a. *Maps and the Columbian Encounter*. Milwaukee, WI: The Golda Meir Library.

———. 1990b. "Texts and Contexts in the Interpretation of Early Maps." In David Buisseret, ed., *From Sea Charts to Satellite Images*, 3–15. Chicago: University of Chicago Press.

Harley, J. Brian, and M. J. Blakemore. 1986. "Concepts in the History of Cartography: A Review and Perspective." *Cartographica*. Monograph 26.

Harvey, David. 1989. *The Condition of Postmodernity*. London: Basil Blackwell.

Harvey, P. D. A. 1987. "Local and Regional Cartography in Medieval Europe." In Harley and Woodward 1987:464–501.

Helgerson, Richard. 1986. "The Land Speaks: Cartography, Chorography, and Subversion in Renaissance England." *Representations* 16 (Fall): 50–85.

———. 1992. *Forms of Nationhood: The Elizabethan Writing of England*. Chicago: University of Chicago Press.

Heller, Henry. 1971. "Marguerite de Navarre and the Reformers of Meaux." *Bibliothèque d'Humanisme et Renaissance* 33:279–89.

Henry, Patrick. 1987. *Montaigne in Dialogue: Censorship and Defensive Writing*. Saratoga, CA: Anma Libri.

Hervé, Roger. 1955. "L'oeuvre cartographique de Nicolas de Nicolay et d'Antoine de Laval (1544–1619)." *Bulletin de la Section de Géographie* 68:224–63.

Hillard, Denise, and Emmanuel Poulle. 1971. "Oronce Finé et l'horloge plantétaire de la bibliothèque Sainte–Geneviève." *Bibliothèque d'Humanisme et Renaissance* 33:311–51.

Hjelmslev, Louis. 1969. *Prolegomena to a Theory of Language*. Translated by Francis J. Whitfield. Madison: University of Wisconsin Press. In French as *Essais linguistiques*. Paris: Minuit 1971.

Hugo, Victor. 1865. *William Shakespeare*. In *Oeuvres complètes: Philosophie. II.* Paris: Hetzel-Quantin.

Ingegno, Alfonso. 1988. "The New Philosophy of Nature." In Quentin Skinner, ed. *The Cambridge History of Renaissance Philosophy*, 236–63. Cambridge, Eng.: Cambridge University Press.

Jacob, Christian. 1992. *L'empire des cartes: Approche théorique de la cartographie à travers l'histoire*. Paris: Albin Michel.

Jacob, P. L., ed. 1858. *Les cent nouvelles nouvelles*. Paris: Adolphe Delahays.

Jay, Martin. 1988. "Scopic Regimes of Modernity." In Hal Foster, ed., *Vision and Visuality*, 3–28. Seattle, WA: Bay Press.

Jeanneret, Michel. 1981. "Du mystère à la mystification: Le sens caché à la Renaissance et dans Rabelais." *Versants* 2 (Winter): 3–21.

———. 1982. "Quand la fable se met à table: Nourriture et structure narrative dans le *Quart livre*." *Poétique* 54 (April): 163–80.

———. 1987. *Des mets et des mots: Banquets et propos de table à la Renaissance*. Paris: José Corti.

———. 1991. "Débordements rabelaisiens." *Nouvelle revue de psychanalyse* 42:130–52.

———. 1993. "Modular Narrative and the Crisis of Interpretation." In John D. Lyons and Mary B. McKinley, eds., *Critical Tales: New Studies of the Heptameron and Early Modern Culture*, 85–103. Philadelphia: University of Philadelphia Press.

———. 1994. *Le défi du sens*. Orléans-Caen: Editions Paradigme.

Jourda, Pierre, ed. 1965. *Conteurs français du XVIᵉ siècle*. Paris: Gallimard-Pléiade.

Kantorowicz, Ernst. 1956. *The King's Two Bodies: A Study in Medieval Political Theology.* Princeton: Princeton University Press.

Karrow, Robert W., Jr. 1993. *Mapmakers of the Sixteenth Century and Their Maps.* Chicago: Speculum Orbis Press for the Newberry Library.

King, James E. 1949. *Science and Rationalism in the Government of Louis XIV, 1661–1683.* Baltimore: Johns Hopkins University Press.

Kinser, Samuel. 1990. *Rabelais's Carnival.* Berkeley and Los Angeles: University of California Press.

Kish, George. 1965. "The Cosmographic Heart: Cordiform Maps of the Sixteenth Century." *Imago Mundi* 19:13–21.

Knoespel, Kenneth J. 1987. "The Narrative Matter of Mathematics: John Dee's Preface to the *Elements* of Euclid of Megara (1570)." *Philological Quarterly.* 60:26–46.

Konvitz, Josef. 1987. *Cartography in France, 1600–1848.* Chicago: University of Chicago Press.

Kritzman, Lawrence. 1991. *The Rhetoric of Sexuality and the Literature of the French Renaissance.* Cambridge, Eng.: Cambridge University Press.

Kuhn, David. 1967. *La poétique de François Villon.* Paris: Armand Colin.

Lacan, Jacques. 1966. *Ecrits.* Paris: Editions du Seuil.

———. 1973. *Les quatre concepts fondamentaux de la psychanalyse.* Paris: Editions du Seuil.

La Charité, Raymond C. 1979. "Réflexion-divertissement et intertextualité: Rabelais et l'Ecolier limousin." In Floyd Gray and Marcel Tetel, eds., *Textes et intertextes: Etudes sur le XVIᵉ siècle pour Alfred Glauser,* 93–103. Paris: Nizet.

Lafond, Jean, ed. 1984. *Les formes brèves de la prose et le discours discontinu (XVIᵉ–XVIIᵉ siècles).* Paris: Vrin.

Lancelot du Voisin, Seigneur de La Popelinière. 1582. *Les trois mondes.* Paris: L'Huillier.

Langlois, Charles V. 1923. "Etudes sur deux cartes d'Oronce Finé de 1531 et 1536." *Journal de la Société des Américanistes de Paris* 15, new series: 83–97.

Leclerc, Jean. 1619. *Le théâtre géographique du royaume de France.* Paris.

Lecoq, Anne-Marie. 1987. *François Iᵉʳ imaginaire.* Paris: Editions Macula.

Lefranc, Abel. 1905. *Les navigations de Pantagruel.* Paris: Henri Leclerc.

Le Goff, Jacques. 1991. *L'imaginaire médiéval.* Paris: Gallimard.

Léry, Jean de. 1578 and 1580. *Histoire d'un voyage faict en la terre du Brésil.* Geneva: Chuppin. In English as *History of a Voyage Made to the Land of Brazil,* translated with an introduction by Janet Whatley. Berkeley and Los Angeles: University of California Press, 1990.

Lestringant, Frank. 1980a. "Calvinistes et cannibales." *Bulletin de la Société du Protestantisme français* 126:9–26.

———. 1980b. "Insulaires." In *Cartes et figures de la terre,* 460–70. Paris: Catalogue du Centre Georges-Pompidou.

———. 1980c. "Suivre la guide." In *Cartes et figures de la terre,* 424–35. Paris: Catalogue du Centre Georges-Pompidou.

———. 1981. "Fictions de l'espace brésilien à la Renaissance: L'exemple de Guanabara." In Christian Jacob and Frank Lestringant, eds., *Arts et légendes d'espaces: Figures du voyage et rhétoriques du monde,* 205–56. Paris: Pressses de l'Ecole Normale Supérieure.

———. 1982. "Rabelais et le récit toponymique." Reprinted in *Ecrire le monde à la Renaissance*, 109–27. Orléans-Caen: Editions Paradigme, 1993.

———. 1984. "Théâtres de cruauté." In André Marchand and Alain Parent, eds., *La Renaissance et le nouveau monde*, 206–10. Montreal: Bibliothèque nationale.

———. 1985a. "Jean Bodin, cosmographe." *Actes du Colloque interdisciplinaire d'Angers* (24–27 May 1984), 133–45. Angers: Presses Universitaires d'Angers. Reprinted in *Ecrire le monde à la Renaissance*, 277–90. Orléans-Caen: Editions Paradigme.

———. 1985b. "Millénarisme et l'age d'or." *Réformes, enracinement socio-culturel*, 25–42. Paris: Guy Trédaniel.

———. 1988a. "L'insulaire de Rabelais, ou la fiction en archipel: Pour une lecture topographique du Quart livre." In Jean Céard and Jean-Claude Margolin, eds., *Etudes Rabelaisiennes* 21, Rabelais en son demi-millénaire, *Actes du Colloque de Tours* (24–28 December 1984), 249–74. Geneva: Droz. Reprinted in Lestringant 1993: 159–85.

———. 1988b. "Les Indiens antérieurs (1575–1615): Du Plessis-Mornay, Lescarbot, De Laet, Claude d'Abbeville." In Gilles Thérien, ed., *Les figures de l'indien*, 51–85. Montreal: Cahiers de l'Université de Montréal.

———. 1990. *Le Huguenot et le sauvage*. Paris: Aux Amateurs de Livres.

———. 1991a. *André Thevet: Cosmographe des derniers Valois*. Travaux d'Humanisme et Renaissance, 251. Geneva: Droz.

———. 1991b. *L'atelier du cosmographe ou l'image du monde à la Renaissance*. Paris: Albin Michel.

———. 1991c. "Crisis of Cosmography at the End of the Renaissance." In Philippe Desan, ed., *Humanism in Crisis: The Decline of the French Renaissance*, 153–79. Ann Arbor: University of Michigan Press. In French in Lestringant 1993: 319–40.

———. 1993. *Ecrire le monde à la Renaissance: Quinze études sur Rabelais, Postel, Bodin, et la littérature géographique*. Orléans-Caen: Editions Paradigme.

Lévi-Strauss, Claude. 1955. *Tristes Tropiques*. Paris: Plon.

———. 1958. *Anthropologie structurale 1*. Paris: Plon.

———. 1962. *Mythologiques 1: Le cru et le cuit*. Paris: Plon.

———. 1985. *La potière jalouse*. Paris: Plon.

———. 1988. *Le regard de loin*. Paris: Plon.

———. 1991. *Histoire de lynx*. Paris: Plon.

———. 1993. *Regarder écouter lire*. Paris: Plon.

Lindberg, David C. 1976. *Theories of Vision from Al'Kindi to Kepler*. Chicago: University of Chicago Press.

———. 1992. *The Beginnings of Western Science: The European Scientific Tradition in Philosophical, Religious, and Institutional Context, 600 B.C. to A.D. 1450*. Chicago: University of Chicago Press.

Longeon, Claude, ed. 1990. *Premiers combats pour la langue française*. Le livre de poche. Paris: Librairie Générale Française.

López de Gómara, Francisco. 1569. *Histoire generalle des Indes occidentalles & Terres neuves, qui iusques à present ont esté descouvertes, traduite en françois par M. Fumée Sieur Marly le Chastel*. Paris: B. Turrisan.

———. 1943. *Historia de la conquista de Mexico.* 2 vols. Reprint, Mexico City: Pedro Robredo.

Lorian, Alexandre. 1973. *Tendances stylistiques de la prose narrative française au XVIe siècle.* Paris: Klincksieck.

Lucian of Samosata. 1961. *Dialogues 7.* Edited and translated by M. D. MacLeod. Cambridge, MA, and London: Loeb Classical Library, Harvard University Press and William Heinemann.

Lyons, John D. 1989. *Exemplum: The Rhetoric of Example in Early Modern France and Italy.* Princeton: Princeton University Press.

Lyotard, Jean-François. 1973. *Discours, figure.* Paris: Klincksieck.

———. 1983. *Le différend.* Paris: Editions de Minuit.

———. 1985. *Le post-moderne expliqué aux enfants.* Paris: Galilée.

MacCannell, Dean. 1976. *The Tourist: A New Theory of the Leisure Class.* New York: Schocken.

Macpherson, C. B. 1962. *The Political Theory of Possessive Individualism: Hobbes to Locke.* New York: Oxford University Press.

Macrobius, Ambrosius. 1483. *In somnium Scipionis expositio.* Brescia.

Mahn-Lot, Marianne. 1982. *Bartolomé de Las Casas et le droit des Indiens.* Paris: Payot.

Marchand, André, and Alain Parent, eds., 1984. *La Renaissance et le nouveau monde.* Montreal: Bibliothèque nationale.

Marin, Louis. 1973. *Utopiques: Jeux d'espace.* Paris: Editions de Minuit.

———. 1981a. "Les fins de l'interprétation ou les traversées du regard dans le sublime d'une tempête." In *Les fins de l'homme à partir du travail de Jacques Derrida,* 317–44. Paris: Galilée.

———. 1981b. *Le portrait du roi.* Paris: Editions de Minuit.

———. 1988. *The Portrait of the King.* Translated by Martha M. Houle. Minneapolis: University of Minnesota Press. Translation of Marin 1981b.

———. 1993. *Des pouvoirs de l'image.* Paris: Editions du Seuil.

Martin, Henri-Jean. 1994. *The History and Power of Writing.* Translated by Lydia G. Cochrane. Chicago: University of Chicago Press.

Martineau, Christine, Michel Veissière, and Henry Heller, eds. 1975 and 1979. *Correspondance entre Marguerite de Navarre et Guillaume Briçonnet.* 2 vols. Travaux d'humanisme et Renaissance. Geneva: Droz.

Massin. 1973. *Lettre et image.* Paris: Gallimard.

Mathieu-Castellani, Gisèle. 1988a. "La parleuse muette." *L'esprit créateur* 28, no. 2: 25–35.

———. 1988b. *Montaigne, l'écriture de l'essai.* Paris: Presses Universitaires de France.

———. 1990. "Anatomie de l'emblème." *Littérature* no. 78 (May): 3–21.

———. 1991. *Le corps de Jézabel.* Paris: Presses Universitaires de France.

Mauss, Marcel. 1969. *Oeuvres.* 3 vols. Paris: Editions de Minuit.

———. 1973. *Essais de sociologie et anthropologie.* With an introduction by Claude Lévi-Strauss. Paris: Plon.

McDougall, Joyce. 1989. *Theaters of the Body.* New York: Norton.

———. 1991. *Theaters of the Mind.* New York: Brunner/Mazel.

———. 1992. *Plea for a Measure of Abnormality.* New York: Brunner/Mazel.

McKinley, Mary. 1981. *Words in a Corner: Studies in Montaigne's Latin Quotations.*
Lexington, KY: French Forum Monographs 26.

Meiss, Millard. 1974. *French Painting in the Time of the Duc de Berry.* 2 vols. New
York: Braziller.

Meschonnic, Henri. 1975. *Le signe et le poème.* Paris: Gallimard.

Métraux, Alfred. 1928. *La religion des Tupinamba et ses rapports avec celle des autres
tribus tupi-guarani.* Bibliothèque des Hautes Etudes en Sciences religieuses, 45.
Paris: Ernest Leroux.

Metz, Christian. 1991. *L'énonciation impersonnelle ou le site du film.* Paris: Klincksieck.

Mijolla-Mellor, Sophie de. 1991. "Le travail de pensée dans l'interprétation." *Topique:
Revue freudienne* 46:193–203.

Miller, Orson K. 1971. *The Mushrooms of North America.* New York: Dutton.

Mitchell, William. 1992. *The Reconfigured Eye.* Cambridge, MA: MIT Press.

Molinet, Jean. 1933. *Les faictz et dictz.* Ed. Noël Dupire, 3 vols. Paris: Société des
Anciens Textes Français.

Mollat du Jourdain, Michel, and Monique de la Roncière. 1984. *Sea Charts of the Early
Explorers, Thirteenth to the Seventeenth Century.* New York: Thames & Hudson.

Montaigne, Michel de. 1962. *Oeuvres complètes.* Edited by Albert Thibaudet and
Maurice Rat. Paris: Gallimard-Pléiade.

———. 1580–1592. *Les Essais.* Edited under the direction of Pierre Villey and with a
preface by V.-L. Saulnier. Reprint, Paris: Quadrige/Presses Universitaires de France,
1988.

Mortimer, Ruth. 1964. *Harvard College Library Department of Printing and Graphics
Arts, Catalogue of Books and Manuscripts.* Part I: *French 16th Century Books.*
Cambridge, MA: Belnap Press of Harvard University Press.

Naudé, Françoise. 1992. *Reconnaissance du nouveau monde et cosmographie à la
Renaissance.* Problemata Iberoamericana 2. Kassel: Reichenberger.

Nebenzahl, Kenneth. 1986. *Maps of the Holy Land: Images of Terra Sancta through Two
Millenia.* New York: Abbeville Press.

———. 1990. *Atlas of Columbus and the Great Discoveries.* Chicago: Rand McNally.

Nerlich, Michael. 1988. *Ideology of Adventure: Studies in Modern Consciousness.* 2 vols.
Translated by Ruth Crowley. Minneapolis: University of Minnesota Press.

Nicolaï, Nicolas de. 1568. *Les navigations, peregrinations et voyages, faicts en la
Turquie . . . contenants plusieurs singularitez que l'auteur y a veu & observé. . . .*
Lyons: Roville.

Nordenskiöld, Adolf Erik. 1973. *Facsimile-Atlas to the Early History of Cartography with
Reproductions of the Most Important Maps Printed in the XV and XVI Centuries.*
With a new introduction by J. B. Post. New York: Dover Books.

O'Neill, John. 1988. *Essaying Montaigne: A Study of the Renaissance Institution of
Writing and Reading.* London: Routledge & Kegan Paul.

Ong, Walter J., S.J. 1983. *Ramus, Method, and the Decay of Dialogue.* 1958. Reprint,
Cambridge, MA: Harvard University Press.

———. 1959. "From Allegory to Diagram in the Renaissance Mind." *Journal of
Aesthetics and Art Criticism* 17:423–40.

Pächt, Otto. 1940–41. "Jean Fouquet: A Study of His Style." *Journal of the Warburg
and Courtault Institutes* 4:85ff.

————. 1986. *Book Illumination in the Middle Ages: An Introduction.* Translated by Kay Davenport. Oxford: Oxford University Press/Harvey Miller Publishers.

Pagden, Anthony. 1982. *The Fall of Natural Man: The American Indian and the Origins of Comparative Ethnography.* Cambridge, Eng.: Cambridge University Press.

Panofsky, Erwin. 1955. *Meaning in the Visual Arts.* New York: Doubleday/Anchor Books.

————. 1971. *Early Netherlandish Painting.* 2 vols. Reprint, New York: Harper Torchbooks.

————. 1972. *Renaissance and Renascences in Western Art.* 1960. Reprint, New York: Harper & Row.

————. 1991. *Perspective as Symbolic Form.* Translated by Christopher S. Wood. Cambridge, MA: MIT Press.

Pastoureau, Mireille. 1980. "Les atlas imprimés en France avant 1700." *Imago mundi* 32:45–72.

————. 1984. *Les atlas français (XVIᵉ-XVIIᵉ siècles).* Paris: Bibliothèque nationale.

————. 1992. *Voies océanes: Cartes marines et grandes découvertes.* Paris: Bibliothèque nationale.

Peurbach, Georg von. 1515. *Theoricarum nouarum textus.* Paris: M. Lesclencher for J. Petit and R. Chandière. Paris.

Poulle, Emmanuel. 1978. "Oronce Finé." *Dictionary of Scientific Biography* 15:153–57.

Proust, Marcel. 1954. *A la recherche du temps perdu.* Edited by Pierre Clarac and André Ferré. 3 vols. Paris: Gallimard/Pléiade.

Ptolemy, Claudius. 1991. *The Geography.* Translated and edited by Edward Luther Stevenson. With an Introduction by Joseph Fischer, S.J. 1460. Reprint, New York: Dover; reprint of New York Public Library, 1932.

Rabelais, François. 1955. *Oeuvres complètes.* Edited by Jacques Boulenger. Paris: Gallimard/Pléiade.

Ranum, Orest. 1980. *Artisans of Glory: Writers and Historical Thought in Seventeenth Century France.* Chapel Hill: University of North Carolina Press.

Rasmussen, Jens. 1958. *La prose narrative en France au XVᵉ siècle.* Copenhagen: Munksgaard.

Renucci, Toussaint. 1943. Critical Edition of Gabriele Symeone, *Description de la Limaigne d'Auvergne.* Paris: Didier.

————. 1944. *Un aventurier des lettres au XVIᵉ siècle: Gabriele Symeoni, florentin (1509–1570).* Paris: Didier.

Riffaterre, Michael. 1994. "L'illusion d'ekphrasis." In Gisèle Mathieu-Castellani, ed., *La pensée de l'image: Signification et figuration dans le texte et dans le peinture,* 211–29. Paris: Presses de l'Université de Paris-VIII.

Rigolot, François. 1976. "Pantagruélisme et cratylisme." *Etudes Rabelaisiennes* 13:115–32.

————. 1977. *Poétique et onomastique: L'exemple de la Renaissance.* Geneva: Droz.

————. 1982. *Le texte de la Renaissance.* Geneva: Droz.

————. 1988. *Les métamorphoses de Montaigne.* Paris: Presses Universitaires de France.

Ripa, Caesare. 1624. *Iconologia.* 2 vols. Padua.

Rose, Gillian. 1992. *Feminism and Geography.* Minneapolis: University of Minnesota Press.

Rosolato, Guy. 1978. *La relation d'inconnu.* Paris: Gallimard.

———. 1985. *Eléments de l'interprétation.* Paris: Gallimard.

———. 1993. *Pour une psychanalyse exploratrice dans la culture.* Paris: Presses Universitaires de France.

Ross, Richard. 1971. "Studies on Oronce Finé (1494–1555)." Ph.D. diss., Columbia University.

———. 1975. "Oronce Finé's *De Sinibus Libri II.*" *Isis* 66:379–86.

Saenger, Paul. 1977. "Geoffroy Tory et la nomenclature des écritures livresques françaises au XVe siècle." *Le Moyen Age* 3–4:494–520.

———. 1982. "Silent Reading: Its Impact on Late Medieval Script and Society." *Viator* 13:367–414.

———. 1989. "Physiologie de la lecture et séparation des mots." *Annales E. S. C.* 939–52.

Saenger, Paul, and Michael Heinlen. 1991. "Incunable Description and Its Implications for the Analysis of Fifteenth-Century Reading Habits." In Sandra Hindman, ed., *Printing the Written Word: The Social History of Books, circa 1450–1520,* 225–58. Ithaca, NY: Cornell University Press.

Sahlins, Marshall. 1972. *Stone Age Economics.* Chicago and New York: Aldine-Atherton.

Sanfaçon, Roland. 1971. *L'architecture flamboyante en France.* Montreal: Presses de l'Université de Laval.

Sansi, Danièle. 1992. "Texte et image dans les incunables français." *Médiévales* nos. 22–23:47–70.

Saulnier, Verdun-L. 1957. *Le dessein de Rabelais.* Paris: Société d'Edition d'Enseignement Supérieure.

Sayce, Richard A. 1972. *The Essays of Montaigne: A Critical Exploration.* London: Northwestern University Press.

Schapiro, Meyer. 1977. *Romanesque Art.* New York: Braziller.

Schefer, Jean Louis. 1976. *Paolo Uccello: Le déluge, la peste.* Paris: Galilée.

Schlesinger, Roger, and Arthur P. Stabler. 1986. *André Thevet's North America: A Sixteenth-Century View.* Kingston and Montreal: McGill-Queen's University Press.

Schulz, Juergen. 1978. "Jacobo de' Barbari's View of Venice: Map Making, City Views, and Moralized Geography before the Year 1500." *The Art Bulletin* 60:425–74.

Schwab, Gabriele. 1984. "Genesis of the Subject: Imaginary Functions and Poetic Language." *New Literary History* 15 (Spring): 453–74.

Screech, M. A. 1958. *The Rabelaisian Marriage.* London: Edward Arnold.

———. 1979. *Rabelais.* Ithaca, NY: Cornell University Press.

Shirley, Rodney W. 1987. *The Mapping of the World: Early Printed World Maps, 1472–1700.* London: Holland Press.

Signot, Jacques. 1515. *La totale et vraie description de tous les passages, lieux et détroits par lesquelz on veut facilement entrer et passer des parties de Gaule que nous disons maintenant France ès parties d'Italie.* Lyon: Benoist Rigaud.

Simonin, Michel. 1987. "Les élites chorographes ou de la 'description de la France' dans la *La cosmographie universelle* de Belleforest." In Jean Céard and Jean-Claude Margolin, eds. *Voyager à la Renaissance,* 433–51. Paris: Maisonneuve et Larose.

———. 1992. *Vivre de sa plume au XVIe siècle ou la carrière de François de Belleforest.* Travaux d'Humanisme et Renaissance, 268. Geneva: Droz.

Skelton, Raleigh A. 1966a. Introduction to Benedetto Bordone, *Libro . . . de tutte l'isole del mondo* (Venice 1528). Amsterdam: Theatrum Orbis Terrarum, Ltd.

———. 1966b. Introduction to Sebastian Münster, 1540 edition of Ptolemy's *Geographia* (Basle, 1540), xii–xiii. Third series, vol. 5. Amsterdam: Theatrum Orbis Terrarum Ltd.

———. 1969. *Magellan's Voyage: A Narrative Account of the First Circumnavigation by Antonio Pigafetta*. New Haven, CT: Yale University Press.

Smith, Catherine Delano. 1992. *Maps in Bibles*. Geneva: Droz.

Stahl, William Harris. 1951–1952. "Ptolemy's Geography: A Select Bibliography." *Bulletin of the New York Public Library* 55:419–32; 484–95 (*Gallia* treated on 484–85); 554–64; 604–14; and 56:18–41; 84–96.

Starobinski, Jean. 1982. *Montaigne et le mouvement*. Paris: Gallimard.

Sweetser, Franklin, ed. 1966. *Les cent nouvelles nouvelles*. Critical edition. Paris: Droz (TLF 127).

Tabourot, Etienne. 1583. *Les bigarrures du seigneur des Accords*. Critical edition by Francis Goyet. 2 vols. Geneva: Droz.

Taylor, Eva C. 1930. *Tudor Geography, 1485–1583*. London: Methuen.

Terdiman, Richard. 1992. "The Response of the Other." *Diacritics* 22, no. 2: 2–10.

Terverant, Guy de. 1958. *Attributs et symboles dans l'art profane, 1450–1600: Dictionnaire d'un langage perdu*. Geneva: Droz. With supplement and index, 1964.

Thevet, André. 1556. *La cosmographie de Levant*. Paris. Critical edition with introduction by Frank Lestringant. Travaux d'Humanisme et Renaissance 203. Geneva: Droz

———. 1557. *Les singularitez de la France antarctique*. Paris.

———. 1558. *Les singularitez de la France antarctique*. Antwerp.

———. 1575. *La cosmographie universelle. . . . Illustrée de diverses figures des choses plus remarquables veuës par l'Auteur, et incogneuës de noz Anciens et Modernes*. 2 vols. Paris: Chez Pierre l'Huillier.

———. 1584. *Les vrais pourtraits et vies des hommes illustres*. 2 vols. Paris. New York: Scholars' Facsimiles & Reprints.

———. 1586–1587. *Le grand insulaire et pilotage d'André Thevet angoumoisin, cosmographe du Roy. Dans lequel sont contenus plusieurs plants d'isles habitées, et deshabitées, et description d'icelles*. Paris: Bibliothèque Nationale. Ms. fr. 15452–15453.

Tooley, R. V. 1978. *Maps and Map-Makers*. New York: Crown.

———. 1979. *Dictionary of Mapmakers*. New York: Less.

Tormey, Alan, and Judith Farr Tormey. 1982. "Renaissance Intarsia: The Art of Geometry." *Scientific American* 247 (July): 136–43.

Tory, Geoffroy. 1529a. *Champ fleury . . .* Paris: Geoffroy Tory and Gilles Gourmont. Edited and introduced by J. W. Jollife. The Hague: Mouton, 1970.

———. 1529b. *La Table de l'ancienne philosophe Cèbes . . . Avec Trente Dialogues moraulx de Lucien autheur iadis Grec . . .* Paris: Jehan Petit.

Tuan, Yi-Fu. 1990. *Topophilia*. New York: Columbia University Press.

Van Den Abbeele, Georges. 1991. *Travel as Metaphor: From Montaigne to Rousseau*. Minneapolis: University of Minnesota Press.

———. 1992. "Duplicity and Singularity in André Thevet's *La cosmographie de Levant*." *L'esprit créateur* 32, no. 3: 25–35.

Vincent, André. 1975. *Las Casas, apôtre des indiens*. Paris: Nouvelle Aurore.

Wallis, Helen, ed. 1981. *The Maps and Text of the Boke of Idrography Presented by Jean Rotz to Henry VIII, Now in the British Library.* Oxford: Roxburghe Club.

Wheat, Carl I. 1957. *Mapping the Transmississippi West 1: The Spanish Entrada to the Louisiana Purchase, 1548–1804.* San Francisco: Institute of Historical Cartography.

White, John. 1987. *The Birth and Rebirth of Pictorial Space.* Reprint, Cambridge, MA: Harvard University Press.

Winnicott, D. B. 1971. *Playing and Reality.* London: Tavistock.

Woodward, David. 1987. "The Manuscript, Engraved, and Typographic Traditions of Map Lettering." In David Woodward, ed., *Art and Cartography: Six Historical Essays,* 174–212. Chicago: University of Chicago Press.

———. 1990. "Roger Bacon's Terrestrial Coordinate System." *Annals of the Association of American Geographers* 80, no. 1 (March): 109–22.

———. 1991. "Maps and the Rationalization of Geographic Space." In Jay A. Levinson, ed., *Circa 1492: Art in the Age of Exploration,* 83–87. New Haven, CT, and London: Yale University Press.

Woodward, David, and J. Brian Harley, eds. 1987. "Cartography" In *Prehistoric, Ancient, and Medieval Europe and the Mediterranean.* The History of Cartography, vol. 1. Chicago: University of Chicago Press.

Yates, Frances. 1966. *The Art of Memory.* Chicago: University of Chicago Press.

Zerner, Henri. 1969. *The School of Fontainebleau: Etchings and Drawings.* New York: Abrams.

Zumthor, Paul. 1978. *Le masque et la lumière: La poétique des Grands Rhétoriqueurs.* Paris: Editions du Seuil.

———. 1987. *La lettre et la voix: De la 'littérature' médiévale.* Paris: Editions du Seuil.

———. 1993. *La mesure du monde.* Paris: Editions du Seuil.

Index

Tom Conley is Abbott Lawrence Lowell Professor in the departments of Romance Languages and Visual and Environmental Studies at Harvard University. He is the author of *An Errant Eye: Poetry and Topography in Early Modern France* (2010), *Film Hieroglyphs: Ruptures in Classical Cinema* (1991 and 2006), and *Cartographic Cinema* (2007), all published by the University of Minnesota Press.